The
Literatures
of the
Soviet Peoples

The Literatures of the Soviet Peoples

A Historical and Biographical Survey

Edited by Harri Jünger

With 96 photographs

FREDERICK UNGAR PUBLISHING CO.
NEW YORK

Translated from the German
Literaturen der Völker der Sowjetunion
by arrangement with VEB Bibliographisches Institut, Leipzig
Based on a translation by Vladimir Nekrasoff

Copyright © 1970 by Frederick Ungar Publishing Co., Inc.
Printed in the United States of America
Designed by Emilio Squeglio
Library of Congress Catalog Card No. 73-125964
ISBN 0-8044-3126-4

Publisher's Preface

This volume is the first English edition of a reference book published in East Germany (German Democratic Republic) and dealing with Soviet literature and with Russian writing before 1918. Throughout, its approach is from the viewpoint of "official" criticism oriented to the school of socialist realism. The evaluation of writers such as Boris Pasternak and Boris Pilnyak, who are known to the Western reading public, is thus quite different from that of Western critics. It must be assumed that literary figures who are generally unknown in Europe and the United States, except to specialists in Russian history and literature, are presented from the same viewpoint.

With this understanding in mind, readers will find here a useful guide especially to contemporary Soviet writing, offering an excellent opportunity to see Russian literature past and present as the citizens of the Soviet bloc nations see it. Nothing as wide in scope exists in English for the general reader.

Those consulting this work should note, as mentioned in the editor's preface that follows, that several literatures in existence for many centuries before the establishment of the Soviet Union are included here as Soviet literatures.

Preface

Russian classical literature has been familiar to readers elsewhere for many decades. Writers such as Pushkin, Lermontov, Gogol, Turgenev, Dostoyevski, L. Tolstoi, and Chekhov are among the most widely read authors in world literature. Soviet Russian literature, including the works of Mayakovski, Sholokhov, A. Tolstoi, Vishnevski, and Tvardovski, has been instrumental in stimulating an awareness of socialism in many areas throughout the world. The writings of these authors have been the faithful companions of millions of cultured people.

Soviet literature, however, is a wider field than just the most recent Russian literature: it represents a multinational literature as yet far too little known. The Georgian, Ukrainian, Uzbekistanian, Armenian, and Latvian literatures have their own centuries-old history, and have produced such great masters of the written word as Firdausi, Rustaveli, Hafis, and Shevchenko. Other literatures, including that of the Komi, have been able to develop only since the October revolution.

Interest in all these literatures has greatly increased in the last few years, despite the difficulty encountered in obtaining information, which is the essential tool of a cultured nation. The contributors to this volume, in their capacity as historians of Slavic literature, faced considerable difficulties in researching the more than five hundred names and titles discussed. Only a fraction of the literatures mentioned may in fact be termed Slavic. Few preliminary studies and definitive works were available.

This reference work, which aims to give an overall picture of the socialist cultural revolution, is the result of a collective effort by historians and literary critics from Jena, Leipzig, Halle, and

Erfurt. Soviet historians of the Literature and Language Departments of Sovetskaya Entziklopediya in Moscow have provided generous help in the selection of individual authors for inclusion in the work. Valuable suggestions have been offered by Professor Raab (Rostock) and Dr. Ziegengeist (Berlin), as well as by Professor Pätsch (Jena), the specialist in Caucasiology. Our thanks go to the members of the Bibliographical Institute and their assistants, for their advice.

It is our hope that this reference work will aid many people in finding a door to the great cultural treasures of the peoples of the Soviet Union; and that it will nurture friendship toward our Soviet brothers.

Jena, May 1966   Harri Jünger

Contents

List of Illustrations

Photographs were obtained from the following sources: Bildarchiv of the VEB Bibliographisches Institut, Leipzig; Deutsche Fotothek, Dresden; Presseagentur Nowosti, Berlin; Zentralbild, Berlin

Note

In the following pages English titles of published works have been given for the convenience of the reader. Wherever a work has been issued in an English translation, that published title is given within parentheses. In other cases a literal translation of the original has been supplied and given within square brackets, for the sake of clarity.

For those languages that do not lend themselves easily to transliteration in the Western alphabet, only the English titles are used.

Birth and death dates, where ascertainable, are given according to the New Style. The so-called Old Style (the Julian calendar) was replaced in Russia on February 1, 1918, by the New Style (the Gregorian calendar). February 1 thus became February 14. Should the reader wish to convert any date to the Old Style, he can do so by deducting 11 days from the day given (in the eighteenth century); 12 days (in the nineteenth century); and 13 days (in the twentieth century).

The survey articles were the work of the following contributors:

RUSSIAN LITERATURE, M. Wegner; SOVIET RUSSIAN LITERATURE, H. Jünger; ARMENIAN LITERATURE, H. Gründler; AZERBAIDZHANI LITERATURE, H. Schmidt; BYELORUSSIAN LITERATURE, K. Kasper; ESTONIAN LITERATURE, N. Sillat; GEORGIAN LITERATURE, G. Warm; KAZAKH LITERATURE, E. Hexelschneider; KIRGHIZ LITERATURE, R. Opitz; LATVIAN LITERATURE, N. Sillat; LITHUANIAN LITERATURE, R. Eckert; MOLDAVIAN LITERATURE, G. Schaumann; TADZHIK LITERATURE, R. Opitz; TURKMENIAN LITERATURE, B. Hiller; UKRAINIAN LITERATURE, M. Wegner; UZBEKISTANIAN LITERATURE, G. Dudek;

The individual entries were prepared by W. Beitz, G. Dudek, R. Eckert, H. Fliege, H. Gründler, E. Hexelschneider, B. Hiller, H. Jünger, K. Kasper, R. Opitz, H. Rennert, G. Schaumann, H. Schmidt, N. Sillat, E. Trautmann, G. Warm, M. Wegner.

An Historical Survey of Ethnic Literatures

RUSSIAN LITERATURE

Development of Russian literature from its earliest beginnings to the time of the socialist October revolution in 1917 can be divided into Old Russian (tenth to seventeenth century) and New Russian (eighteenth to the beginning of the twentieth century).

I Old Russian Literature

The so-called Russ, or Russian, folklore for many years constituted the only form of poetic art in Old Russia. This art form was closely connected with the life of the East Slavic tribes, with their pagan customs and practices. In the ninth and tenth centuries, during the transition of these Eastern Slavic tribes from tribal structure to a feudal class society, written literature based on folklore came into being. This development was made possible by the appearance of the Cyrillic alphabet; the alphabet was probably created by two Byzantine missionaries, the so-called apostles of the Slavs, Cyril and Methodius. The Christianization of the Eastern Slavs in 988 under Prince Vladimir Sviatoslavich and the adoption of Christianity as the state religion expedited the union of the East Slavic tribes into a uniform state—the Kievan Russ—and consolidated the powers of the more cultured feudal classes. It also had the effect of bringing the newly developing East Slavic culture into contact with the cultures of the other Christian states in Europe, and of promoting the development of Old Russian literature.

Old Russian literature shows certain definite characteristics. It emerged from a highly developed form of national poetry and always remained closely connected with the verbal literature of

1

the people. The fruitful interchanges that developed between the oral vernacular and the written literature resulted in Old Russian literature having markedly popular features despite its feudal character. The creative encounter between Old Russian literature and verbal poetry—in which the feelings of the people were expressed in a manner largely free from the influence of the predominantly religious ideology—reinforced the existing tendencies toward cultural liberation. In many works of Old Russian literature we find the influences of national poetry so strong that they force Christian humility and asceticism into the background. These national influences promoted the introduction of secular thought into Old Russian literature and resulted in a move toward the depiction of actual events occurring in the life of Russian medieval society. These national aspects are of great sociological importance to Old Russian literature.

A further characteristic of Old Russian literature is its relationship to the utilitarian writings of the Russian Middle Ages. Old Russian literature cannot be regarded as an autonomous body above the level of general writing. It forms a part of the historical, juridical, liturgical, and political writing of the time. In almost all instances we find that the art of ancient Russia simultaneously exhibits religious as well as secular elements. Writings of a general historical character—sermons, liturgical texts, accounts of manners—are therefore regarded as belonging to Old Russian literature.

1. The Kievan Period of Old Russian Literature
(Eleventh and Twelfth Centuries)

The oldest documents of Old Russian literature handed down to us is the "translation literature" of the Kievan Russ. Translation literature entered the East Slavic area from Byzantium after Christianization. These writings are translations of religious and semireligious texts from the Greek into Old Church Slavonic; the translated texts—chiefly written in Bulgaria in the tenth century—came to Russia in the form of copies. Russian translators, however, occasionally made an appearance. The writings translated were for the most part biblical texts and books relating to church services, biographies of saints (*vitae*), theological works, religious treatises on themes of natural philosophy, apocryphal books, and historical chronicles and stories.

One of the most important relics of early Old Russian translation literature is the oldest surviving manuscript of the Eastern Slavs, the *Ostromir Gospel*. This was written in 1055–57 for the governor Ostromir of Novgorod. Some of the secular works frequently translated at this time included the well-known *Alexandria*, a story about Alexander the Great of Macedon written in the second century in Northern Egypt; the Greek epic on the Byzantine national hero Basilios Digenis Akritas, which appeared in Russia under the title *Zhitiye i deyaniya Devgeniya Akrity* [The Life and Deeds of Digenis Akritas], and the story of the Indian empire, originally a Byzantine work, which reached Russia by way of Western Europe. *The Jewish War* (97–100), by the noted Jewish writer Flavius Josephus, became known in Old Russian literature as *Povest o razorenii Jerusalima* [Account of the Destruction of Jerusalem].

One of the oldest and most important works of original Kievan literature is the *Povest vremennykh Cet* [The Story of Times Past], the so-called Chronicle of Nestor. This was named after its probable author, the monk Nestor, and was completed circa 1120. The original has not survived, but the story has come down to us in various manuscript versions. The *Lavrentyevski spisok* (the "Laurentius manuscript," written by the monk Laurentius in 1377 in a cloister near Nizhni Novgorod for the grandduke of Suzdal) and the *Ipatyevski spisok* (the "Hypatius manuscript," writtten in the mid-fifteenth century and named after the Hypatius cloister near Kostroma, where it was found) reflect most accurately the character of the original chronicle.

The Chronicle of Nestor is an important document of both literary and historical interest. The themes of the work are manifold. It contains, in addition to actual descriptions of historical events that occurred in the East Slavic region up to the year 1187, texts of national treaties, legends of pre-Christian times, prose renderings of ancient heroic songs, short biographies of princes, and reports on the personal experiences of their liegemen. Of particular interest is the marked tone of patriotism that permeates the Chronicle, lending an internal unity to the heterogeneity of its themes.

Other works belonging to the oldest original writings of the Kievan period include homilies and sermons of a moral or solemn, rhetorical nature. *Poudeniye Vladimira Monomakha* [The Catechism of Vladimir Monomachus] and the rhetorical, pompous sermons of the metropolitan Ilarian (*Slovo o zakone i blagodati* [Sermon on Law and Mercy, 1037–50]) represent outstanding examples of their kind. Other works of the period include the historical legend of the murdered brothers Boris and Gleb (created around 1200); the *Paterik* of the Kievan cave cloister (a collection of legends and stories describing the lives and exploits of the Russian saints); and the so-called pilgrim literature, which consists of travelogues compiled by East Slavic pilgrims on their journeys to various shrines. A good example of pilgrim literature is *Khozhdeniye igumena Daniila* [The Pilgrimage of Prior Daniel to the Holy Land], written in 1106–08, which has survived in a number of manuscript copies.

Old Russian literature of the Kievan period reached its climax with the *Slovo o polku Igoreve* [The Lay of the Host of Igor]. Created between 1185 and 1187, this heroic epic deals with the unsuccessful campaign of Prince Igor Sviatoslavich of Novgorod-Seversk against the nomadic tribe of the Polovetzy in 1185. The unknown author of this work did not content himself with merely chronicling the campaign. He took the occasion to reflect profoundly on the fate of ancient Russia. His patriotic sentiments culminated in a solemn appeal for the unification of all Russian tribes in the fight against outside enemies, described by Marx as an "admonition of the Russian princes to unify shortly before the invasion of the Mongolian hordes." The basic patriotic idea of the *Slovo o polku Igoreve* finds artistic expression in a profoundly symbolic style rich in rhetoric, images, and parables. The vocabulary of this work is of an extraordinary diversity, and the entire poem shows traces of national, popular poetry. The patriotic, humanist ideas expressed are combined with a rare artistic skill that places this work among the most important masterpieces of world literature.

2. Old Russian Literature between the Thirteenth and Fifteenth Centuries

The increasing feudal disunity of the mid-twelfth century, which was accompanied by the decline of the Kievan Russ, inhibited literary development. The center of literary life moved from Kiev, which had been destroyed by the Tartars in 1240, to other cities, especially those in the northeast—Suzdal, Ryazan, Moscow, Nizhni Novgorod, Tver, Novgorod—and in the southeast (Galicia-Volhynia). The Tartar-Mongolian invasion that poured across the internally disrupted Kievan state early in the thirteenth century severely affected Old Russian culture. The attacks by the Tartars, in the course of which vast areas of Russia were razed and burned to the ground, were very damaging to the cultural life of the time, but did not succeed in totally overwhelming it. Even under Tartar rule the newly developing literary centers in the northeast continued the traditions of Kievan literature. The decentralized literary development during the following centuries still drew its inspiration from the cultural inheritance of the Kievan Russ.

The effect of the Tartar invasion was reflected in a number of literary works, including the *Povest o Kalksom poboishche* [The Story of the Battle on the River Kalka, 1224], the *Povest o razorenii Batyyem Ryazani* [The Story of the Destruction of Ryazan by Batu, 1237], and the *Slovo o pogibeli Russkoi zemli* [The Lament on the Destruction of the Russian Country], which was probably written during the first three decades of the thirteenth century. Other important literary documents from this period are *Moleniye Daniila Zatochnika* [The Petition of Daniil the Exile], which represented a valuable testimony to medieval thought and rhetoric, and the biography of the last grand duke of Kiev, Aleksandr Nevski, *Zhitive Aleksandra Nevskovo*, which was probably compiled at the end of the thirteenth century.

Most of the literary works created under the yoke of the Tartars during the thirteenth and fourteenth centuries are indebted to the literature of the Kievan period for their ideological content. The newly awakened national consciousness, which had found mature artistic expression in *Slovo o polku Igoreve*, also permeated the literature of the period, gradually becoming the spiritual basis for literature. The literature of the Moscow principality began to emerge after Moscow had won the great victory over the Tartars of the Golden Horde in the battle of Kulikovo (the Battle of the Woodcock Field) in 1380. This battle resulted in the predominance of Moscow among the neighboring principalities, and eventually led to the liberation of Russia from the Tartar yoke. The battle itself has been the theme of numerous works, the most important of which is *Zadonshchina*. This epic, created around the end of the fourteenth century by the Ryazan monk Sofronia, clearly shows the influence of *Slovo o polku Igoreve*. The rise in national consciousness also is reflected in the *Povest o vzyatii Jzargrada* [The Story of the Capture of Zargrad], a colorful fifteenth-century description of the capture of Constantinople by the Turks in 1453. This historical event is treated by the author, Nestor Iskander, in a way that emphasizes the gradually developing idea of Moscow as the "Third Rome," an idea used by the dukes of Moscow to bolster their claim for Russian unification.

Literature also began to flourish in the cities of Tver, Novgorod, and Ryazan. A prominent literary work emerged from the city of Tver—*Khozhdebiye za tri morya* [Journey beyond the Three Seas], in which the merchant Afranasi Nikitin described his hazardous voyage to India in 1466–72.

3. The "Moscow" Period of Old Russian Literature (Sixteenth and Seventeenth Centuries)

Formation of a centralized state on Russian soil was completed early in the sixteenth century. By 1520 Moscow had subjugated the last independent Russian principality, and in 1552 Ivan IV ("the Terrible") conquered Kazan, the capital of the Volga Tartars; the incorporation of foreign nationalities into the Moscow state had begun. The establishment of a central power by the

Muscovite grand dukes—an event of great importance—was accompanied by fierce internal strife. In his claim to absolute rule Ivan IV relied mainly on the lower nobility and on a section of the Russian clergy called Josephites, whose spiritual head was the abbot Joseph Volotzki. The higher Russian nobility (boyars) and strong groups of the clergy opposed consolidation of the monarchy.

Political writing developed rapidly in this tense atmosphere, and the struggles and ideologies of the time were expressed by several individuals, including the monk Nil Zorski. The most important political writer of the time was also a monk. Maksim Grek was a truly humanist thinker and a brilliant rhetorician who continually exposed the failings of the church to harsh criticism. His opponent was the pugnacious metropolitan Daniel, who defended official church policies in his political writings. The most important defender of a monarchical state was Ivan Peresvetov. Peresvetov's versatile, polemic writings included *Skazaniye o tzare Konstantine* [Stories about Tsar Konstantin] and *Skazaniye o Magmet Saltane* [Stories about Sultan Mohammed]. In these works he defended the new absolutism in Russia.

An interesting literary document of the second half of the sixteenth century was the *Correspondence of Prince Andrei Kurbski with Ivan Gronznyi*, in which the ideological arguments of the period appeared in all their profundity. The letters of Kurbski in particular reflect the highly verbal nature of literature at that time. Certain ecclesiastical works of the sixteenth century also are of literary value, including the well-known moral code *Domostroi* and the *Stoglav* [The Hundred Chapters], an extensive collection of resolutions adopted by the church council of 1551.

The revival of literary life in Russia coincided with the rise of the Russian state in the seventeenth century. By this time Russia had emerged victorious from the struggles with the invading Polish and Swedish armies. The feudal state, now unified to a far greater degree, was interested in a widening of its intellectual ranks to include all fields. Numerous educational establishments were opened, in which both Slavonic and classical languages, grammar, rhetoric, and poetry were taught. The political reunion with the

Ukraine in 1654 reinforced mutual cultural interests, and the literary influences exerted by the Ukrainian cultural centers at Kiev and Lvov contributed greatly to the increasing interest in literature.

New literary forms began to appear, including syllabic poetry and drama. These were widely employed, chiefly in the form of a "drama of humanism." Several of the plays written during this period, although still in the developmental stage, already contained scenes depicting national life. Characters drawn from the ranks of the people endowed these pieces with a colorful realism. Purely secular plays, which in most cases came from Western Europe, also began to appear. In Moscow, the German pastor Gottfried Gregori directed a theater group under the patronage of the tsar. The *Artakserksovo deistvo* [The Comedy of Artaxerxes] was one of the most frequently performed plays.

In the field of poetry Simeon Polotzki, a student at the Kiev Theological Seminary, stands out as a remarkable phenomenon. His satirical poems prepared the way for the satire of the eighteenth century. The other important writer of the seventeenth century was the priest Avvakum, a fanatical opponent of the much disputed church reforms being attempted by the Moscow patriarch Nikon. Avvakum's most important literary work, *Zhitiye protopopa Avvakum* [The Life of the Archpriest Avvakum], written in 1672–76, is the first autobiography to appear in Russian literature. Numerous epics and legends occupy a prominent position in the colorful panorama of literary events taking place in the seventeenth century, including *Povest o Gore-Zloshchastii* [The Story of Sorrow-Trouble], *Povest o Shemyakinom sude* [The Judgment of Shemyak], *Povest o Yershe y Yershovich* [The Story of the Ruff and the Ruff's Son] among others. The satirical, descriptive content of these stories prepares the way for the realistic prose of later Russian literature.

The period of Old Russian literature ended in the seventeenth century. The regional tendencies in literary development had been definitely broken, and the writings of the seventeenth century were marked by a more nationalist, truly Russian character; the realities of daily life penetrated deeper and deeper into the realm of literature, pushing religious themes into the background. Simple country people appeared with increasing frequency as literary characters. The influence of the folk tale and of national poetry grew stronger, and the democratization of literature began. Criticism of the inadequacies of social life became more and more common; new literary forms, including drama and poetry, began to emerge. The merging of the alive, vibrant vernacular with the more formal Church Slavonic created a favorable atmosphere for the development of a Russian literary language. New Russian literature was to develop from this transitional period.

II New Russian Literature

1. Russian Literature of the Eighteenth Century

The Russian nation in its definite form was established in the eighteenth century. The extensive reforms undertaken by Peter I gave more power to the landed proprietors and merchants, and accelerated the economic and cultural development of Russia. Peter I energetically attempted to rescue his country from the darkness of medievalism and to raise Russia to the level of the more highly developed Western European nations. The successful wars against Turkey and Sweden increased the international prestige of Russia and made the empire of the tsar one of the mightiest nations of Europe. The rise of Russia was partially accomplished by the ruthless exploitation of the serfs, who were continually rebelling.

The development of eighteenth-century literature took place at a time of gradual transition. Russia was developing into a bourgeois, capitalist state; there was constant instability in the feudal system and an increased sense of tension between the nobility and the peasants. The social carriers of that development were the members of the aristocratic intelligentsia, whose ideological views and aesthetic ideals were reflected in the literature of the time. Literature nevertheless also reflected the national interests of the Russian people as a whole, especially in the works of those writers who finally found themselves taking a critical view of autocratic rule and serfdom and searching for a more honest and unbiased view of the common people.

The prominent literary personality to emerge in the first thirty years of the eighteenth century was Feofan Prokopovich, a passionate champion of the reforms of Peter I and one of the first Russians of his time to spread the ideas of humanism. By the middle of the eighteenth century classicism had begun to develop, stemming for the most part from France, whose "Age of Enlightenment" was to dominate the entire literature of this period. The views of the Russian nobility, who supported the new humanist movement, are reflected in classical Russian literature. Proud and chauvinistic, they wished to create a noble culture, one that would be representative of the entire nation.

Russian classicism has certain characteristic features. Despite their orientation toward antique Greek and Roman art and their preference for subjects taken from ancient history, many classicist writers adopted national, contemporary themes. The satirical element became particularly well developed, while Russian classicism's close relationship with oral folk poetry also exerted a specific influence on classicist poetry as a whole.

The first important representative of Russian classicism was Antiokh Kantemir, who castigated the lack of culture, corruptibility, avarice, and depravity of the Russian nobility of his time in his famous satires. Vasilii Tredyakovski was successful in his attempts to reform the Russian literary language, particularly in the field of poetry. Mikhail Lomonosov, the first Russian scholar, poet, and writer of worldwide reputation, exerted his efforts in the same direction. Aleksandr Sumarokov was the most important representative of the classic dramatists. He attempted to give national color to his tragedies, which were written strictly in accordance with the rules of classicism.

Russian classicism virtually ended during the last years of the eighteenth century, although the form remained the predominating literary movement for some time. The bourgeois revolutions in America and France, as well as the peasant uprisings under

Pugachev in 1773 and 1775, severely damaged the "enlightened absolutism" theory, and struck at the very roots of ideological classicism. In the face of the steadily increasing class differences, the classicist movement slowly disintegrated. This disintegration became manifest in the 1760s, when a group of classicist writers, among them Mikhail Kheraskov (the successor of Sumarokov), Vasilii Maikov, Ippolit Bogdanovich, and Ivan Khemnitzer, abandoned the rational, liberal spirit of their predecessors and accepted the official ideology of autocracy. In the following decade a second group—Yakov Knyazhnin, V. Kapnist, and N. Nikolov among them—took up a position that was highly critical of the works of the former group.

The most important poet in the closing years of Russian classicism was Gavriil Derzhavin. Almost all his odes and poems are classic in form, but they show clearly the incipient disintegration of the creative principles of classicism. In his candid descriptions of the social environment, Derzhavin opened a new road for Russian literature.

The leading dramatist at the end of the eighteenth century was Denis Fonvizin, whose poetry owed something of a debt to classicism. His dramas, however, prepared the way for the nineteenth century's literature of realism. The increasing number of ideological struggles taking place at the end of the eighteenth century brought political writing to the fore. One of the more progressive political writers was Nikolai Novikov, the publisher and editor of a number of satirical magazines.

In the last decades of the eighteenth century a new literary movement—sentimentalism—developed as a reaction to the now outmoded classicism. Distinctly antirational, the sentimentalists gave precedence to sentiment over intellect. They drew on the emotional experiences of the individual for their literary creations, preferring descriptions of the lives of simple, ordinary people, and contemporary themes. On the whole, sentimentalism advocated a literature that was close to life, although writers of the sentimental school frequently left reality far behind in their rosy, idealistic presentations. These writers, who were involved with the needs and feelings of the individual, with his emotional life in all its complexity, paved the way for romantic literature. The most important of the sentimentalists was N. Karamzin, a somewhat conservative writer whose *Bednaya Liza* [Poor Liza] became the leading work of sentimental literature. Russian sentimentalism had another talented representative in I. Dmitriyev.

Russian realist literature—known as the early realism of enlightenment—started to develop toward the end of the eighteenth century within the boundaries of classicist and sentimentalist writing. The focal point of early realist literature is occupied by certain typical writers who described the problems of serfdom. Their works are distinguished for fidelity to detail and popular, colloquial style. These works, which show a certain didactic fervor, also exhibit marked critical and satirical tendencies. The beginnings of realism are reflected in the later dramatic works of Fonvizin and in the political writing of Novikov. A definite climax was reached in the work of A. Radishchev, whose *Puteshestviye iz Peterburga v Mosku* (The Voyage from Petersburg to Moscow), written in 1790, gives a comprehensive description of the barbaric system of serfdom then practiced in Russia. The Russian picaresque novel, which appeared toward the end of this period, also showed realist trends. This particular literary form became popular with the appearance of works by A. Izmailov and V. Marezhny. I. Krylov, a fabulist, became the most important representative of the early realist tradition. His brilliant criticism of his times and the popularity achieved by his work helped to pave the way for Russian critical realism.

2. Russian Literature of the Nineteenth Century

At the beginning of the nineteenth century, emotion-stressed sentimentalism changed into a new literary movement—romanticism. The development of Russian romanticism, which reached its peak between 1806 and 1825, paralleled the crises then coming to a head in the feudal system. Two historical events greatly influenced the character of Russian romanticism—the War of 1812, and the uprising of the noble revolutionaries which resulted in the Decembrist insurrection of 1825. The expulsion of the French and the fall of Napoleon increased national awareness and made the need for instituting radical changes in the Russian social structure extremely urgent. The struggle of the Russian nobility against autocratic rule and the miseries of serfdom had begun to bring the greater circles of Russian society into opposition against the absolutist system. Sociopolitical thinking became considerably more radical during this period. Russian romanticism, born of a dissatisfaction with social realism, reflected the hopes and disappointments of an entire generation of young writers.

V. Zhukovski, the founder of Russian romanticism, inaugurated the period of romantic literature in Russia. Together with Karamzin, he prepared the ground for the literature of psychological realism to come. Zhukovski, like his talented contemporary Batyushkov, represented the passive, esoteric direction taken by Russian romanticism after 1816.

The progressive direction within Russian romanticism was represented by the writers of the Decembrist movement, including the young Pushkin and Lermontov. The work of the later authors represents the gradual rise of Russian literary development, while the work of Zhukovski, especially after 1815, gradually became more and more difficult and reactionary. The crosscurrents of political life in the 1820s are reflected in the works of the Decembrists, including Ryleyev, Kuechelbecker, Bestuzhev, and Odoyevski. The Decembrists regarded their literary activities as part of the political battle. This explains their unanimous demand for an involved political literature filled with intense patriotism, as well as their preference for subjects concerned with the heroic periods of Russian history. The Decembrists equated the right of Russia to a national literature with the right of the Russian people to political freedom. The revolutionary, romantic writings of the Decembrists and the young Pushkin which characterized the literary output until 1825 set the example later followed by all liberal artistic activities in Russia.

The literary importance of the Decembrist movement is not limited to the work of the revolutionary romanticists. Writers whose creative activities were removed from romanticism were also influenced by the revolutionary movement taking place among the nobility. Foremost in the group was A. Griboyedov, whose comedy *Gore or uma* (The Mischief of Being Clever) is Decembrist in its ideological content. Griboyedov, together with Krylov, thus belongs to the group of writers who progressed from classicism to realism without ever having been attracted by romanticism.

After the defeat of the Decembrists in 1825, a bleak period of reaction affected the cultural life of Russia, and romanticism gradually lost its raison d'être. The new historical developments confronted literature with problems romanticism could not solve. A split began to be evident in the movement as ideology and aesthetics started to move in opposite directions. The most talented representatives of the movement—Pushkin, Lermontov, and Gogol —moved from romanticism to realism without entirely giving up their romantic style, while others, chiefly those belonging to the conservative camp (Kozlov and Benediktov among them) continued to write in the passive, romantic style of Zhukovski. Their works gradually became rigidly anachronistic and imitative; by the end of the first half of the nineteenth century romanticism had disintegrated completely as a literary movement.

After 1825 critical realism became the dominant literary movement. Its arrival was closely connected with the development of a consciously critical attitude on the part of the progressive social forces toward Russian feudalism and absolutism. The increasingly critical view of the tsarist state taken by the literary intelligentsia led to disillusionment and the abandonment of their romantic attitude toward society and its problems. Writers no longer attempted to disassociate themselves from reality, but came to regard it dispassionately. They began to examine social conditions and to analyze the inner core of the political system of tsarist autocracy, an autocracy that had withstood the assault of the Decembrists. The role of the people became more important, and the possibilities of revolution in order to change the social structure were examined seriously.

These and other sociopsychological conditions resulted in the development of realistically critical writing, a literary movement for which the entire course of Russian literature up to this time had paved the way. Basic artistic preconditions for the development of the new movement had been created by progressive romanticism. Although the connections with all previous literary movements (classicism, sentimentalism, romanticism, and early realism) are evident, critical realism represented a qualitatively new phenomenon in Russian literature. The endeavor to understand the character of social phenomena, the molding of characteristic features, the historical outlook, nationalism in the sense of concern and support for the people, the choice of ordinary people as literary heroes, the preference for everyday situations, comprehensive characterization, profound psychological understanding, and an objective and imaginative reflection of reality became the characteristics of the new critical realism.

The development of critical realism is chiefly linked with A. Pushkin. Pushkin, the first of the Russian writers to arrive at the new aesthetic interpretation of reality, was instrumental in propagating Russian realism. Pushkin's works depicted for the first time the greatest and most noble aspects of the national character—love of liberty, patriotism, humanity, and a vigorous optimism. His literary work is encyclopedic in character, embracing all branches of literature and almost all forms of poetic expression. As the greatest poet of his nation, Pushkin gave final form to the modern Russian literary language.

Mikhail Lermontov and Nikolai Gogol inherited Pushkin's literary traditions. Lermontov's pensive, intellectual novels and lyrical poetry represented an important milestone in the development of Russian literature. With Gogol, the realistic prose movement finally and completely arrived. He pitilessly exposed the differences between the classes in the feudal order, and declared his affection for "the little people" of the tsarist capital and the exploited peasants of the Russian provinces. Gogol's tense, satirical style opened new possibilities for expression. The union of Russian literature with national hopes and aspirations is particularly clearly marked in the poetic works of Aleksis Koltzov, whose folksong-like poems expressed the feelings and emotions of the Russian serfs.

Capitalism expanded during the 1840s and continued to do so until the 1860s. The feudal system, which had reached a state of crisis, brought about the revolutionary reactions of 1859–61. The abolition of serfdom in 1861 smoothed the way for bourgeois development. The struggles between the serfs and the feudal landowners, which had become intensified during this period, involved all areas of society. The leading role in the Russian liberation movement passed from the hands of the noble revolutionaries to the revolutionaries of common descent (*rasnochintze*). The bourgeois, democratic period of revolutionary movement began in Russia around 1861.

The politics of the time favored literary development. Critical realism had become the predominant movement. Strongly influenced by Gogol, the Natural School was founded in the 1840s, issuing in an important new stage in the development of critical realism. The Natural School was important in that it widened the base of critical realism, establishing Russian literature permanently as an art involved with the depiction of life. Important members of the School, all of whom were united in their criticism of the tsarist state, included N. Nekrasov, A. Herzen, M. Saltykov-Shchedrin, I. Turgenev, F. Dostoyevski, and I. Goncharov. The acknowledged theoretical leader of the group was V. Belinski.

Literary development in the 1840s was characterized by the advancement of narrative prose. The writers of the Natural School preferred the short story or essay form, but a number of novels written at that time are suggestive of the great epic writings of the years to come. Lyric poetry was a popular genre, and especially well represented was poetry of a definite political nature. The political poem was one of the forms of lyric expression most preferred by the leading writers of the time—Nekrasov, Ogariov, and Pleshcheyev.

The members of the Natural School disbanded toward the end of the 1840s, the increasing class struggles in Russia and the revolutionary events taking place in Western Europe in 1848 having led to many ideological differences among the writers. Humanism and the search for truth were still the chief concern of the Russian realists, however, and the masterpieces that emerged during the second half of the nineteenth century ensured Russian literature world-wide recognition.

The rise of Russian realism occurred at a time when there was considerable and fruitful exchange of ideas between the writers themselves and the critics in favor of revolutionary measures who were to take over the leadership of the progressive forces in the 1840s. Their most important representatives were Belinski and Herzen in the 1840s and Chernyshevski and Dobrolyubov and Pisarev in the 1860s. Belinski, in demanding a realistic literature that would reflect with great artistry all aspects of reality, created the cornerstone on which all future democratic criticism of literature would rest. It was under Belinski's guidance that the magazine *Sovremennik* [The Contemporary], the representative organ of the Russian liberation movement, became the most important weapon of the democratic critics.

After Belinski's early death his critical work was continued by Chernyshevski and Dobrolyubov. Dobrolyubov intervened in the literary battles of his time with brilliantly written critical articles. It was from the revolutionary democratic critics that the most thorough analyses of the works of the important Russian realists eventually came. Belinski had by 1835 discovered the extraordinary talent of Gogol and predicted a great future for him; he was also the first critic to recognize the great achievements of Pushkin. Chernyshevski in the mid-1850s drew attention to the work of Lev Tolstoi, who had just started to write. Dobrolyubov wrote much important criticism of the the work of Goncharov, Turgenev, Ostrovski, and Dostoyevski.

Critical realism was in full flower by the 1850s and 1860s. The sociocritical attitude toward social realism was intensified among the more prominent writers as they became aware of the disintegrating feudal system and the rise of the liberation movement. As the major problem of the time—the abolition of serfdom—came to a head, other related difficulties concerned with the peasants also moved to the fore, involving writers associated with the revo-lutionary-democratic movement. Foremost among these was N. Nekrasov, the leading lyric poet of the era, whose poems made him famous as the spokesman for the Russian peasant. Saltykov-Shchedrin, using an especially biting satirical style, depicted the brutality and immorality of the provincial nobility, pointing out the irreconcilable gulf that separated landowners and serfs.

The flowering of the Russian social novel, which may be said to represent the highest achievement of Russian nineteenth-cen-tury literature, came in the 1860s. Turgenev, Goncharov, Cherny-shevski, Saltykov-Shchedrin, Dostoyevski, and Lev Tolstoi, the leading novelists of the time, raised the sociocritical novel to the height of perfection. The Russian novelists made great advances in their epic treatment of the significant historical events of their times and of the fate of the people involved in these events. The artistic objectivism seen in novels by these writers—emotions viewed from the sociocritical viewpoint—is a characteristic feature of Russian critical realism. The novels show both critical and psychological understanding. The employment of a "dialectics of the soul"—the term used by Chernyshevski to characterize the peculiar nature of Lev Tolstoi's work—may be regarded as the distinguishing feature of the Russian social novel in general.

The classical period in Russian epic literature in the second half of the nineteenth century was inaugurated by Turgenev. Turgenev pointed out the weaknesses of the liberal noble intelli-gentsia, chiefly by showing such weaknesses as they appeared in intimate personal relationships. His novels, which question the social forces destined to bring about a renewal of Russian society, indicate an awareness that the aristocratic period of the liberation movement had ended and that the *rasnochintzes* had taken over the leading role in the battle against absolutist rule. Turgenev, however, did not hide the fact that his sympathies were with the Russian nobility. The characters in Turgenev's novels symbolizing the revolutionary figures of the epoch, especially Inzarov and Bazarov, were viewed with great sympathy by the progressive forces, although a number of the democratic critics did not at that time fully realize their compelling importance.

The decline of the Russian landed gentry is the subject of Goncharov's novel *Oblomov*. Oblomov, the typical representative of degenerate aristocracy, became a world-famous literary figure, and "Oblomovism" became the symbol for all the passive and non-viable aspects of tsarist society. Dostoyevski manipulated characters drawn from the lowest dregs of a nation smothering in the dark atmosphere of an obsolete order. The tragic destruction of the individual in bourgeois capitalist society became the basic theme of his work. Dostoyevski pitilessly exposed the morals of the ruling classes and the terrible effect of such morals on the underprivileged. He created many great characters and told of the deeply moving conflicts taking place at that time, thus opening a unique world of literary figures. Dostoyevski's passionate protests against the degradation of the individual forced his more abstract teachings and his prejudiced attacks on the revolutionary movement into the background.

The flowering of the sociocritical novel in Russia was paralleled by the development of the political novel. A social event of some importance was the appearance of Chernyshevski's *Chto delat?* (What Is to Be Done?), in which the revolutionaries of the 1860s are depicted for the first time. Chernyshevski's profound belief in the approaching social changes and his grandiose visions of the socialist future of Russian society led the democratic public to feel that this novel represented the political testament of the revolutionaries then suffering in the tsarist jails. A number of young democratic writers of the time wrote in the spirit of Chernyshevski: N. Pomyalovski, V. Sleptzov, F. Reshetnikov, G. Uspenski. These writers for the most part took present-day, sociopolitical subjects as their themes.

The great upsurge in Russian literature in the second half of the nineteenth century involved all literary genres. A. Ostrovski, the greatest dramatist of the period, brought the "dark empire" of the Russian merchant class into the light, laying bare their despotic, medieval habits and their lust for profit. Ostrovski energetically supported the rights of the underprivileged for equality and recognition. His drama *Groza* (The Thunderstorm) became the most important event to take place on the Russian stage since Gogol's *Revizor*. In the 1860s A. Sukhovo-Kobylin effectively contributed to the satirical drama of the time.

Developing alongside the critical realist school was a group of writers who avoided social themes and made the subjective world of human emotions their chief concern. This "pure art" movement was composed for the most part of poets; the work of A. Fet-Shenshin, a member of the group, found a permanent place in Russian poetry. A. K. Tolstoi and F. Tyutchev were closely linked with this movement, although their work frequently went beyond the confines of the aesthetic program recommended by the followers of "pure art." Despite their rather unrealistic, subjective methods, these poets enriched Russian literature with their subtle presentations of the most intimate spheres of human life. Some of these writers developed new poetic styles to suit their individual needs.

Development of Russian literature during the final third of the nineteenth century and the beginning of the twentieth is related to the significant historical events occurring at the time. The capitalist economic system had triumphed, although economic development was still greatly inhibited by the restraints inherent in the feudal system. The capitalist entrepreneurs were yet a new class of exploiters anxious to put the yoke around the neck of the Russian people. However, side by side with capitalism there also developed the industrial proletariat; the members of this class gradually lost their narrow-minded, bourgeois illusions and became ready to fight under the socialist banner. After the failure of the heroic attempt of the *narodnost* (a populist group) to rally the Russian peasant masses to revolt in 1895, the revolutionary proletariat, led by the Marxists, stepped into the forefront of the Russian liberation movement. In the bourgeois revolution of 1905 the Russian working class demonstrated its strength for the first time.

Russian literature between 1870 and 1917 reflects the complex, sometimes self-contradictory development of the Russian revolution. Critical realism, the representatives of which sympathized with democratic ideas to some extent, remained the determinant literary movement, reaching a peak during this period. The most prominent literary figure to emerge was Lev Tolstoi, whose realistic art represents the crowning achievement in nineteenth-century Russian literature. Tolstoi's works brought to life the historic changes taking place in the period between the early peasant reforms and the first Russian revolution. Tolstoi raised questions of vital importance for the Russian people and gave expression to the feelings and hopes of the suppressed masses. From his position as a member of the patriarchal Russian peasant classes he passionately protested the injustice, mendacity, perfidy, and degeneracy of the bourgeois aristocratic society. Tolstoi's criticism of certain aspects of the tsarist state finally crystallized and became a rejection of any antagonistic class society. His work reflects the strengths and weaknesses, the greatnesses and limitations of the peasant movement against tsarism, and in this sense it represents a "mirror of the Russian revolution," as Lenin once described it. Tolstoi created fictional characters of worldwide literary significance. The moral views of these characters were shaped by their search for a positive solution to the historical and social problems of the times, and by their total involvement with the lives and thoughts of the people.

N. Leskov was one of the great Russian novelists of the late nineteenth century. He was eminently successful in depicting characters drawn from both the lower and upper strata of the Russian clergy. Another highly regarded narrator of the period was D. Mamin-Sibiryak, who described the capitalist development of the mining districts in the Urals. A number of important belletrists also emerged from the ranks of the *narodniks*, including G. Uspenski, S. Karonin, N. Naumov, N. Zlatovratski, and S. Kravchinski.

The dominant literary form of this period was the short story. One extremely individual writer was the novelist V. Garshin, whose psychologically profound short stories described the conflicts of sensitive, everyday people in an unjust society. V. Korolenko was one of the leading novelists of the period. His lyrical, romantic stories written in the Turgenev tradition are among the finest works of the realistic school. The most important novelist of the closing years of the nineteenth century was Anton Chekhov, who saw through the weakness of tsarist society and realized the dubiousness of capitalist progress. Dryly and with a lyrical melancholy he endowed commonplace incidents and people with an aesthetic significance, pointing his finger at the sores of the old class-dominated society. He condemned the parasitic life of both aristocrat and bourgeoisie with biting, satirical severity. Filled with love for the working people, Chekhov demanded a reformation of human society. His stories represent a small encyclopedia of Russian life around the turn of the century. Preceded by the works of Gogol and Ostrovski, Russian drama at the turn of the century reached its climax with the plays of Chekhov. These plays, which take up the same message as his stories, also pointed to the brittleness and shortcomings of the old order, and announced the coming of a new way of life.

L. Tolstoi and Chekhov were the two most important writers of Russian realism to appear at the end of the prerevolutionary developmental period. Realist traditions were still noticeable at the beginning of the twentieth century, although in a somewhat less active form. Aleksandr Kuprin, Ivan Bunin, Leonid Andreyev, Vikentii Veresayev, and others adhered for the most part to the principles of realist writing. A number of them, however, including Andreyev, gradually took up decadent positions after the defeat of the Russian revolution of 1905. The publishing cooperative *Snaniye* [Knowledge] directed by Maksim Gorki played a significant role in amalgamating democratic writers in the battle against political reaction and literary decadence.

With the strengthening of the Russian bourgeoisie certain modern, decadent literary movements developed. Russian symbolism became active, following the pattern set by Western European decadent art. Its most prominent representatives included

Dmitri Merezhkovski, Valerii Bryusov, and Feodor Sologub. A less active, more bourgeois form of naturalism tried to gain a foothold in Russian literature at this time, as is exemplified in the works of Petro Boborykin and Mikhail Artzybashev. It speaks well for the strength of the realist literary tradition that the effect of these decadent movements was episodic. The most talented poets—Blok, Bryusov, and Mayakovski (who began his artistic development in the ranks of the Russian futurists)—disassociated themselves from their symbolist beginnings at the start of the twentieth century, and later found their way to an acceptance of the revolution.

The new progressive element in the development of Russian literature in its final period was represented by proletarian literature, which developed in conjunction with the rising socialist worker movement. The proletarian writers, including D. Bednyi and Serafimovich and led by Gorki, first followed the traditions of critical realism but later extended these traditions to include socialist realism. Gorki created the bridge from critical realism to the new socialist literature. His novel *Mat* [The Mother] was the first work of socialist realism. Together with other proletarian writers, whose model and teacher he was, Gorki fertilized Russian writing with socialist ideas, and laid the cornerstone for the history of Soviet literature after the October revolution.

SOVIET RUSSIAN LITERATURE

The great socialist October revolution created for the first time in history an environment favorable to the flowering of the culture of an entire nation. Despite economic confusion, civil war, hunger, and poverty, the first years following the revolution were a time of learning and the general assimilation of cultural values. Millions of people conquered illiteracy. Literature, also involved in this cultural renaissance, had to make allowances for the difficult conditions of the times. Publishing houses, printing plants, and theaters were now in the hands of the people. Organizations such as Proletcult were destined to help promote new talents in the arts.

A free literature developed as predicted by Lenin, who as early as 1905 had said that such a literature would emerge—one in which man's revolutionary thoughts would mingle with the living experiences and work of the socialist proletariat. Socialism and sympathy for the workers had become the driving force behind literature; literary careers and the needs of the individual writer now mattered but little. Literature no longer served only the "pampered heroine" or the "bored, obese, upper ten thousand," but catered to the thinking of millions of workers.

The bitter class struggle taking place during the revolution had demanded a clear decision from every writer: he had to decide to join the counterrevolutionaries. "There was no middle ground left," Mayakovski wrote. For many writers who before the revolution had been connected with modernist movements or other bourgeois tendencies, there now began a complex, contradictory phase, a time of searching and indecision. In short, it was a period of radical change.

Some of these writers, among them Dmitri Merezhkovski, Zinaida Gippius, and Artzybashev, emigrated and became enemies of the Soviet. Some of the well-known writers of socialist realism, including Ivan Bunin, Aleksandr Kuprin, Leonid Andreyev, and Aleksei Tolstoi, became so entangled in contradictions that they too emigrated. Many of these writers began to walk a via dolorosa that eventually led some of them, including A. Tolstoi and A. Kuprin, back to their home country.

The majority of the more important Russian writers, however, stayed within the barricades. The founders of symbolism Aleksandr Blok and Valerii Bryusov, together with Vikenti Veresayev, Sergei Sergeyev-Tzenski, Sergei Yesenin, Mikhail Prishvin, Andrei Belyi, Anna Akhmatova, and Kornei Chukovski, elected to remain. In the early years following the revolution the nucleus of Soviet literature was formed by the writers whose works had helped to prepare the way for the revolution—Maksim Gorki, Aleksandr Serafimovich, Demyan Bednyi, and Vladimir Mayakovski. The work of these writers, the traditions of the classical literature of the nineteenth century, and the legacy left by the

Russian revolutionary democrats represented the aesthetic foundations upon which Soviet literature began to develop.

From the beginning Soviet literature was a literature of revolution. In the first years after the revolution Soviet literature depicted with great skill the complex relationships developing between the people and the politics of the time. Existing conditions combined with the limited possibilities for publication resulted in the development of lesser literary genres such as lyric poetry and journalism. The poets, whose work at the time was for the most part romantic and revolutionary, attempted in their writings to reveal the true nature of the historic changes taking place.

The poets of the Proletcult—Aleksei Gastev, Vladimir Kirillov, Vasilii Aleksandrovski, Mikhail Gerasimov, Nikolai Poletayev—showed a true feeling for liberty and a fervent revolutionary spirit. Their work extolled the universe, the earth, the factory, and the workers. In the important revolutionary poem *Dvendtzat* (The Twelve) A. Blok tried to voice the "music of the revolution." The most effective civil war poet was D. Bednyi, whose direct, provocative, and simple poems fired the minds and hearts of the Red Army soldiers. V. Mayakovski, whose much-loved drawings and lyrics were published by the revolutionary press agency Rosta, contributed to the mobilization of the Red Army.

The dogmas pronounced by some of the leaders of the Proletcult, including Aleksandr Bogdanov, who denied the existence of cultural traditions and rejected talents of nonproletarian origin, represented a serious impediment to the development of literature during the first years after the revolution. By contrast Lenin, in his address before the Third Komsomol Congress in 1920, and in a number of other speeches, established the Marxist view on the question of tradition. He stated that the proletarian culture could only develop if based on an amalgamation of all cultural values created by mankind. The most important representatives of Soviet literature underlined the importance of world literature; M. Gorki composed literary portraits of Lev Tolstoi and Vladimir

Korolenko, while D. Bednyi wrote a number of poems on Pushkin. The Proletcult was dissolved in 1920.

After the civil war the Communist Party of the Soviet Union prepared the way for a peaceful reconstruction of the national economy by introducing new economic policies and plans. Economic reconstruction brought about improved possibilities for the development of literature. Many new, rich literary talents began to be recognized: Dmitri Furmanov, the commissar of the famous Chapayev Division; Aleksandr Fadeyev, the commissar of a partisan unit in the Far East; Nikolai Ostrovski and Isaac Babel, two fighters in the glorious Budionny cavalry army. Others included Leonid Leonov, Boris Lavreiov, Fiodor Panfiorov, Vsevolod Vishnevski, Stepan Shchipatchov, Valentin Katayev, Fiodor Gladkov, and Petro Pavlenko.

A great number of writers united in literary organizations such as the group known as the "Serapion Brothers," among them Vsevolod Ivanov, Mikhail Zoshchenko, Konstantin Fedin, Nikolai Tikhonov, Venyamin Kaverin, Lev Lunz, and others. The "Group of Lev" included Ilya Selvinski, Vera Inber, and Eduard Bagritzki among their members. A number of the writers who formerly had belonged to the Proletcult organization, among them V. Aleksandrovski, F. Gladkov, and Nikolai Lyashko, united in the group known as *Kuznitza* [The Steel Forgers]. The largest proletarian writers' organization, RAPP, which had its beginnings in 1923 and was formally organized in 1925, counted D. Furmanov, A. Fadeyev, F. Panfiorov, Aleksandr Bezymenski, and Aleksandr Afinogenov among its members. These and other organizations catered to the individual interests, origins, and aesthetic philosophies of the individual writers. They promoted—although to different degrees—talented and gifted writers. Their ideologies were frequently based on idealist, aesthetic concepts. The more important works of Soviet literature, however, do not reflect these concepts.

The main theme of the literature of the 1920s was the civil war. Epic genres prevailed, and works with a solid historical background became popular. The hero of many such works was the revolutionary individual who showed a strong, unyielding character during times of stress.

A number of writers, such as Aleksandr Malyshkin in *Padeniye Daïra* [The Fall of Dair, 1923], and Aleksandr Serafimovich in his classic novel on the civil war *Zhelezny potok* (The Iron Flood, 1942), pictured the revolution as a mass movement able to create a literary hero drawn from the ranks of the people themselves. Other writers concentrated on depicting the revolutionary individual. Yuri Libedinski was one of the first writers to show the heroism of the revolutionary fighter in his novel *Nedelya* [A Week, 1922]. The class struggles taking place in the villages at this time were described by Aleksandr Neverov in his unfinished novel *Gusi-Lebedi* [Geese and Swans, 1923]. His novel *Tashkent-gorod khlebny* (Tashkent, the City of Bread), which remains popular to this day, describes a young boy's struggles against hunger and other incredible hardships during the civil war. The battles of the partisans were immortalized in stories by V. Ivanov.

The great talent of Mikhail Sholokhov first found expression in his *Donskiye rasskazy* [Stories from the Don]. D. Furmanov was the first writer to describe the flowering of the individual personality after the revolution; his *Chapayev* (1923) is a permanent memorial to the legendary hero of that name. L. Leonov's *Barsuki* (The Badgers) revealed the truth about the revolutionary villages during the period of political change. It demonstrated the resistance and backwardness of the Russian merchant class and of the wealthy peasants (*kulaks*).

A number of works created at this time show the new man as he appeared in difficult postrevolutionary situations. The prose works of N. Lyashko, Anna Karavayeva, F. Panfiorov, L. Leonov, Y. Libedinski, Kuzma Gorbunov, and other writers, together with the plays of Boris Romanshov and A. Faiko, chiefly pictured the individual and his new relationship to his work. These efforts were especially well expressed in F. Gladkov's novel *Tzement* (Cement). Together with many other writers, including K. Fedin,

L. Leonov, and A. Fadeyev, Gladkov regarded himself as the pupil of Gorki. Gorki had repeatedly pictured the relationship of individuals to work under exploitative conditions and continued to do so in his postrevolutionary works *Moï universitety* (My Universities) and *Delo Artamonovykh* (The Artamanovs), which are written from a broader, more philosophical point of view. Gorki's work and personality exerted an influence on the development of Soviet literature as a whole to an extent that can hardly be overestimated.

The present was also depicted in a versatile, satirical manner; certain writers of the old order were censored by writers of the new. Writers who became very popular were V. Kaverin, V. Katayev, Olga Forsh, and M. Zoshchenko as well as Ilya Ilf and Yevgenii Petrov, who were noted for their satirical novels *Dvenadtzat stulev* (The Twelve Chairs) and *Zolotoi telionok* (The Golden Calf). V. Mayakovski created dramatic masterpieces of satirical comedy including *Klop* (The Bedbug) and *Banya* [The Sauna]; he also showed himself to be one of the greatest Soviet poets.

By the mid-1920s a tendency toward more profound psychological writing developed, together with a deep concern for the early masters of Russian literature and with the literary legacy of the nation as a whole. This feeling found expression in the works of Gorki, A. Tolstoi, Sholokhov, Leonov, and Fedin.

In this respect the work of I. Babel, especially *Konarmiya* (Red Cavalry), a collection of short stories, is of particular importance. Fadeyev's novel *Razgrom* (The Nineteen), with its profound insight into the character of the chief protagonists, represents a peak in the various fictional studies of the civil war.

The inner conflicts of the "new man" were subjects chosen by the dramatists and poets of the time. The Komsomol poets Aleksandr Zharov, A. Bezimenski, and Mikhail Svetlov all aimed at a synthesis of the social and individual aspects of the revolution —V. Mayakovski, N. Aseyev, and N. Tikhonov, among others— now tried to express the romantic aspects of the present and of everyday life. Important writers of the 1920s included E. Bagritzki, a truly modern lyric poet and romanticist, and S. Yesenin, whose lyric heroes constantly struggle to overcome the past in the name of the new world. The literature of socialist realism reached its peak between 1920 and 1941. The socialist individual man in the conflicts of his time, and the struggles taking place between the classes were the factors determining the face of literature at this period. From the overall point of view literature presented an impressive artistic chronicle of the era, showing considerable philosophical depths and an epic breadth. These aspects found clear expression in the lyrical, epic works of V. Mayakovski.

The more important Soviet dramas also have an epic quality. M. Gorki's postrevolutionary plays, including *Yegor Bulychov i drugiye* [Igor Bulychov and the Others] and *Dostigayev i drugiye* [Dostigayev and the Others], uniquely reflect the major social conflicts in evidence on the eve of the revolution, as pictured in the emotions of the chief protagonists. Innovative changes can be observed in *Shtorm* [Storm] by Vladimir Bill-Belotzerkovski. The revolutionary fight is shown as the battle of the masses. The effects of the revolution on the intelligentsia are shown by Konstantin Trenev in *Lyubov Yarovaya*; on the officers by B. Lavrenev in *Razlom* [The Breach]; on the anarchistic sailors by V. Vishnevski in *Optimisticheskaya tragediya* [An Optimistic Tragedy]; and on the peasants by Vsevold Ivanov in *Bronepoyezd 14–69* (Armored Train No. 14–69).

The epic novel developed during this period. Its creators attempted to paint a sweeping portrait of their times; they frequently delineated historical events and sketched artistic pictures of an entire people. In his postrevolutionary work M. Gorki had already attempted to create a panorama of the entire Russian society. The culmination of these attempts and one of the greatest works of Soviet literature is his philosophical and psychological novel *Zhizn Klima Samgina* (The Life of Klim Samgin), in which the author succeeded in creating both an artistic chronicle of the

Russian intelligentsia over four decades and an encyclopedia of bourgeois individualism.

M. Sholokhov in his four-volume novel *Tikhi Don* (And Quiet Flows the Don) shows the complex path taken by the Cossacks toward the acceptance of Soviet rule. In his unfinished novel *Posledni is Udege* [The Last of the Udehes] A. Fadeyev created a great portrait of the period.

A. N. Tolstoi, who had depicted the fate of contemporary and future civilizations in his science-fiction novels, drew an epic picture of the civil war and the sufferings of the Russian intelligentsia in his trilogy *Khozhdeniye po mukam* (The Way of Suffering).

The theme of the intelligentsia was a popular one during the 1920s. The heroes of works by V. Veresayev were exposed to conflicts created by the difficult struggles of the war (*V tupike* [The Deadlock]). In his novel *Goroda i gody* (Cities and Years)—the action of which takes place in Germany, Petrograd, Moscow, and the Russian provinces before the war, during the years of revolution, and during World War I—K. Fedin described a hero from the intelligentsia, who was unable to find a place in the new life because of his abstract views. In his other important novel, *Bratya* [Brothers], Fedin discussed the complex problems of art in revolutionary times. In his novel *Sevastopol* A. Malyshkin wrote of an intellectual's search for a solid position in life, exposing the pseudoromantic illusions of an individualist who had been influenced by Kant's philosophy.

The important Soviet writers of this time were linked to the Russian classicists by surprisingly strong traditional ties. This is evident in the writings of M. Prishvin, whose philosophical, lyrical works showed the new relationships developing between the people and nature.

The task of the historical novel is to present a unified panorama of an epoch. The Soviet novelists concentrated on depicting the subjugation and enslavement of the people, and on recalling the tragic fights of all progressive movements in the past. They thus made their readers aware of the victory over the oppressors and strengthened their will to defend these new freedoms. Many writers made the historic class struggles the subject of their novels, as did Aleksei Chapygin in *Razin Stepan* and Vyacheslav Shishkov in *Yemelyan Pugachov*. Other writers, following Lenin's precepts, regarded the cultural values of the past as the foundation of the culture of the future; among these were O. Forsh (*Radischev*) and Yurii Tynyanov (*Kyukhlya* and *Pushkin*). Still others, including A. N. Tolstoi, concerned themselves with Russian politics of the past. A. N. Tolstoi in *Piotr Pervy* pictured the young Tsar Peter and his relationship to the society of his time. This work may be regarded as the most important Soviet historical novel written to date.

Soviet novelists writing about contemporary life also attempted to give an accurate picture of the historical changes taking place by sharply delineating the reality of the present in the hope of influencing it for the better. These writers succeeded in showing the gradual development of an entirely new kind of relationship that was then taking place among the people. Many writers described the changes in the country and the villages. In *Bruski* (And Then the Harvest), F. Panfiorov offered a large-scale picture of the development of a peasant artel during the time between the early 1920s and collectivization. M. Sholokhov's *Podnyataya zelina* (Seeds of Tomorrow) is the most important novel to describe the collectivization period. Aleksandr Tvardovski described the same period in his poem *Strana Muraviya* [The Land Muravia]. Problems arising in connection with industrialization were described in epic terms by writers such as L. Leonov and A. Malyshkin.

By the mid-1920s a uniformity of basic attitudes on the part of writers no longer permitted their division into either proletarian writers or *poputchiki* (political fellow travelers); up until this time RAPP had been able to classify them in this way. In a resolution adopted in 1925, the Communist Party of the Soviet Union appealed to all writers to adopt a fully socialist ideology; they felt that this would be helpful for the advancement of literature, and would enable writers to compete freely with the various movements and groups working at the time. This amalgamation, they felt, would bring about a new renaissance in literature and promote the development of a more unified moral, political, 'and aesthetic point of view. The many different literary organizations then in existence represented a serious block for the future development of literature. In 1932 the party therefore decided to dissolve all these various groups, suggesting the formation of a unified writers' association.

The First Soviet Writers' Congress was held in August, 1934 under the chairmanship of M. Gorki. As a result the development of Soviet literature in general was put on a broader theoretical base, the methods of creative Soviet literature were specifically stated to be the methods of socialist realism, and future projects and directions were outlined. The Writers' Congress promoted the opening of new fields for aesthetic consideration.

The literature of the 1930s presented the new man; it showed him in all his complicated and varied aspects. The short story and the short article, particularly well suited to fast, accurate pictures of the newly developing trends, began to gain in importance as literary genres. Works written at that time included some by the most important exponents of Soviet literature—M. Gorki, V. Ivanov, L. Leonov, F. Gladkov, Konstantin Paustovski, N. Tikhonov, Boris Gorbatov, Vladimir Stavski, and M. Prishvin. The general atmosphere of life in Russia during the first Five-Year Plan was depicted by L. Leonov in Sot (Soviet River), by Marietta Shaginyan in Gidrotzentral [The Hydroelectric Plant], by V. Katayev in Vremya vperiod (Time, Forward), and by Ilya Ehrenburg in Den vtoroi (Out of Chaos).

Although socialist man was at first only sketched in these novels they represent fine attempts on the part of the writers to depict their times and events with accuracy. By the mid-1930s this type of genre writing became more differentiated. Human problems connected with the socialist construction of the new order took over the focal point of the more recent works. Gladkov's Energiya (Energy) pictured man and his relationship to the socialist collective. L. Leonov's Skutarevski described his heroes "on the way to the ocean"—striving for a communist future. The heroism of everyday life, the creative restlessness of the people who founded the Stakhanov movement, and the development of socialist relationships within the collectives are the major themes of Yurii Krymov's *Tanker "Derbent"* (1938). The building of the city of Komsomolsk in the Far East was the subject of Vera Ketlinskaya's novel *Muzhestvo* (Courage).

Writers were now interested primarily in the new "socialist man." People and their relationships to work became the principle subject, whatever the writers' preferred genre might be; this ultimately lent a new dimension to the novel devoted to the portrayal of an individual character. In his autobiographical *Shkola* [The School of Life], Arkadi Gaidar pictured the formation and development of socialist thought and action in the adventures of his fourteen-year-old hero.

N. Ostrovski's novel *Kak zakalyalas stal* (How the Steel Was Tempered) is one of the most effective works of Soviet literature. In *Pedagogicheskaya poema* (The Road to Life), Anton Makarenko presents a model example of the Soviet educational novel. The development of young heroes is depicted by V. Katayev in *Beleyet parus odinoki* (A White Sail Gleams).

Soviet children's literature began to emerge in the 1930s. In addition to writers such as Kornei Chukovsky, Lev Kasil, and M. Ilyin, A. Gaidar became especially popular with *Timur i yevo Komanda* (Timur and His Squad) and *Chuk i Gek*. Also very popular were verses written for children by Olga Bergholz, Agniya Barto, and Samuil Marshak, whose skillful *Mister Twister* is a model example of the genre.

A more intensified study of character and an increase in ideological struggles took place in Soviet drama in the 1930s, as is shown in the works of V. Vishnevski, N. Pogodin, L. Leonov, Aleksei Arbuzov, B. Romanshov, Viktor Gusev, and others. The "new reality" emerged in the work of N. Pogodin, as can be seen in his *Poema o topore* [Poem of the Axe] and *Moi drug* [My Friend]; in Aleksandr Afinogenov's *Chudak* [The Crank] and

Strakh [Fear], as well as in the works of L. Leonov, V. Katayev, and A. Faiko. A severe conflict of opinion began to develop among playwrights at this time regarding the character of the new drama. While Vishnevski, Pogodin, and others saw in the new theater an epic broadening of the scope of the drama, Afinogenov, Vladimir Kirshon, and others wished to present life in a more traditional manner and within a relatively narrow framework. These two movements reflect the manifold possibilities then existing for Soviet drama. The 1930s produced a whole new generation of writers—Mikhail Isakovski, A. Tvardovski, Aleksandr Prokofyev, Aleksei Surkov, Konstantin Simonov, S. Shchipachov, O. Bergholz, I. Selvinski, N. Tikhonov, and Mikhail Golodni among others.

The most important prose works written during the 1930s were the romantic *Pobediteli* [The Victors] and *Poslednaya notch* [The Last Night] by E. Bagritzki; *Yurga* and *Stikhi o Kaketii* [Poems on Kakhetia] by N. Tikhonov, as well as Vladimir Lugovskoi's *Bolshevikam pustyni i vesny* [To the Bolsheviks of the Wasteland and of the Spring]. The 1930s also produced numerous important Russian songs. The important ballad-writer Isakovski wrote intimate, colorful lyrics (*Katyusha*); Vasilii Lebedev-Kumach, on the other hand, made direct, strong ballads about life in the country (*Shiroka strana moya rodnaya* [My Great Homeland]). In the second half of the 1930s lyric poetic writing developed to an even greater degree. S. Shchipachov, Yevgeni Dolmatovski, A. Surkov, and A. Prokofyev wrote in a versatile, original manner about the thoughts and emotions of the new Soviet man. A. Tvardovski, M. Isakovski, N. Tikhonov, I. Selvinski, Dmitri Kedrin, P. Vasilyev, and Nikolai Dementev, among others, joined the ranks of the lyric poets.

Socialism was winning great victories during these years, but they were also the years in which the gradual rise of fascism brought about fears for a world war. Soviet writers did their best to ward off this danger. A. Tolstoi, I. Ehrenburg, N. Tikhonov, Boris Pasternak, V. Vishnevski, A. Barto and others made personal appearances at international meetings to warn against war and fascism. Mikhail Koltzov, one of the most talented Soviet political writers, reported in his *Ispanski dnevnik* [Spanish Journal] on the antifascist fight in Spain. Gorki, A. Tolstoi, Ehrenburg and others wrote articles in political journals calling for the world to do battle against fascism. In his novel *Padeniye Parizha* (The Fall of Paris), which depicted the tragedy of the French people, I. Ehrenburg exposed the fascist aggression within France as well as the treacheries of the French government.

The development of the literature of the 1930s contradicts the rumors circulated by enemies of Soviet literature, who spoke of a "decline of literature"; these rumors were simply a variation on the "ruin of literature" attitude frequently mentioned during the first years after the revolution. The "decline of literature" theories were supposedly supported by certain manifestations of the personality cult.

The personality cult did, in fact, cause considerable damage to Soviet literature in the Thirties. The creative means of a number of writers was limited; in many instances creative discussion was replaced by a bureaucratic administration. Development of a living literature and its gradual upsurge was nevertheless not halted. The cultural policies of the party as evidenced in the resolutions adopted in 1925 and 1932 proved to be the correct ones, as is demonstrated by the glorious history of the united fight of Soviet writers against fascism in World War II. During the war Soviet writers united on the side of the people. More than one thousand writers early exchanged the pen for the sword in order to take an active part in the fight. Soviet literature suffered considerable losses: J. Petrov, J. Krymov, A. Gaidar, V. Stavski, A. Lebedev, and many others lost their lives. These writers did not fight with the sword alone, however; they searched for suitable ways in which to write effective propaganda about wartime events.

A great many authors wrote regularly in *Pravda*; others, including Tvardovski, Vadim Kozhevnikov, A. Surkov, K. Simonov, A. Prokofyev, N. Tikhonov, and V. Vishnevski, worked as correspondents for army newspapers. They told of the heroic deeds of the Soviet fighters and of the atrocities committed by the enemy.

A. Tolstoi, one of the most original and popular writers of the time, took the theme of the fatherland and the Russian people as the subject of numerous philosophical articles. The history of the fatherland was also a familiar subject in the work of L. Leonov, who made his readers understand that the responsibility for the victory over fascism rested in part with them.

The writings of M. Sholokhov were very popular at this time. In his sketch *Nauka nenavisti* (The Science of Hatred), the hero, a Soviet prisoner of war in Germany, loses his respect for the Germans and his former regard for their culture on the basis of his own experiences; he develops an irreconcilable hatred of the fascists. In another short piece written during the first months of the war, *Voyennoplenniye* [Prisoners of War], Sholokhov gave a different view of the Germans, showing on the one side the arrogant representative of the master race and on the other the thoughtful soldier worrying about the future of his homeland. While Tolstoi, Leonov, and Sholokhov placed the national element in the foreground of the antifascist political writing, I. Ehrenburg depicted the dangers of fascism to all mankind and the damage it could do to world culture.

Like the political journalists, Soviet poets also employed their creative talents in the fight against fascism. The poems of writers such as Tvardovski, Isakovski, Shchipachov, Surkov, Simonov, Marshak, and others became familiar to great numbers of soldiers at the front. During the war many important poems were written, all of which reflected the experiences and thoughts of the people at war. One of the first works of this kind to appear was *Kirov s nami* [Kirov Is with Us] by N. Tikhonov, which—with the poems *Febralski dnevk* [February Journal] and *Leningradskaya poema* by O. Bergholz and the lyrical diary *Pulkovski meridian* [The Pulkovo Meridian] by V. Inber—is a dignified memorial to the people of the heroic city of Leningrad.

The poems of this period—Antokolski's *Syn* [The Son] and A. Prokofyev's *Rossiya* [Russia]—sing in universal terms of the homeland and its people. A. Tvardovski's *Vasilii Tiorkin* presented the simple soldier as the hero of a true national epic.

The dramatists, too, contributed to the defeat of fascism. A few months after the commencement of hostilities plays with wartime themes had begun to appear, written by Afinogenov, K. Trenev, and others. Plays about the war were part of the theatrical repertoire during the war years, for the theater, even in those difficult times, fulfilled its duty to the people. One of the most popular works was *Russkiye lyudi* (Russian People) by K. Simonov, which depicted Soviet patriotism and the moral growth of the people during the war. Of particular importance were Leonov's *Nashestviye* [Invasion] and A. Tolstoi's historical drama *Ivan Groznyi* [Ivan the Terrible].

Careful characterization was needed on the part of an author in order for him to inspire his readers with the heroic deeds of his heroes. Toward the end of the war years and immediately after the war numerous writers produced short stories of considerable merit, among them Tikhonov, Leonid Sobolev, K. Paustovski, K. Simonov, K. Trenev, B. Gorbatov, V. Grosman, and F. Gladkov. A short story by A. Tolstoi, *Russki kharakter* [The Russian Character], is typical of the genre. In it the author traces the forces that made heroes out of simple Russian people during those difficult times.

In 1941 V. Grosman wrote his lyrically expressive novel *Narod bessmerten* [People Immortal], in which he predicted that the coming victory would be due to the inner strength of the nation. The invincibility and the inflexible will of the nation are also shown by B. Gorbatov in his novel *Nepokorionnye* [The Inflexible Ones]. A. Bek's *Volokolamskoye shose* [The Volokolamsk Highway] describes the battles near Moscow, while the great turning point of the war at the Volga was described by K. Simonov in his heroic epic *Dni i nochi* (Days and Nights).

With the arrival of the postwar period, the writers' task was to immortalize the heroic deeds of the people during the war as an encouragement to coming generations and as a warning to the indifferent. One of the most important memorials of this kind is A. Fadeyev's *Molodaya gvardiya* (The Young Guard). At this time M. Sholokhov began work on his still unfinished novel *Oni zrazhalis za rodinu* [They Fought for Their Homeland], in which he depicted the depths of patriotic feeling among the soldiers, their thoughts and feelings of responsibility for the fate of the entire nation. Boris Polevoi re-created the fate of a hero in his novel *Povest o nastoyashchem cheloveka* (A Story about a Real Man); I. Ehrenburg described the events of the entire war in his epic novel *Burya* [The Storm], which is closely related in style to his other war novels—*Padeniye Parizha* (The Fall of Paris) and *Devyati val* (The Ninth Wave).

World War II represented a time of severe trial for the Soviet people, and its aftermath was felt by them for many years. Postwar writers frequently recalled the different phases of the war. The first months of the war were the subject of M. Bubennov's novel *Belaya berioza* [The White Birch]. Nikolai Chukovski retold the story of the siege of Leningrad in *Baltiiskoye nebo* [Under Baltic Skies]. E. Kazakevich, in *Vesna na Odere* (Spring on the Oder), described the last days of the war and the decisive battles in Germany. The humane character of the Soviet army's missions and the details of the liberation are very convincingly described by Kazakevich in *Dom na ploshchadi* (The House on the Place) which is a continuation of *Vesna na Odere.* Here he shows the soldiers of a Soviet command post working with the German antifascists in a small town in the Hartz Mountains during the first hours following the liberation. P. Pavlenko in *Shchastye* (Happiness) depicts his hero's search for a deeper meaning to life.

Many novels tell of the tragedies and scars of war left on the lives of the people of the interior. Azhayev's *Daleko ot Moskvy* [Far from Moscow] describes the formation of a collective during the construction of an oil pipe-line in the Far East.

In works with similar themes, authors now began to form a link between the established tradition of the 1930s; the new interpersonal relationships of socialist reconstruction came to the fore as subject matter. The talents of Vera Panova, who had become known earlier for her novel *Sputniki* (The Train), began to develop further after the war. Her novels *Krushilikha* (Looking

Ahead), *Yasnyye berega* [Bright Shores], *Vremena goda* (Span of the Year), and the short story *Seriozha* (Times Walked) tenderly describe the new life.

The profound problems evident in Soviet agriculture, which had become completely disorganized as a result of the war, were pictured by Yalizar Maltzev, Grigori Medynski, Semion Babayevski, and, particularly successfully, by Galina Nikolayeva in *Zhatva* (The Harvest), which has been translated into several languages. The beauty and poetry of the human soul is shown in a number of original works by Paustovski. Continuing the tradition of folklorist poetry, M. Prishvin, who frequently used the fairy tale as his medium, created works depicting man and his relationship to nature.

A large and varied collection of works based on historical events of the past appeared soon after the war. In his novel *Stepan Razin*, Stepan Zlobin described the early, desperate uprising of the peasants. F. Gladkov in a four-part autobiographical novel told of the lot of the poor country people and the fishermen in Russia before the turn of the century. K. Fedin wrote about preparing and carrying out the revolution and the civil war. The first two parts of his trilogy *Pervyye radosti* (Early Joys) and *Neobyknovennoye leto* (No Ordinary Summer) occupy a special position in Russian postwar literature. In contrast to most works taking the intelligentsia and their life as a theme, Fedin's work was focused on professional revolutionaries and party workers.

The poets, too, concerned themselves for a long time with the events, trials, sufferings, and heroic deeds of World War II. Widely differing artistic interpretations were given by A. Tvardovski, A. Surkov, O. Bergholz, A. Prokofyev, and S. Shchipachov. The harsher sentiments of war, however, were soon replaced by a more universal feeling of peace. The lyric hero, having succeeded in escaping from the horrors of war once again, breathes the fresh air of peace; he becomes intoxicated with the joys of reconstruction, but is disquietened by the new dangers of war once again evoked by the dark forces of the old world.

In his poem *Dom u dorogi* [The House at the Wayside], A. Tvardovski captured the feelings and thoughts of those returning from war who swore never to forget what they had experienced. By 1948 the problems and joys of peaceful reconstruction were finding expression in the poems of N. Tikhonov, O. Bergholz, Nikolai Gribachov, Mikhail Lukonin, Semion Kirsanov, and S. Shchipachov. Many poets dedicated their talents to the fight for peace; among these were K. Simonov in *Druzya i vragi* (Friends and Foes), A. Surkov in *Miru-mir* [Peace to the World], and N. Tikhonov in *Dva potoka* [Two Streams].

Dramatic writing underwent a particularly difficult period after the war. The transition from the conflict-loaded years of the war to the era of reconstruction made heavy demands upon the playwright. At first a definite upsurge was noted in the life of the theater. A number of new plays appeared dealing with the problems of war, including B. Lavrenev's *Za tekh, kto v more* [To Those on the High Seas]. Several plays focused on the political questions of the time—*Russki vopros* (The Russian Question) by K. Simonov, and *Golos Ameriki* [The Voice of America] by B. Lavrenev. Conflicts of Soviet postwar life were also handled with great versatility by B. Romashov in *Velikaya sila* [The Great Force], by Aleksandr Stein in *Zakon chesti* [Law of Honor], K. Simonov in *Chuzhaya ten* [Foreign Shadow], and by Anatolii Sofronov in *V odnom gorode* [In a Town] and *Moskovski kharakter* [The Character of Moscow].

A number of plays appeared between 1950 and 1953 the value of which was greatly diminished by poor construction, didacticism, and pseudoconflicts. The "theory of the absence of conflict," based on the idyllic notion of a society without conflicts and contradictions, greatly damaged the development of the drama. Such deficiencies, however, do not justify the conclusion that a decline in literature had taken place after the war. In many works in all genres Soviet literature discussed the difficult questions of existence raised by the war. By reflecting the peaceful reconstruction taking place at that time Soviet literature was able to form a link with the great traditions of the 1930s and, at the same time, venture forth into new fields.

The Second Soviet Writers' Congress was held in December, 1954. Its participants were able to look back on two decades of literary development and to outline plans for the future of literature. The Twentieth Congress of the Communist Party of the Soviet Union was also of great importance since it brought about a noticeable revival in literature. In a relatively short period of time a great number of young writers had come to the fore. New themes emerged, and anything that could inhibit socialist development was critically examined. These tendencies had already become evident in some of the finest works of Soviet literature written before the Twentieth Congress. L. Leonov based his patriotic novel *Russki les* (The Russian Forest) on very real problems. His heroes fight against intrigue, indifference, and bureaucracy. In this particular novel the concern expressed for the Russian forest is symbolic of the author's concern for the welfare of the nation. In his essays published in 1953–54, Valentin Ovechkhins exposed the abuses existing in agriculture and suggested remedies. In *Iskateli* (Those Who Seek) Daniil Granin opposed all immoral tendencies in science and technology, thus aiding the creative forces of science by means of literature. Vsevolod Kochetov's *Zhurbiny* (The Zhurbins) depicted the simple Russian worker as the supporter of socialist society.

The dramatists, who wished to contribute to a consolidation of communist ethics and morale, probed deeply into the complex thoughts and feelings of their characters, and by creating true, conflicting situations developed a psychological drama. V. Rozov in his play *V dobryi chas* [Happy Landings!] demanded the recognition of human dignity. In *Gody starnstvi* [Intricate Roads], A. Arbuzov made moral tenets the focal point in the lives of his characters. New foundations for family life were portrayed by A. Sofronov in *Serdtze ne proshchayet* [The Heart Does Not Forgive]. In *Zolotaya kareta* [The Golden Carriage], L. Leonov was interested in true human happiness. All the tendencies mentioned above were further developed in the course of the next few years. N. Pogodin's *Tretya pateticheskaya* [The Final Chord]—the last part of the author's Lenin trilogy—may be regarded as the most important phenomenon in Soviet drama of the time.

Plays about contemporary problems are very popular in Russia today. Among these are *Irkutskaya istoriya* [Irkutsk Story] by A. Arbuzov, and works by A. Sofronov, V. Rozov, Nikolai Virta, Yevgeni Shvarts, Samuil Alioshin, A. Salynski, and A. Stein. The most important work of postwar Soviet poetry is A. Tvardovski's *Za dalyu dal* [A Distant Place beyond Distant Places], the lyric hero of which perfectly represents the ideas and feelings of today's Soviet man. Tvardovski's poem *Tiorkin na tom svete* [Tiorkin In the Other World] is a controversial attempt to picture the abuses of the recent past in satirical form. Many poets, including Tvardovski, felt the need for a more universal treatment of subjects. V. Lugovskoi experienced an increase in artistic activity in the last years of his life. His most important work, *Seredina veka* [Halfway through the Century], is a collection of twenty-four poems—an "autobiography of the century"—written in the course of fifteen years.

The most important lyric writers of the 1950s and 1960s turned their attention to the demanding questions of the time. Their work is characterized by a freshness and richness of impression and emotion. Typical of the period are such writers as N. Aseyev, A. Prokofyev, Nikolai Zabolotzki, S. Shchipachov, M. Isakovski, M. Aliger, N. Gribachov, Leonid Martynov, Mikhail Dudin, and Yaroslav Smelyakov.

A remarkable phenomena of Soviet literature in recent years has been the appearance of numerous young poets. These writers —frequently still a little awkward and inexperienced—have enriched Soviet lyric poetry to a significant extent by their fresh approach, elan, exuberance, and joie de vivre. They have continued to maintain their critical attitudes and to experiment boldly despite setbacks and disappointments. Such poets include Yegor Isayev, Yevgenii Vinokurov, Konstantin Vanshenkin, Vasili Fio-

dorov, Yevgenii Yevtushenko, Robert Rozhdestvenski, Andrei Voznesenski, Bella Akhmadulina, and Vladimir Zybin. These names
represent only a few of the vast number of talented poets now
beginning to develop. We may be certain that they will do justice
to the great inheritance left them by Mayakovski, Bloc, Bednyi,
Yesenin, and Tvardovski.

The works of M. Sholokhov represent a high point in the development of Russian prose since 1954. His story *Sudba cheloveka*
(One Man's Destiny, and Other Stories) is a minor masterpiece
about the fate of a great man. It represents a warning to all mankind not easily forgotten.

In the second part of the novel *Podnyataya tzelina* (Seeds of
Tomorrow), Sholokhov examines significant contemporary questions of the present in the light of the past. One of the main
concerns of present-day social development—to work with the
people for the people in order to create a communist society—is
extraordinarily well presented.

Attempts to elucidate present-day problems with the aid of material from the more recent past, generally speaking, occupy a prominent place in the literature of today. In *Zhestokost* (Cruelty),
Pavel Nilin shows the sincerity and passion of the young communists during the early 1920s. Sergei Zalygin in *Na Irtyshe* [On
the Irtysh] and Mikhail Alekseyev in *Klehb—imya sushchest-
vitelnoye* [Bread Is a Substantive] give a new view of the days
of collectivization. In his memoirs *Lyudi, gody, zhizn* (see under
entry for full titles and translations) I. Ehrenburg depicts half
a century of Russian history in short, exciting, episodic scenes.
The new writers are constantly moved by the events of World
War II. Yurii Bondarev, Grigori Baklanov, and, above all, K.
Simonov, were extremely skillful in re-creating the heroism and
tragedy of the war years, frequently utilizing newly discovered
material. In his novel *Kostior* [The Flame], which is part of a
trilogy, K. Fedin depicts the civil war heroes as they have developed in the days just prior to and right after World War II.

Numerous writers, using contemporary material, have created

works that may serve others as guides through life. The great conflicts of the 1950s are treated by G. Nikolayeva in her novel *Bitva v puti* (Battle Along the Road), with its headstrong hero Bakhirev. The works of D. Granin—*Posle svadby* [After the Wedding] and *Idu na grozu* [Toward the Thunderstorm]—are also characterized by their immediacy. In addition to experienced writers such as V. Kochetov, B. Polevoi, Y. Maltzev, M. Bubennov, V. Kozhevnikov, F. Panfiorov, Mikhail Shestev, Georgi Markov, Vladimir Tendryakov, and Yurii Trifonov, many young and talented writers have appeared in the course of the last few years. Among them are Vasilii Aksionov, Yurii Kazakov, Anatoli Kuznetzov, Aleksandr Rekemchuk, Georgii Vladimov, Vladimir Soloukhin, and others, including many of the most widely read writers of today.

ARMENIAN LITERATURE

The Keilin documents, originating from the slave state of Urartu between the end of the ninth century B.C. and the beginning of the sixth century B.C. are among the oldest proofs of an Armenian culture to come down to us. The beginnings of a written Armenian language, used for both original works and for translations, resulted in the appearance, in the fifth century A.D., of histories, poetry, and various philosophical, theological, and religious writings. It was at this time that the great scholar Mesrob Mashtots (361–440) created the Armenian alphabet. Theological and polemic prose and church poetry were the dominant genres between the seventh and ninth centuries—the time of the Arab invasion and of Byzantine expansion. Secular themes began to appear in literature, art, and the sciences in the tenth century, with the restoration of Armenian independence.

The literary representative of the early renaissance in Armenia was Grigor Narekatzi (951–1003). During the twelfth century literature, art, and the sciences continued to develop in a secular direction. The foremost representative of literature at this time was the fabulist Mkhithar Gosh (1133–1213) and the poet Nerses Shnorali ["Nerses the Gracious"] (1102–72).

In the thirteenth century church-oriented poetry began to decline and was replaced by a feudal, increasingly reactionary literary movement. This was in strong contrast to the work of the two best writers of the time—Frik, the author of numerous sociocritical poems, and the fabulist Vardan Aigektzi. The early Armenian feudal state of Cilicia had ceased to exist around the end of the fourteenth century. During the sixteenth to nineteenth centuries, Armenia was divided between Turkey and Persia. The yearning of the people for liberty was never dimmed, and it repeatedly found expression in the literature of the period, in the songs of Naapet Kachag (sixteenth century) and Sayat-Nova (pseud. of Arutin Sayadian). The sixteenth century saw the first books printed in Armenian. Most were printed abroad, first in Venice and then in many Western European countries. The first Armenian periodical, *Azdarar* [The Messenger], was published in Madras, India, in 1794.

The liberation of Transcaucasia and East Armenia, and the gradual union with Russia between 1801 and 1827, created a favorable climate for further literary development. Classicism had begun to develop during the eighteenth century, and it remained the dominant movement during the first quarter of the nineteenth century. The representatives of this movement—O. Vanandetzi and Arsen Bagratuni, among others—wrote of traditional historical events and were the authors of several important translations. These writers, however, were hampered by the fact that they wrote in a language very difficult to understand—Grabar, which even in the twelfth century was regarded as antiquated.

The modern Armenian literary language (Ashkharabar) was created by the democratic humanist Khachatur Abovian. His literary work, which encompassed many genres, strengthened both progressive romanticism and realism; it also acted as a counterbalance to classicism. His work was continued by Mikael Nalbandian in the 1880s. This was a time of considerable development in all literary genres.

Prose first developed in liberated East Armenia; Pertsh Proshian (pseud. of Ter-Arakelian, 1837–1907) and Gazares Agaian were the outstanding representatives of Armenian prose literature at this time. These writers described the early capitalist class differences observable in the Armenian villages. Proshian's novel *Unon* (1900) described the spontaneous uprising of the peasants; his hero was an avenger, one who came to relieve the sufferings of the oppressed. An important representative of West Armenian prose of the 1870s and 1880s was Akop Paronian, who wrote sociopolitical satires in varying genres.

The tendency to return to the traditions of national liberation were fanned by the events of the Russo-Turkish war of 1877–78, giving impetus to the current rise in popularity of the historical novel. The more important representatives of this genre in the 1870s and 1880s were O. Tzerentz (pseud. of Shikhmanian) and Raffi (pseud. of Akop Melip-Akopian); Raffi's most important work, the novel *Sav mel*, is based on events that occurred during the fourth century. In both East and West Armenia prose writing reached its peak in the 1880s and 1890s. With the rise of Aleksander Shirvanzade (pseud. of Movesian), Grigor Muratzan, Nar-Dos (pseud. of M. Ovanisian), and Vartanes Papasian critical realism became the leading literary movement of the period. These writers took for their major themes the gradual disintegration of bourgeois society, village life, and the fight for national liberty. Nar-Dos wrote of the tragic fate of the middle classes.

A national drama began to develop toward the end of the 1870s and 1880s in West Armenia. The founder and most important figure in Armenian realistic drama was Gabriel Sundukian, whose comedy *Pepo* appeared in a Russian translation in 1896. The main theme of progressive Armenian poetry was the country's fight for liberation, both in the past and in the 1890s, at which time West Armenia still remained under Turkish rule. The most important representatives of East Armenian literature between 1860–80 were Rafael Patkanian and Smbat Shakhasis; the important representatives of West Armenian literature of the 1860s were Mkrtich Peshiktashlian and Petros Durian. The sociopolitical poetry of Yoannes Yoannisian and Aleksander Zaturian, written in the last two decades of the nineteenth century, represents the transition of literature from the eighteenth to the twentieth century.

The institution of Soviet power in Armenia created an atmosphere favorable to the development of a socialist national literature. In the 1920s the older writers gradually began to differ from each other in their attitudes; the more distinguished openly declared themselves in favor of the socialist revolution—Ovanes Tumanian, O. Yoannisian, Avetik Issakian, A. Shirvanzade, Nar-Dos, and Derenik Demirchan. Numerous writers' associations came into being at this time. The *Federatziya sovetskikh pisatelei Armenii* (Armenian Writers' Union) was founded in 1929; it accepted the so-called *poputchiki* (political fellow travelers) for membership. The literature of this time encompassed all the major genres, and utilized an extensive palette of colorful themes. The civil war was the most favored topic; the theme of liberated man and his work became very popular.

The most important representatives of poetry at this time included Akop Akopian, a classic writer of socialist Armenian literature, Egish Charentz. (pseud. of Sogomanian), and Asat Vshtuni. Prose writers included Arasi (pseud. of Movses Arutyunian), D. Demirchian, and Aksel Bakuntz.

This promising literary development continued into the 1930s. Contemporary and historical themes remained popular. A new generation of writers joined the ranks of the established authors. Wartime literature was at first dominated by the minor genres in both poetry and prose, but historical novels soon reappeared. The main themes of the time were the heroic, patriotic, and humane qualities of the people. Among the most significant works on World War II was Kochar's *The Children of the Great House* (1952). Prevolutionary events in Armenia are depicted in L. Guruntz's novel *Golden Morning* (1953), as well as in Nairi Sarian's drama *Mr. Petros and His Ministers* (1958).

Many authors have written on contemporary and fantastic themes—Sero Khansadian (*The Country*) and A. Shaibon (*Captains of the Oceans of Space*), and have produced adventure tales —Vakhtang Ananian. A generation of young poets—Paruir Sevak,

Vaagu Davtian, and Amo Sagiian among them—have contributed
to the riches of Armenian poetry.

AZERBAIDZHANI LITERATURE

Azerbaidzhani literature has a centuries-old tradition. The oldest
monuments of literature originating in the area now known as
Azerbaidzhan are legends of the ancient Medes, recorded by
Herodotus, and the *Avesta*, or sacred book of the Zoroastrians—
a collection of prayers, myths, and laws. Both works go back to
the seventh century B.C. After the disintegration of the ancient
empire of the Medes, a new literary language—Albanian—began
to develop in ancient Albania, that is, in the northeastern part of
present-day Azerbaidzhan. Azerbaidzhani poetry written in Albanian reached a high level in the sixth and seventh centuries,
but the invasion of the Arabs and the forced introduction of Islam
in the seventh century brought the development of independent
art and literature to an abrupt halt.

From the seventh to the eleventh century, during the period
of Arab domination, the Azerbaidzhani people produced a great
number of distinguished poets—Babakukhi Baku, Pir Hussein
Shirvani, and Khatib Tabrizi among others—who wrote in Arabic,
at that time the predominant language. The epic *Kitab-i dede
Korkut*, which was written in Azerbaidzhani, appeared in the
eleventh century. The Azerbaidzhani language had by this time
developed to a considerable extent, and the epic—which consists
of twelve songs extolling courage, patriotism, and truth—has
greatly influenced the development of Azerbaidzhani national
poetry.

The consolidation of the small individual states into ancient
Shirvan at the end of the eleventh and during the twelfth century, the gradual economic development of the towns, and the
growth of social contradictions brought about a favorable condition
for the development of scholarship and culture. It was at this time
that Abu'l-Ula Gandshevi, the "King of the Poets," dedicated his
panegyric verses to the rulers of Shirvan. Hagani (1120–99) at

first also extolled the rulers of his country; later, however, he wrote courageous poems against their religious fanaticism, their feudal despotism, and their tyrannic rule. As a result he was persecuted and forced to flee the country. The poetic work of the master of lyric love songs Feleki (1118–81), the sensitive nature poems of Katran Tebrizi as well as those by Mekhseti Hanum were characterized by their freedom-loving spirit. With the work of the genial Nizami Gandzhevi (1141–1209) twelfth-century Azerbaidzhani poetry reached its peak.

During the reign of the thirteenth- and fourteenth-century Mongols poetry developed a mood of pessimism. But soon—in the religio-mystical disguise of Sufism and pantheism—the protest against the Mongol yoke awoke and grew. The works of Shams Tebrizi, Maragaly, Akhvedi, Makhmud Shabusteri (who, toward the end of the thirteenth century, wrote the well-known *Gulshan-ras* [The Flower Garden of Secrets]), and that of Esar Tebrizi, a pupil of Zizam and the author of the poem *Mekhri Mushtari*, developed during this movement of protest.

The poems of Nezimiz are of great significance in Azerbaidzhani literature. They were the product of the Hurufite movement of the late fourteenth century, and protested the feudal yoke and bloody rule of Tamerlane (1336?–1405). In these philosophical ghazals the poet extolled the greatness and divine nature of man; he was the first to create a large divan, or collection of poems, in his native tongue. Hasim Anvar (d. 1434), Habibi and Shah Ismail Hatai, author of *Dekhname* [Ten Open Letters] and *Nasikhet-name* [The Book of Instructions], also contributed significantly to Azerbaidzhani literature. The great Azerbaidzhani poet of the sixteenth century was Mohammed Fizuli (1498–1556) whose progressive, humanist writings brought the Azerbaidzhani literary language to maturity.

The development of Azerbaidzhani literature in the sixteenth century was characterized by the flowering of oral, folklorist poetry and the appearance of numerous romantic national epics. These included *Kör-Ogly, Ashug-Garib,* and *Abbas and Gülges.* This strong movement in national poetry significantly encouraged classical poetry to be directed more toward the people and their interests, a view which found expression in the seventeenth century in the simple, lucidly vivid poems of Govsi Tebrizi, Aga Masikh Shirvani, and Saib Tebrizi. Azerbaidzhani literature of the eighteenth century continued to be of a popular nature; Vidadi's social poems are frequently tinged with sadness, however, and in Molla-Panach Vagif's work we see realistic poetry filled with optimism. The union of Azerbaidzhan with Russia in 1828 opened new perspectives for the development of Azerbaidzhani literature.

The progressive literature of Azerbaidzhan found strong and valuable allies in the revolutionary, democratic thinking of Russia and in the Russian literature of critical realism, which was at that time gaining acceptance. The humanist poet and scholar Abbas Kuli-Aga Bakikhanov and Mirsa Shafi Vasekh may be regarded as the first representatives of the new Azerbaidzhani literature. Their works prepared the way for the most significant Azerbaidzhani poet of the nineteenth century and the founder of the Azerbaidzhani theater, Mirsa Fath Ali Akhundov. Akhundov's works greatly influenced the development of the satirical movement within Azerbaidzhani literature, which counted among its members Kasum-bek Sakir and Said Asim Shirvani. Among the playwrights can be included Nadshafbek Vesirov (*From Bad to Worse* and *The Suffering of Fokhraddin*); Dshalil Mamed-Kuli-Zade (*Corpses*), Abduragim Akhverdov, and Suleiman Sani Akhundov.

The development and strengthening of the proletarian movement led to the formation and consolidation of the strong revolutionary and revolutionary-democratic movement. Members of this movement supported *Molla Nasreddin*, the most important satirical magazine of the Western Orient. They drew certain conclusions from the events of the Russian revolution, and applied them to their own struggles with the nationalist Azerbaidzhani bourgeoisie, the feudal counterrevolution, and their literary exponents and supporters (Hussein Dzhavid, Akhmed Dzhavad, among others). Nariman Narimanov and Alekper Sabit were the most important representatives of revolutionary-democratic Azerbaidzhani literature in the closing years of the nineteenth and the beginning of the twentieth century.

The victory of Soviet power in Azerbaidzhan (1920) opened vast possibilities for the development of Azerbaidzhani literature. The revolutionary changes led to a liberation of the creativity of the people, and new, healthy forces came to literature. This young generation of writers was supported by the important writers of the older generation (D. Mamed-Kuli-Zade, A. Akhverdov, S. S. Akhundov, Mamed Said Ordubady, and others) who, even before the revolution, had devoted their artistic abilities to the task of liberating the people.

A further consolidation of the united front of Soviet Azerbaidzhani writers took place during the following years. Under the leadership of the Communist Party they struggled against bourgeois nationalism and the theories of "pure art." Since 1934, Azerbaidzhani writers have been members of the Soviet Writers' Union. The first decade of its development saw Azerbaidzhani Soviet literature gaining remarkable successes on its road to socialist realism. The new vital energies, socialist reconstruction, and the secure feeling generated in Azerbaidzhan by its friendly relationship with the many other peoples of the great Union were artistically reflected in poetry, drama, and the novel. Samed Vurgun, Suleiman Rustam, Mamed Ragim, Adhmed Dzhamil, and Rasul Rsa, among other writers, came to the fore, lending Azerbaidzhani poetry of the 1930s its own individual character. S. S. Akhundov's play, considered the first Soviet drama, *The Eyrie of the Falcon*, was written in 1921.

During the following years, drama became the most successful genre in Azerbaidzhani literature, its practitioners including writers such as Dzhafar Dzhabarly and S. Vurgun. The achievements in the field of the novel are hardly less impressive; novelists included M. S. Ordubady, Mir Dzhalal (*Risen Man; The Manifesto of a Young Man*), Suleiman Ragimov (*Shamo*), Alekper-

Zade Abulhassan (*The World is Crumbling*), Mekhti Hussein, and Mirsa Ibrahimov. In the days of World War II, Azerbaidzhani literature followed the lead taken by Soviet literature as a whole in battling against Hitlerism. The body of works written during the war reflect the ideals of Soviet patriotism, hate for the fascist aggressors, and belief in the just cause and in the victory of the Soviet Union.

A number of important realist works on social reconstruction, the socialist village, and the life of the oil workers in Baku appeared during the early postwar years. A new generation of young Azerbaidzhani Soviet writers are now successfully engaged in depicting the stormy development of their country toward communism. Among these are the novelists Bairam Bairamov (*Leaves*, 1958), Ilyas Efendiyev (*Yew-trees at the Water*, 1959 and *Three Friends Beyond the Mountains*, 1963), and G. Musayev (*The Northwind*, 1963). Poets include E. Alibeili, S. Chalil, N. Chasri, Taliat Eyubov, I. Kibirli, S. Rustam, I. Safarly, A. Seinalli, and Bachtiyar Vagab-Zade.

BYELORUSSIAN LITERATURE

Byelorussian literature began to develop in the eleventh and twelfth centuries. It was based on the Old Russian literature of Kiev, a background it shares with both Russian and Ukrainian literature. In the fourteenth century, Byelorussia was incorporated into Lithuania. The Byelorussian nation and its language, the official language of Lithuania at this time, developed amidst the conflict of the lower classes with the feudal oppressors and with Catholicism. Laws, chronicles, and all diplomatic documents were written in Byelorussian.

The Lublin agreements concluded with Poland in 1569 made Lithuania a part of Poland. The Byelorussian people struggled hard against social, national, and religious oppression, and this struggle is reflected in the literature of the sixteenth and the seventeenth century. Two opposing trends appeared at this time, one reactionary, feudal-Catholic trend directed toward Poland, and one progressive movement directed toward union with Russia.

The chief representative of the anti-Catholic movement was Georgi Skorina (circa 1490–1541), who printed both the Bible and other writings in Byelorussian, adding commentaries of his own which reflected humanist and patriotic views. The idea of a union between Byelorussia and Russia is also reflected in the works of the scholar-poet Simeon Polotzki. In 1697 the Polish Diet passed a law prohibiting the use of Byelorussian. The subsequent reaction on the part of the Catholics resulted in the disintegration of written Byelorussian literature. During this period, only oral national poetry was able to produce anything worthy of note; these achievements were the seeds of the new Byelorussian literature.

The union of Byelorussia with Russia after the first partition of Poland toward the end of the eighteenth century led to an increase in literary development. Anonymous poems written in the early years of the nineteenth century contain realistic pictures of the life and work of the Byelorussian peasant. Tsarism continued to suppress national cultures, however, and most of the works of Byelorussian literature created in the first half of the nineteenth century were disseminated in manuscript form only; many have been lost. The liberal nobleman Vikentii Dunin-Martzinkevich (1807–84), made a great contribution to the development of Byelorussian literature. Despite a certain idealization of the relationships between serfs and landowners, he described the conditions of life in the Byelorussian village quite realistically; his socio-critical comedies were the foundation stone for the national Byelorussian drama.

Critical realism in Byelorussian literature finally gained acceptance with the publication of poems by the well-known democrat Frantzisk Bagushevich. Byelorussian literature at this time was directly influenced by the revolutionary democratic literature of Russia. The revolution of 1905–07 was of great importance to the development of Byelorussian literature. The revolutionary efforts of the people were expressed in the poems of Yanka Kupala, Yakub Kolas, and Tziotka (pseud. of Aloiza Pashkevich).

These poets adopted the ideas of social and national liberation and, because of their close association with the people, produced a literature of great importance. It represents a peak of the pre-revolutionary period. The poetic works of Y. Kupala and Y. Kolas exerted a great influence on numerous writers who started their literary careers at a later time, among them Tishka Gartny, Maksim Bahdanovich, Smitrok Byadula, and others, whose works offered an impressive picture of the lives of the workers, artisans, and peasants as well as of the poverty in the villages. These writers contributed to the dissemination in Byelorussian of progressive works of Russian and Polish literature.

The October revolution opened new doors for Byelorussian literature. The Byelorussian SSR was founded on January 1, 1919; a part of its territory, however, was ceded to Poland upon completion of the peace treaty of 1921. During the civil war, two groups of Byelorussian literature opposed each other. One group sided with the ideas of social revolution, while the other, for bourgeois, nationalist reasons, supported the counterrevolution. In the 1920s fierce ideological struggles took place in Byelorussian literature. A number of literary associations played a significant role in these differences. The Byelorussian Association of Proletarian Writers was of considerable help in bringing about the eventual union of all writers on the basis of proletarian cultural policies.

The leading Byelorussian writers of the 1920s, Y. Kupala and S. Byadula, were not entirely free from nationalist tendencies. On the basis of their close association with the people and their history, however, they were able to overcome this ideological crisis. Kupala translated *The Lay of the Host of Igor* and wrote a number of poems about loyalty, while Kolas took the revolution for his major theme.

Kupala's poems extolled the free life of the workers and farmers; Kolas published two volumes of his autobiographical novel trilogy, in which he described the changed life of the Byelorussian people and the relationship of the intelligentsia to the people, the revolution, and socialism. T. Gartny published a number of new poems as well as a novel. The new poems, verses, and short stories of S. Byadulya show that he succeeded in overcoming his bourgeois, nationalist views.

Among the young people who came to literature in the 1920s we find the dramatist Kandrat Krapiva (b. 1896); the prose writers Kuzma Chorny (1900–44), Mikhas Charot (1897–1938), Pyatro Glebka (b. 1905), and Pyatrus Browka (b. 1905).

The First Byelorussian Writers' Congress was held in June, 1934; the resolutions adopted were of importance for the literary development of the future. The improvements taking place in agriculture became one of the main literary themes of the 1930s, as can be seen from the works of Y. Kupala, Y. Kolas, K. Chorny, M. Lynkow, E. Samuilionak, P. Browka, and others. These writers described the class battle in the country and the development of new human relationships. The newly important relationship of man to his work was developed in themes drawn from the life of working-class people in Byelorussian cities. Another major theme of the 1930s was the events of the revolution and the civil war. After the reunion of Western Byelorussia with the Soviet Union in 1939, writers such as Tank (b. 1912) and Kubyashow (b. 1914) became popular. Socialist realism became the leading literary movement in Byelorussia. The poems, fables, ballads, and short stories of Y. Kupala, Y. Kolas, K. Chorny, M. Lynkow, A. Kulyashow, P. Browka, M. Tank, P. Glebka, K. Krapiva, and others greatly influenced the people in their understanding of the aims of the war. Among the best works of Byelorussian literature to be published in the course of the first postwar years were the third volume of Y. Kolas' autobiographical trilogy, the war novels of M. Lynkow, Ivan Melesh (b. 1921) and Ivan Shamyakin (b. 1921), the plays of K. Krapiva, and the stories of Filip Pestrak (b. 1903).

Byelorussian literature has been experiencing a new rise since the mid-1950s. This is reflected in the greater universality of its themes, in its closer association with real life, and in the greater number of problems and conflicts to appear. Writers such as I.

Shamyakin, P. Browka, Yanka Bryl (b. 1917) have presented the problems of our times in their novels. The works of I. Melesh and Vasil Bykov (b. 1924) are among the most important to emerge from the World War II period; the poets A. Kulyashow and P. Browka may be considered as representative of the most popular poets of the time.

ESTONIAN LITERATURE

When Sweden lost the Northern War (1700–21), her Baltic possessions, including Estonia (Livonia), were incorporated into the Russian empire. This turn of events boded well for the future, objectively speaking, but the Estonian peasants remained subjugated to the German barons, whose ancestors had conquered the area in the thirteenth century under pretense of Christianization.

Melancholy songs, fairy tales, and heroic sagas all reflect the unquenchable desire of the Estonian people for liberty. The beauty of the Estonian national songs was already recognized by the end of the eighteenth century by Herder and Schlegel, who introduced the German reader to some of them. A systematic survey of Estonian folklore was not undertaken before the nineteenth century.

Estonian literature has its roots in the sixteenth century. Its first book was a catechism in Low German and corrupt Estonian printed in Wittenberg, Germany, in 1535. A series of religious works followed, and, beginning in the seventeenth century, secular writings also; the latter, however, were all written by Baltic German authors who represented the interests of the nobility. The crisis of feudalism and the rise of capitalist conditions at the beginning of the nineteenth century created an atmosphere favorable for the development of an Estonian national literature.

The work of the first Estonian writer, J. Peterson, already contained an appeal to the patriotic feelings of his countrymen. The activities of the democratic humanists F. R. Faehlmann and F. R. Kreutzwald led to the dissemination of national and antifeudal ideas among the masses. The preparation and publication of national poetry was of great significance for the development of Estonian literature and the Estonian language. The national epic *Kalevipoeg* [The Son of Kalev], by Kreutzwald, was one of the most influential works of this period. Friendship between Russians and Estonians was the main concern of J. Sommer, while the lyrical poems of L. Koidulas were permeated with her love for her country. The work of E. Bornhöhe is also linked with the rise of the national movement; Bornhöhe enriched Estonian literature by his use of the historical genre; his story *Tasuja* [The Avenger, 1880], which depicts the peasant revolt of 1343, was particularly popular.

The end of the nineteenth century and the beginning of the twentieth are characterized by the acceptance of critical realism. The revolutionary events of 1905–07 contributed to this development. The works of E. Vilde give a large-scale picture of the social contradictions existing not only at that time but also during the preceding century. The stories of E. Särgava and the plays of A. Kitzberg were of a sociocritical nature, while J. Liiv was one of the most important poets. Other representatives of this movement were the poets J. Tamm and A. Haava, and the prose writers J. Mändmets and O. Luts. Luts's first novel, *Kevade* [The Spring], a humorous account of events taking place in a village school, has remained very popular.

In 1905 a proletarian literature and criticism began to develop. These two genres are represented by H. Poogelmann, J. Lilienbach, and V. Buk, among others. The influence of progressive Russian literature on Estonian became very evident at this time, and a certain orientation toward Finnish literature—the Finnish language is related to Estonian—was also noticeable. The literary association *Noor Eesti* [Young Estonia] was founded under the leadership of G. Suits at this time. Its members first wrote mostly realistic works influenced by the revolution. During the more reactionary years, however, they turned to a more decadent style of writing. Following the victory of the bourgeois republic, a highly complex situation developed in the field of literature. Proletarian literature was being suppressed, and a number of its representatives were imprisoned, including J. Lauristin and, P. Keerdo. Others fled to the USSR. A number of literary magazines were published in Estonian in Leningrad.

Bourgeois literature in Estonia was politically extremely diverse. While some writers either supported the established order (nationalism and anticommunism) or took a nonpolitical stand, others remained faithful to democratic and realist traditions. A. Kivikas, A. Mälk, A. Gailit (who emigrated in 1944) were among the nonpolitical writers. A. Tammsaare, F. Tuglas, M. Metsanurk, M. Raud, and A. Jakobson created superb prose works. J. Barbarus and J. Sütiste must be mentioned as being among the most important poets of the period. When Soviet order was established in 1940, the more important democratic writers, together with the already established communist writers, helped in the reconstruction of a new socialist literature.

During World War I, the writers continued to work, often under frontline conditions or after evacuation. J. Lauristin and the playwright E. Tammlaan lost their lives during the war. A number of young writers, whose ideological views had been formed by the new socialist order, were working after the liberation, as well as some of the older writers who at times had had to reassess their political and aesthetic views. The younger writers published their first collections of poems and short stories at this time. They included D. Vaarandi, A. Kaal, and E. Männik. Socialist realism became the prominent literary movement. Between 1945 and 1948 a number of important works appeared. They described wartime events, the socialist transformation of the village (H. Leberecht), and the life of the intelligentsia (J. Semper). An upsurge of new authors appeared in the mid-1950s. In addition to the works of H. Leberecht and J. Smuul, which are known outside the republic, the novels of R. Sirge (*Maa ja rahvas* [Nation and People, 1956]), J. Semper (*Punased nelgid* [Red Carnations, 1955]), A. Hint (*Tuuline rand* [The Shore of the Winds, 1951–66]), and Lilli Promet (*Meetsteta küla* [The Village Without Men, 1962]) deserve particular mention. A number of successes have been registered in the minor literary genres by writers such as E. Krusten.

Poetry is represented by the works of D. Vaarandi, J. Smuul, P. Rummo, M. Kesamaa, V. Laht, V. Beekman, and others. Dramatic writing is represented by A. Jakobson, E. Rannet, V. Gross the Younger, J. Smuul, and Å. Liives.

GEORGIAN LITERATURE

Georgian literature is one of the oldest literatures in the USSR. The many differing sub-genres of literature—heroic epics, sagas, fairy tales, and songs flourished in Georgian national poetry. The Greek historian Xenophon reported the existence of secular songs in Georgia in the fourth century B.C. The national myth *Amiraniani* exerted a great influence on the development of Georgian literature. It contains themes similar to those found in the Prometheus story, and was familiar to poets as early as the second millennium B.C. The heroic epics *Eteriani* and *Tarieliani* have their origins in the eleventh and the twelfth century B.C. Georgian folklore continued to develop up to the present time. *The Song of Arsen* is of great literary significance. It was created in the beginning of the nineteenth century during the peasant uprisings against serfdom.

Georgian writing developed during the fourth century after the introduction of Christianity. An inscription found in Israel was made at the beginning of the fifth century and is regarded as the oldest testimony of Georgian writing. Georgian literature was at first greatly influenced by the Byzantine church, bringing about the development of a religion-directed literature. In addition to numerous translations, biographies of saints and saints' legends soon appeared, written by Georgian authors such as Jakov Zurtaveli (fifth century) and Ion Sabanizdze (eighth century). These writings had certain patriotic aims: the martyrs described had resisted the enemies of the people—the Persians and the Arabs.

The creation of the Georgian central state under Davit the Founder (1089–1125) resulted in an economic rise and a cultural flowering. The hegemony of the church was broken by this event. Secular poetry began to develop, in the course of which Georgian secular script ("mkhedruli") was created. Many poets worked at the Georgian court at this time. They included M. Choneli, the author of the heroic epic *Amiran-Daredshaniani*, Shavteli, who wrote a poem in honor of King Davit, and Chakhrukhadse, who dedicated his poem *Tamariani* to Queen Tamar. They were either precursors or contemporaries of Shota Rustaveli, the most important Georgian poet of this period, who created his great epic *Vepkhis-tgaosani* [The Knight in the Tiger's Skin] around 1200. This work—written in the Middle Georgian language—demonstrates the peak reached by Georgian literature. Certain ideas are developed in this work that became more widely circulated only during the Renaissance.

The conquest of Georgia by the Mongols in the thirteenth century and the subsequent oppression by the Mongols, the Persians, and the Turks brought about an economic and cultural decline. By the seventeenth and the eighteenth century political thought gradually revived, and a new rise in literature followed. Among the leaders of this creative period were Teimuras I (1589–1663), Josif Tbileli, whose historical poem *Didmouraviani* tells of Georgi Saakadze, the great fighter for the unification of Georgia, and Sulkhan-Saba Orbeliani (1658–1725), the author of *Sibrdsne sizrnisa* [The Book of Wisdom and Lies, 1894], a book on princely personages. Patriotic ideas, sorrow for the sad fate of Georgia, the striving for liberation, and the idea of friendship between Georgians and the Russian people are most strongly reflected in the work of Devit Guramshvili (1705–92).

Unification of Georgia with Russia in 1801 made the land secure against foreign invaders; Georgian literature now began to be influenced by Russian literature. The tsarist colonial administration, however, was a socially oppressive one; it attempted to prevent a new flowering of Georgian literature. Social and national liberation became the predominating literary idea. This was particularly evident in the field of Georgian romanticism, a movement that was of decisive importance in the literary development of the 1930s and the 1940s. Its Georgian founder was the poet and translator Alexander Chavchavadze, who had been educated in Europe. The work of the poet N. Baratashvili, whose main themes were sorrow for the lost liberty of Georgia, the willingness to die for liberty, and the exile's longing for freedom, marked a peak in Georgian romanticism. Baratashvili introduced new themes into the poetry of his country, bringing it closer to Russian and Western European literatures. Similar problems were treated by Srigor Orbeliani. Writers such as S. Rasmadze, T. Tumanishvili, and A. Orbeliani were also members of the romanticist movement. Writing of the period was greatly influenced by the philosopher and critic Solomon Dodashvili, who edited the progressive Georgian news magazine *Thilisis Uzekebani* [The News from Tbilisi].

Around 1850 the accelerating downfall of the feudal order and the development of capitalism brought about an increasing polarization of social contrasts, a fact which favored the development of realism in Georgian literature. The social problems of the times were strongly reflected in the plays of Eristavi, including *The Division* (1850) and *The Trial* (1850). A dramatist and the founder of the new Georgian theater, Eristavi was also the author of the novel *The Castle of Surami* (1859). The theme of serfdom was handled by Daniel Chonkadze and also, in the first great novel on the Georgian bourgeoisie *Solomon Isakich Medshganuashvili* (1861), by Lavrenti Ardasiani (1815–70).

The new social conflicts that developed following the abolition of serfdom in the 1860s led to a great upsurge in Georgian literature, which at that time was being influenced favorably by the Russian revolutionary democrats. Critical realism in Georgian literature was brought to a peak by the "Group of Tergdaleuli" (literally, those who drank from the waters of Terek, i.e., who went to Russia to obtain a higher education). The leading representatives of this group were initially materialists who created works aimed at social and national liberation. The leading writers of the period were Ilya Chavchavadze (who wrote realistic stories and novels as well as patriotic and philosophical poems) and Akaki Tzereteli whose historical poems, dramas, novels and songs always stressed the inseparability of social and national liberation; a number of his works are dedicated to the events of the revolution of 1905–07. The group also included the epic writer Georgi Tzereteli whose works, including *Gulkan* (1868; The First Step, 1891), dealt with the new social conflicts, the lyric writer Rafael Eristavi, and the novelist Anton Purtzeladze. This movement received considerable impetus from Alexander Kasbegi, a dramatist and novelist, and from the versatile Vasha-Pshavela, who created truly heroic characters and who became well known for his masterly descriptions of nature. The dramatist Davit Eristavi became prominent in the 1880s.

Literary development was also influenced by the materialistic philosopher and critic Niko Nikoladze, whose work was closely linked with that of Nikolai Chernyshevski. A new period of development in Georgian literature began in the nineties with the formation of the workers' movement. The social-democratic organization *Messamedasi* [The Third Group] was founded in 1893, and contributed greatly to the dissemination of Marxist ideas in Georgia. What was once the revolutionary minority of the movement became the leading force in the workers' movement. One of the minority leaders, E. Ninoshvili (pseud. of Egnato Ingorokva), wrote short stories and novels about the peasants, the social contrasts existing in the villages, and the decadence of the nobility. Irodion Evdoshvili (pseud. of Khositashvili) was the first writer to extol the fight of the workers and to tell of the revolution of 1905–07. Realistic descriptions of the declining nobility, the bourgeoisie striving for power, the misery and growing resistance of the peasants and workers were given by Davit Kldiashvili in his novels and comedies, by V. Vasili Barnovi, and by Shio Aragvispireli (pseud. of Dedabrishvili). The realistic traditions of M. Gorki were particularly evident in the works of the dramatist Shalve Dadiani (1874–1959), of Leo Kiacheli (1884–1963), and, in his novel on the revolution of 1905, *Tariel Golua* (1915); also in the stories about life in the villages written by Niko Lordkipanidze (1880–1944). Antirealistic currents, which after the defeat of the revolution (1907) became evident in the works of a few writers such as Salaktion Tabidze (1892–1959) and Josif Grishashvili (1889–1965), did not greatly influence literary development. Before the October revolution proletarian writers such as Sandre Euli (b. 1890) and Josif Vakeli (pseud. of Megrelidse, b. 1900) gained prominence.

A new period in the development of Georgian literature began after the establishment of Soviet power in Georgia in 1921. The literature of the 1920s was characterized by a clash of opinions about the new Soviet power, the search for new subjects, for the new hero, and for new artistic methods and the means by which to describe them. This complex process, which was judiciously guided by the Communist Party, resulted in the establishment of the principles of socialist literature, which were recognized by all writers in the first years of the 1930s. This development was greatly influenced by the progressive writers, who adopted the demands for the general support of Soviet power made by G. Tabidze in his poem *We, The Poets of Georgia!* (1925) as their platform. These writers united in 1922 to form the Association of Proletarian Writers. The First Congress of Georgian Writers, at which all groups declared their willingness to support socialist reconstruction, took place in 1926. Subsequent developments confirmed the effectiveness of this movement. The building of the new order and the formation of the socialist man found reflection in the early 1930s in the poems of G. Tabidze and Alio Mashasvili (pseud. of Mirzkhalava, b. 1903); in the works of Yashvili (1895–1937), who after a symbolist phase had returned to realism; Tizian Tabidze (1895–1937), and Georgi Leonidze (1899–1966), and in those of former futurists such as Simon Chikovani (b. 1903), as well as in the verses of young poets including Irakli Abashidze (b. 1909). Literature of epic proportions continued in books about the socialist reconstruction in the country, on the development of the workers' movement in Georgia, and on the October revolution. In the field of drama, Polikarp Kakabadze, Serge Kldiashvili, S. Dadiani, and I. Vakeli discussed the new conflicts in socialist reconstruction.

During World War I, the defense of the socialist country, the battle for the destruction of fascism, and the fight for peace became the main literary themes. The poems of G. Tabidze, Karlo Kaladze (b. 1904), I. Abashidze, S. Chikovani, and G. Leonidze were extremely well received. Josif Noneshvili (b. 1920) and Revas Marginiani (b. 1914) started to write during the war years; these authors are now among the leading Georgian lyricists. In the epic genre, L. Kiacheli, Konstantin Lordkipanidze (b. 1904), Rashden Gvetadze (1897–1952), S. Kldiashvili, Demna Shengelaya (b. 1896), and Akaki Beliashvili (1903–61) were the leading figures.

Following the defeat of fascism, wartime events and the gradual transition to a peaceful existence were pictured in Georgian literature. At the same time, a number of superficial and idealistically optimistic re-creations of reality were written under the influence of the "Theory of Non-Conflict." These hindered literary development to a certain extent. By the 1950s, however, these tendencies had been overcome, and literature was employed to settle the conflicts that had arisen with the formation of new ideas. A more profound characterization of human fate and the search for new ways in which to express these thoughts were the dominant factors in literature. Prose writing took a leading role in Georgian literature with the publication of the historical novels of Konstantin Gamsakhurdia (*The Flowering of the Vine*, 1953), A. Beliashvili (*The Mountain Pass*, 1956), K. Lordkipanidze (*Rustavi*, 1959–60), S. Kldiashvili (*The Silent Hermitage*, 1958), K. Gamsakhurdia, Grigol Abashidze (b. 1913), and Levan Gotua (b. 1905). The works of Vladimir Avaliani (b. 1914), Nadar Dumbadze (b. 1926), and other writers became well known. In poetry, the poems of I. Abashidze (*On the Trail of Rustaveli*, 1959; *Approach to the Middle of the Century*, 1959); the verses of Anna Kalandadze (b. 1924), and Mikha Kvlividze (b. 1925) among others; and the plays of Mikhail Mrevlishvili (b. 1904), G. Abashidze, and Grigori Berdsenishvili (b. 1909) earned the approbation of the reading public.

KAZAKH LITERATURE

Kazakh literature is characterized by a century-old national epic and lyric tradition extending into contemporary times. Up to the middle of the nineteenth century, this rich national poetry, which contains all genres—heroic songs, lyric poetry, ballads, fairy tales, and legends—was the only means of expression by which the Kazakh people were able to voice their views of times past and present, and to tell of their dreams for a more beautiful future. Individual poetic works became important in the *akyne* (folklore) poetry of the eighteenth century; the most important representatives of this type of poetry were Bukhar-shirau Kalkamanov (1693–1787), Makhambet Utemisov (1804–46), and Sherniyas Sharylgasov (1817–81). Two attitudes were evident in the repertoire of these folklorists, whose artful and complex chronicles were presented at the *aitys* (song festivals) and in the *tolgan* (lyric meditations): 1) a democratic attitude, which expressed the desire of the people for a better standard of living; this was seen in the establishment of friendly relations with Russia; 2) an attitude of subservience to the ruling feudal classes of the beys and to the propaganda favoring the existing conditions, which was then being presented by the followers of Islam.

A distinct Kazakh literature began to develop only after the final political and cultural unification of Kazakhstan with Russia in 1846. The first Kazakh book appeared in 1807—written in a Kazakh script based on the Arabic alphabet—a Kazakh script based on the Cyrillic alphabet was only introduced in 1941.

It was only after the Kazakh people had been in combat with Russian revolutionary democratic circles that the intellectual and cultural development of the area began to take place. Russian Orientalists such as Vasili Radlov (1837–1918) first wrote down the treasures of Kazakh folklore. Influenced by the ideas of the Russian revolutionary democrats, a broad movement toward enlightenment developed in the last third of the nineteenth century which, in turn, prepared the ground for the development of a national Kazakh literature. Of great importance were the works of the first prominent Kazakh scholar Chokar Valikhanov (1835–65) and of the humanist Ibrai Altynsarin (1841–89), a translator, writer of children's books, and teacher, who also developed a Kazakh alphabet based on Cyrillic script. Kazakh poetry (other genres had as yet not been developed) reached its peak with the works of Abai Kunanbayev (1845–1904), who may be considered the father of modern Kazakh literature. It is due to Kunanbayev's great talent as a translator that Russian literature became familiar to members of the Kazakh intelligentsia, which at that time was still only a small group.

A movement also existed at this time concerned with the consolidation of patriarchal and feudal conditions, the representatives of which were Shortenbai Kanayev (1818–81) and Dubat Babatayev (1802–71); their work, however, showed certain realistic aspects. This conservative movement in Kazakh national literature continued into the beginning of the twentieth century with the works of such writers as Abubakir Kerderi (1856–1912), Nurshan Naushabayev (1859–1919), and Shangerej Bukeyev (1847–1920).

These early stirrings of critical realism evident in the work of Abai Kunanbayev continued to develop in the works of writers such as Spaudiyar Kubeyev (1878–1956), who wrote the first Kazakh novel, *Kalym* [The Bartering of the Bride, 1908], Shabit Dunentayev (1894–1933), who was one of the first Kazakhs to extol the new socialist life, and the realist poet Sultanmakhmud Toraigyrov (1893–1920), who may perhaps be regarded as the most important successor to Abai.

Despite the work of these writers, prerevolutionary Kazakh literature was unable to fulfill its inherent possibilities because of poor existing conditions—in 1917, 98 per cent of the population was illiterate. It was only after the industrial and agricultural reforms that took place with the establishment of Soviet power in 1918, and with the success of the socialist cultural revolution, that a favorable atmosphere for the development of a Kazakh national literature emerged. In its conquest of new spheres of reality, Kazakh Soviet literature made use of all the traditions of democratic folklore—its epic universality, its depiction of heroic characters, and its poetic language. In the course of this process, certain didactic features and reactionary prejudices gradually disappeared from Kazakh literature. Modern Kazakh literature, furthermore, is supported by the achievements of prerevolutionary critical realist literature. Interesting interactions between folklore and literature became evident, and are particularly well reflected in the works of the modern folklorist Dzhambul Dzhabayev (1846–1945).

Among the founders of Kazakh Soviet literature who were involved to a significant degree in making the methods of socialist realism a success were S. Seifullin (1894–1939), I. Dzhansugurov (1894–1938), B. Mailin (1894–1938), and S. Mukanov (b. 1900). These writers established continuity between the prerevolutionary democratic traditions and modern socialist literature. The poems and verses of S. Seifullin, I. Dzhansugurov, the short stories of B. Mailin, the novels of S. Mukanov and I. Dzhansugurov, and the dramas of S. Seifullin greatly influenced the development of Kazakh Soviet literature of the 1920s and 1930s. The new reality meant a constant search for new forms and means of artistic expression. These were found either in Kazakh traditions or in Russian and other Soviet literatures. In the 1920s, the main themes of lyric poetry, which was then the leading genre, were the exuberance of the revolution and the joys of the new life, which were contrasted with the hard times of the past. Gradually a deeply meaningful, artistic form of political, militant poetry became predominant. In their poems, S. Seifullin and I. Dzhansugurov attempted to show their appreciation of the new reality. The satirical poems of S. Donentayev, the plays of S. Shanin (1891–1938), and the prose works of S. Seifullin, B. Mailin, and Mukhtar Auezov (1897–1961) became well known at this time.

The foundation of the Kazakh Writers' Union in 1934 was of great importance for the subsequent development of Kazakh literature, which was now being strongly influenced by Russian Soviet literature. Collectivization (Sabit Musrepov, b. 1902) and industrialization (S. Mukanov, and Satrar Yerubayev, 1914–1937) became the basic themes of the writing developing at that time. In World War II, literature—in particular the songs of Dzhambul Dzhabayev—played an important role in the patriotic education of the masses.

In the postwar years prose writing became the leading genre in Kazakh literature. The more important writers, most of whom had started their careers earlier, include Sabider Mustafin (b. 1902), Askar Tokmagambetov (b. 1905), Abdilda Tashibayev (b. 1909), Kasym Amansholov (1911–55), Tair Sharokov (1908–65), Sali Ormanov (b. 1907), Srybai Maulenov (b. 1922), and Olshas Suleimenov (b. 1936). M. Auezov's multi-volume epic *Abai Golo* and the novels of G. Mustafin have brought Kazakh Soviet writing to the forefront of world literature.

KIRGHIZ LITERATURE

The Kirghiz people have had their own alphabet only since 1924. These people, who lived as nomads before the revolution, have a national poetry rich in tradition. In addition to fairy tales and epigrams, their heroic epics and lyric poetry represent permanent achievements. The epic *Manas* is justly famous far beyond the borders of Kirghizia. The minor epics, especially *Kurmanbek,* which appeared during the feudal period, are of some importance. The songs, which, like the epics, have been handed down to us by the folklorists (*akynes*), are divided into several distinct genres, including *Opmaida* (working songs), *Koshok* (laments), and *Terms* (didactic poems reflecting the wisdom of the people). The two founders of Kirghiz Soviet literature—Toktogul Zatylganov (1864–1933) and Togolok Moldo (1860–1942)—occupied an intermediate position between *akynes* and writers. They attained mastery as folklorists, transmitting ancient cultural treasures to the present generation, but they also created new works. T. Satylganov developed the lyric genres while Togolok Moldo concentrated on objective poetry. In contrast to their work as folklorists, these poets gained a reputation as individual writers; Moldo recorded his own songs. The poetic creativity of the people as a whole is still an active force in literature today; song festivals remain a tradition throughout the country, and the *akyne* on these occasions must demonstrate his improvisatory art and his ability to find the appropriate poetic images.

The first Kirghiz newspaper, *Erkin-Too* [The Free Mountains], appeared in 1924, while the Kirghiz state publishing house and a theater were founded in 1926; the first Kirghiz writers' union was founded in 1927. The ground was therefore already ripe for the development of literature. In addition to Toktogul Zatylganov and Togolok Moldo, the poets Asly Tokombayev (b. 1904) and Mukai Elebayev (1905–43) produced great works in these developmental years. Later Dzhoonart Bokonbayev (1910–44) and Kubanychbek Malikov (b. 1911) became well-known. Tokobayev (b. 1905) wrote the first Kirghiz multi-act play, *Kaigyluu Kakei* [The Unhappy Kakei], in 1924, and a few years later Kazymaly Dzhantoshev (b. 1904) wrote the first dramatic pieces. Prose writing developed more slowly. K. Bayalinov's (b. 1902) short story *Adzhar* (1928) was the precursor of the great novels that were to be written in the 1930s. The process of coalescence, involving the many national literatures of the Soviet Union and the increasing influence of Russian literature, had a very positive effect on the development of Kirghiz literature. M. Elebayev's *Uzak dzhol* [The Long Road, 1936] would not have been possible without Gorki's autobiographical trilogy, just as Tugelbai Zydykbekov's (b. 1912) novel *Ken-Suu* (1935) would not have been possible without Sholokhov's *Podnyataya tzelina* (Seeds of Tomorrow). A. Tokombayev's stories, which appeared in 1941 under the collective title *Dsharalangan dshürök* [The Wounded Heart], are of great literary importance. At this time, D. Bokonbayev wrote his drama *Altyn-kys* [The Golden Girl, 1937]; in cooperation with K. Malikov and D. Turusbekov (1910–43), he wrote the libretto for the first Kirghiz opera, *Aitshurek*, which used themes from the *Manas* epic. The first performance of this opera was given with great success in 1939. The versatility of themes seen in the other Soviet literatures is also characteristic of the Kirghiz literature of the 1930s, which bore the stamp of writers such as Togolok Moldo and A. Tokombayev and, above all, that of D. Bokonbayev, D. Turusbekov, Tomirkul Umetaliyev (b. 1908), and Alykul Osmonov (1915–50).

During the war years writing was characterized by themes describing the harsh life and heroic deeds of the people at the front. D. Turusbekov, M. Elebayev, T. Umetaliyev, D. Bokonbayev and, in the interior of the country, A. Tokombayev and A. Osmonov were writing at this time. M. Elebayev and D. Turusbekov were killed at the front. In addition to the work of the lyric poets, some of whom reached their peak in these years, we must mention the heroic drama *Kurmanbek* (1943) by K. Dzhantoshev as representative of one of the greatest achievements of Kirghiz Soviet literature.

In the postwar years several well-known writers published new works: K. Bayakinov wrote his novel *Bakyt* [Happiness, 1947]; K. Dzhantoshev wrote a drama on the *akyne* Toktogul, *El yrchysy*, [The Folklorist, 1952]; and T. Umetaliyev published many poems and verses. In addition to these a number of masterpieces written by lesser known young writers appeared. In addition to the novel *Zaltanat* (1949) by Nazirdin Baitemirov (b. 1916), the poems of Zuyunhai Eraliyev, and the dramas (*Ashyrbai*, 1957, among others) of Toktobolet Abdumomunov (b. 1922), the short stories of Chingis Aitmatov (b. 1928) are of great importance. These stories are characterized by extraordinary incidents and passionately exaggerated language as well as by the psychological profundity of their characters. They have found a wide readership in many countries. Most of these stories tell of the rapid rise of Kirghizia, a land once so far behind the times.

LATVIAN LITERATURE

The history of the Latvians has much in common with that of the Estonians. In their case, too, unification with the Russian state, which took place at different times in the various areas (1721, 1772, and 1795), represented the beginning of a new epoch, although the oppression of the people continued. A national language and a national poetry were all that remained of Latvian literature following the conquests of the Teutonic knights. For more than half a millennium the Latvians drew new hope for a better future from their songs (*dainas*), fairy tales, riddles, and epigrams. The Baltic German nobility and the clergy attempted in vain to suppress their national poetry by means of a distorted Latvian language. This language had been created in the sixteenth century with the appearance of church literature and in the eighteenth century with the coming of secular literature. The Old Letts—Indrikis (1783–1828) among them—supported these attempts. The Old Letts gave an idealized picture of the existing conditions, presenting obedience to the powerful ruling classes as a virtue. By the end of the eighteenth century and the beginning of the nineteenth the ideas of humanism had begun to spread among the German lower-middle classes; these ideas were of a distinctly liberal character. G. Merkel was the only writer to appear as an implacable enemy of feudalism. His work, which included *The Latvians*, published in Leipzig in 1796, had a considerable effect on the growing Latvian intelligentsia.

Formation of the Latvian bourgeois nation took place in the second half of the nineteenth century. The national movement may be divided into two phases. Between 1850 and 1870 bourgeois, democratic tendencies (Young Letts) predominated; in the 1880s and 1890s reactionary, nationalist tendencies came to the fore. In the ranks of the Young Letts there were a number of important humanists and writers. The Young Letts emphasized the strict rejection of feudal conditions, based on inability to comprehend contradictions existing in the capitalist order. The group numbered among its members K. Valdemārs, J. Alunāns, and K. Barons. The Young Letts published several collections of national poetry, and were involved with the cultivation of the Latvian language.

The newspaper *Peterburgas Avīzes* (1862–65), founded by K. Valdemārs and J. Alunāns in St. Petersburg, became an effective instrument in the campaign for enlightenment. In the 1870s and

1880s, the works of Auseklis (pseud. of M. Krogzemis) and A. Pumpurs appeared; these contrasted strongly with the literature of reactionary romanticism and sentimentalism cultivated by the nationalists. The democratic, romantic poems of Auseklis show strong elements of both realism and satire. Realism finally gained acceptance in the works of the brothers Kaudzītis (Reinis and Matīss). The form was developed further in stories by A. Jēkabs. One noticeable weakness in their work is the glorification of the patriarchal order. R. Blaumanis occupied a prominent position in the literature of realism. Nationalist literature became stronger toward the end of the century. A. Niedra, who is regarded as its most typical representative, glorified the founders of growing Latvian capitalism. He and his followers attempted unsuccessfully to found a neoromantic literary movement.

The awakening consciousness of the Latvian proletariat gradually led to the so-called New Movement in the mid-1880s. The center of this movement was at first located in Tartu (Estonia); its most prominent representative was E. Veidenbaums. Later came Jānis Rainis and P. Stucka, who belonged to the left wing of the movement. These two writers were responsible for turning the newspaper *Dienas Lapa* [Daily News] into the organ of the proletariat. Rainis, Aspazija, and several other writers developed a literature that was closely connected with the struggles of the working class. After the victory of the reactionary forces these writers took up the fight against decadent tendencies in literature. A. Upīts entered the fight as a proletarian writer.

After the October revolution Soviet power was able to retain control in Latvia only for a short period. The Soviets had to yield to the superior strength of the intervening powers and the bourgeois nationalists. Nonetheless, despite very difficult conditions, the cornerstone for Soviet Latvian literature was laid. The communist press, especially the central organ *Cīņa* [The Battle], played an important role in the propagation of Marxist aesthetics. The works of A. Upits, L. Paegle, L. Laicens, A. Arājs-Bērce, and other writers were being published at this time. Some of the bourgeois writers, including J. Subrabkalns, supported the idea of Soviet power. During the rule of the bourgeois government, which after the events of 1934 took on a fascist character, bourgeois literature glorified the existing conditions, falsified the history of the past, and cultivated mysticism and eroticism, as may be seen in the works of J. Veselis, A. Grīns, and others. Supporters of revolutionary literature were persecuted by those in power. The editor of *Cīņa*, A. Arājs-Bērce, was shot and killed on June 10, 1921.

Despite these trials progressive literature continued to develop. New forces led by Subrabkalns and V. Lācis cultivated the democratic traditions. The lives of workers and farmers, the revolutionary battle, and the historic events of the past were reflected truthfully in the works of A. Upīts, L. Paegle, L. Laicens, and E. Birznieks-Upīts. The democratic poets writing at this time attempted to find a way to escape from the narrow confines of bourgeois society. They included J. Subrakalns, A. Čaks, J. Grots, and A. Grigulis.

In the 1930s many young writers, among them V. Lukss and J. Vanags, found their allegiance to social democracy changing in favor of the united antifascist front. The period was characterized by an increasing interest in Soviet literature; while progressive literature in Latvia had to fight strenuously and under difficult conditions to retain its position, the same literature in the USSR was offered an excellent chance for development. As one of the multinational Soviet literatures, progressive Latvian literature in Russia turned its attention to both the problem of socialist reconstruction and improvement of the conditions existing in the home country. The theme of the battle for liberation of the Latvian people was popular with all these writers. During the first years of Soviet power political poems and verses occupied the most important position in Latvian literature. Prose writing and dramatic works gained in importance. R. Eidmanis, K. Pelēkais, and S. Edzus, who was a member of the older generation, made considerable contributions in the field of poetry. E. Eferts-Klusais, A. Ceplis, O. Rihters, and K. Jokums published novels. In 1940, following the re-establishment of Soviet power, the best elements united in order to contribute to the building of a new culture: this peaceful development was interrupted by World War 'II. The writers continued their activities at the front and in the interior. Poems filled with patriotism predominated, by writers such as J. Subrabkalns, V. Lukss, F. Rokpelnis, J. Vanags, and A. Balodis. The postwar period opened with a number of important works by A. Upīts, V. Lācis, and Anna Sakse.

Since the mid-1950s new successes in all fields of literature have been achieved. Important novelists were V. Ḅērce, Ž. Grīva (pseud. of Folmanis), J. Grants, R. Selis (pseud. of Germanis), I. Lēmanis, and A. Brodele. The minor prose forms were cultivated by A. Brodele, A. Grigulis, Ž. Grīva, B. Saulītis, I. Muižnieks, and E. Salenieks. Among the poets M. Ķempe, P. Vīlips, and the representatives of the younger generation O. Vācietis, A. Vējāns, and A. Skalbe deserve mention. A. Grigulis, A. Brodele, and E. Zālīte stand out in the relatively weak field of drama. A new generation of writers has made its mark in the course of the last few years. Most of them are novelists such as Z. Skujiņš, D. Zigmonte, and I. Indrāne, but lyric writers such as I. Ziedonis and A. Elksne are gaining in importance.

LITHUANIAN LITERATURE

The earliest monuments of Lithuanian literature, originating in the fourteenth century, were written either in the Old Russian language, which was of Byelorussian origin, or in Latin or Polish. The legal code (*Litovski statut*), one of the first written legal documents of the area, was written in Old Russian. During the feudal period the Lithuanian people expressed their views and hopes in their rich national poetry. Numerous songs (*dainos*), fairy tales, legends, and epigrams came into being during this time. Written Lithuanian came into use only in the sixteenth century.

The first Lithuanian book, the catechism of Martynas Mazvydas (d. 1563), appeared in 1547. In addition to church literature, a secular literature—epigrams, poems, and letters written in verse form—began to develop in the seventeenth and eighteenth centuries. First place in eighteenth-century Lithuanian literature is occupied by the work of K. Donelaitis, whose poem *Metai* [The Seasons] laid the foundation stone for the subsequent development of Lithuanian aesthetic literature. This form of literature was successfully developed by the poet and linguist D. Poska, the folklorist S. Stanevičius, and the writer-historian S. Daukantas. The work of the poet A. Strazdas was also of major importance in the field of poetry at this time. Many of Strazdas's poems have become folksongs; the thoughts of the simple peasants and the force of their unbroken will resound throughout these poems. The work of A. Baranauskas, which has done much for the development of Lithuanian poetry, appeared tword the close of the feudal period. Baranauskas was associated with the activities of several of the great German linguists, including H. Weber and F. Specht. K. Brugmann, A. Leskien, and A. Bezzenberger were important literary figures who aided in the propagandization of Lithuanian national poetry and old Lithuanian literature.

The revolutionary ideas gradually coming into Lithuania from Russia, together with the activities of progressive intellectuals at the University of Vilnius, exerted a positive effect on the rapid development of Lithuanian literature at the beginning of the nineteenth century. Interest in Lithuanian history, folklore, and language was also beginning to grow abroad. L. Rhesa, a language professor in Königsberg, in 1818 arranged for the first publication of the collected works of Donelaitis, and was a great collector of Lithuanian folksongs. Many famous German scholars, including Kant, Herder, and Goethe, showed a deep interest in Lithuanian national poetry.

After the defeat of the peasants' revolt of 1863, a cruel period of reaction set in. The tsarist government imposed a ban on Lithuanian writings (1864–1904), and a revival of Lithuanian culture began to develop only during the closing years of the nineteenth century with the formation of the Lithuanian nation and the development of the bourgeois movement for national liberation. The first Lithuanian magazines—*Ausra* [The Dawn] and *Varpas* [The Bell]—began to appear in Eastern Prussia in the 1880s and

1890s. Lithuanian literature was greatly aided at this time by the works of the political journalist V. Kudirka and by the work of the most important Lithuanian poet J. Maironis. The aims of the national movement of the Lithuanian intelligentsia toward liberation were most clearly reflected in the work of the poet J. Macys-Kekštas.

Critical realism gained acceptance in Lithuanian literature around the turn of the century, reaching its peak in the work of the folklorist J. Žemaitė. J. Biliunas was the first writer to introduce the figure of the worker into Lithuanian literature; realistic traditions were further developed by the poet Jovaras (pseud. of J. Krikščiunas) and L. Gira, the novelist A. Vienuolis, the sisters Sofija Psibiliauskiene and Marija Laustauskiene, who both wrote under the pseudonymn Lazdynu Peleda. The romantic movement in Lithuanian literature was represented by J. Maironis, V. Krèvè-Mickevičius, and J. Tumas-Vaižgantas. All these writers and poets based their work on Lithuanian national poetry.

The beginnings of proletarian Lithuanian literature came in the closing years of the nineteenth century with the work of the important Lithuanian revolutionary literary critic V. Mickevičius-Kapsukas. The voice of the talented worker-poet J. Janonis was first heard during World War I. The battle for Soviet power flared up in 1918–19 under the aegis of the victorious October revolution, although at that time the reactionary forces gained the upper hand. The proletarian writers continued working to build a Lithuanian proletarian literature; they were forced to work illegally, often after having emigrated to the Soviet Union. The communist magazines *Kibirkstis* [The Spark] and *Priekalas* [The Anvil] were founded at this time.

During the period of bourgeois fascist development there were two opposing groups of writers in Lithuania: the democratic anti-fascists such as P. Cvirka, S. Neris, V. Montvila, T. Tilvytis, A. Venclova, J. Simkus, and K. Korsakas on the one hand, and the reactionary writers on the other. The former group were opposed to fascism and clericalism and supported realistic art. The poets B. Sruoga, V. Mykolaitis-Putinas, K. Binkis, and others were among the best-known representatives of the modernist movement in Lithuanian literature. In the 1930s, however, their works took on a definite realist slant. A great number of other writers—J. Grusas, I. Simonaityte, J. Paukstelis, the playwrights P. Vaičiunas and S. Čiurlioniene among them—recorded the decay of bourgeois society.

Literature in Lithuania entered a new stage of development after the establishment of Soviet power in 1940, when the creativity of the democratic, antifascist writers showed a marked increase.

During World War II the majority of Lithuanian writers lived in the parts of the Soviet Union that remained unoccupied, or served in the Red Army. Lithuanian poetry achieved a peak at this time, as may be seen in the work of S. Neris, L. Gira, A. Venclova, and K. Korsakas. Nationalism, lyricism, hatred of the fascist aggressors, and a firm belief in victory were reflected in the poems of these writers.

Side by side with the talents of younger writers, the established writers of the older generation—A. Vienuolis, I. Simonaityte, V. Mykolaitis-Putinas, and B. Sruoga, among others—formed a link with the Soviet literature of the postwar years. All literary genres began to develop during this period of social and communist reconstruction. The stories of P. Cvirka, A. Vienuolis's novel *The Manor of the Puodziunas* (1949), A. Gudaitis-Guzevičius's *Kalvio Ignoto teisybe* [The Truth of the Blacksmith Ignotas, 1948–49], the poems of A. Venclova, E. Mieželaitis, and other writers played an important role in this development. The new heroes, the builders of socialism and of communism, are the leading figures in many of these works. The association between literature and the life of the people was gradually strengthened at this time and contemporary themes, problems of communist morality, of socialist humanism, and of proletarian internationalism occupied a considerable place in the realm of belles-lettres.

Lithuanian literature is at present characterized by much poetry of considerable importance. E. Mieželaitis received the All-Union Lenin prize in literature for his collection of poems *Žmogus* [Man, 1961], while J. Marcinkevičius was nominated for the highest artistic award of 1965. Contemporary Lithuanian literature has also made considerable strides in the area of literary criticism.

The creative interaction between the literature of Lithuania and her neighbors, which began toward the end of the nineteenth century, received a new impetus under Soviet rule. This is reflected in the increasing number of translations of world literature and of the other Soviet literatures appearing in Soviet Lithuania. In the course of the last few years the number of works translated from Lithuanian into Russian and other languages has shown a substantial increase.

MOLDAVIAN LITERATURE

The history of Moldavian literature until 1917 parallels that of Rumanian literature.

The first literary documents, written in ancient Slavonic, originated in the fourteenth century; most of these are archives and letters. A great many chronicles emerged by the end of the fifteenth century, some of them developed to such an extent one might well call them examples of artistic historiography. During the seventeenth and eighteenth centuries, important historians such as Miron Costin (1633–91), Grigore Ureche (1590[95?]–1647), and Jan Neculce (1672–1745) were active; their works have continued to exert some influence on the writers of the nineteenth century. The spirit of national awareness was strengthened at this time during the battles against the Turks. The life of the people and their fight for freedom found its artistic reflection in national poetry, the ballad being the most popular form employed.

A new epoch in the history of Moldavia and its literature commenced with the unification of Bessarabia and Russia in 1812. The ideas of the Decembrists, of Pushkin, and of other Russian writers had a positive effect on the development of Moldavian literature. Writers such as Costache Conachi (1777–1849), George Asachi (1788–1869), and Constantin Stamati (1786–1869) worked during the beginning of the nineteenth century to create the foundation for the development of a modern national litera-

ture. Alexandru Donici (1806–66), the novelist Charache Ne-
gruzzi (1808–68), the revolutionary democrat Alocu Russo
(1819–59), the versatile dramatic and lyric writer Vasile Alec-
sandri (1821–90), and the critic Bogdan Petriceicu Hasdeu
(1838–1907) began to develop a realistic literature. Two major
writers came to the fore at this time: the Rumanian poet Milai
Eminescu (1850–89) and the popular short-story writer Ion
Creanga (1837–89). Their works helped Moldavian literature to
join the ranks of world literature.

Since 1917 Moldavian literature has been developing under
new social conditions. A socialist, realist literature has developed
since the founding of the Moldavian SSR in 1924. The best-
known representatives of this literature include D. Milev (1888–
1944), M. Andriescu (1898–1934), T. Malai (b. 1890), G.
Cosereu (1861–1934), I. Canna (b. 1902), N. Markov (1907–
1937), and L. Corneanu (1909–57). Using many different
genres, these authors have re-created the history of their home
country, especially the struggles of the revolutionary period and
the socialist reconstruction of the Moldavian village. Early Moldavian Soviet literature was positively influenced by the works
of Gorki and Mayakovski. The cross-currents developing between
Moldavian literature and that of the Russian and Ukranian Soviet
have been most productive.

Between 1918–40 Moldavian writers working in Rumania-
owned Bessarabia were considered to belong to the progressive
wing of Rumanian literature; their works for the most part supported the fight of the Rumanian and Moldavian workers and
peasants against a feudal, bourgeois order. Important representative of this group included Emilian Bucov (b. 1909), Andrei
Lupan (b. 1912), Georgi Meniuc (b. 1918), Bogdan Istru (pseud.
of Ivan Bodarev; b. 1914), and Liviu Beleanu (b. 1911). After
the unification of Bessarabia with the USSR and the foundation
of the Moldavian SSR, Moldavian Soviet literature continued to
develop under social conditions similar to those existing in other
parts of the Soviet Union.

In contemporary Moldavian literature numerous talented young authors have developed alongside the established writers. Ion Druta (b. 1928), in particular, has become known in both the USSR and abroad for his impressive short stories.

TADZHIK LITERATURE

The Tadzhik people have a literature extraordinarily rich in tradition. Originally an offshoot of Persian, Tadzhik literature today —like Iranian, Afghanistanian, Ossetian, and certain other literatures—is heir to the great Persian literature of the Middle Ages. The oldest surviving document of that literature is the *Zend-Avesta*, the holy book of Zoroastrianism—a collection of prayers, religious laws, hymns, songs, sagas, and historical legends—written in ancient Persian dialects.

The *Avesta* developed over a long period; the oldest sections, the *gathas* (songs) and the *yashchs* (hymns), go back to the first millennium B.C. Both these sources and popular tradition permit the assumption that there existed at that time a rich national poetry, especially in the Eastern regions where Iranian was the national language. A strong literature developed in the eighth century A.D. during the flowering of the Persian (Samanid) dynasty and in the course of the liberation from Arab oppression, which proceeded from East to West. Earlier documents of a poetic nature may be found in the work of Bahram Gor (420–438) and in that of other authors; these works were in part the outcome of the interaction between Persian and Arab culture and in part a truly national poetry.

Around 900 A.D. the appearance of Rudaki (858?–941) opened the glittering era of Persian classicism, an era by which Goethe was to be strongly influenced. Rudaki and his contemporaries were the originators of the following poetic forms: the *kasside* (a poem glorifying a personage, but frequently also of a satirical or didactic nature); the *ghazal* (a lyric poem, which possibly developed from the introductory part of the kasside); the *rubai* (stanzas consisting of four lines and having an epigrammatic character), which almost always consist of different combinations of double verses (*baits*) thematically interconnected, as well as the *masnavi* (rhyming, paired double verses, joined together in arbitrary numbers and representing the form employed in the didactic and narrative literatures).

Firdausi's (934?–1020[26?]) monumental work *Shah-Nameh* indicates the high quality attained by the epic at this time. Avicenna (980–1037) composed philosophical poems (*rubai*) in Daric, the written Persian language of those times. These poems greatly influenced Nasir-i Husrau (1004–1072[77?]) and, later, Omar Khayyam (1021[22?]–1123). Gurgani's romantic poem *Vis u Ramin* [Vis and Ramin] was written circa 1048 but was actually taken from an earlier source. This adventure story of two lovers appears to have been as popular as the amusing little epic *Mus u gurbe* [The Muse and the Cat] and the other acerbic compositions produced by the satiricist Obaid-i Sakani (1300–71) three hundred years later.

Uneasiness stemming from the material dependence of writers on court favors on the one hand, and the desire for ideologic independence on the other, became the source of considerable conflicts for many poets at this time, including Firdausi and Sakani. We would, however, be doing them an injustice if we were to regard the works of these court poets as merely false glorifications of the rulers, lacking in any lyric qualities. The work of the mystic, religious poets such as Dzhalal-ad-Din Rumi (1207–73), which is characterized by the conflicts existing between the different forms of Islam, have a songlike quality. These poets took the problems of their own lives, social themes, etc., as their chief subjects.

The thirteenth and fourteenth centuries are characterized by the great creations of Sadi (1213[19?]–91[95?]) and the remarkable flowering of the ghazals (Sadi; Kamal Hudshandi, d. 1400; Hafis, circa 1325–90). Dshami (1414–92) was the last of the important classical writers. It should, however, be kept in mind that the great Azerbaidzhani poet Nisami Gandshevi (circa 1141–

1209) also wrote ghazals and poems in the Persian language, and that there was a strong link between the Near Eastern and the Central Asian literatures.

In 1491 the Uzbekistanian writer Navoi (1441–1501) compiled an anthology of Persian Uzbekistanian poetry.

Feudal disunity finally brought about the end of the great Persian classical age. Later writers usually represented only a small section of the country, with the result that individual national literatures began to develop. Very few writers and poets were able to match the brilliance of the past. Among those whose work attained importance were Bidil (1644–1721), who lived in India and whose work greatly affected Tadzhik literature; and the two national poets Abdarrahman Mushfiqi (1539–88) and Mir Abid Sayyida Nasafi (d. 1707[11?]). A. Mushfiqi employed themes taken from daily life; an eighteenth-century Till Eulenspiegel, his satirical poems were aimed at the hearts of nobility and royalty alike. Nafasi's classic kassides extolled the artisan; his witty fables criticized the upper classes.

The idea of friendship with Russia began to gain acceptance in the work of Danish (1827–97). Sadriddin Aini (1878–1954) recognized the errors of a gradually developing nationalism. Friendship with Russia was associated with the acceptance of revolutionary and social aims. The realization of these aims turned the retarded Tadzhik land into a highly developed cultural and industrial state, in which for the first time native literature found a mass audience. This development was associated with the acceptance of modern prose forms. S. Aini especially played a large part in this development. However, certain crude forms of prose writing had become evident in the Persian Middle Ages. Also developing at this time was the struggle against a slavelike adherence to the poetic traditions of the classical period. This complex search for a synthesis between tradition and an acceptance of the achievements of European literature characterizes recent Tadzhik literature.

Together with S. Aini we may regard Abulqasim Lahuti (1887–1957) as the founder of Tadzhik Soviet literature. These two authors left an imprint on this literature during the first decade after the revolution. Very soon, however, new names came to the fore, some of which have become internationally known. Mirso Tursum-sade's (b. 1911) lyric poems of the postwar period, inspired by the worldwide fight for peace, are among the best achievements of the era. Sotym Ulug-soda (b. 1911) may be regarded as the most prolific playwright of Tadzhik literature.

The psychological novel is a genre gaining wide acceptance in contemporary Tadzhik literature. One of its chief exponents is D. Ikramis (b. 1909) in whose novels we find a deep understanding of psychological motivation.

TURKMENIAN LITERATURE

The beginnings of Turkmenian literature go back to the tenth and eleventh centuries. A dictionary compiled by Mahmud Kashgari contains parts of poems and epigrams from the tenth and eleventh centuries, while the most important piece of national literature, the epic *Kor-ogly*, was created between the sixteenth and seventeenth centuries. It deals for the most part with the struggles against foreign invaders, and calls for a united front on the part of all Turkmenian tribes. This call for unity remained one of the main themes of Turkmenian literature until well into the nineteenth century, since feudal disunity represented a major obstacle in the defense against Uzbekian and Iranian attempts at annexation.

The oldest known Turkmenian literary documents are chiefly of a religious nature, and show the influence of Islam. These include *The Helper of the Myurid* by Sheref-chodsha (fourteenth century), *Rounak il islam* [Rounak, or The Islam], and *The Light of Islam* by Vepai (fifteenth century). The influences of Islam are still strongly in evidence in the literature of the eighteenth century, especially in the works of the poet Shabende. A story in verse by Abdy-Settar-Kasi in the 1860s about the fight of the Turkmenian tribes against the Shah of Iran clearly shows the influence of Islam. The literary form most widely distributed in the eighteenth century was the destane, an extensive epic work sung or recited by folk singers (bakhshi) before an audience over a period of several days. The best-known destanes are *Shasenem and Garib,* the story of the love of Shasenem, the daughter of the Shah, for the poor boy Garib, and *Khyurlyukga and Khemra.* Lyric poetry in the second half of the eighteenth century was represented by Dovletmamed Asadi (1700–60), who also wrote a didactic tract, *The Sermon of Asadi,* and by Gaibi and Sheidai.

Classic Turkmenian literature was founded by the poet and thinker Makhtum-Kuli (circa 1730–80[90?]). Although he was still influenced by Islam, Makhtum-Kuli based his poems on incidents drawn from the daily life of the Turkmenian people. Patriotic themes dominated later poetic works, including those of Seid-Nasar Seidi (1768–1830) and Kurbandurdy Selili (circa 1790–1844); the latter was best known for his history of Turkmenia. The feelings of the poorer classes were the subject of poems by the democratic poet Mamedveli Kemine (1770[80?]– 1840) who also castigated the exploiters of the poor. Similar themes were treated by Talibi, Sinkhari and Ashiki.

The traditions of Makhtum-Kuli were considerably extended in the middle of the nineteenth century by the poet Mollanepes (circa 1810–62.) His work is illuminated by intimate lyrics which contrast strongly with his biting protests against the despotism of the rulers. The works of the poet Myatadshi (1824–84), too, were chiefly of a lyrical nature.

In the 1880s Turkmenia came under Russian rule, a move that resulted in the beginning of capitalist development. The democratic theme now became dominant as a result of close contacts with Russian literature. The poet and musician Miskin-klych (1845–1905) sang of the beauty of his native land; poetic writing more and more reflected the writer's need to protest against suppression and despotism; this is shown in the works of Bairam Shahir (1871–1948), Kör-Molla (1872–1934), Durdy Klych (1886–1950), and Molla Murta (1879–1930).

The great socialist October revolution liberated the Turkmenian people from feudal and capitalist oppression. A great renaissance became evident in Turkmenian literature. Kör-Molla created his poem *Bolshevik* in honor of the Communist Party; Durdy Klych welcomed the revolution and called for the building of a new life in his *Poem on Lenin, The Time Has Come to Learn,* and *Girls.* By the mid-1920s the first Turkmenian-language newspapers and magazines had begun to appear. The first Turkmenian theater was opened in Ashkhabad in 1929, thus laying the foundation for the development of Turkmenian dramatic writings. Among the founders of Turkmenian Soviet literature, we find Berdy Kerbabayev (b. 1894), Karadsha Burunov (b. 1898), Ata Kaushutov (1903–53), and Jakib Nasyrli (b. 1899). These writers mainly discussed the changes taking place in the Turkmenian village, as did Ata Salikh (b. 1908), Atakopek Mergenov (b. 1898), and Nuri Anna-Klych (1911–58). Turkmenian prose writing developed particularly well after the revolution. The writer Nurmurad Sarykhanov (1904–44), who was strongly influenced by both Chekhov and Gorki, wrote a series of stories on the revolution taking place in the Turkmenian village. The same theme was treated by Agakian Durdyev (1904–47) in his stories. Anandurdy Alamyshev (1904–43), Kodsha Shukurov (1897–1944), Aman Kekilov (b. 1912), and certain other writers produced poems on the class struggle taking place in the villages. A. Kaushutov and Ata Niyasov (1906–1942) wrote praiseworthy dramas.

During World War II, Turkmenian writers fought side by side with their own people for the liberation of the Soviet homeland. The brotherhood of all Soviet nationalities became a major poetic theme, as can be seen in the works of Khalurdy Duryev (b. 1909), Rukhi Aliyev (b. 1910), A. Kekilov, A. Niyasov, Kara Seitiyev (b. 1915) among others. The heroic battles taking place at the front and in the interior of the country have been described by A. Kaushutov in his stories and in his novel *Mekhri i Vepa* (1944–46); by Kh. Ismailov (1913–48) in his story *Rivals* (1944); by Hussein Mukhtarov (b. 1914); and by Belgo Purliyev (b. 1919). In the postwar years the problems of the socialist reconstruction of Turkmenia again became a popular theme. The stories and novels of B. Kerbabayev, A. Kaushutov, Kh. Ismailov, and Beki

Seitakov (b. 1914), in particular, have become well-known. A. Kekilov, Chary Ashirov (b. 1910), Pomma Nurbedyev (b. 1909), Rakhmet Seidov (1910–54), K. Seitliyev, and Ata-Aradshanov (b. 1922) gained importance in the field of poetry. Hussein Mukhtarov (b. 1914), K. Seitliyev, and Alty Karliyev (b. 1909) have become known as dramatic writers.

UKRAINIAN LITERATURE

The beginnings of Ukrainian literature, like those of the two other East Slavic literatures (Russian and Byelorussian), go back to the ancient literature of the Kievan Russ. The literary works of that period, including *The Lay of the Host of Igor* and the highly developed verbal national poetry, greatly influenced the development of Ukrainian literature during the feudal period. Traces of what appear to be distinctly Ukrainian cultural and linguistic peculiarities were found as early as the thirteenth and fourteenth centuries in the so-called Galician-Volhynian chronicle as well as in the Western Russian ("Lithuanian") chronicles of the fourteenth and fifteenth centuries. A uniquely Ukrainian literature, closely connected with the historical development of the Ukrainian people, began in the fourteenth and fifteenth centuries. Large areas of the ancient Kievan Russ—Kiev, Chernigov, Podolsk, Galicia—were at that time absorbed into Lithuania and Poland, with the result that the Ukrainian people became separated from the originally united association of the East Slavic tribes.

The development of trade and the beginning of cultural contacts with other areas led to a noticeable upswing in the cultural and literary life. This was particularly evident in rapidly growing towns such as Kiev and Lvov, which became cultural centers. Schools were instituted, printing shops were founded, and numerous religious and didactic books were translated. This cultural growth was forcibly interrupted in the second half of the sixteenth century. The political union between Lithuania and Poland, signed in 1569 at Lublin, led to a long period of spiritual and economic oppression.

The Poles attempted to bring the Orthodox Ukrainian Church

under the rule of Catholicism. They were helped in this by members of the Jesuit order, with whom the Poles signed the Union of Brest in 1596.

Sixteenth- and seventeenth-century literature developed gradually; the Ukrainian people renewed their fight for social and national liberation and were eventually successful in having the Ukraine returned to Russian rule after the victorious revolt of the Cossack hetman Bogdan Khnelnitsky. The dominant ideas of Ukrainian literature of this period stemmed from antifeudalism and the fight for liberation. Thinly disguised as a religious struggle, the battle of the Ukrainian people for national liberation became the most important feature of their cultural resistance to the catholicization policies of the Polish oppressors.

The centers of literary activity were the so-called fraternities (Orthodox religious communities) and their schools at Lvov, Ostrog, and Kiev. Religious, political works of a polemic character —approximately 140 in number—developed at these centers. The most important representatives of this religious and polemic literature were Mileti Smotrytzkyi (1577–1633), who was also a well-known grammarian (*Slavic Grammar*, 1619), and Ivan Vyshenskyi (circa 1550–after 1620). In open church letters, dialogues, and tracts—forms that were frequently combined in a very individual style—these men passionately fought against Catholicism, criticized both the church and the secular order, and demanded an ascetic mode of life. The work of I. Vyshenskyi is both the cornerstone of Ukrainian satire and an important peak in the Ukrainian literature of feudalist times.

The so-called Baroque poetry developed in the seventeenth century under the influence of Western European movements. It was strongly influenced by the work of the Kievan Academy founded in 1615 and transferred, in 1651, to the Kiev-Mohyla college. Syllabic poetry (virshi), concerned chiefly with religious, moral, didactic, and historical themes, predominated. The historic virshi in particular was widely distributed. At the same time the drama, similar in style to that of the Jesuit Latin school, came to represent the favored genre in Baroque literature. Individual scenes in these didactic dramas were already strongly nationalist in feeling, depicting folk heroes and people of the times. Prose writings were less sophisticated; they consisted almost exclusively of biographies of saints, apocryphal books, and translations of Western European chivalric romances. Baroque literature did promote cultural progress despite its isolation from the interests of the people and despite its scholastic, formal creative principles. Baroque poetry enriched Ukrainian literature by the introduction of a series of new poetic genres, and it eventually led to an Europeanization of native writings.

One of the most interesting features of Ukrainian eighteenth-century literature is the increase in realistic descriptions of the milieu; such descriptions had already become evident in the interludes of a number of didactic dramas. True pictures of life and the use of the vernacular indicate that the usually anonymous authors were turning to an increasing extent toward real life for their subjects. Wandering scholars and the lower-ranking clergy were for the most part responsible for the gradual secularization of literature in the eighteenth century. Among these we find Klyment Zynovyev, Ivan Nekrashevych, and the poet and philosopher Hryhorii Skovoroda (1722–94). The latter is considered the most important representative of Ukrainian enlightenment. His biting criticism of the life led by estate owners, merchants, and high church dignitaries; his satirical, critical view of the official religion; and his interest in the human personality make his versatile work the high point of feudal Ukrainian literature. Skovoroda greatly influenced the subsequent development of literature; later burlesque, satirical poetry, and sentimental secular poetry together introduce a new period in Ukrainian literature.

Development of the Ukrainian literature of the nineteenth century took place despite signs of growing capitalism, the crisis in the feudal system, and the formation of the Ukrainian bourgeois nation. The most important representative of literature at the beginning of this century was Ivan Kotlyarevskyi (1769–1838). His poems and dramas took the parasitic existence of the Ukrainian upper classes for their themes. His work shows a deep knowledge of the national life. Kotlyarevski completely reformed the Ukrainian literary language by basing it, for the first time in its history, on the living, colloquial language of the people. He was the first Ukrainian poet to introduce a syllabic-tonal verse form.

The literary traditions of Kotlyarevski were directly continued by Pavlo Biletzki-Nosenko, the fabulist Petro Hulak-Artemovskyi (1796–1865), and Yevheni Hrebinka (1812–48), as well as by the founder of the new Ukrainian prose writings Hrykori Kvitka-Osnovyanenko (1778–1843).

Romanticism began to develop in the 1830s. Its development was closely linked with the increasing interest in Ukrainian history and folklore. The collections of works of national poetry, especially the *Dumy* or epic heroic songs of the Cossacks, greatly influenced the work of the Ukrainian romanticists. Publication of these national poetic works was arranged by folklorists such as Nikolai Tzertelev (1790–1869), Mykhailo Maksymovych (1804–73), and Amyrosi Metlynskyi (1814–70). Ukrainian romanticism, like its Russian counterpart, exhibited one progressive movement (Leyko Borovykovskyi, 1806–89; Markiyan Shash-kevych, 1811–43) and one conservative movement (Mykola Kostomarov, 1817–85; A. Metlynskyi; Panteleimon Kulish, 1819–97).

The transition from romanticism to critical realism in Ukrainian literature came with T. Shevchenko (1814–61), the national poet of the Ukrainian people. The spontaneous resistance of the oppressed masses, the dreams and hopes of the Ukrainian peasants and their rich world of feelings and emotions, found classical poetic expression in the works of this revolutionary democratic writer. Shevchenko's writings were deeply rooted in the national soil; they represented a synthesis of philosophical ideas, progressive political ideals, and high artistic standards. His work has had a decisive influence on the subsequent development of Ukrainian literature.

Shevchenko directed the way of Ukrainian literature toward democracy, national solidarity, and critical realism. All the important Ukrainian writers of subsequent periods saw in his work artistic standards they themselves could follow. In the steps of

Shevchenko came Marko Vovchok (1834–1907), whose popular stories about the serfs saw the beginning of a more critically realistic prose style.

By the second half of the nineteenth century critical realism had become the dominant literary movement in Ukrainian literature. The leading literary role at this time was played by the democratic writers. Stimulated by the example of Shevchenko and that of classical Russian literature, their works commented on the decay of the feudal system, the stormy growth of capitalism, the increased exploitation of the masses, the dissension within the groups of Ukrainian peasants, their increasing resistance to social oppression, and the gradual ripening of the revolution. Ivan Nechui-Levytzkyi (1838–1918) greatly extended the literary themes used by depicting the lower intellectuals and the clergy. His novels and stories, together with those of Anatoli Svydnytzkyi (1834–71) and Oleksander Konyskyi (1836–1900), exhibit strong ethnographic features.

The prominent personality of the critical-realist movement in the 1870s and 1880s was Panas Myrnyi (1849–1920), who re-created the social contrasts existing in the Ukrainian village after the reforms of 1861. The heroes of his epic novels are for the most part peasants in revolt against the yoke of the estate owners and the capitalists. The revolutionary, democratic poet and political journalist-writer Paulo Hrabovskyi (1864–1902) continued the progressive traditions of Shevchenko. His poems, which call for a revolution against tsarism, exhibit the influences of socialist ideas. Other well-known poets of this period were Stepan Rudanskyi (1833–73), Ivan Manzhura (1851–93), and Leonid Hlibiv (1827–93), whose fables received particular attention in progressive circles.

Realistic dramatic writing showed a remarkable rise in the second half of the nineteenth century. Mykhailo Starytizkyi (1840–1904), Marko Kropyvnytzkyi (1841–1910), and, in particular, Ivan Karpenko-Karyi (1845–1907) wrote numerous plays that helped the Ukrainian professional theater achieve national representation.

Ivan Franko (1856–1916) was the greatest Ukrainian writer of the revolutionary, democratic movement. His works are among the most mature achievements of critical realism in Ukrainian literature. Franko's handling of the stormy development of capitalism and his description of the miserable conditions under which the exploited workers and peasants lived are particularly impressive. Other notable writers in the field of critical-realist literature around the turn of the century included the novelists Mykhilo Kotzyubynskyi (1864–1913), Arkhyp Teslenko (1882–1911), Stepan Vasylchenko (1878–1932), and the novelist, dramatist, and poet Lesya Ukrayinka (1871–1913). All these writers took an active part in the fight for social liberation and devoted their work to the service of progressive ideals. Using contemporary social and philosophical themes, they severely criticized the deplorable conditions existing in bourgeois, capitalist society, and voiced their sympathy for the common people. Critical realism in Ukrainian literature reached its peak in the works of these revolutionary, democratic writers.

The great socialist October revolution created basically new social and ideologic conditions for a successful development of Ukrainian literature under Soviet rule. This development began with a profound ideological dissension within the community of Ukrainian writers stemming from the historic events of the revolution. The finest representatives of the old democratic intelligentsia—P. Myrnyi, S. Vasylchenko, and others—joined the ranks of the proletariat. This step was also taken by a number of younger bourgeois writers, including Pavlo Tychyna (1891–1967), Maksim Rylskyi (1895–1964), and Ivan Kocherha (1881–1952). A few writers, however, preferred emigration, among them Vyinnychenko and Cherkasenko. Ukrainian Soviet literature was formed during the years of civil war and foreign intervention. The new literature relied chiefly on the classical inheritance of both Russian and Ukrainian literatures—on the works of A. Pushkin, N. Nekrasov, T. Schevchenko, I. Franko and, in particular, on the proletarian writings of M. Gorki. The first works of the new socialist Ukrainian literature appeared mainly in the revolutionary worker and peasant press and in army newspapers. The Communist Party paid a great deal of attention to the growing proletarian literature and aided in its development as much as possible. Collections of poems by P. Tychyna, V. Sosyura (1898–1965), V. Chumak (1900–19), and V. Ellan (1892–1925) may be considered the first examples of Ukrainian Soviet literature.

The new socialist literature grew strong in defending the decisive class battles of the period—the battles against bourgeois, nationalist ideology and antirealistic movements. Many proletarian writers started their careers during that decade, including novelists A. Holovko (b. 1897), P. Panch (b. 1891), I. Le (b. 1895). Y. Yanovskyi (1902–1954); the poets M. Bazhan (b. 1904), P. Usenko (b. 1902), A. Malyshko (b. 1912); the dramatic writers Y. Mamontiv (1888–1940), M. Irchan (1898–1937), M. Kulish (b. 1892). These writers wrote about the revolution and the civil war, and, for the first time, about the problems arising in connection with early socialist reconstruction.

The position of socialist realism in Ukrainian literature was strengthened in the thirties. New and talented writers included the dramatist O. Korniichuk (b. 1905), the lyricists I. Honcharenko (b. 1908), L. Pervomaiskji (b. 1908), L. Dmyterko (b. 1911), and the novelists A. Shyan (b. 1906), L. Smilyanskyi (b. 1904), and N. Rybak (b. 1913). A number of writers who had hitherto not become involved with the socialist reconstruction movement now took an active part in literary life. Among these was M. Rylskyi, who subsequently became one of the most important representatives of Ukrainian Soviet literature. The literature of the 1930s was especially concerned with the artistic presentation of the new socialist aspects of the Soviet people, as well as with the theme of patriotism and friendship among nations.

The Ukrainian writers made great literary and political contributions to the victory over fascism in World War II. The heroism of the Soviet people both at the front and in the interior was depicted in the various literary genres. Writers exposed the antihuman ideology of fascism in their political writings.

The period of peaceful reconstruction after the war was associated with a renewed flowering of Ukrainian Soviet literature. Writers already known—M. Rylskyi, P. Tychyna, M. Bazhan, and O. Korniichuk—were involved in this, together with many representatives of the younger generation of writers. After 1945 several young writers appeared with works that came to the public attention, including O. Honchar (b. 1918), M. Stelmakh (b. 1912), S. Oliinyk (b. 1908), V. Sobko (b. 1912), H. Tyutyunnyk (1920–61), and O. Levada (b. 1909). Contemporary Ukrainian literature continues to enrich the development of the multinational Soviet literature.

UZBEKISTANIAN LITERATURE

Uzbekistanian literature is one of the oldest literatures in the Soviet Union. The earliest writings originated with the Turkic and Iranian tribes living in Central Asia, who wrote their poetry in Sogdian, Ugrian, ancient Turkic, and other related scripts. Almost all early written documents were destroyed in the seventh and eighth centuries by Arab invaders. Only a few funerary inscriptions of the eighth century have come down to us. These inscriptions represent the oldest written documents of Uzbekistanian literature.

Verbal national poetry also goes back to ancient times. Some of this poetry was written down by Mahmud Kashgari, a linguist living in the eleventh century, in his *Divan lugat at turk* [Collection of Turkic Dialects]. National poetry is still very much alive in Uzbekistan; the figure of Nasreddin Hodsha, the Turkic Till Eulenspiegel, enjoys great popularity. After the Arab invasion of the seventh and eighth centuries, the development of Uzbekistanian literature was impeded by the introduction of Islami and Arabic. Up until the fourteenth century religious, mystical poetry written in the spirit of Islam or in accordance with the ascetic teachings of Sufism was the chief form of literature to develop. Its most important representatives were Ahmed Yasevi (circa 1105–66), author of a collection of poems entitled *Hikmat* (Epigrams); Suleiman Bakirgani's *Ahir samon kitabi* [The Book on the End of the World]; Ahmad-ibn Mahmud Yugnaki's *Hibat-*

ul-hakoik (The Gift of Truth); and Rabgusi's religious, didactic stories *Kisas-ul-anbiia* [Legends about the Prophets]. The love poem *Yusuf and Suleikha* by the Uzbek poet Durbek (fourteenth–fifteenth centuries) is notable as one of the rare examples of secular literature written at this time. Most secular poetry consisted chiefly of translations from the great poets of Asia Minor (Nizami's *Khosgran and Shirin*; Sadi's *Gulistan*).

Secular Uzbekistanian literature experienced a rebirth in the fifteenth century, reaching its peak in the work of the poet-scholar Nismaddin Alisher Navoi (1441–1501), one of the greatest poets in world literature. Navoi wrote in the ancient Uzbekistanian language; his ten volumes of poems and lyrics laid the foundation for the subsequent development of all Uzbekistanian literature as well as for the other literatures of Central Asia. The historic writings of the fifteenth and sixteenth centuries, which tell of the great war expeditions of the Uzbekistanian khans, are of great interest from the standpoint of cultural history. Sahireddin Mohammed Baber described in his *Baber-name* [The Book of Baber] the military expeditions into Afghanistan and India. Mohammed Salikh, a contemporary of Baber, in his *Sheibani-name* [The Sheibani Book] described the conquest of Central Asia by Khan Sheibani, the leader of the Uzbekian nomad tribes. The author glorifies the heroism of the khan, but at the same time describes the great losses suffered by the people and the catastrophic results of feudal power struggles and civil war.

Feudal, religious, and secular writings all continued to develop in the sixteenth to nineteenth centuries. The secular movement led the way, however, and showed marked democratic tendencies. In the seventeenth century the poet Turdy created a series of satirical works in which he opposed the khan, his dignitaries, and the clergy. The poet Mashrab (1657–1711) was widely praised for his satires on the feudal upper classes in the nineteenth century. Mohammed Makhmur wrote important socio-critical poems in which he depicted oppression and plundering of the peasants by the khan. The popular allegoric fables *Sarbul-masal* [Epigrams, 1890] by Gulkhani raise accusations against social injustices.

Democratic Uzbekistanian literature experienced a tremendous upsurge following the annexation of Central Asia by Russia in the mid-nineteenth century. Development of literature was based on the national traditions and on realistic Russian writings. The center of the movement for democratic revival in Uzbekistanian literature was in Kokand, the home of the important poets Mohammed Amin Mukimi (1851–1903) and Furkat (1858–1909). During the early years of the twentieth century, the leading democratic writers—Ubaidulla Salikh Savki (1853–1921), Avas Otar-Ogly (1884–1919), Hamim-Zade Hamza (1889–1929)—supported the people, national independence, and social liberation. They opposed the bourgeois nationalism of the Dshadides, and indicated the need for cooperation with the progressive Russian culture.

After the October revolution of 1917, Uzbekistanian literature developed as a national, independent unit within the multinational Soviet literature. The range of the themes and forms of expression were greatly extended, thus enabling the writers to deal in proper artistic terms with the enormous social changes taking places as a result of the Socialist Revolution. To verse writing, which had been cultivated for centuries, was now added realistic prose and dramatic writing, as well as independent literary criticism.

The founder of Uzbekistanian socialist literature was H. Hamza, whose plays and poems praised the revolution and its achievements. Hamza was the creator of the modern Uzbekistanian theater, which became directly involved in the social battles of the times. He was also a militantly political journalist and a composer. Hamza exerted a considerable influence on the development of socialist literature in Uzbekistan and in the other Soviet republics of Central Asia. Shortly after the October revolution the newly developing Uzbekistanian prose became an important factor in the cultural life of the country. These writings were greatly stimulated by Sadriddin Aini (1878–1954), the founder of Tadzhik Soviet literature, a number of whose novels and short stories were first published in the Uzbekistanian language and later translated into Tadzhik.

In the 1920s and 1930s a new generation of poets appeared; these writers treated the real problems of Uzbekistanian life. Among them we find the poets Gaful Gulyam (1903–66) and Alimdzhan Khamid (1909–44), whose poems form a link with the revolutionary poetry of V. Mayakovski; the versatile writer Aibek (b. 1905); the master of the Uzbekistanian short story Abdulla Kakhkhar (1907–68); the dramatist Kamil Yashen (pseud. of Nugmonov; b. 1909); the poet and dramatist Uigun (pseud. of Rakhmatulla Atakusiyev, b. 1905); the realist poet Gairati (pseud. of Abdurakhim Abdullayev, b. 1905), and others. These writers described life in the towns and villages changed by the revolution. They supported socialism and the power of the Soviets. In doing so, they often had to fight against the counter-revolutionary intrigues of the Dshadides, who killed the democratic writer Hamza in 1929. With the aid of the Communist Party, these young writers succeeded in fully establishing socialist literature in Uzbekistan.

The industrialization of the country and the social changes connected with it were the subject of poems by the lyric writers Gafur Gulyam (*On the Rails of the Turksib; Petroleum; The Textile Cooperative and the Egyptian Pyramids; The Water Main*) and Alimdzhan (*The Land Has Mobilized; We Have Won; The Story of Two Girls*) as well as in the poetry of Aibek. Similar themes have been treated in the short stories of A. Kakhkhar and Gairati. The collectivization of the land and the development of the socialist village were reflected in Uzbekistanian literature, becoming the subject of poems such as *Kukan* by Gafur Gulyam; *Dzhantemir* (1936) by Uigun; *Seinab and Aman* (1938) by Alimdzhan; as well as of the stories *Utbasar and Mastan* by A. Kakhkhar, and in the dramatic pieces *Comrades, Let's Burn!, Honor and Love* by K. Yashen. The emancipation of women represented an additional central theme of Uzbekistanian Soviet literature, since women in old Uzbekistan had been completely excluded from public life and had been permitted to appear outside their homes only when veiled. This problem has been treated by Aibek in his poem *Dilbar, a Daughter of Her*

Times (1932), and by K. Yashen in his musical dramas *Gulsara* and *Honor and Love.* The presentation of Uzbekistanian Soviet history—in particular the fight for social liberation—occupies considerable space in Uzbekistanian Soviet literature. In his novel *Holy Blood* (1943) Aibek told of the life of the Uzbekistanian people during World War I and he showed how the poorest classes in the Uzbekistanian village gained an awareness of the revolution and joined in the movement for national liberation in 1916.

During World War II, Uzbekistanian writers actively participated in the battles against fascism. The patriotic, militant poems of Alimdzhan, *Mother and Son* (1942), *Take Up Your Rifles!* (1942), *The Dshigites Go to the Front* (1942), and others, enjoyed great popularity. Alimdzhan also wrote several political articles during the war—*The Artists of Uzbekistan Call for Victory.* The war lyrics of Galfur Gulyam (*I Am a Jew, You Are Not an Orphan, I Am Waiting for You, My Son*) were also very popular. During the war years, Uigun and Isat Sultanov (b. 1910) created the important drama *Alisher Navoi* (published in 1948). Aibek completed his novel *Navoi* in 1945, receiving the State Prize for it in 1946.

Authors

ABAI KUNANBAYEV
Born August 10, 1845, in Chingistan; died there July 6, 1904.
Founder of modern Kazakh literature; philosopher and composer.
A., the son of a feudal nobleman, received a good Kazakh and
Russian education in Semipalatinsk. His ideology was formed by
the tenets of Eastern humanism and the doctrines of the Russian
revolutionary democrats. In his poems A. denounced social abuses
and supported social action in art. He enriched the existing poetic
forms by reviving poetry and introducing new genres. His best
poems, which he himself frequently set to music, were to become
well known for their intellectual and humanistic qualities. A. was
deeply involved in making Russian classical literature known
throughout Kazakhstan.

Editions: Shygharmalarynyng tolyq shynaghy [Collected Works],
2 vols., Alma-Ata, 1957; *Sobraniye sochinenii* [Collected Works],
Moscow, 1954

ABOVIAN, KHACHATUR
Born in 1805, Kanaker, near Yerevan; died April 14, 1848.
Armenian writer, philosopher, democrat, teacher, and ethnographer; founder of modern Armenian literature and of the Armenian
literary language; translator of classical Greek and Latin works and
of classical Russian and German literature.
All A.'s work was directed against feudal authority and the
reactionary clergy. His work includes stories, sketches, plays, works
of a scientific and artistic nature, and poems and fables written in
modern Armenian. In 1841 A. wrote a novel (*The Wounds of
Armenia*)—which was not to be published until 1948—using the
Russo-Persian war (1826–28) as a background. This work, which
is considered to be the first secular Armenian novel, tells of the
fight of the Armenian people for liberation from Turkish domi-

nation. A. saw the friendship between the Russian and Armenian peoples as a token of hope for the rebirth of Armenia.

Editions: Izbrannoye [Selected Works], Moscow, 1948; *Stikhotvoreniya* [Poems] (in Russian), Yerevan, 1948

ABRAMOV, KUZMA

Born November 12, 1914, Staryye Naimany. Mordvinian poet and short-story writer.

A. has been publishing poems (*Poems*, 1940) and stories on kolkhoz life since 1935. In 1957 he wrote the peasant novel *Naiman*, which deals with the consolidation of Soviet power in Mordvinia.

AFANASYEV, ALEKSANDR NIKOLAYEVICH

Born July 11, 1826, Boguchar (District of Voronezh); died October 23, 1871, Moscow. Russian folklorist and ethnographer.

A. must be highly commended for his life's work—the collection and publishing of Russian fairy tales. The collection *Narodnyye russkiye skazki* [Russian Fairy Tales, 1855–63] is the first scholarly edition of fairy tales in Russia, and has remained the basic work for research into the genre. A.'s work in three volumes *Poeticheskiye vozzreniya slavyan na prirodu* [The Poetic View of the Slavs on Nature, 1865–69] is based on his research into Russian national poetry.

Editions: Narodnyye russkiye skazki (Russian Fairy Tales, 3 vols., 1957), Moscow

AFINOGENOV, ALEKSANDR NIKOLAYEVICH

Born April 4, 1904, Skopin (District of Ryazan); died October 29, 1941, Moscow. Soviet Russian dramatist.

After overcoming certain influences of the Proletcult, toward the end of the 1920s A.'s work began to follow the traditional forms of realistic drama. He was championed in these efforts by Gorki. His dramas *Chudak* [The Crank, 1929] and *Strakh* [Fear, 1930] dealt with the fight against bureaucratism and the problem of intelligence in Soviet society. His themes are concerned with the "small but great man,"—with the simple Soviet man whose fate he has shown in his dramas *Daliokoye* (1935; Distant Point, 1941) and *Mashenka* (1940; Listen, Professor! 1944), as the fate of the Russian people. His plays *Salyut, Ispaniya!* [Salute to Spain, 1936], and *Nakanunye* [On the Eve, 1941] deal with the burning problems of these difficult times.

A.'s dramatic works are characterized as dramas of spiritual struggle, and are endowed with a specific intellectuality. They have a tendency to investigate the psychological ramifications and depths of the intellectual struggles that are a major factor in his works. He presents these conflicts in the form of polished dialogues reminiscent of Chekhov and Gorki. A.'s plays, which may be regarded as a significant contribution to the Soviet drama of the 1930s, reflect the mental growth of the Soviet people of this period, revealing the moral and political problems that arise in the mind of the indvidual during the process of maturation.

Editions: Pyesy [Plays], Moscow, 1956

AGATANGEKHOS
Armenian historian of the fourth century. Author of the vividly written *History of Armenia* rich in dialogues, a work which also exhibits elements of national poetry. This valuable literary document has significantly influenced ancient Armenian literature.

AIBEK (Pseud. of *Mussa Tashmukhammedov*)
Born January 10, 1905, Tashkent. Uzbekistanian Soviet poet and novelist; member of the Uzbek Academy of Sciences; Deputy of the Supreme Soviet of the USSR.

In his poems A. supported the social reconstruction of his homeland. His poem *Hamsa* (1948) is dedicated to the founder of Uzbekistanian Soviet literature. *Holy Blood* (1943) was the first great realistic novel of Uzbekistanian literature. It describes the increasing revolutionary movement among the Uzbekistanian peasantry, and the road traveled by the peasants to their fight for national liberation in 1916. A. received the State Prize of 1946 for his novel *Navoi* (1945), based on the life of the greatest ancient Uzbek poet. His novel *Solntze ne pomerknet* [The Sun Will Not Stop Shining, 1965] is dedicated to the heroic fight of the Soviet soldiers during World War II.

A. has translated numerous works of world literature; his versions of Pushkin's *Yevgenii Onegin* and of Goethe's *Faust* deserve particular mention.

Editions: Sochineniya [Works], 5 vols., 1962–64
Further Works: Navoi (1945); *V poiskakh sveta* [In Search of Light] (1959)

AIMURZAYEV, SHOLMURSA
Born May 9, 1910. Kara-Kalpak Soviet poet, novelist, and playwright.

A.'s literary career began in the 1920s. His first volume of poetry appeared in 1937 in Moscow in the Kara-Kalpak language. In 1958 he published his novel *Amudarya boyynda* [On the Banks of the Amu-Darya] about a Kara-Kalpak village of the postwar period. His poems *Gures* [The Battle, 1934–35] and *We have Won in Battle* (1938), as well as his play *Aigul-Abat* (1959), deal with the establishment of Soviet power in his homeland and the class battles in the country during the time of collectivization. His play *Berdakh* (1958) is about the life of the famous Kara-Kalpak poet of that name.

Editions: Shygarmalary [Works], Vol. 1, Nokis, 1961; *Poety sovyetskoi Kara-Kalpakii* [The Poets of Soviet Kara-Kalpak] (in Russian), Nukus, 1956

AINI (Pseud. of *Sadriddin Saidmuradovich*)
Born April 27, 1878, Soktare; died July 15, 1954, Dushanbe. Tadzhikian novelist and literary scholar; founder of Tadzhik Soviet literature and also of the Uzbek novel.

From 1951 to his death A. was president of the Tadzhik Academy of Sciences. Following the death of his parents in 1890, A.

worked as a cook in Bukhara. He acquired a good education by private studies, and, later, by attending religious schools. Under the influence of Danisch he became a writer. His concern for the reform of the Tadzhik literary language was evident in even his early works. A. soon became the leader of the left wing of an illegal liberal organization. In 1917 he was cruelly ill-treated by the ruling emir. He visited Samarkand and in 1920 took part in the liberation of Bukhara. A. worked for a number of Uzbek and Tadzhik newspapers and was active as teacher. A. wrote about his adventures and the results of his historical research, publishing a number of prose works which appeared simultaneously in Uzbek and Tadzhik. These include *Gallodoni Bukhoro* [The Hangmen of Bukhara, 1920–35], a short story, *Odina*, published in 1924, and *Dokhunda* (1930) which is considered the first Tadzhik novel. *Gulomon* [Slaves], published in 1935, is a novel about the last one hundred years of the Tadzhik people. In 1950 A. was awarded the State Prize for his volume of reminiscences *Joddostho* (1949–54).

In 1925, A. published an anthology of Tadzhik literature in three volumes entitled *Namunayi adabijoti togik*. During the years 1936–38, he prepared a dictionary of the Tadzhik literary language.

Editions: Kullijot [Collected Works], 15 vols., Stalinabad, 1958 f.

AITMATOV, CHINGIS

Born December 12, 1928, Sheker. Kirghiz Soviet playwright and journalist.

Following World War II, A. studied the science of animal breeding and veterinary medicine until 1953. From 1956 to 1958 he attended a two-year course for young writers in Moscow.

A.'s short story *Dyamila* (1958), "the most beautiful love story in world literature" (Aragon), has been translated into many languages. Here A. described the love of a young Kirghiz girl, who defends her right to this love against the traditional moral view held in her homeland. His short stories *Botokös* [The Eye of the Camel, 1961], *Birinchi mugalim* [The First Teacher, 1962], and *Samanchynyn dsholu* [The Harvester's Road, 1963] are of similar importance. The latter story, with its psychologically profound characterizations, tells of the great sacrifices and bravery of the Kirghiz people during the war years. A. was awarded the Lenin Prize of 1963.

AKHMATOVA (Pseud. of *Anna Andreyevna Gorenko*)

Born June 23, 1889, Odessa; died March 5, 1966, Moscow. Soviet Russian poet.

A.'s first collection of poems, *Vecher* [Evening, 1912], exhibited many features characteristic of Acmeism. She gave expression to the sensitive feelings of a lonely woman, and attempted to retain links with the traditions of classical Russian literature, especially with the work of Pushkin. After prolonged efforts, A. succeeded in breaking through her isolation, as shown in her poem *Is shesti knig* [From Six Books, 1940]. Her poetic works on beleaguered Leningrad—*Klyatva* [The Oath, and Other Poems, 1941]—belong to the best achievements of Soviet lyric writing. A cycle of peace poems was followed by *Poema bes geroya* [Poem without a Hero, 1942–64], A.'s masterful verses are deeply thoughtful, artistically original, and unpretentious.

A. is also well known for her many translations of works of world literature. She has received an honorary doctor's degree from Oxford University.

Editions: Stikhotvoreniya stikhotvoreniya [Poems], Moscow, 1958; *Beg vremeni* [Poems, The Course of Time], Moscow, 1965

AKHMED YASEVI

Lived circa 1105–66. Uzbekistanian poet and preacher; follower of Sufism, a system of ascetic mysticism developed in the Islam world.

A.'s collection of poems *Hikmat* [Epigrams]—which has come down to us together with many stories written later—contains, in addition to mystic, religious themes, criticism of the representatives of the official Islam religion and appeals for help for the needy. A.'s poems, which were written in a popular, vernacular style, were known throughout Central Asia.

AKHUNDOV, MIRSA FATH ALI

Born July 12, 1812, Nukha; died February 26, 1878, Tbilisi. Founder of modern Azerbaidzhani literature, educator and democrat, materialistic philosopher and statesman.

After studying Russian language and literature A. joined the Russian Army in the Caucasus in 1874, where he made the acquaintance of the Decembrists who had been exiled there. A.'s ideology and his aesthetic views were influenced by Pushkin, Lermontov, and the Russian revolutionary democrats of the 1840s and 1850s. He broke with the set laws of Oriental poetry, and laid the foundation for a realistic Azerbaidzhani national literature—a modern literature that was militant and antifeudal. In his works A. unmasked the backwardness of patriarchal conditions, and described the life of the Azerbaidzhani people as it was during the middle of the nineteenth century.

Between 1850 and 1856 A. wrote six comedies of social criticism. *Hadshi Gara* (1852), a satire on a greedy and cowardly merchant, is regarded as the best of these plays. With these comedies A. became the founder of the Azerbaidzhani theater. His satirical story *Deceived Stars* gave the first impetus to the development of Azerbaidzhani realistic prose. Here A. depicts the Persian despot Shah-Abbas and the harness-maker Jusuf, who used the powers temporarily entrusted to him to execute a number of intelligent state reforms. A.'s philosophical tract, *The Three Letters of the Indian Prince Kemal-Ud-Dovle to the Persian Prince Dshalal-Ud-Dovle* (1864–65), represents a prominent work of materialistic philosophy, and is an example of militant, atheistic political writing.

Editions: Asarlary [Works], 3 vols., Baku, 1948–55
Further Works: Na smert Pushkina [On Pushkin's Death] (1837)

AKHVERDOV, ABDURAGIM

Born May 17, 1870, Shusha; died December 12, 1933. Azerbaidzhani Soviet dramatist and short-story writer.

A.'s first work, published in 1896, influenced by A. N. Ostrovski, was the drama of social criticism *The Destroyed Nest*. He was active in the development of the Azerbaidzhani national theater founded by Akhundov, and brought it closer to the European, enriching it with new themes and genres. In his social dramas (*The Unhappy Young Man*, 1900) and historical tragedies (*Aga Mamed-shah Kadshar*, 1907), A. described the fight of the Azerbaidzhani people for liberty. A.'s minor prose works, permeated by revolutionary, democratic ideals, are concerned with the unmasking of feudal backwardness and bourgeois narrowness, and of bureaucracy and sanctimoniousness. These works appeared in the magazine *Molla Nasreddin* (1906–30), and also in the collections *My Stags* and *Letters from Hell*.

Editions: Setshilmish asarlary [Selected Works], 2 vols., Baku, 1955

AKOPIAN, AKOP

Born May 29, 1866, Gandsha (now Kirovabad); died November 13, 1937. Armenian Soviet poet; founder of Armenian proletarian poetry.

After the revolution of 1905, A. extolled the might, the faith in ultimate victory, and the solidarity of the working people [*A New Morning*, 1909]. After the establishment of Soviet power, A.'s work reflected the formation of socialism and the friendship of the Soviet people [*The Volkhov Construction*, 1925].

Editions: Izbrannoye [Selected Works] (in Russian), Moscow, 1950; *Sochineniya* [Works] (in Russian), Moscow, 1956

AKSAKOV, KONSTANTIN SERGEYEVICH

Born April 10, 1817, Novo-Aksakovo (District of Orenburg); died December 19, 1860, Tzakynthos.

A., the son of S. T. Aksakov, was a Russian political writer, literary critic, and linguist. Like his brother Ivan Sergeyevich

Aibek

Aini

C. Aitmatov

M. F. A. Akhundov

M. Auezov

(1823–86), was a theoretician of Slavophilism. He idealized the patriarchal, pre-Petrian Russia, but nevertheless stood for social reform in his time, advocating the abolition of serfdom. He submitted his reform program to the tsar in the form of a learned memoir entitled *O vnutrennem sostoyanii Rosii* [On the Internal State of Russia].

During the Crimean War (1853–56) A. developed a nationalistic program of conservative Pan-Slavism which aimed at the union of all Slavic people. This program was later further developed by his brother Ivan. As a literary critic, A. supported a conservative but socially oriented literature. His 1842 essay on Gogol's novel *Miortvyye dushi* (Dead Souls) was severely criticized by Belinski because of its concept, which he regarded as being contrary to historical fact.

Editions: Polnoye sobraniye sochinenii [Complete Works], 3 vols., Moscow, 1861–80

AKSAKOV, SERGEI TIMOFEYEVICH
Born October 1, 1791, Ufa; died May 12, 1859, Moscow.

A. was a Russian realistic writer of patriarchal stamp. Through his two sons, Konstantin and Ivan, he was closely connected with the Slavophiles. He became famous late in life, following the publication of his memoirs *Semeinaya khronika* (1856; The Family Chronicle, 1961), which are of cultural and historical significance, and of *Detskiye gody Bagrova-vnuka* (1858; Years of Childhood, 1960). In these two works A. described the northern Russian character of feudal Russia, including the horrors of serfdom, in a vividly fluent epic style.

Editions: Sobraniye sochinenii [Collected Works], 4 vols., Moscow, 1955–56
Further Works: Vospominaniya [Memoirs] (1856)

AKSIONOV, VASISILII PAVLOVICH
Born August 20, 1932, Kazan. Russian Soviet novelist and short-story writer.

A. studied medicine in Leningrad and became a physician; he has been publishing stories and short novels since 1959. In his much discussed works, which are written in a rational and laconic manner, A. has examined the problems of Soviet youth and the ways in which the people prove themselves in their daily work. These themes are presented in the strongly autobiographical short novel *Kollegi* [Fellow-Workers, 1960], and in *Zviozdny bilet* [Ticket to the Stars, 1961]. In *Apelsinv is Marokko* [Oranges from Morocco, 1963], A. again attempted to describe the life of the young Soviet workers.

Further Works: Pora moi drug, pora [It Is Time, My Friend, It Is Time] (1965); *Na polputi k lune* [Halfway to the Moon] (1965)

ALEKSANDROVSKI, VASILI DMITRIYEVICH
Born January 3, 1897, Baskakovo (District of Smolensk); died November 13, 1934. Russian Soviet poet.

In 1918–19 A. was a follower of the Proletcult; he later became a member of the literary union *Kuznitza*. Prior to 1925 he wrote numerous heroic poems—using the symbolistic, realistic style—on the civil war, the period of the New Economic Policy, and on the changes that took place during that time in the Russian villages. Selections of his lyric poems may be found in *Vostaniye* [The Revolt, 1919], *Veter* [The Wind, 1925], and in a number of other collections. He also has written several longer poems, including *Derevnya* [The Village, 1921].

Editions: Stikhotvoreniya i poemy [Poems and Verses], November, 1957

ALIGER, MARGARITA IOSIFOVNA
Born October 7, 1915, Odessa. Russian Soviet poet and dramatist.

A. became known following the publication in 1938 of both her volume of poetry *God rozhdeniya* [The Year of Birth] and her poem *Zima etovo doga* [The Winter of That Year]. Her lyric writings on the fight of the Soviet Union during the war reached a climax in 1943 with the narrative poem *Zoya*, for which she was awarded the State Prize. This poem told the story of the heroic young partisan girl Zoya Kosmodemyanskaya, who did not show fear even when she faced the hangman. A.'s poems *Tvoya pobeda* [Your Victory, 1945] and her postwar dramas including *Skazka o pravde* [The Tale about the Truth, 1945] as well as her late volume of poetry *Leninskiye gory* [The Lenin Mountains, 1953] distinguish her as a prominent writer.

Editions: Stikhotvoreniya [Poems], Moscow, 1958

ALIMDZHAN, KHAMID

Born in 1909 in Dshisak; died July 3, 1944. Uzbekistanian Soviet poet, dramatist, political writer, and literary critic.

Under the influence of Gorki and Mayakovski, A. created modern Uzbekistanian poetry, in which themes on the socialist present predominate. His most mature works were written during World War I, and are dedicated to the fight of the Uzbekistanian people for liberation from the Arab conquerors. Two of his best-known works are the poem *Roksana's Tears* (1944) and his drama *Mukanna* (1942–43). A.'s work in the field of literary criticism included essays on classical Uzbekistanian poetry and on the beginnings of Uzbekistanian socialist realism.

AMANZHOLOV, KASSYM

Born in 1911, near Karkaralinsk; died January 17, 1955, Alma-Ata. Kazakh Soviet poet.

A. was a forestry school graduate and later worked as a journalist. He began publishing poems and verses in 1932. These poems, which included *Agynölimi turaly angys* [On the Poet's Death, 1944] and *Bisding dastan* [Our Dastan, 1947], reflected the life of the Kazakh people during peace and war. He also has translated Russian and other Soviet lyric works into Kazakh.

Editions: Shygharmalarynyng tolyo shinaghy [Collected Works], 3 vols., Alma-Ata 1955–57; *Stikhi i poemy* [Poems and Verses], Alma-Ata, 1958

ANANIAN, VAKHTANG

Born August 8, 1905, Shamakhyan. Armenian Soviet novelist and short-story writer.

A's *Stories of a Huntsman* (1947–59) contain impressive descriptions of nature; he is also known as a writer of children's books, including *At the Banks of the Sevan* (1951) and *The Prisoner in the Panther Ravine* (1956).

ANDREYEV, LEONID NIKOLAYEVICH

Born August 21, 1871, Orel; died September 12, 1919, Neivola (Finland). Russian novelist and playwright.

A., who came from a civil servant's family, graduated from the law school of the University of Moscow. Active in literature since 1898, he continued the humanist traditions of critical realistic writing. After the suppression of the Russian revolution of 1905–1907, A. became alienated from the progressive literary circles led by Gorki, with which he had been closely connected. He finally occupied a position of literary decadence.

After 1910 A.'s work—some aspects of which are reminiscent of the poetry of the expressionists—is characterized by metaphysical symbolism. A. used such symbolism to give poetic expression to his profoundly pessimistic feelings.

A.'s antiwar story *Krasnyi smekh* (1904; The Red Laugh, 1915) and the story *Rasskaz o semi poveshennykh* (1908; The Seven Who Were Hanged, 1958) form a permanent literary monument to the unselfish fight of the Russian revolutionaries, and can be considered among his best achievements.

Editions: Povesti i rasskazy [Stories], Moscow, 1957; *Pyesy* [Plays], Moscow, 1959

ANNENKOV, PAVEL VASILYEVICH

Born July 1, 1813, Moscow; died March 20, 1887, Dresden, Germany.

A. was a Russian liberal literary critic and a representative of "the Westernizers," a social movement among the Russian nobility that attempted to achieve a reformation of feudal Russia after the pattern of bourgeois Western methods. Its theories were opposed to those held by the Slavophiles. In 1846 A. corresponded with Karl Marx. Through his *Pisma is Parizha* [Letters from Paris, 1847] A. introduced the thoughts of the French utopian socialists to the Russian reader.

In the 1850s A. became an advocate of "pure art." He edited the first posthumous edition of the works of Pushkin and the *Materialy dlya biografi A. S. Pushkina* [Material for a Pushkin Biography, 1855]. His memoirs, especially his *Zamechatelnoye desyatiletiye 1838–1848* [A Remarkable Decade, 1838–1848, 1881], are of value historically.

Editions: Literaturnyye vospominaniya [Literary Reminiscences], 3 vols., Moscow, 1877–81, and Moscow, 1960

ANTOKOLSKI, PAVEL GRIGORYEVICH

Born July 1, 1896, St. Petersburg. Soviet Russian lyric writer.

A. studied law at the University of Moscow. In 1915 he began to work at the Vakhtangov theater studio, later becoming producer there, a position he held until 1934. A., whose first poems were published in 1921, developed into an individualistic lyric writer who has treated versatile themes in his intellectually profound, symbolically intense poems. He frequently views contemporary problems in the light of historical reminiscences. In his verses he has treated themes from French and German history from the point of view of historical philosophy—*Robespyer i Gorgona* [Robespierre and the Gorgo, 1928], *Kommuna 71 goda* [The Commune of 1871, 1933], and *François Villon* (1934).

Toward the end of the 1930s, A.'s work turned toward themes from contemporary Soviet life, a direction that is also expressed in his choice of translations from the lyric works of other nationalities. His poem *Syn* [The Son, 1943], one of the most important Soviet war lyrics, reflects the sorrow of a father for his only son, who has been killed in the war. *Syn* contains a passionate condemnation of fascism. A.'s work also includes literary and critical essays and studies as well as numerous translations from the French and other languages.

Editions: Izbrannyye proizvedeniya [Selected Works], 2 vols., Moscow, 1961

ANTONOV, SERGEI PETROVICH
Born May 16, 1915, Petrograd. Soviet Russian writer.
After graduating from a technical school in 1938, A. worked as a construction engineer in road building. His first poems were published in 1944; these were followed by short stories. He was awarded the State Prize for his volume of stories entitled *Po dorogam idut machiny* [Cars Roll on Roads, 1950]. His basic themes are modern village life and the beauty of daily work, which he describes lyrically and in minute detail. A., whose work is indebted to Chekhov's narrative prose style, has recently turned to the discussion of moral and ethical conflicts.

Editions: Izbrannoye [Selected Works, 1947–53], Moscow, 1954; *Povesti i rasskazy* [Short Stories], Moscow, 1961
Further Works: Alionka (1960); *Porozhiireis* [Empty Passage] (1960)

ANTONOVICH, MAKSIM ALEKSEYEVICH
Born May 9, 1835, Belopolye (District of Kharkov); died November 14, 1918. Russian philosopher, political writer, and literary critic.
A. received his education at various religious schools, and then turned to the study of natural sciences. He became a follower of revolutionary democracy and was influenced by Darwin, becoming a supporter of scientific materialism. Between 1859 and 1866 A. was literary critic for the magazine *Sovremennik* to which he also contributed. He resolutely supported Chernyshevski's materialist aesthetics as well as the views held by contemporary democratic realistic writers. His essays, however, did not reach the

theoretical level of his classical precursors Belinski, Chernyshevski, and Dobrolyubov.

Editions: Izbrannyye filosofskiye sochineniya [Selected Philosophical Works], Moscow, 1945; *Literaturno-kriticheskiye stati* [Critical Essays on Literature], Moscow–Leningrad, 1961

ARASI (Pseud. of *Movses Arutyunian*)
Born April 1, 1878, Shulaver; died December 27, 1964, Yerevan. Armenian Soviet novelist.

A. was a master of the short story. His stories *Enker Mukuch* [Comrade Mukuch, 1924] and *Asar Glkhany* [The Men with a Thousand Heads 1931], in which he achieved a masterful synthesis of poetic content and artistically polished form and structure, deserve particular mention. The main themes in A.'s work were the misery of the working people under capitalism, and the dialectics of character formation and of participation in socialist reconstruction. A. also wrote a strongly autobiographical novel entitled *Airvokh gorison* [Hot Horizon] and, in 1959, the historical novel *Israel Ori.*

Editions: Izbrannyye rasskazy [Selected Stories] (in Russian), Moscow, 1952

ARBUZOV, ALEKSEI NIKOLAYEVICH
Born May 26, 1908, Moscow. Soviet Russian dramatist.

A. attended the Theater School in Leningrad. From 1923 he worked in the theater: his early works were pieces written for the agitprop stage. The characteristic features of his work—his presentation of complex, profound changes in the awareness of young people and his preference for a lyrically romantic, loosely dramatic form—were already apparent by the 1930s. These features have gradually been modified, and certain aspects have become more penetrating. Contemporary problems and activity form the subject matter for many of A.'s plays.

Among A.'s dramatic works published in the 1930s *Dalnaya doroga* [The Long Road, 1935] and *Tanya* (1938) deserve special mention. In the latter play, A. shows how a young woman finds meaning in life after overcoming illusory ideas of private happiness. The builders of Komsomolsk are shown in *Gorod na zare* [A Town at Dawn, 1940]. A. directed a frontline theater during World War II. After 1945 he wrote a number of pieces constructed in epic form, among the most important of which are *Gody stranstvi* [Intricate Roads, 1954] and *Irkutskaya istoriya* [Irkutsk Story, 1959]. In these plays A. deals with problems connected with the development of socialist consciousness.

A.'s best plays belong to the standard repertoire of the Soviet theater; many of them have also been presented abroad.

Editions: Pyesy [Plays], Moscow, 1957
Further Works: Vstrecha s yunostyu [A Meeting with Youth] (1947); *Yevropeiskaya khronika* [European Chronicle] (1951); *Dvenadtzatyi chas* [The Twelfth Hour] (1960); *Moi bednyi Marat* [My Unfortunate Marat] (1964)

ARTZYBASHEV, MIKHAIL PETROVICH

Born October 18, 1878, Akhtyrka (District of Kharkov); died March 3, 1927, Warsaw. Russian novelist.

A.'s development characteristically reflects the transition of numerous bourgeois intellectuals from liberalism to counterrevolution; his literary work very impressively shows the typical features of decadence.

In his early stories, written between 1901 and 1906, A. combined liberal ideas with a predilection for erotic motives and naturalistic description of the violent actions of the reactionaries during the revolutionary years. In his notorious, almost pornographic novel *Sanin* (1907), A. advocated a life of extreme individualism, without ideals or social duties. His later works, including the novel *U poslednei cherty* (1909; The Breaking Point, 1915), defamed the revolutionaries. A. emigrated to Warsaw after the October revolution, and acted against the Soviet state.

Further Works: Chelovecheskaya volna (1907); *Milliony* (1908; The Millionaire, 1916); *Sobraniye sochinenii* (10 vols., 1913–17); *Vragi* (1914; Enemies, 1923); *Zapiski pisatelya* (1917); *Dikiye* (1923; The Savage, 1924); *D'yavol* (1925)

ASEYEV, NIKOLAI NIKOLAYEVICH
Born July 10, 1899, Lgov; died July 16, 1963, Moscow. Soviet Russian lyric poet.

Prior to World War I A.'s poems exhibited symbolistic and futuristic tendencies. The experience of World War I, however, gave his work a certain antimilitaristic accent, and he depicted the October revolution as a heroic, romantic event. A.'s search for unusual rhymes and for poetic individuality became more directed after 1917, but his work still, to some extent, exhibited formalistic elements.

After 1922 the development of A.'s work was greatly influenced by his friendship and close association with Mayakovski. In the poems *Dvadtzat shest* [Twenty-six, 1921], *Sverdlovskaya burya* [Sverdlovsk Storm, 1926], and *Semyon Proskakov* (1926–28) depicting contemporary heroes, A. complied with the fluctuations of the political situation during the N.E.P. period.

Many of A.'s poems describe the transformation that has been taking place in the Soviet Union, changes which he himself observed in the course of his frequent journeys across the country. His most important work is the long poem *Mayakovski nachina-yetsya* [Mayakovski Begins]. This work, which was written between 1937 and 1939 and which received the State Prize in 1941, is a loyal, polemical defense of A.'s great friend and hero Mayakovski. A.'s other poetic works—*Rasdumya* [Reflections, 1955] and *Lad* [Unity, 1961] (which received the Lenin Prize of 1962) —have a mature wisdom that convinces the reader that A. was a poet still young in heart when he wrote them.

Editions: Sobraniye sochinenii [Collected Works], 5 vols., Moscow, 1963
Further Works: Nochnaya fleita (1914); *Bomba* (1921); *Dnevnik poeta* (1929); *Izbrannyye stikhotvoreniya poemy* (1951)

ASPAZIJA (Pseud. of *Elza Rozenberge*)
Born March 16, 1868, Daukvas (County of Zalenieks); died November 5, 1943, Riga. Latvian poet and dramatist; lifelong companion of Jānis Rainis (1865–1929).

In her early work A. opposed the false morality of bourgeois society and was an active feminist. After the dissolution of the naturalist movement at the end of the nineteenth century, the pessimistic tones exhibited in her work prior to that time were replaced, in 1905, by more militant themes. After the revolution of 1905, A. emigrated to Switzerland with Rainis, returning to Latvia only after its independence in 1920.

A.'s later work lost its earlier aggressiveness and became predominantly lyrical. Her most important works are the volume of poetry *Sarkanas pukes* [Red Flowers, 1897] and the drama *Sidraba škidrauts* [The Silver Rug, 1905].

Further Works: Vaidelote [The Vestal] (1894); *Asteru laika* [In Aster Time] (1927); *Dvēseles celojums* [A Soul's Journey] (1933)

AUEZOV, MUKHTAR

Born September 28, 1897, Chingistan; died June 27, 1961, Moscow. Kazakh Soviet novelist and playwright, linguist, and folklorist.

A. was the son of a nomad family. He graduated in 1919 from the teachers college in Semipalatinsk, and in 1928 from the department of Oriental studies at Leningrad University. He wrote his doctoral thesis in Tashkent, and became a member of the Kazakh Academy of Sciences in 1946.

By 1917 A. had been writing stories and some twenty plays, including *Engliki-Kebek* (1917; rev. ed., 1957). Most of A.'s works are concerned with the Kazakh people's road to revolution. His multi-volume epic poem, *Abai Golo* (1942–56), is based on the life of the national Kazakh poet Abai Kunanbayev. This work gives an epic picture of Kazakh life during the second half of the nineteenth century.

A. also wrote a number of sketches on Turkestan and India, and has translated works of the Russian classicists. He was awarded the State Prize in 1949, and the Lenin Prize in 1959.

Editions: Tangdamaly shygharmalar [Selected Works], 6 vols., Alma-Ata, 1955–57

AVVAKUM, PETROVICH

Born ca. 1620 or 1621, Grigorovo near Nizhni Novgorod; died April 14, 1682, Pustosyorsk. Russian Orthodox archpriest.

A. was the head of the conservative but basically antifeudal Old Believers, or *Raskolniki*, who were opposed to the church reforms which had been instituted by the patriarch Nikon. These reforms had led to a schism (*Raskol*) in the Russian church. A. was cruelly persecuted and twice exiled to Siberia (in 1667 to Pustosyorsk in the arctic north), where he was finally burned at the stake.

A. wrote more than fifty works, mostly of a religious nature; among these is his linguistically forceful autobiography *Zhitiye protopopa Avvakuma*, (1672–76; The Life of the Archpriest Avvakum, 1924), in which he combined the language of the church —the literary church-Slavonic—with that of the people. This work contains a psychological analysis of himself, which is in contrast to the traditional form of such vitae.

Editions: Zhitiye protopopa Avvakuma [The Life of the Archpriest Avvakum], Moscow, 1960

AZHAYEV, VASILII NIKOLAYEVICH

Born February 12, 1915, Sotzkoye; died April 27, 1968, Moscow. Soviet Russian novelist.

After completing a correspondence course, A. graduated in 1944 from the Gorki Institute of Literature in Moscow. He became known following publication of his novel *Daleko ot Moskvy* [Far from Moscow, 1948], for which he was awarded the State Prize of 1949.

One of A.'s main themes is the heroism of the Soviet people during the construction of a strategically important oil pipe-line in the taiga during the first years of World War II. Another major theme is his concern with the socialist education and direction of people. A.'s short story *Odd Man Out* deals with a similar subject.

Further Works: Zoloto [Gold] (1948); *Predisloviye k zhizni* [An Introduction to Life] (1961)

BABAYEVSKI, SEMION PETROVICH

Born June 6, 1909, Kunye (District of Kharkov). Soviet Russian novelist.

B. graduated from the Gorki Institute of Literature in 1939; he worked as a frontline correspondent during World War II. His work (sketches, short stories, and novels) is closely connected with his home district—the Kuban region and the country around Stavropol.

In his novels *Kavaler zolotoi zvezdy* [2 vols., The Knight of the Golden Star, 1947–48], and *Svet nad zemlei* [2 vols., Light on Earth, 1949–50], B. described the problems of postwar development in the Soviet kolkhoz village. *Svet nad zemlei* in particular has a tendency to take an overly rosy view of things.

Further Works: Sukhaya buivola (1958); *Synovny bunt* [The Son's Rebellion] (1963)

BABEL, ISAAK EMMANUILOVICH

Born July 13, 1894, Odessa; died March 17, 1941. Soviet Russian short-story writer.

B. came from a bourgeois Jewish family. In Odessa he attended a commercial school. His first two stories were published in 1916 in Gorki's magazine *Letopis*.

In 1917 he served in the civil war with Budyenni's First Cavalry Army. In 1923 he started writing his two cycles of short stories *Konarmiya* (1926; Red Cavalry, 1939) and *Odeskiye rasskazy* [Odessa Stories, 1931]. In his civil war stories B. described his impressions in a concise, laconic, and vivid manner, stressing the psychological contradictions apparent in his characters. He saw in the Red Guards both deep humanity and cruelty, lack of discipline and true heroism, an awareness of the revolution and of anarchism. His stories—most of which are written in the first person—are characterized by romantic and naturalistic elements.

Editions: Izbrannoye [Selected Works], Moscow, 1957
Selected English translation: The Collected Stories, New York, 1955

BABER, SAHIREDDIN MOHAMMED

Born February 14, 1483, Fergana; died December 28, 1530. Uzbekian statesman, army leader, and writer; great-grandson of Timur and related to Genghis Khan.

B. became ruler of Fergana in 1494; he conquered Afghanistan and northern India in the early years of the sixteenth century and founded the Mogul empire. In his autobiographical memoirs, the *Baber-name* [The Book of Baber, 1905], B. depicted the life, society, culture, and nature of the Central Asia, Afghanistan, and India of his time. This work continues to be of importance today as a source of historical information. It has been translated into numerous European languages. B. also left a small but noteworthy collection of poetry.

BAGRITZKI (Pseud. of *Edvard Georgiyevich Dzyubin*)

Born November 3, 1895, Odessa; died February 16, 1934, Moscow. Soviet Russian poet.

B.'s early work was influenced by various literary styles—Acmeism, symbolism, and futurism. The exotic world of his early verses is somewhat removed from reality. B.'s work after the revolution described the heroic, romantic features of those times on the one hand in relatively abstract "cosmic" statements, and on the other in poems that were artistically more convincing. These poems were written in addition to his work in the field of propaganda. Heroes from world literature appeared in his balladlike works as revolutionary symbols.

A reorientation of his work commenced with his long poem *Duma pro Opanasa* [The Story of Opanas, 1926], in which he used themes from Ukrainian folklore in imitation of Shevchenko's poetry. This poem, which in 1933 was reworked for use as an opera libretto, shows—in the fate of the peasant Opanas—that one cannot take up a neutral position during a time of great decision.

The theme of Soviet reality finally appeared in B.'s work during the time of the first Five-Year Plan. As may be seen in his two poems written in 1932, *Pobediteli* [The Victors] and *Poslednaya noch* [The Last Night], B.'s ideals found adequate embodiment in the everyday life of reconstruction. Both are works of great impressive impact. B. is one of the most important lyricists of Soviet literature.

Editions: Stikhotvoreniya i poemy [Poems and Verses], Moscow, 1958
Further Works: Jugo-zapad [Southwest] (1928); *Fevral* [February] (1934)

BAHDANOVICH, MAKSIM ADAMAVICH
Born December 9, 1891, Minsk; died May 25, 1917, Yalta. Byelorussian poet and essayist.

B., the son of a teacher, first began to write during the years of reaction that followed the defeat of the 1905 revolution. Melancholy and loneliness were the themes of B.'s early poems, but he was able to overcome these elements once he became involved in Byelorussian folklore and began to champion the cause of national and social liberation. His poems expressed more and more strongly the hopes of the oppressed and their demands for radical changes in society.

B. also translated from Russian, Ukrainian, Polish, and German, and was the author of a number of critical essays on literature.

Editions: Tvory [Works], Minsk, 1957

BAHGUSHEVICH, FRANTZISHAK KASIMIRAVICH
Born March 21, 1840, Svirany; died April 28, 1900. Byelorussian democratic poet.

B., the son of an impoverished nobleman, took part in the uprising of 1863. He belonged to the founders of realism in Byelorussian literature. His collections *Dudka belaruskaya* [The Byelorussian Shawm, 1891] and *Smyk belaruski* [The Byelorussian Fiddle-bow, 1894] contain poems that tell of the poet's compassion for the misery of his oppressed people.

Editions: Vybranyya tvory [Selected Works], Minsk, 1946

BAKLANOV, GRIGORII YAKOVLEVICH

Born September 11, 1923, Voronezh. Soviet Russian narrator, short-story writer, and novelist.

B. volunteered for service in the army during World War II. He graduated from the Gorki Institute of Literature in Moscow in 1951 and commenced work as a journalist. His first publications appeared in 1950.

B. has contributed greatly to recent Soviet war literature. His short stories *Yuzhneye glavnovo udara* [To the South of the Main Attack, 1958], *Pyad zemli* [A Foot of Ground, 1959], and *Myortvyye sramu ne imut* [The Dead Cannot Be Blamed, 1961] combine dramatic descriptions of complex battle episodes with the psychological presentation of characters. His first novel, *Iyul 1941 goda* [July 1941, 1965], gives an impressive description of the very difficult situation in which the Soviet armies found themselves during the first months of the fascist attack on the Soviet Union.

Editions: Tri povesti [Three Short Stories], Moscow, 1963

BALMONT, KONSTANTIN DMITRIYEVICH

Born June 15, 1867, Gumnishchi (District of Vladimir); died December 24, 1942, Noisy-le-Grand (near Paris). Russian poet, translator, and essayist.

B. was the son of a nobleman; in 1886 he began to study law at the University of Moscow, but was expelled for leading some of the student outbreaks. His first volumes of poetry show the influence of populist thought. In the 1890s B. became one of the leading representatives of symbolism. B.'s poetry is rich in impressions, and is distinguished by a marked musicality; it makes considerable use of alliteration. Occupying a liberal position, B. welcomed the revolution of 1905–07, denouncing tsarism in his *Pesni mstitelya* [The Song of the Avenger, 1907].

B. emigrated to Europe in 1906, and spent a considerable amount of time in world travel. As a result, he published volumes of lyric writings of a strongly exotic nature, as well as collections of Egyptian, Mexican, Peruvian, and Indian folklore. B. translated numerous works of English, American, French, and Georgian literature, including those of Shelley, Baudelaire, Whitman, and Rustaveli. B. left his homeland permanently in 1921. From that time until his death in 1942 he published collections of poetry and autobiographical prose works.

Editions: Palnoye sobraniye stikhotvoreniy [Complete Collection of Poems], 10 vols., 1908–13

BARANAUSKAS (BARANOVSKII; BARONAS), ANTANAS

Born January 17, 1835, Anyksciai; died November 26, 1902, Seinai. Lithuanian classicist and dialectologist.

B., the son of a peasant, became a Roman Catholic priest and was later appointed bishop. B.'s work reflects the contradictions present in an epoch of declining feudalism and increasing capitalistic conditions. His major work, the poem *Anyksciu silelis* (1858–59; The Forest of Anyksciai, 1956), is significantly close to being nationalist in style. Together with Donelaitis's poem *Metai*, it represents the greatest poetic work in Lithuanian literature.

Further Works: Kelione Peterburgan (1858); *Neramumas* (1863)

BARATASHVILI, NIKOLOS

Born December 27, 1817, Tbilisi; died October 21, 1845, Gandsha (Abkhazia). Georgian poet.

Under the influence of the Georgian philosopher S. Dodashvili, B., the son of an impoverished nobleman, was from his earliest years interested in humanism and the liberation movement. After 1885 he worked as civil servant in the judicial system of his homeland, obtaining deep insight into the social abuses prevalent at the time; he was deeply concerned by the nationwide oppression of his people under the tsarist rule.

B.'s poetry was directed against this oppression. Although his poems are filled with sorrow for the lost independence of Georgia, at the same time they proclaim the willingness of the poet to sacrifice his life for the liberation of his homeland. These poems, especially *Lonely Souls* (1839) and *Pegasus* (1842), also reflect B.'s belief in humanity and in the power of reasoning. His poem *The Fate of Georgia* (1839) describes the invasion of Georgia by the Persians in 1795. B. favored the union of Georgia with Russia.

National traditions and those of Russian and Western literatures are combined in the work of this very significant representative of Georgian romanticism.

Editions: Chsulebani [Poems], Tbilisi, 1945

BARATYNSKI, YEVGENII ABRAMOVICH
Born March 2, 1800, Mara (District of Tambov); died July 11, 1844, Naples. Russian romantic poet.

B. was expelled from the Imperial Corps of Pages because of some youthful pranks. Between 1820 and 1825 B. served as corporal in Finland. His early poems indicate that he was a literary follower of Pushkin. In one of his principal narrative poems (*Eda*, 1826) B. made a peasant girl his central figure.

Individual political motives in which he indicated his intellectual closeness to the Decembrists soon faded, to be replaced with profound but frequently pessimistic philosophical considerations. The elegy thus emerged as his true genre.

Further Works: Bal [The Ball] (1828); *Sumerki* [Dusk] (1842)

BARBARUS (Pseud. of *Johannes Vares*)
Born January 12, 1890, Viljandi; d. November 29, 1946, Tallin. Estonian poet and statesman.

After he graduated from high school B. studied medicine in Kiev. As a physician he took part in World War I, and between 1920 and 1940 practiced medicine in Pärnu. After the fall of the bourgeois government, B., a convinced democrat and humanist, became president of the council of ministers in June 1940. He later became chairman of the Presidium of the Supreme Soviet of the Estonian SSR.

B. published a series of poems during the bourgeois period. He overcame both the original influences of symbolism and his inclination toward the use of a complex linguistic structure. The themes of his poetry became determined more and more definitely by the ideas and the reality of socialism in the USSR. B. produced a notable collection of poems during the Soviet era. These included *Relvastatud värsid* [The Armed Verse, 1943], *Rinde-teedel* [On Front Roads, 1944], *Vastu voolu* [Against the Current, 1946], and *Samm-sammult voidule* [Step by Step Forward to Victory, 1946]. In 1945 B. received the award of Meritorious Writer of the Estonian SSR.

BARTO, AGUIYA LVOVNA
    Born November 17, 1906, Moscow. Soviet Russian poet.
    B.'s topics included the life of the child in school and at home. Her first poems, which appeared in the collection *Kitaichonok Van Li* [The Little Chinese Boy Wan Li], already exhibited the characteristic features of her total *oeuvre*. In a humorous and vivid manner B. instills in her small readers respect for man and his work. This basic idea is reflected in numerous collections of poems, including *Igrushki* (1936; Toy Times, 1938) and *Stikhi detyam* (1949; Little Verses for Little Folk, 1955). B. has also written scripts for children's films. She was awarded the State Prize in 1950.

Editions: Tvoi stikhi [Your Poems], Moscow, 1960; *Stikhi* [Poems], Moscow, 1961

BASHIROV, GUMER
    Born January 7, 1901, Yanasala. Tatar Soviet short-story writer and novelist.
    B., the son of a peasant, graduated from the Institute of Marxism and Leninism in Kazan, and became a teacher. Between 1956 and 1959 B. was president of the Writers' Union of the Tatar ASSR; he is a member of the Secretariat of the Writers' Union of the RSFSR, and Deputy of the Supreme Soviet of the USSR.
    B. was first employed as a newspaper correspondent, later becoming a literary writer. Drawing on his own experience, B. has written (*Sivash*, 1937) of the heroic battles of the Red Army under the leadership of Frunse. His most important work is the

novel *Namus* [Honor, 1947], for which he received the State Prize in 1951. This work gives a realistic picture of life on a Tatar kolkhoz which achieved record crops during wartime.

BATYUSHKOV, KONSTANTIN NIKOLAYEVICH

Born May 29, 1787, Volodga; died there July 19, 1855.

Together with Zhukovski, B. is considered the most important Russian poet of the pre-Pushkin period. He took part in the battle of Leipzig in 1815. In 1823 his literary career was ended by mental illness.

B. wrote lyric poems filled with anacreontic sentiments and emotions, including *Soviet druzyam* [Advice to Friends, 1806], which he reworked and then published as *Vesioly chas* [Happy Hours, 1810], and *Vakkhanka* [The Bacchante, 1814–15], which, as unaffected, concrete presentations of natural sensual pleasures and of simple life (see B.'s open letter *Moi penaty* [My Penates, 1811–12]) are of significant importance.

B.'s popularity was based on his pamphlet *Videniye na beregakh Lety* [Vision on the Banks of the Lethe, 1809], in which he attacked the reactionary, archaistic Shishkovists and the imitators of Karamzin (1776–1826). The events of the War of 1812 for a while helped B. to overcome his increasing depression. During this period B. wrote patriotic poems and historical elegies including *Ten druga* [The Shadow of the Friend, 1814], *Perekhod cheres Rein* [The Crossing of the Rhine, 1817], and *Podrazhaniya drevnim* [Imitation of the Ancients, 1821]. Tragic tones then began to dominate his work, as in *Umirayuschchi Tass* [The Dying Tasso, 1817].

B. prepared the way for realistic prose with his sketches *Progulka po Moskve* [A Walking Tour through Moscow, 1812], *Vecher u Kantemira* [An Evening with Kantemir, 1816], and other similar works. His language captivates the reader with its harmony, objectivity, and clarity. He thus may be regarded as the teacher of Pushkin and as a pioneer of the realism of the nineteenth century.

Editions: Sochinenya, Moscow, 1955

BAZHAN, MYKOLA

Born October 9, 1904, Kamenetz-Podolski. Ukrainian Soviet poet and translator.

B. graduated from a cooperative technical school and in 1921 studied at the Institute for International Relations in Kiev. During World War II he edited the newspaper *Za Radyansku Ukrayinu* [For a Soviet Ukraine]. B. is Deputy of the Supreme Soviet of the USSR and a member of the Presidium of the Writers' Union of the USSR.

B. overcame certain formalistic and constructivist tendencies evident in the poems and pamphlets he produced in the 1920s, and, by the middle 1930s, had become a socialist realist. He became more widely known in 1926 following the publication of *17–y patrol* [Reconnaisance Patrol No. 17], a collection of poems about the civil war. Among his most mature works are his poetic trilogy on Kirov, *Bezsmertya* [Immortality, 1937] and *Bakty i syny* [Fathers and Sons, 1938]. This last poem, together with *Mati* [Mother, 1939], is about the heroism of the plain Soviet man during the civil war and the period of socialist reconstruction. Also important are B.'s cycles of poems about friendship between peoples, written in 1939–40, and his cycle of war poems *Stalingradski zoshyt* [Stalingrad Notebook, 1943]. He also wrote *Klyatva* [The Oath, 1941] and *Angliski vrazhennya* [English Impressions, 1948].

B.'s lyric writing exhibits strong philosophical features, and is distinguished by individual, bold linguistic pictures. B. is known for his sensitive rendition of the thirteenth-century Georgian national epic poem *The Hero in the Tiger Skin* by Shota Rustaveli. He also translated works by Pushkin, Mayakovski, and contemporary Soviet poets. He was awarded State Prizes in 1946 and 1949.

Editions: Tvory [Works], 2 vols., Kiev, 1954.
Further Works: Bilya Spaskoyi vezhi [Near the Spas Tower], (1952); *Mitzkevych v Odesi* [Mickiewicz in Odessa], (1957)

BAZHOV, PAVEL PETROVICH
Born January 27, 1879, Sysertski Savod; died December 3, 1950, Moscow. Soviet Russian writer.

After attending a theological seminary, B. taught Russian and began to assemble his collection of folk literature and poetry. He volunteered for service in the Red Army. During the years 1923–29 he was a member of the editorial staff of *Krestyanskaya gazeta* [Farmers' Journal]. B.'s literary career began with the publication of a collection of sketches, *Uralskiye byli* [Stories from the Urals, 1924]. In 1943 he received the State Prize for his most important work, *Malakhitovaya shkatulka* (1939; The Malachite Casket: Tales from the Urals, 1962). Prior to his death B. added a number of new legends and sagas to this collection.

His work is characterized by its folkloric features and a combination of realistic and fantastic elements.

Editions: Sochineniya [Works], 3 vols., Moscow, 1952

BEDNYI, BORIS VASILYEVICH
Born August 25, 1916, Yaroslavskaya, near Krasnodar. Soviet Russian short-story writer.

B. worked as a forestry engineer in the Komi ASSR. In 1952 he graduated from the Institute of Literature in Moscow. B. has published stories on the development of young people and on their ethical and moral problems, including *Devchata* [Girls, 1961].

Editions: Rasskazy [Stories], Moscow, 1954

BEDNYI, DEMYAN (Pseud. of *Yefim Alekseyevich Pridvorov*)
Born April 13, 1883, Glubovka (District of Kherson); died May 25, 1945, Moscow. Soviet Russian poet; one of the founders of Soviet poetry.

The son of a poor peasant, B. attended the local village school. Between 1904 and 1908, after serving with the army, he studied at the Faculty of History and Philosophy of the University of St. Petersburg.

B. was a regular contributor to the Bolshevik magazine *Pravda* from its first issue on May 5, 1912. Continuing traditions established by Krylov and Nekrasov, he developed the genre of the fable. His first collection, *Basni* [Fables], appeared in 1913. A favorable comment on this work was made by Lenin in a letter sent to Gorki. In 1917 *Pravda* published B.'s story in verse, *Pro zemlyu, pro volyu, pro rabochuyu dolyu* [On the Soil, on Liberty, and on the Destiny of the Workers], a heroic and satirical epic about the revolution.

B. was one of the most active Soviet poets during the civil war. His lyric, fervent verses, collected in *Vognennom koltze* [In the Ring of Fire, 1918], his Red Guard songs—*Provody* [Company, 1948], and his satire on the White Guards *Manifest barona von Vrangelya* [The Manifesto of Baron von Wrangel, 1920] were greatly appreciated by the soldiers at the front. His poem *Glavnaya ulitza* [Main Street, 1922] is also well known.

In the 1920s and 1930s B.'s poems extolled the heroic, everyday work of the Soviet man—*Tyaga* [The Train, 1924]. During World War II B. developed the antifascist satire (*Volk-moralist,* The Wolf as Moralist, 1943). An authority in the field of folklore, B. frequently made use of the genre of the song and the ditty. As a satiricist, too, he exerted great influence on the development of Soviet literature.

Editions: Sobraniye sochinenii [Collected Works], 5 vols., Moscow, 1953–54

BEK, ALEKSANDR ALFREDOVICH

Born January 3, 1903, Saratov. Soviet Russian short-story writer and novelist.

B.'s main interest was the Soviet worker, particularly the technical innovator, to whom he dedicated numerous sketches, short stories, and novels. His work contains many literary and historical figures. By 1934 his artistic conception was already in evidence, as can be seen in the short story based on the life of a well-known blast-furnace worker, *Kurako*. B. also has made a great contribution to Soviet war literature. In his novella *Volokolamskoye shose*

[Volokolamsk Highway], written between 1934 and 1944 and based on events that occurred during the battles around Moscow in 1941, B. took up a polemic position against biased and over-simplified presentations of Soviet man during the war. He showed here how difficult it really is to depict true heroism. The theme of this novella is continued in the two novels written in 1960, *Neskolko dnei* [A Few Days] and *Reserv Generala Panfilova* [General Panfilov's Reserves]. The problems of technical creativity are treated in the documentary novel *Zhizn Berezhkova* (1956; Berezhkov: The Story of an Inventor, 1958).

Editions: Zerno stali. Rasskazy i ocherki [The Grain of the Steel: Stories and Sketches], Moscow, 1950; *Timofei-Otkrytoye serdtze. Povesti i rasskazy* [Openhearted Timofei: Short Stories], Moscow, 1955

BELINSKI, VISSARION GRIGORYEVICH

Born June 11, 1811, Sveaborg; died June 7, 1848, St. Petersburg. Russian revolutionary democrat, literary critic, and philosopher.

B., the son of an army surgeon, attended the high school in Pensa between 1825 and 1829. He studied at the University of Moscow, but was expelled for his progressive views. In 1834 he began to work as a journalist and critic for the Moscow magazine *Teleskop*, which published his first essay, *Literaturnyye mechtaniya* [Literary Musings, 1834]. After *Teleskop* was prohibited by the censors in the fall of 1836, B. worked for the *Moskovski nablyudatel* [The Moscow Observer]. Three years later he moved to St. Petersburg, and between 1839–46 edited the critical section of the revolutionary democratic magazine *Otechestvennyye zapiski* [Patriotic Notes]. From 1846 to 1848 he edited *Sovremennik* [The Contemporary]. Poverty, tuberculosis, and reprisals by the tsarist authorities made his last years very difficult.

After a complex and contradictory intellectual development, which was first influenced by the idealistic philosophy of Schelling and, above all, by that of Hegel, between 1840 and 1841 B. underwent a basic change in ideology. He turned toward revolutionary democratism, materialism, and utopian socialism. As the founder of classical Russian revolutionary democratic aesthetics and literary criticism, in the 1840s B. became the central figure in the Russian movement for liberation from tsarist autocracy, and the leading personality in Russian intellectual and literary development. B.'s political, philosophical, and aesthetic views represent important highlights in the history of all European pre-Marxist thought.

B.'s theories included the importance of realism and democracy in literature and its ties with the people themselves, as well as its value as an awakening and educative force. Through these theories B. was able to develop a tightly knit, complete artistic concept which, in the 1840s, was to become the basis for the unification of the younger generation of talented Russian writers. This unification resulted in the foundation of the Natural School and in turn led to the rise of critical realism in Russia. B. was the first Russian literary critic to point out the significance of both Pushkin and Gogol for Russian literature. In the work of these two novelists B. also saw the future of Russian realism. He paid much attention to Western European literatures.

In his famous *Pismo k Gogolyu* [A Letter to Gogol, 1847]—the most significant political literary manifesto of the Russian revolutionary democrats as well as his own political manifesto—B. formulated the most important national aims for the entire anti-feudal movement. In it he appealed to the Russian realists to move forward into the frontlines of the fight against serfdom and tsarism. B.'s aesthetic and critical views became the theoretical program on which Russian critical realism was based. His views—in conjunction with those developed in the theoretical works of Chernyshevski and Dobrolyubov—have determined the development of classical Russian literature and its rise to one of the leading national literatures in Europe. These views today are a living tradition in socialist realism.

Editions: Polnoye sobraniye sochinenii [Complete Works], 13 vols., Moscow, 1953–59
Selected English Translation: Selected Philosophical Works, 1948

BELYI, ANDREI (Pseud. of *Boris Nikolayevich Bugayev*)

Born October 26, 1880, Moscow; died there January 8, 1934. Soviet Russian poet, novelist and essayist; leading representative and theoretician of symbolism.

B., the son of a professor of mathematics, graduated in 1905 from the Faculty of Mathematics of the University of Moscow. Under the strong influence of V. Solovyov, the late-bourgeois philosopher, B.'s ideology acquired a religious, mystical character. His poetry is characterized by impressionistic features, and he endeavored to bring lyrics and prose closer to music with respect to both structure and sound.

In his early works B. combined his regret for the decline of the old Russia with satirically grotesque incidents exposing her rulers and bureaucracy. These aspects are especially evident in his collection of lyric writings *Zoloto v lazuri* [Gold in Sky-Blue, 1904] and in *Pepel* [Ashes, 1909]. It can also be seen in his novel *Petersburg* (1913–14; St. Petersburg, 1962), in which B. depicted the atmosphere of St. Petersburg society during the revolution of 1905–7 in a manner reminiscent of Dostoyevski. *Petersburg* exhibits characteristics of the modern novel; these characteristics were to become more prominent in B.'s later prose writings.

B. failed to understand the historical significance of the October revolution; his principles of creative work changed very little. After 1917 he wrote poems, autobiographical prose works, literary essays, and the historical trilogy *Moskva* [Moscow, 1926–33].

Editions: Sobraniye sochinenii [Collected Works], vols. 4 and 7, Moscow, 1917; *Stikhotvoreniya* [Poems], Leningrad, 1940

BERDAKH (Pseud. of *Berdimurat Karkabayev*)

Born 1827; died 1900. Kara-Kalpak poet.

B., who came from a poor family, wrote lyric, satirical, and historical poems and verses. B.'s poems reflect the misery of the people and their revolt against despotism and injustice. Before the October revolution his works were mainly distributed by story-

M. Bazhan

D. Bednyi

V. G. Belinski

A. A. Blok

P. Browka

tellers. His most important work is the verse-novel *Akmak pasha* [The Autocratic Pasha].

Editions: Tanglamaly shygaramalary [Selected Works], Nokis, 1956; *Izbrannoye* [Selected Works] (in Russian), Nukus, 1958

BERGELSOHN, DAVID RAFAILOVICH
    Born August 12, 1884, Okhrimovo (District of Kiev); died 1952. Jewish Soviet novelist.
    B. came from a wealthy family. Between 1921 and 1929 he lived abroad, mostly in Berlin, where he worked for the democratic Jewish press. B.'s first novel, *Arom voksal* [At the Station], appeared in 1909. This novel presents, in a psychologically impressive manner, the fate of people broken by life. His novel *Nokh alemen* [The End of the Story, 1913] is also distinguished by the subtle psychological treatment of its characters. This story is concerned with the social decline of the Jewish bourgeoisie and the tragic fate of Jewish intellectuals.
    B. developed the modern Jewish psychological novel and the lyrically emotional story based on the traditions of critical realism. The impressive epic poem *Bam Dnepr* [At the Dnieper, 1932–40], which made B. the leading representative of Jewish literature in the USSR, relates incidents from the life and battles of the people during the revolutionary times of 1905.

Editions: Werke, 5 vols., *Werke* [Works, in Hebrew], 5 vols., Berlin, 1922; *Izbrannoye* [Selected Works] (in Russian), Moscow, 1957

BERGHOLZ, OLGA FIODOROVNA
    Born May 16, 1910, St. Petersburg. Soviet Russian poet.
    During World War II B. lived and worked in beleaguered Leningrad. Her first volume of poetry appeared in 1934. In her early poems, B. told of the exciting everyday life of the Komsomol youth movement. She became known during the war years for her poems on the siege of Leningrad. In these poems, based on her own experiences, she described the sufferings of her compatriots and their firm belief in ultimate victory. *Leningradski*

dnevnik [Leningrad Diary, 1942], *Leningradski poema* [Leningrad Poem, 1942], and her drama *Oni zhili v Leningrade* [They Lived in Leningrad, 1944] are among such works.

B.'s lyrical, philosophical prose work *Dnevnyye zviozdy* [Star That Shines During the Day, 1959] offers a picture of her time and of her generation based on personal experience. She was awarded the State Prize in 1950.

Editions: Sochineniya [Works], 2 vols., Moscow, 1958
Further Works: Pervorossiisk [Pervossiish] (1950); *Vernost* [Faithfulness] (1954)

BESTUZHEV (MARLINSKI), ALEKSANDR ALEKSANDROVICH

Born November 3, 1797, St. Petersburg; died June 19, 1837, Cap Adler. Russian novelist and literary critic belonging to the Decembrist movement; after 1827, leading exponent of the romantic movement.

B. was one of the leaders of the Decembrist Northern Society uprising in 1825. As a result he was reduced in rank and exiled to the Caucasus, where he was killed in battle.

B. extolled the heroic in his lyric writings, in the *Agitatzionnyye pesni* [Agitatory Songs, 1823–25], which he co-authored with the poet Ryleyev, and in his historical novels, including *Roman i Olga* (Roman and Olga, 1823). He drew attention in numerous essays to the folk-oriented originality of Russian literature. The great popularity of B.'s romantic stories stemmed from the extraordinary events and unusual heroes depicted in them, as well as from his flowery language—a language, however, which was soon recognized as being bombastic in nature. Among his best known works are *Leitenant Belozor* [Lieutenant Belozor, 1831], *Fregat "Nadezhda"* [The Frigate "Hope", 1832], *Morekhod Nikitin* [The Sailor Nikitin, 1834], and *Mulla-Mur* (Mulla-Mur the Robber, 1836).

Editions: Sochineniya [Works], 2 vols., Moscow, 1958; *Vospominaniya Bestuzhevykh* [Memoirs of the Bestuzhevs], Moscow–Leningrad, 1951

BEZBORODOV, MIKHAIL ILYICH
Born January 10, 1907, Staryye Pichengushi; died March ́11, 1935. Mordvinian Soviet poet.

B. was one of the founders of Mordvinian poetry. In 1927 he began publishing poems and verses on the situation of the Mordvinian people before 1917, on the fight for liberation—*Jefks, kona uls* [A Fairy Tale, 1930]—and on collectivization—*Matovs kyashetz* [Suppressed Fury, 1930].

Editions: Sochineniya [Works], 2 vols., Saransk, 1939–41

BEZYMENSKI, ALEKSANDR ILYICH
Born January 19, 1898, Zhitomir. Soviet Russian poet and dramatist.

B.'s literary beginnings are closely connected with the October revolution and the civil war. His first two volumes of poetry *Oktyabrskiye zori* [October Dawn, 1920] and *K solntzu* [Toward the Sun, 1921] reflected a certain abstract fervor which B. later overcame by turning toward themes of everyday life and by following—to some extent—Mayakovski's poetry in a form of literary imitation.

In the 1920s B. was active in the Komsomol movement; he belonged to the so-called Komsomol poets, who selected their themes chiefly from the life of Soviet youth. His work reached its climax with the satirical drama *Vystrel* [The Shot, 1929] and the poem *Tragedinaya noch* [Tragic Night, 1930]. His later work has failed to maintain the standards set by these two titles.

Editions: Izbrannyye proizvedenii, 1918–1958 [Selected Works, 1918–1958], 3 vols., Moscow, 1958

BIANKI, VITALI VALENTINOVICH
Born February 11, 1894, St. Petersburg; died June 10, 1959, Leningrad. Soviet Russian writer of children's books.

B., the son of a scientist, studied natural sciences in Petrograd. His literary career began in 1923. During his numerous travels, expeditions, and hunting trips, B. made many observations on nature, which he later incorporated into his books for children.

In the frequently reissued *Lesnaya gazeta na kazhdyi god* [Forest Magazine for Every Year (1st ed. 1928, 10th ed. 1961], he introduced children to poetry and the laws of nature.

Editions: Rasskazy i skaski [Stories and Fairy Tales], Leningrad, 1960

BIDIL, ABDUL-QADIR
Born 1644, Akbarabad; died 1721, Delhi. Indian, Persian, and Tadzhik poet and philosopher.
B.'s book *'Irfan* [Knowledge, 1712] contains the love story *Komde and Modan*, as well as philosophical ghazals. B. here couched liberal ideas in a language intentionally complex and structured, with resulting negative effects on the Tadzhik written language. *'Irfan* and other philosophical works (*The Four Elements, The Talisman of the Miracle*) contain rationalistic ideas and natural explanations of natural phenomena. One therefore cannot call B. a true mystic.

Editions: Kulliyyat [Collected Works], Bombay, 1882

BILL-BELOTZERKOVSKI, VLADIMIR NAUMOVICH
Born January 9, 1885, Alexandria (southern Ukraine). Soviet Russian short-story writer and playwright.
In his youth B. lived the hard life of a sailor in the merchant marine. He also held different jobs in the U.S.A. In 1917 he returned to Russia where he joined the Communist Party and took part in the civil war. B. held several responsible positions and learned first hand of the difficulties encountered by the Soviets during the first years of power, and of the hard battles required to overcome them.
B. turned to literature with the intention of using his writings as propaganda in the revolutionary battle. B. wrote numerous stories, but he was better known for his plays, which were written in the style of the agitprop theater. These included *Ekho* [Echo, 1924] and *Levo rulya* [Turn the Helm to the Left, 1925]. His play *Shtorm* [Storm, 1925], in which he showed the struggle of the young Soviet republic against the White Guards and internal

enemies in a series of laconic, dynamic pictures, was an important landmark in the development of the Soviet drama. For the first time in the history of the Russian stage, he depicted the Bolshevists as the leading force in the revolution by presenting individual, realistically convincing figures.

In his comedy *Luna sleva* [The Moon from the Left, 1927], B. showed a communist girl torn between her duty as a revolutionary and her need for love. In *Golos nedr* [The Voice from the Depth, 1928], B. wrote of the mass enthusiasm of the workers. This later work did not reach the level of his earlier plays. His merit lies in his cofoundership of the revolutionary, realistic drama; his play *Shtorm* belongs to the classical repertoire of that drama.

Editions: Izbrannoye [Selected Works], Moscow, 1954; *Pyesy* [Plays], Moscow, 1955

BLAUMANIS, RUDOLFS

Born January 1, 1863, Ērgļi; died September 4, 1908, Takaharju (Finland). Latvian novelist, poet, and playwright.

B. was the son of a cook. He graduated from a commercial college in Riga, and held several different jobs which he was able to combine with his literary activities. From 1890 he worked as a journalist.

B.'s literary work consisted chiefly of realistic novels and plays, distinguished for their descriptions of the village milieu. B. is also known for his lyrical, humorous, and satirical poems.

Editions: Kopoti raksti [Gesammelte schriften], 12 vols., 1954–57

BLOK, ALEKSANDR ALEKSANDROVICH

Born November 16, 1880, St. Petersburg; died August 7, 1921, Leningrad. Soviet Russian poet, critic, and dramatist.

B. was the son of a university professor, but he was reared by his mother and her family, who were members of the leading Russian noble intelligentsia. From 1898 to 1906 he studied law and philology in St. Petersburg, and later devoted all his time to literary activities. His first phase of creative work (1898–1904) was influenced by the idealistic, mystical philosophy of Soloviov. He became a follower of symbolism, the most important movement within Russian decadence. In his first collection of poems, *Stikhi o prekrasnoi dame* [Verses about a Beautiful Lady, 1904], B. sublimated his love for his future wife—Lyubov Mendeleyeva, the daughter of the famous chemist—into a mystical encounter with the Eternal Feminine.

The Russian revolution of 1905 deeply affected B. He detached himself from symbolism and developed a reality-related but still largely symbolic style of representation. In his collection of verses (*Sytyye* [The Satiated Ones, 1905]) B. castigated the intellectual poverty of the bourgeoisie. He wrote a parody on the transcendental, symbolistic ideology in his lyric drama *Balaganchik* [The Small Booth, 1906]. In *Neznakomka* [The Unknown Girl, 1905], which he wrote in both poetic and dramatic form, B. introduced his ideal of beauty and purity into the world of the capitalistic city. His intellectual disassociation from tsarist Russia became evident in the lyric poem *Snezhnaya maska* [The Snow Mask, 1907]. B.'s final transition to realistic poetry is reflected in his collection of poems *Volnyye mysli* [Free Thoughts, 1907]. The poet at that time was searching for close links with both the Russian people and the democratic intelligentsia.

In addition to writing lyric poems, B. now turned more toward epic verse forms and to the drama. In his poems *Solovyinyi sad* [The Garden of Nightingales, 1915], B. acknowledged the correctness of the social view of art. In 1913 B. completed his most important drama, *Roza i krest* [The Rose and the Cross, 1936], the action of which takes place in medieval France. The question of the historical mission of Russia became of central importance for B. at this time. In his poetic cycle *Stikhi o Rosii* [Poems on Russia, 1915], B. expressed his love for his country, the realization of the history-forming power of the people, and his feelings about the coming revolution. In the unfinished poem *Vozmezdiye* [Retaliation, 1910–21], B. created a realistic story in verse, in which he combined his personal experience and the fate of his father with the development of Russia between the years 1878 and 1910.

B. dedicated his passionate poem *Dvenadtzat* (1918; The Twelve, 1920)—which soon became world-famous—to the historic October revolution. He defended the revolution against the attacks made by bourgeois Western Europe in his poem *Skify* [The Scythians, 1918]. In his essay *Intelligenziya i revolyutziya* [The Intelligentsia and the Revolution, 1918], he appealed to the Russian intelligentsia to come forward and serve the revolution. B. himself took an active part in the construction of the new culture. He also was a prominent literary critic and translator.

Editions: Sobraniye sochinenii [Collected Works], 8 vols., Moscow, 1960–63; *Stikhotvoreniya i poemy* [Poems and Verses], 2 vols., Leningrad, 1961; *Pisma* [Letters], 2 vols., Leningrad, 1927–32; *Dnevnik* [Diary], Leningrad, 1928

BOGDANOV, NIKOLAI VLADIMIROVICH
Born March 3, 1906, Kandoma (now the District of Ryazan). Soviet Russian novelist.

B. is the son of a country doctor. His greatest literary success was his novel *Pervaya devushka* [The First Girl, 1928, rev. 1958]. Here he described the activities of young Komsomols filled with the spirit of revolutionary romanticism during the first years of Soviet power. His heroine is the "first girl" to be active in a county orgranization of the youth movement, her proving, her failure, and her tragic end. During the following years, B. described chiefly young people and children, as in his story *Vyzov* [The Challenge, 1931], and in the novel *Plenum drusei* [The Assembly of Friends, 1934].

Further Works: Zapiski voyennovo korespondenta, I-II [Notes of a War Correspondent, 1941]; *V pobeshdionmoi Yaponii* [In Conquered Japan, 1947]

BOGDANOVICH, IPPOLIT FIODOROVICH
Born January 3, 1744, Perevolochnaya (District of Poltava); died January 18, 1803, Kursk. Russian poet.

B. came from a noble Ukrainian family; he studied in Moscow.

His first literary activities came under the direction of M. Kheraskov. B.'s works included the volume of lyrics *Lira* [The Lyre, 1773], the poem *Suguboye blazhenstovo* [Double Bliss, 1765], and a collection of Russian proverbs, written in 1785. He also wrote the lyric comedy *Radost Dushenki* [Dushenka's Joys, 1786] and the play *Slavyane* [The Slave, 1788].

B. published a number of magazines and newspapers. He translated Voltaire, Rousseau, Diderot, and other foreign authors. His best work, written between 1778–83, is said to be the poem *Dushenka*, an excellent paraphrase of La Fontaine's *Psyché et Cupidon*. This poem, written in the lighter, sentimental style of the Russian fairy tale, is in strong contrast with the heroic poems of classicism.

Editions: Stikhotvoreniya i poemy [Poems and Verses], Leningrad, 1957

BOKONBAYEV, DZHOOMART

Born May 16, 1910, Masar-Sai; died August 1, 1944. Kirghiz Soviet lyricist and dramatist.

B. came from a poor family. His poems first appeared in print in 1927. He depicted the new life of the Kirghiz people—*Kökösh kösum achty* [Kökösh Opened his Eyes, 1928]—the stormy process of industrialization—*Suluktu*, 1933—and the battles in defense of the Soviet homeland—(*Kosh, Ala-Too* [Farewell, Ala-Too]). In his poems B. combined a militant political spirit with profoundly individual feelings.

Editions: Tshygarmalarynyn toluk dshyinagy [Collected Works], Vols. I and II, Frunse, 1950–54
Further Works: Altyn kys (1937); *Toktogul* (1939)

BONDAREV, YURII VASILYEVICH

Born March 15, 1924, Orsk (southern Urals). Soviet Russian short-story writer and novelist.

B. was a gun-commander during World War II. His first literary works appeared in 1949. B. graduated from the Gorki Institute of Literature in Moscow in 1951, and since then has become one of the most prominent representatives of recent Soviet war literature. In his short stories *Batalyony prosyat ognya* [The Battalions are Asking for Fire, 1957] and *Posledniyye salpy* [The Last Salvoes, 1959], B. has demonstrated, with impressive psychological characterization, the heroism of soldiers during the routine of war. In his two novels *Tishina* [Silence, 1962] and *Dvoye* [The Two, 1963], B. has investigated the effects of the personality cult.

BROWKA, PYATRUS (PYOTR USTINAVICH)

Born June 25, 1906, Putilkavich. Byelorussian Soviet poet and novelist. People's Poet of the Byelorussian SSR since 1962; corresponding member of the Academy of Sciences of the Byelorussian SSR since 1953.

B. was born into the family of a poor peasant, and began to write in 1926. His first major work was the poem *Pras gory i step* [Through the Mountains and the Steppe, 1932], which depicts the heroism of the Red Guards in the civil war. B. soon overcame a tendency toward rhetoric evident in his early work, and arrived at an artistically convincing presentation of the nature of Byelorussia and the intellectual world of its people. The heroes of his poems *1914* and *Katerina* (both written in 1938) are the people who participated in the social events of their time.

During the war B. wrote numerous patriotic poems and verses, some of which are in the style of the epic heroic ballad or exhibit features of Byelorussian folklore. B. was awarded the State Prize of 1947 for his poem *Khlyab* [Bread, 1946], describing postwar kolkhoz life, and for a series of other poems. He was awarded a second State Prize in 1951 for another series of poems. In 1962 he was awarded the Lenin Prize for his volume of poetry *Days Will Come*, published in 1961.

In his novel *Kali zlivayutztza reki* [When the Rivers Flow Together, 1957], B. described the construction of a hydroelectric plant at the border where the Byelorussian, Lithuanian, and Latvian SSR meet; the main theme of this work is the friendship existing between the socialist peoples. B.'s works are closely related to contemporary events, and they frequently exhibit a marked political accent; they are generally characterized by an original, national color. B. has translated the works of Shevchenko, Mayakovski, Tvardovski, Isakovski and of other authors into Byelorussian.

Editions: Sbor tvorav [Collected Works],·2 vols., Minsk, 1957

BRYL, YANKA (Pseud. of *Ivan Antonavich Bryl*)
Born August 4, 1917, Odessa. Byelorussian Soviet novelist.
B. comes from a working-class family. His literary activities commenced with realistic short stories about life in the western Byelorussian villages. Numerous short stories and novels distinguish B. as one of the most prominent prose writers of Byelorussia. His novel *The Last Encounter*, published in 1959, demonstrates B.'s skill in depicting the complexity of human emotions. The novel *The Birds and Their Nests* (1964) is an interesting example of the emergence of lyrical and philosophical embellishments in B.'s work. He was awarded the State Prize in 1952 for his story *Land without Pan*.

Editions: Sbor tvorav [Collected Works], 2 vols., Minsk, 1960

BRYUSOV, VALERI YAKOVLEVICH
Born December 13, 1873, Moscow; died there October 9, 1924. Soviet Russian poet, translator, literary critic, and historian.
B., the son of a merchant, was educated in the spirit of philosophical materialism and democracy, and was one of the most educated personalities of his time. He was a free-lance writer from an early age.
B. belonged to the founders of Russian symbolism, and published as their manifesto the collection of poems *Ruskiye simvolisty* [The Russian Symbolists, 3 vols., 1894–95]. In the early 1900s B. divorced himself from the personal, decadent symbolist tendencies strongly evident in his first collections—*Chefs d'œuvre* [Masterpieces, 1895], *Me eum esse* [This Is Me, 1897], and *Tertia Vigilia* [The Third Watch, 1900]. In his volumes of poems

Urbi et orbi [To the City and the World, 1903], *Stephanos* [The Wreath, 1906], and *Vse napevy* [All Melodies, 1909], B. used historical themes as well as the social contradictions arising in the capitalistic city. He recognized the power of the proletariat—see his poem *Kamenschchik* [The Bricklayer, 1901]—and welcomed the revolution of 1905, although he failed to understand its true aims.

It was only after a period of complex ideologic and artistic development—proceeding from a rational, scientific view and approved by Gorki—that B. arrived at the rejection of the existing society and of the imperialist war. He supported the October revolution, and joined the Communist Party in 1920. B. was a pioneer in the cultural development of the Soviet Union, and a supporter of young writers. He lectured at the University of Moscow.

After 1917, B.'s poetry, including the poem *Lenin*, published in 1924, became filled with revolutionary and scientific ideas. He was a master of the precise, pregnant word, and of the perfect form. In addition to his extensive original work, B. has left valuable adaptations and translations of works by Vergil, Goethe, Poe, Verhaeren, and Rolland, as well as of Armenian poetry.

Editions: Izbrannyye proizvedeniya [Selected Works], 3 vols., Moscow–Leningrad, 1926; *Stikhotvoreniya i poemy* [Poems and verses], Leningrad, 1961
Further Works: Altar pobedy [Altar of Victory] (1913); *Ognionnyi angel* (1908; The Flaming Angel, 1930); *V takiye dri* [On Such Days] (1921); *Mig* [Mix] (1922); *Mea! Speshi!* [Mea! Hurry!] (1924)

BUBENNOV, MIKHAIL SEMIONOVICH
Born November 21, 1909, Vtoroye Polomoshnevo (Altai). Soviet Russian novelist.

B.'s literary career commenced with short stories about collectivization (*Gremyaschchi god* [The Year of Thunder, 1932]) and the civil war (*Besmertiye* [Immortality, 1940]). B. became known in 1947 following the publication of the first volume of his long novel *Belaya berioza* [The White Birch], for which he was awarded the State Prize in 1948. The second volume of this work appeared in 1952. In Volume I, B. describes the intellectual and emotional maturation of the ordinary Soviet soldiers during the battles taking place around Moscow in 1941; the second part of the novel, however, is not entirely free from the effects of the "passive resistance" theory. B.'s novel *Orlinaya step* [The Steppe of Eagles, 1959] tells of the heroism of the Komsomols in the new virgin lands.

BUCOV, EMILIAN

Born July 28, 1909, Novoya Kiliya (Bessarabia). Moldavian Soviet poet, short-story writer, and novelist.

B.'s work developed in bourgeois Rumania and was closely connected with activities of the illegal revolutionary workers' movement. B. wrote a series of political propaganda poems and popular workers' songs; after 1934 he produced cycles of lyric poems based on broad social themes. These were subsequently rewritten by him as short stories.

The liberation of Bessarabia represented the beginning of a new period in B.'s work, and he has developed into one of the best Moldavian lyricists. In the poetic style of Mayakovski, whose works he has translated, B.'s poems are concerned with the battles of his people during World War II.

After the war B. wrote several short stories and novels of contemporary life in addition to his poems. Among his best works are the fairy tale *Andriesh* (1945) and the poem *My Country* (1945).

BUNIN, IVAN ALEKSEYEVICH

Born October 22, 1870, Voronesh; died November 8, 1953, Paris. Russian poet, novelist, short-story writer, and critic.

B. came from the impoverished landed nobility. His lyric talent developed in the 1890s, and is evident in his nature poems. It was during this period that B. wrote his first stories about the suffering and starving Russian village. His friendship with Chekhov, Gorki, and the progressive Snaniye circle led to an intensification of the social testimony offered in his works. The life of the Russian peasantry and the decline of the landed nobility became his main themes, themes which he used in a psychologically impressive and fluid manner in many of his important stories.

B.'s presentation of the tragic fate of the people reached a climax in his story *Derevnya* (1910; The Village, 1923). After 1910 B. frequently wrote of the destruction of moral character by inhumane conditions. Because of his aristocratic prejudices and his rejection of the revolutionary movement, B. was unable to see the beginnings of the social and intellectual changes taking place in the Russian village. His attitude toward capitalistic morals and civilization was definitely a negative one, as is shown by his short stories *Bratya* [The Brothers, 1914] and *Gospodin iz San Francisco* (1915; The Gentleman from San Francisco, 1935).

B. emigrated to France in 1920. His subsequent work was impaired by his anti-Soviet sentiments, making the awarding of the Nobel Prize in 1933 a questionable decision. B.'s views on the Soviet Union underwent certain changes after World War II. The best part of his total work—contradictory with respect to both theme and ideology—is linked to the traditions of Russian critical realism and represents the final chapter of that genre.

Editions: Sobraniye sochinenii [Selected Works], 5 vols., Moscow, 1956
Further Works: Zhizn' Arsenyeva (1930; The Well of Days, 1933); *Tiomnyye allei* (1943; Dark Avenues, 1935)

BYADULYA, SMITROK (Pseud. of *Samuil Yafimavich Plavink*)
Born April 23, 1886, Posadetz; died November 3, 1941, near Uralsk. Byelorussian Soviet poet and novelist.

B. was born into a poor Jewish family. He began to write poems and verse in 1910 in both the Byelorussian and the Russian language. His work written prior to 1917 reflects a true picture of the thoughts, customs, and ways of the Byelorussian peasantry. They contain, however, only a superficial presentation of the processes of social development, and indicate a hostile attitude on the part of the author toward socialist revolution. B.'s attitude in this respect changed only in later years.

In a number of stories written during the 1920s, B. created heroes who fought against the hitherto existing exploitative order. His best work is the historical novel *Salavei* [Nightingale, 1927], in which he described the decline of serfdom and the fight of the peasants against the estate owners.

Editions: Sbor tvorav [Collected works], 4 vols., Minsk, 1951–53

BYKOV, VASIL VLADIMIRAVICH
    Born June 19, 1924, Cherenovschchina (District of Vitebsk). Byelorussian Soviet short-story writer.

B. came from a peasant family, and at the age of seventeen volunteered for frontline duty in the army. His war experiences provide the main themes of his stories; he depicts the routine of war and the intellectual attitude of the soldiers in a laconic, expressive style. B.'s most important work so far is his long story *The Third Rocket*, published in 1962.

Editions: Voyennyye povesti [War Stories] (in Russian), Moscow, 1965

BYLINY
    Old Russian epic or heroic folksongs based on events of the eleventh to sixteenth centuries. They may be grouped in cycles around Kiev ("heroic" *byliny*) or around Novgorod (*byliny* about historical figures). In an artistically generalized form, these songs describe the fight of the Kievan Russian people for independence from the Tatars of the steppes, as well as commenting on the internal social problems then existing in Russia.

The main characters are the ancient heroes. The older heroes (including Mikula Selyaninovich Svyatogor) represent spontaneous natural forces or original peasant figures; the younger ones (in particular Aliyosha Popovich, Dobrynya Nikitich, and the favorite hero Ilya Murometz) represent the best characteristics of the Russian people. Sadko and Vaska Buslayev are the best-known figures among the fictional heroes.

Forced into the background since the sixteenth century, the *bylinys* today are regarded as a significant cultural inheritance. Other artistic fields are frequently stimulated by *bylinys*.

Editions: Drevniye rossiiskiye stikhotvoreniya, sobrannyye Kirsheyu Danilovym [Old Russian Poetry, Collected by Kirsha Danilov], Moscow–Leningrad, 1958

CHAADAYEV, PIOTR YAKOVLEVICH
Born June 8, 1794, Nizhni Novgorod; died April 26, 1856, Moscow. Russian humanist and philosopher.

As a Guards officer C. participated in the war against Napoleon in 1812. He influenced the youthful Pushkin with his liberal ideas.

Between 1820–21 C. was a member of a Decembrist secret society. After a voyage across Western Europe in 1823–26 C. turned toward Catholicism. During the years 1829–31 he wrote eight philosophical letters, the first of which appeared in 1836 in the magazine *Teleskop*. Because of the strong criticism of tsarism voiced in these letters C. was officially declared insane.

Further Works: Apologiya sumeshedshevo [An Apology for the Insane] (1837)

CHAKOVSKI, ALEKSANDR BORISOVICH
Born August 26, 1913, St. Petersburg. Soviet Russian novelist and journalist. Author of several biographies, including those of H. Barbusse, H. Heine, and M. Andersen Nexö.

C. was editor-in-chief of the magazine *Inostrannaya literatura* [Foreign Literature] between 1959 and 1963. C. has been editor of *Literaturnaya gazeta* [Literature Magazine] from 1938. C.'s World War II experiences and his life during the postwar years are reflected in his novel *Eto bylo v Leningrade* [This Happened in Leningrad, 1946], and in *Mirnyye dni* [Peaceful Days, 1947]. In his later novels C. has analyzed a number of contemporary ideologies and moral problems, especially those concerning the way young people living in the far north handle conflicting situations. Among works dealing with these subjects are *God zhisni* [A Year of Life, 1956], *Dorogi, kotoryye my vybirayem* [The Roads That We Have Chosen, 1960], and *Svet dalyokoi svesdy* [Light From A Star Far Away, 1962].

CHAPYGIN, ALEKSEI PAVLOVICH

Born October 17, 1870, Kargopolski Uyesd (District of Olonetz); died October 21, 1937, Leningrad. Soviet Russian short-story writer and novelist.

The son of a peasant, C., whose work was much influenced by Gorki, published his first story in 1903. In the stories written between 1904 and 1911, *Igoshka, Marushka*, and *Poslednyaya doroga* [The Last Road], he gave an accurate description of the hard life of the lower strata of the city population. His novel *Bely skit* [The White Cloister, 1913] described the life of a northern Russian village on the eve of the revolution of 1905–07. C. published a number of his hunting stories in one volume under the title *Po zverinoi trope* [At the Hunting Ground, 1918].

The Soviet historical novel has been permanently influenced and enriched by C.'s *Razin Stepan* (1926–27; Stepan Razin, 1946), in which—for the first time in Soviet literature—a true interpretation of Razin is given. C. presents a realistic picture of that great mass movement and shows the relationship between the leader and the mass. The early history of the same revolt was described by C. in his novel *Gulyashchuye lyudi* [Wandering People, 1937].

C. has also written the autobiographical novels *Zhizn moya* [My Life, 1929], *Po tropam i dorogam* [On the Paths and the Roads, 1930], and *Oskolok togo zhe zerkala* [A Fragment of the Same Mirror]. This last title, published in 1933, remained unfinished at the time of the author's death.

Editions: Sobraniye sochinenii [Collected Works], 7 vols., Moscow, 1928

CHARENTZ (Pseud. of *Egishe Sogomanian*)

Born in 1897, Karsa; died 1937. Armenian Soviet dramatist, poet, and translator of works from Russian, Soviet, and Western literature.

C.'s early work was influenced by the symbolists, particularly by the writings of A. Blok. After the October revolution C. wrote poems, permeated by romantic fervor, in which he described the movement of the masses. He also created individual portraits in verse of revolutionary fighters. His ballad cycle on Lenin (*Uncle Lenin; Ballad on Vladimir Illyich, The Farmer, and A Pair of Boots; Lenin and Ali*) was written in 1924–25. In numerous dramas, comedies, and in his novel *The Land of Kairi*, C. exposed the enemies of the revolution, especially the Transcaucasian nationalists.

By 1924 C. had traveled through Turkey, France, Italy, and Germany; his travel impressions are recorded in the verses and poems he wrote shortly after his return. C.'s last poems exhibit a nihilistic attitude toward Armenian history.

Editions: Tri poemy o Lenine [Three Poems on Lenin], Moscow, 1955; *Izbrannoye* [Selected Works] (in Russian), Moscow, 1955

CHAROT MIKHAS (Pseud. of *Mikhail Syamonavich Kudzelka*)

Born November 7, 1896, Rudsensk (District of Minsk); died December 14, 1938. Byelorussian Soviet poet and dramatist.

C., the son of a poor peasant, commenced writing in 1919; his poems were very popular in the 1920s. Under the influence of the symbolist poet A. Blok he wrote the poem *Bosyya na vognishchy* [Barefoot into the Fire, 1921], which is about the revolution and the civil war in Byelorussia. T. also has written short stories and several plays.

Editions: Sbor tvorav [Collected Works], 2 vols., Minsk, 1958

CHAVCHAVDSE, ILIA

Born October 27, 1837, Quareli (in Kakhetia); died September 12, 1907. Georgian novelist and poet.

C. came from a noble family. He studied at the University of St. Petersburg but, because of his involvement in student disturbances, was forced to leave that city in 1861. C.'s ideology was formed by the ideas of the Russian revolutionary democrats, and his work was influenced by the Russian lyricist N. A. Nekrasov.

In 1863 C. founded the magazine *Sakartvelos Moambe* [The Messenger from Georgia], and between 1877 and 1902 published the literary and political newspaper *Iveria* [Georgia]. He became the leading representative of the progressive forces in Georgia in the second half of the nineteenth century. A materialistic philosopher, C. stood for the unity of social and national liberation movements. He demanded a realistic art which would serve as an "improvement of life." The problems arising in connection with capitalistic development and the class character of the revolution of 1905–07 were not fully understood by C. In his novels, which included *Tales of a Beggar* (1859), *Notes of a Traveler* (1861), and *Is That Still a Human Being?* (1859–63), C. depicted social contradictions, the declining nobility, and the humanity of the peasants.

C.'s poems passionately advocated the progressive ideas of his times. He lamented the defeat of the Commune of Paris. C. also discussed philosophical problems in his poems. His poem *Vision* (1859, published 1872–73) depicts the progressive forces of Georgia. C.'s poetic and prose works, together with his essays on literature, aesthetics, and other problems, have exerted a decisive influence on the development of realistic literature in Georgia.

Editions: Izbranniye proizvedeniya [Selected Works] (in Russian), 1950

CHEKHOV, ANTON PAVLOVICH

Born January 29, 1860, Taganrog; died July 15, 1904, Badenweiler, Germany. Russian short-story writer, novelist, and dramatist.

C. was the son of a small shopkeeper. He attended the local high school in Taganrog and then studied medicine in Moscow (1880–84). As a student he had already become known for his amusing short stories. In 1890 C. went to the island of Sakhalin, a penal settlement, where he investigated the harsh living conditions of the prisoners. He submitted his findings to the tsarist authorities in a biting paper entitled *Ostrov Sakhalin* (1893–94; A Journey to Sakhalin, 1967).

Between 1892 and 1899 C. lived in Melikhovo near Moscow, where he worked as a country doctor and writer. In 1892 he organized a relief movement for the inhabitants of Novgorod in central Russia when that region was severely hit by a cholera epidemic. It was during this time that C. critically reviewed the prevailing intellectual movements—liberal populism, Tolstoiism, and decadence—and formed his own democratic ideology based on scientific knowledge.

In 1899, already suffering from the tuberculosis that was to result in his death, he moved to Yalta in the Crimea. It was in Yalta that he met Lev Tolstoi and became a friend of M. Gorki. In 1900 C. was elected honorary member of the Russian Academy of Sciences. He resigned from the Academy in 1902, in protest against the annullment of Gorki's election to that body by Tsar Nicholas II. C.'s participation in political events increased during the last years of his life, and he expressed his hopes for early changes in Russia.

In the 1880s C. published approximately 400 short stories, some of which have been collected in the volumes entitled *Shazki Melpomeny* [Tales of Melpome, 1884], *Piostryye rasskazy* [Colorful Stories, 1886], and *V sumerkakh* [At Twilight, 1887]. For a time he contributed to the humorous magazine *Oskolki* [Splinters] published by N. L. Leikin. C.'s humor was at first concerned only with the external phenomena of society, but a number of stories already show him to be an incorruptible critic of social conditions. This may be clearly seen in *Smert chinovnika* [The Death of the Official, 1883], *Tolstyiitonki* (1883; Fat and Thin, 1922), *Khameleon* (1884; A Chameleon, 1916), *Unter Prishibeyev* [Corporal Prishibeyev, 1885], and *Vanka* (1886; Eng., 1915).

During the final years of the 1880s, C. matured into the master of the great short novel. With the trained eye of a physician he laid bare the illnesses and abuses of tsarist Russia, leading Russian critical realism to its climax. His work in the field of the novella is characterized by a wealth of ideas, a profound depth of characterization, and a rich emotional content. With *Step* (1888; The Steppe, 1916), C. introduced the technique of association; he frequently gave a symbolic value to his realistic descriptions. The basic theme of his narrative work—the question of a correct "total idea" for the individual as well as for Russia —was broached by C. in *Skychnaya istoriya* (1889; A Tedious Story, 1915), *Duel* (1891; The Duel, 1950), *Ward No. 6* (1892), *Palata No. 6* (1903), *Dom s mesoninom* (1896; The House with the Mezzanine, 1917), and *Moya zhisn* (1896; My Life, 1917).

In many of his short stories, including *Uchitel slovesnosti* [The Teacher of Literature, 1894], *Ionych* (1898), *Kryzhovnik* (1898; The Gooseberry Bush, 1915), and *Chelovek v futlyare* (1896; The Man in the Case, 1914), C. attacked the bourgeoisie and the spiritual aridness of the contemporary intelligentsia. C. exposed the parasitic degeneration of the Russian upper middle class in his novels *Babye tzarstvo* [Womenfolk Doings, 1894], *Tri goda* [Three Years, 1895], and *Slucha iz praktiki* [A Case from the Practice, 1898].

The misery of life in the Russian village and the advancement of capitalism in peasant society are described in C.'s stories *Muzhiki* (1897; Muzhiks, 1908) and *V ovrage* [In the Ravine, 1902]. C. also diagnosed contemporary love, marriage, and the family in stories of great artistic sensibility, including *Supruga* [The Spouse, 1895], *Ariadna* [Eng., 1895], *Dushechka* (1898; The Darling, 1950), and *Dama s sobachkoi* (1895; The Lady with the Toy Dog, 1937). C.'s ideal of quiet heroism—the great scientific or humane deed—has been expressed by him in novels such as *Pripado* [The Fit, 1889], *Popryguna* [A Capricious Person, 1891], and *Student* [The Student, 1894]. In his last novel, *Nevesta* [The Bride, 1903], C. expressed his hopes for the renewal of Russia by the revolutionary actions of the young people of his time.

As a dramatist C. has opened new roads for both Russian and world literature. He created the lyrical psychological drama in which the inner conflicts or dramatic undercurrents take precedence over the external action. This new form of drama gained general acceptance following a number of presentations by the Moscow Art Theater, directed by Stanislavski and Nemirovich-Danchenko. C.'s first dramatic works were comic one-act plays such as *Medved* (1888; The Bear, 1908) and *Predlozheniye* (1888; A Marriage Proposal, 1903). His first full-length play, *Ivanov* (1888; Eng., 1912), still followed the traditions of the classical Russian theater, and it was only with *Chaika* (1896; The Seagull, 1912) that C. succeeded in establishing his own personal form of drama. In this play C. showed the fate of various artists, and threw light on the nature of true art. In *Dyadya Vanya* (1897; Uncle Vanya, 1912)—a revision of *Leshi* [The Woodsman, 1889] —C. demonstrated the conflicts arising between cultured idlers (Serebryakov) and hardworking people (Voinitzki, Sonya, Dr. Astrov). The tragedy of an unlived life coming to nothing in the unfulfilled longing for significant activity represents the central theme of C.'s drama *Tri sestry* (1901; The Three Sisters, 1916). C.'s last play, *Vishniovyi sad* (1904; The Cherry Orchard, 1908), reflects the sad gaiety of the nobility in their leavetaking from old Russia. In this play the dramatist depicts the conflict between the declining nobility, the bourgeoisie striving to become the ruling class, and the revolutionary intelligentsia planning for the future. With this work C. welcomed the new Russia, a Russia which he unfortunately was only able to imagine.

Editions: Polnoye sobraniye sochinenii i pissem [Complete Works and Letters], 20 vols., Moscow, 1948–51; *Sobraniye sochinenii* [Collected Works], 12 vols., Moscow, 1954–57
Further Works: Toska (1886; Sorrow, 1897); *Spat Khochetsya* [I Want to Sleep] (1888); *Vragi* [Enemies] (1888); *Chornyi monakh* [The Black Monk] (1893); *Skripka Rotshilda* (1894; Rothschild's Fiddle, 1903); *Anna na Sheye* (1895; Anna on the Neck, 1917); *Podelam sluzhby* [On Business Matters] (1898); *Arkhiyerei* [The Bishop] (1902)

CHERNYSHEVSKI, NIKOLAI GAVRILOVICH

Born July 24, 1828, Saratov; died there October 29, 1889. Russian revolutionary democrat, journalist, and literary critic; leader of the Russian revolutionary movement of the 1860s; one of the most important precursors of Marxism in Russia.

C. was the son of a priest; he attended the theological seminary in Saratov between 1842 and 1846, and between 1846–50 studied at the University of St. Petersburg. He then worked as a teacher of Russian language and literature in Saratov and St. Petersburg. From 1853 he was a contributor to and editor-in-chief of the leading revolutionary democratic magazine *Sovremennik* [The Contemporary]. C. was arrested in 1862 and following a truly disgraceful trial in 1864 was exiled to Siberia; he returned in 1883, a physically broken man. He was forbidden to engage in any literary activity after his return.

C.'s first important literary work was his master's thesis *Estecheskiye otnosheniya iskusstva k deistvitelnosti* [The Aesthetic Relationship between Art and Reality, 1853–55], a brilliant, materialist criticism of Hegel's idealist aesthetics. Here C.—following in the footsteps of Belinski—formulated the basic aesthetic principles for realistic artistic creativity. This paper represents one of the most significant achievements of pre-Marxist aesthetics.

In numerous critical essays, including the well-known *Ocherki gogolevskovo perioda russkoi literatury* [Sketches on the Gogolian Period of Russian Literature, 1855–56], C. demonstrated the significance of critical realism for Russian literature. His essay *Lessing, yevo vremya, yevo zhizn i deyatelnost* [Lessing: His Times, His Life, and His Work, 1856–57] represents the first extensive interpretation of German liberalism as seen from the point of view of the Russian revolutionary democrats.

In his most important work, the political novel *Chto delat* (1863; What Is to Be Done?, 1886), C., using the language of the fabulist, rich in allegorical images, speaks of the life of the "new man," and his attempt to change Russian society in the utopian, socialist sense. The figure of the revolutionary Rakhmetov is one of the most impressive examples of the positive hero in classical Russian literature. The novel called for a revolutionary transformation of society.

In his second political novel, *Prolog* [The Prologue, 1877], C. drew a colorful picture of the social arguments and difficulties connected with the abolition of serfdom on the eve of the peasant revolt of 1861, and compared the self-sacrificing fight of the revolutionary democrats with the shameful lack of action of the Russian liberals.

C.'s ideas greatly influenced the class struggles of his time as well as the ideological artistic development of the people, especially in the Slavic countries, as well as the entire international labor movement. Marx, Lenin, Bebel, Clara Zetkin, Dimitroff, and other revolutionary leaders saw in C.'s activities the living tradition of socialist world movement.

Editions: Polnoye sobraniye sochinenii [Complete Works], 16 vols., Moscow, 1939–53; *Izbrannyye proizvedeniya* [Selected Works], 3 vols., Moscow, 1950; *Estetika i literaturnaya kritika* [Aesthetics and Literary Criticism], Moscow, 1951

CHORNY, KUZMA (Pseud. of *Mikalya Karlavich Ramanovski*)

Born June 24, 1900, Borki (District of Minsk); died December 1, 1944, Minsk. Byelorussian Soviet short-story writer, dramatist, and novelist.

T. was the son of a farm laborer; he became a village teacher. His first story, *Na granitzy* [On the Border], appeared in 1923. In his later stories and novels he attempted to present the entire history of the Byelorussian people from the times of serfdom to the present. His novels *Syastra* [The Sister, 1927], *Zyamlya* [The Earth, 1928], *Vyasna* [Spring, 1930] *Tretzaya pakaleniye* [The Third Generation, 1935], among others, belong to this cycle.

C. was also the author of a number of stage plays. He was very familiar with village life, and frequently took the ideology of private property and the process of overcoming that ideology as his subject. C.'s war stories and his novels *Vyaliki dzen* [A Great Day, 1941–44] and *Poshuki budchyni* [Toward the Future,

I. Chavchavdse

l.
A. P. Chekhov
r.
N. G. Chernyshevski

D. Demirchian

G. R. Derzhavin

1943] represent high points in the development of a socialistic, psychological Byelorussian prose.

Editions: Sbor tvorav [Collected Works], 6 vols., Minsk, 1954–55

CHUKOVSKI, KORNEI IVANOVICH
    Born March 31, 1882, St. Petersburg; died October 28, 1969. Soviet Russian juvenile author, translator, literary critic, and philologist.
    C. obtained an extensive education through private study. He studied English, and worked for some time in London as a newspaper correspondent. C. soon earned the approbation of the public as a literary critic, and became very popular. Many of his essays have been collected in *Ot Chekhova do nashikh dnei* [From Chekhov to Our Days, 1908] and *Litza i maski* [Faces and Masks, 1914]. During the revolution of 1905–07, C. published the satirical newspaper *Signal*; legal proceedings were instituted against him after the failure of the revolution.
    Since 1905, C. has put considerable effort into the establishment of a meaningful children's literature. His ideas on this subject have been expressed in essays such as *Nat Pinkerton i sovremennaya literatura* [Nat Pinkerton and Contemporary Literature]. In the 1920s he was a passionate defender of the fairy tale for children as opposed to the modern, realistic theory of juvenile literature.
    In addition to essays on contemporary literature, C. has written versatile papers on nineteenth-century Russian literature, including *Lyudi i knigi shestidesyatykh godov* [People and Books of the Sixties, 1934].
    After the October revolution C. was acclaimed for his research into and interpretation of the work of N. A. Nekrasov. In 1919 he edited the first complete edition of Nekrasov's poems; he reassembled original versions and discovered the existence of new texts. His book *Masterstvo Nekrasova* [Nekrasov's Mastery] appeared in 1952.
    In 1912 C. published the children's magazines *Zhar-ptitza* [The Firebird] and—together with M. Gorki—*Yolka* [The Fir]. He

also was the organizer of the publishing house *Raduga*, which specialized in children's books. C. won considerable praise for his study of the unpredictable laws of children's thought and psychology. *Malenkiye deti* [Small Children], published in 1925, represented the first version of his book *Ot dvukh do pyati* (From Two to Five, 1963), which appeared in many foreign languages, including English.

C.'s fairy tales in verse, *Krokodil* (1916), *Moidodyr* [Go and Wash, 1923], *Tarakanishche* [The Cockroach, 1924], *Barmalei* (1926), and *Mukha-Zokotukha* [The Fly Called Buzz, 1927], have enjoyed considerable popularity. The great dynamic force of these fairy tales is due, above all, to the fact that C. uses original observations made in his study of children's language and psychology. C. has also made translations of juvenile classics, including *Baron Munchausen's Travels* and *Doctor Ajbolit*. He has been a prominent translator of English and American works, including those of Whitman, Mark Twain, and Kipling. He has published a number of essays on the theory of translating, including *Vysokoye iskusstvo* [The Great Art, 1941]. He was awarded the Lenin Prize in 1962.

Editions: Sobraniye sochinenii [Collected Works], 6 vols., Moscow, 1964

CHUKOVSKI, NIKOLAI KORNEYVICH

Born June 2, 1905, Odessa; died November 4, 1965. Soviet Russian novelist; son of the writer and literary critic Kornei I. Chukovski.

C. graduated from the Leningrad School of Art History in 1930. He participated in World War II; his most important work, the novel *Baltiiskoye nebo* [Under Baltic Skies, 1954], deals with wartime events. This novel, in which C. created a number of very impressive characters, described the heroic battles fought by a small group of Soviet airmen in defense of Leningrad. The novel is one of the best works of Soviet literature on the subject of World War II.

CVIRKA, PETRAS

Born March 12, 1909, Klangiai near Veliuona; died May 2, 1947, Vilnius. Most important Lithuanian poet, novelist, and short-story writer.

C. came from a peasant family. His first publications were poems; these have been collected in *Pirmosios misios* [Early Mass, 1928]. His greatest success, however, was in the field of the novel. The satirical novel *Frank Kruk* (1934) deals with the life of a bourgeois upstart. C.'s transition from critical to socialist realism became evident in his novel *Zeme maitintoya* [Mother Earth, 1935], in which he exposed the bourgeois agrarian reforms as being inadequate, and demonstrated the necessity for a socialist development of the village. Apart from his novels, C.'s great talent was most evident in the genre of the short story. His best collections include *Kasdienes istorijos* [Everyday Stories, 1938], *Bausmes ranka* [The Hand of Retribution], and *Avysakos apie okupantus* [Stories of the Occupying Forces, 1943], which have as their theme the fight of the people against the fascist invaders.

Editions: Rinktine [Selected Works], Kaunas, 1958

DADIANI, SHALVA

Born May 21, 1874, Sestafoni; died March 15, 1959, Tbilisi. Georgian Soviet playwright and novelist; People's Artist of the Georgian SSR from 1923 until his death.

In the years between 1895 and 1923 D. worked as an actor and producer. In 1908 he directed a group of actors playing revolutionary pieces before the workers. D. continued the traditions of critical realism in his early stories and dramas written between 1905 and 1917. In these he described the life of the people, the decline of the nobility, and the revolutionary movements in Georgia. They include the dramas *Yesterday's People* (1917) and *Gekechkori* (1915).

D.'s dramatic work reached its peak after 1917. He wrote more than thirty dramas, among them the first Georgian satirical comedy *Right into the Heart* (1928) and the historical novels *Yuri Bo-*

golyubski (1926)—about Georgia at the end of the twelfth and the beginning of the thirteenth centuries—and *The Family Gvirgviliani* (1956) on the declining feudal bourgeois order.

Editions: Rcheuli chsulebani [Selected Works], 5 vols.; vols. 1 and 2, Tbilisi, 1958–59

DAL, VLADIMIR IVANOVICH
Born November 22, 1801, Lugansk (District of Yekaterinoslav); died October 4, 1872, Moscow. Russian ethnographer, lexicographer, and short-story writer.

D. helped to establish the Natural School with his adaptations of Russian fairy tales and his stories and sketches depicting the life of the people. These were published under the pseudonym "The Cossack from Lugansk." D.'s lifelong work was the collection and compilation of a dictionary of the contemporary Russian language. His *Tolkovyi slovar zhivovo velikoruskovo yazyka* [4 vols., Analytical Dictionary of the Living Russian Language, 1863–66] has remained a standard reference work.

Further Works: Poslovitzy russkovo naroda [Sayings of Russian Folk People] (1862)

DEMENTYEV, NIKOLAI STEPANOVICH
Born February 17, 1927, Leningrad. Soviet Russian short-story writer.

D. held an engineering position in Siberia, and his first short stories were published there in 1952. They appeared in the literary magazine *Sibirskiye ogni* [Siberian Lights]. D.'s work is primarily aimed at Soviet youth. Among his best-known collections are *Moi dorogi* [My Roads, 1958] and *Kubanetz* [A Man From the Kuban, 1958].

Editions: Idu v zhizn. Povesti i rasskazy [Into Life: Short Stories], Leningrad, 1961

DEMIRCHIAN, DERENIK
Born February 18, 1877, Akhalkalaki; died December 6, 1956, Yerevan. Armenian Soviet poet, novelist, and playwright; received

the Meritorious Artist Award in 1940; a member of the Armenian Academy of Sciences from 1953 until his death.

D. studied in Geneva, Switzerland, and at other universities. He lived in Yerevan from 1925 until his death.

D.'s development as a poet and writer was determined primarily by the revolutions that took place in 1905–07 and in 1917. After the establishment of Soviet power D. extolled the beauty and heroism of the revolutionary struggle and of emancipated labor in an impressive verse collection, *The Spring* (1919). His short stories and novels of the 1930s deal with similar themes.

D.'s dramatic works, especially those written during the 1930s, including *Erkir Aireni* (1939), have greatly influenced the Armenian Soviet drama. His historical patriotic novel, *Vardanidy* (2 vols., 1943–46, revised second edition published in 1951 as *Yardanank*), was inspired by the events of World War II. It is concerned with the Armenian war of liberation in 441 A.D. D. was also active as a linguist, literary critic, and historian.

Editions: Izbrannoye [Selected Works], Yerevan, 1950; *Rasskazy* [Short Stories] (in Russian), Moscow, 1954; *Yardanak* (in Russian), Moscow, 1961

DERZHAVIN, GAVRILLA ROMANOVICH

Born July 14, 1745, District of Kazan; died July 21, 1816, Svanka (District of Novgorod). Considered the most important Russian poet of the eighteenth century.

D. was the son of a poor estate owner. Between 1762 and 1769 he served with the army, first as a common soldier and then as an officer. From 1784 to 1809 he occupied various high government positions.

D. combined the advocacy of monarchism and serfdom with liberal ideas on the welfare and happiness of the people. His fight against despotism and abuse of power brought about rapid changes in imperial favor and disfavor, and some regarded him as a tribune and defender of the people.

D.'s literary models were Lomonosov (1711–65) and Sumarokov (1718–77). In 1779 he started out on his own creative road;

he listened more carefully to the voice of his own genius, closely connected to life, than to poetic dogmas. He introduced Russian reality into the hitherto mostly traditionally classicist genres of his work.

The ode *Felitza* (1782), in which D. combined praise of Catherine the Great with criticism of her nobles and courtiers, is one of the first important examples of this modern method. D.'s anger at the abuses throughout the country reached a climax toward the end of the 1880s, and was expressed in his odes *Vlastitelyam i sudyam* [To the Rulers and Judges, 1787] and in *Valmozha* [The Dignitary, 1794]. His other poetic works reflect the good living and thoughts of the Russian nobility—*Priglasheniye k obedu* [An Invitation to Lunch, 1795]. Russian nature is depicted in *Osen vo vremya osady Ochakova* [Autumn during the Siege of Ochakov, 1788], and in *Vodopad* [The Waterfall, 1794], with surprising objectivity and in characteristic national colors.

D. was the first Russian poet to become interested in the complexity of his own personality as a poet, and to write of the aims, national significance, and relationship to environment of that personality. His poems on these themes include *Yevgeniyu. Zhizn Svanskaya* [To Eugene: The Life in Svanka, 1807], *Pamyatnik* [The Monument, 1795], *Lebed* [The Swan, 1805], and *Na ptichku* [On a Little Bird, 1792–93]. The national characteristics and the marked realism shown in D.'s work made him a pioneer of nineteenth-century Russian realism and a model for Pushkin.

Editions: Sochineniya [Works], 9 vols., St. Petersburg, 1864–83; *Stikhotvoreniya* [Poems], Leningrad, 1957; *Stikhotvoreniya* [Poems], Moscow, 1958

Dmitriyev, Ivan Ivanovich

Born September 21, 1760, Bogorodskoye (District of Kazan); died October 15, 1857, Moscow. Russian poet.

D., the son of an aristocratic estate owner, became an officer and held a high position in the civil service. At the age of seventeen he began to write poetry. His later works included translations from La Fontaine and other French authors.

D. was a follower of Karamzin; he actively supported K.'s efforts to rejuvenate Russian language and literature. He also became prominent as an exponent of sentimentality, and repeatedly attacked the new and inferior ode style, divorced from real life, that had developed in the climate of classicism. He stimulated and influenced Vyazemski, Zhukovski, and Batyushkov, although Pushkin did not value his work highly. D. endeavored to take his themes from life, and many of his poems exhibit features of fairy tale and fable. His poetic work in general, in both content and language, was closely connected with the life of the nobility.

Editions: Sochineniya [Works], 2 vols., St. Petersburg, 1895

DMYTERKO, LYUBOMYR DMYTROEVYCH

Born March 18, 1911, Vinniki (Galicia). Ukrainian Soviet poet, short-story writer, and dramatist.

D. was the son of a country schoolteacher. Between 1928 and 1929 he studied at the Institute of Adult Education in Kamenetz-Podolsk. In the 1930s he worked as a scriptwriter at a film studio in Kiev, and, following a period of active military service during World War II, has been working chiefly as a journalist and managing editor. Since the start of his literary career in 1928 D. has published numerous collections of poems, verses, short stories, and plays. His best-known poem, *Prysyaha virnykh* [The Oath of the Faithful, 1937], deals with the legendary civil war army leader Nikolai Shchors. D.'s literary talent is most evident in the field of lyric writing.

Editions: Vybrani tvory [Selected Works], Kiev, 1950; *Dramatychni tvory* [Dramatic Works], Kiev, 1958

DOBROLYUBOV, NIKOLAI ALEKSANDROVICH

Born February 5, 1836, Nizhni Novgorod; died November 29, 1861, St. Petersburg. Russian revolutionary democrat, political writer, and literary critic.

D. was the son of a village priest. He attended the theological seminary in Novgorod (1843–53) and the Institute of Pedagogy in St. Petersburg (1853–57). In 1856 he met Chernyshevski, who asked D. to work with him on the influential revolutionary democratic magazine *Sovremennik* [The Contemporary]. D. edited the literary section of this magazine until his death. Following in the steps of Belinski, and under the strong influence of Chernyshevski, D. became the leading revolutionary democratic literary critic of the 1860s.

The nucleus of D.'s materialist aesthetics—"realistic criticism"—is his demand for a realistic literature that is close to the people and that influences the course of social events of the time in an illuminating manner. Truthfulness and the depth of artistic presentation of reality represented for D. the decisive criteria in the evaluation of literary works. His essays belong to the classical achievements of Russian international literary criticism. They include *Chto takoye oblomovshchina?* [What Is Oblomovism?, 1859], *Kogda zhe pridyot nastoyashchi den?* [When Will That Day Finally Arrive?, 1860], which is about Turgenev's novel *Nakanune* [On the Eve], and *Luch sveta v tiomnom tzarstve* [A Ray of Light in the Realm of Darkness, 1860] (on Ostrovski's drama *Groza* [The Thunderstorm]).

P.'s literary criticism, together with the essays of Belinski and Chernyshevski, have profoundly affected the development of Russian realism. They represent a living tradition of socialist views on art and literature.

Editions: Sobraniye sochinenii [Collected Works], 9 vols., Moscow–Leningrad, 1961–65

DOLMATOVSKI, YEVGENI ARONOVICH
Born May 5, 1915, Moscow. Soviet Russian poet.

D. graduated from the Gorki Institute of Literature in 1937. His collection *Lirika* [Lyrics] appeared in 1934. D. participated in World War II, and his war poems are collected in the following volumes: *Pesnya o Dnepre* [The Song of the Dnieper, 1942]; *Stepnaya tetrad* [Notebook on the Steppe, 1943]; *Vera v pobedu* [Belief in Victory, 1944]; and *Stikhi iz daleka* [Poems From Far

Away, 1945]. D.'s most important work about the war is the poem
Propal bez vesti [Missing in Action], representing the first part
of the trilogy *Odna sudba* [A Fate], written between 1942 and
1946. D. has written the lyrics for numerous popular songs. He
was awarded the State Prize in 1950 for his collection of poems
Slovo o zavtrashnem dne [A Word on Tomorrow's Day, 1949].

Editions: Isbrannyye proizvedenii [Selected Works], Moscow, 1959

DONELAITIS, KRISTIJONAS

Born January 1, 1714, Lasdinelen (Prussian Lithuania); died
February 18, 1780, Tolminkemen. Founder and classic writer of
Lithuanian national literature.

D., the son of a free peasant, attended the Faculty of Theology
at the University of Königsberg from 1736. In 1743 he became
cantor and later minister in Tolminkemen.

D.'s works reflect a sweeping picture of the social contradictions
existing in Eastern Prussia during the second half of the eighteenth century. Himself originating from the working class, D.
was on the side of the exploited villeins and sharply and satirically
attacked the feudal and national oppressors, the German estate
owners and overseers, and their Lithuanian henchmen.

D.'s most important work is his classical poem *Metai* [The
Seasons], written in hexameters between 1760 and 1770. D. took
for his theme the rebellious peasant and clearly showed the moral
superiority of the latter over his masters. D. must be regarded as
one of the most important representatives of the so-called realism
of enlightenment.

*Editions: Das Jahr in vier Gesängen, ein ländliches Epos aus dem
Litauischen des Christian Donaleitis, genannt Donalitius, in gleichem
Versmaß ins Deutsche übertragen von D.L.J. Rhesa, Prof. d. Theol.*
[The Year in Four Songs: A Peasant Epos from Lithuania, by Chris-
tian Donaleitis, called Donalitius. Translated in the same meter into
the German by D.L.J. Rhesa, Professor of Theology (Incomplete first
edition of the *Metai*)], Köningsberg, 1818; *Christian Donaleitis,
Litauische Dichtungen. Erste vollständige Ausgabe mit Glossar von*

August Schleicher [Christian Donaleitis, Lithuanian Poetry. First complete edition, with a glossary by August Schleicher], St. Petersburg, 1865
Further Works: Prickaus posaka apie lietuviska, svodba.

DOROFEYEV, SAKHAR FIODOROVICH
Born April 5, 1890, Salasgar; died July 8, 1952, Moscow. Mordvian Soviet poet and teacher.
D. was one of the pioneers of Mordvian literature. His work includes the collection of poems *Songs and Thoughts of a Public-School Teacher*, published in 1912.

Editions: Es moroneke [My Songs], Moscow, 1925; *Izbrannoye* [Selected Works] (in Russian), Saransk, 1959

DOSTOYEVSKI, FIODOR MIKHAILOVICH
Born March 11, 1821, Moscow; died February 9, 1881, St. Petersburg. Russian novelist.
D. was the son of an army surgeon. He attended the school of engineering at St. Petersburg Military Academy between 1838 and 1843, and subsequently worked for two years in the Department of Engineering that was concerned with fortress construction. From 1845 on he devoted himself entirely to literature.
Living without funds in St. Petersburg, D. very early in his literary career experienced the humiliating position of the "intellectual proletariat" in an aristocratic, bourgeois society. His ideological development in the 1840s was influenced by the democratic and utopian socialist ideas of Belinski and Nekrasov, in which D. showed great interest. From 1847 he was a regular participant in the meetings held in the home of the revolutionary political writer Petrashevtski. D. was arrested in 1849 and sentenced to death; shortly before the execution, however, his sentence was commuted to four years of hard labor and four years of military service as a common soldier in Siberia, to be served subsequently. D.'s epileptic seizures, from which he had suffered all his life, greatly increased during his exile in Omsk (1850–54).

In 1854–56 D. served as a soldier in Semipalatinsk. He returned to St. Petersburg in 1859.

D. gradually turned away from his earlier socialist ideas, and he strongly opposed the revolutionary democrats Chernyshevski, Dobrolyubov, and Herzen. On his return to St. Petersburg D., together with his brother, published the magazine *Vremya* [Time], which existed between 1861 and 1863. This was followed, between 1864–65, by *Epokha* [Epoch]. D. sided with the oppressed classes in the 1860s, and remained critical of the tsarist state. He observed with increasing uneasiness the development of capitalism in Russia. He condemned the social inequalities and the moral decline of the ruling upper classes, but at the same time he professed more and more strongly the religious dogmas of the Russian Orthodox Church, in the name of which he demanded a "reconciliation" of the nation under the aegis of the tsar and the Orthodox Church. D. firmly believed that a reformation of Russian society was possible only by the moral self-improvement of the individual on the basis of Christian tenets; he categorically rejected all attempts at changing social conditions by the use of revolutionary methods.

In 1862–63 and again in 1867–71, D. traveled extensively in Western Europe, visiting Germany, France, England, and Italy. He was profoundly shaken by the capitalistic exploitation he observed there, and his anticapitalist views consequently became more pointed. His experiences in Europe, on the other hand, also increased his philanthropic illusions, especially his theory that the realization of a "universal brotherhood of man" was possible in Russia only if based on a religious groundwork.

In 1873 D. continued his political writings in the magazine *Grazhdanin* [The Citizen]. His *Dnevnik pisatelya* (1877, Diary of a Writer, 1954) appeared there. In it he explained his social, political, and aesthetic views which, during the last years of his life, were greatly influenced by K. P. Pobedonostzev, the reactionary chief dignitary of the Holy Synod. D.'s social theories reached a climax in his famous "Pushkin speech" given shortly before his death on the occasion of the Pushkin celebrations of 1880.

In his extensive literary work, D., in a manner unique in world literature, created the tragic fate of the insulted and degraded individual in an antagonistic society. He was the inexorable critic of bourgeois capitalism. At the same time, however, he opposed all the possible realistic solutions that could correct the social oppression and degradation of man. This deep conflict represents the key by which one can understand D.'s complex work—work in which a contradictory, realistic narrative encompasses both a pessimistic theory of life and an awareness of its bitter truth.

In his first literary work, the epistolary novel *Bednyye lyudi* (1845; Poor Folk, 1956), D.—following in the steps of Gogol—described the social tragedy of the "little man" in the tsarist city. This novel became the seminal work of the so-called Natural School. D. treated similar social problems in many of his early short stories, including *Dvoinik* (1846; The Double, 1958) and *Belyye nochi* (1849; White Nights, 1958). Such a problem was also the subject of his first great social novel *Unizhennyye i oskorblionnyye* (1861; The Insulted and the Injured, 1955). In *Zapiski is miortvovo doma* (1861; Notes from the House of the Dead, 1958), D. offered a deeply moving picture of convict life in Siberia, based on his own experiences. This work was the first literary description of forced labor in tsarist Russia.

With *Prestupleniye i nakazaniye* (1866; Crime and Punishment, 1958), D. began his cycle of great social novels, all of which attained the rank of classics in the field of world literature. In this work—"the greatest criminal story of all time" (Thomas Mann)—D. employed the stream-of-consciousness technique to reveal the problems of the murderer Raskolnikov. These problems demonstrated the complete bankruptcy of bourgeois individualism, of Napoleonic striving for power, and showed the antisocial ideology of the "superior" person. In *Podrostok* [The Young Man, 1875], D. condemned the uninhibited "Rothschildean" greed for money and the brutal laws of bourgeois society.

The decline of everything beautiful in aristocratic, bourgeois society was handled in D.'s novel *Idiot* (1868; The Idiot, 1958). In the figure of Prince Myshkin D. tried to contrast his positive utopian ideal of man with the depraved practices of the ruling classes. His novel *Besy* (1872; The Possessed, 1948), a malicious, biased presentation of the fight of the Russian revolutionaries, is a much weaker work from the artistic point of view. D. uses the problems of a declining family and of patricide as the basis for his unfinished novel *Bratya Karamazovy* (1880; The Brothers Karamazov, 1958). In this work he discussed the basic philosophical and ethical problems of his historic epoch. The flagrant ideological contradictions in D.'s mood are clearly in evidence in the latter work, which may be regarded as a summing up of his philosophy of life.

D.'s artistic genius combined the gifts of a brilliant psychologist with the intellectual profundity of the philosopher and the passionate vehemence of the political writer. His narrative work introduced numerous new methods of expression to literature, and, especially in his "many-stranded" novels, he has greatly enriched the genre of the realistic novel. D.'s work has exerted an extraordinary influence on the intellectual and literary development of all nations. Progressive literary experts see in the profound humanism of D.'s work a permanent, constantly relevant achievement.

Editions: Polnoye sobraniye sochinenii [Complete Works], 14 vols., St. Petersburg, 1904–06; *Sobraniye sochinenii* [Collected Works], 10 vols., Moscow, 1956–58
Further Works: Selo Stepanchikovo [The Village of Stepanchikovo] (1859); *Igrok* (1867; The Gambler, 1949)

DROSHCHIN, SPIRIDON DMITRIYEVICH
Born December 18, 1848, Niskova (District of Tver); died there December 24, 1930. Russian rural democratic poet.

After a long period of wandering, in 1849 D. settled in his home village of Niskova, where he lived a simple, peasant existence. His lyric writing developed under the influence of the democratic poetry of Nekrasov, Nikitin, and Surikov, among others.

D.'s main themes were life in his own village and the living

l.
N. A. Dobrolyubov
r.
F. M. Dostoyevski

l.
M. Dzhalil
r.
D. Dzhambul

I. G. Ehrenburg

conditions of artisans and workers in large cities; he also wrote of the Russian countryside. In his verses D. aroused the reader's compassion for the workingman, although he himself remained a prisoner of his patriarchal views.

Editions: Stikhi [Poems], Moscow, 1958

DRUTA (DRUTZE), ION

Born September 13, 1928, Khorodishte (Moldavian SSR). Moldavian Soviet short-story writer.

In his prose works D. writes of the village life of the Moldavian people. Based on D.'s own experiences, these works deal with the versatile moral and ethical problems connected with the history of his homeland. D. rapidly became known following the publication of the short-story collections *In Our Village* (1953) and *Stories About Love* (1954). His mature poetic style, his profound psychological analysis, and the freshness and humor of his language, which occasionally verges on the vernacular, are particularly in evidence in his short stories *Gheorghe the Son of the Widow* (1957) and *Longing for People* (1959).

Further Works: Casa mare (1960)

DUDIN, MIKHAIL ALEKSANDROVICH

Born November 20, 1916, Klenevo. Soviet Russian poet.

D. comes from a peasant family. He was a frontline correspondent during World War II, and it was at this time that he began to develop his individual poetic talent. His first collection of poems, *Liven* [Cloudburst], appeared in 1940. His work focuses on the active humanism and patriotism of the Soviet soldier.

D.'s poems written after the war take the life of postwar Europe for their subject, and are dedicated to the fight for peace.

Editions: Stikhotvoreniya. Poemy [Poems, Verses], Moscow, 1956; *Pesnya Voronei gory* [Song of the Crows' Mountain], Leningrad, 1964

DUDINTZEV, VLADIMIR DMITRIYEVICH
Born July 29, 1918, Kupyansk (in the region of Kharkov).
Soviet Russian novelist and short-story writer.
D. studied law. In the years between 1946 and 1951 D. wrote
for *Komsomolskaya pravda*. His novel *Ne khlebom yedinym*
(1956; Not by Bread Alone, 1957) has frequently been misin-
terpreted in the Western countries because in it D. presented a
realistic picture of the negative aspects of life under Stalin. D.
has also written short stories in which he tells of the life of the
Soviet worker, his feeling of solidarity, and his creative abilities.
These stories include *U semi bogatryrei* [With the Seven Heroes,
1951]. His allegorical story *Novogodnyaya skazka* [A New Year's
Fairy Tale] appeared in 1960 and was published in English the
same year as *A New Year's Tale*.

Editions: Povesti i rasskazy [Short Stories], Moscow, 1959

DUNIN-MARTZINKEVICH, VIKENTI IVANAVICH
Born in 1807, near Bobruisk; died July 17, 1884. Byelorussian
poet and dramatist.
D., who came from a noble family, was an estate owner and
civil servant. He wrote sentimental, didactic stories in verse about
life in the country. His realistic and satirical comedies pointedly
exposed both officialdom and the village bourgeoisie. Because of
their controversial content they were published only after the
revolution. They are among the most important works of Byelorussian literature.

Editions: Sbor tvorav [Collected Works], Minsk, 1958

DZHABARLY, DZHAFAR
Born March 22, 1899, Khisy, near Baku; died December 31,
1934, Baku. Azerbaidzhani Soviet poet, dramatist, and short-story
writer.
D. began to write in 1915, producing social dramas, short stories,
and satirical poems. An upswing in his work became evident once

he overcame certain bourgeois, nationalist influences after the victory of Soviet power.

In his effective dramatic works, which are distinguished by the sharpness of the conflicts and the vitality of the dialogue, D. takes the century-old fight of the Azerbaidzhani people for liberation as his theme. In *The Fire Bride* (1927), D. described the problems connected with the emancipation of the Azerbaidzhani women He depicted the revolutionary changes that took place in the life of the Azerbaidzhani village in *Almas* (1930) and *Jashar* (1932). D.'s work has exerted a marked influence on the development of the Azerbaidzhani Soviet drama.

Editions: Sechilmish asarlary [Selected Works], Baku, 1949; *Sechilmish pieslar* [Selected Letters], Baku, 1949

DZHALIL, MUSA

Born February 15, 1906, Mustafa (District of Orenburg); died August 25, 1944, Berlin-Spandau. Tatar Soviet poet.

D., who was the son of a poor peasant, graduated in 1931 from the Faculty of Literature of the University of Moscow. He was the editor of a number of Tatar magazines, and the cofounder of the Tatar State Theater for Opera and Ballet. Between 1939 and 1941 he was Secretary of the Writers' Union of the Tatar ASSR. In 1941 he joined the Soviet Army, and the following year was severely wounded in action and taken prisoner by the Germans. He was killed by the German fascists in 1944 for taking part in an illegal resistance group within the concentration camp.

Many of D.'s poems are dedicated to the Komsomols and the achievements of the Soviet people and their work. Early in the 1930s D. turned to the theme of the kolkhoz farmers and internationalism. His poem *Khat tashuchy* [The Letter Carrier, 1938] depicts Soviet youth at work. D. received a posthumous State Prize in 1948 for his opera libretto *Altyn chech* [The Girl with the Golden Hair, 1941].

D.'s war poems reflect optimism and his belief in an ultimate victory over fascism. Even imprisonment in a fascist concentration camp was unable to silence this honorable fighter and poet. More than one hundred poems written at that time and saved by other prisoners at considerable risk bear witness to the suffering, the courageous spirit, and the heroism of this poet.

D.'s *Moabit Diary*, which won him a posthumously awarded Lenin Prize in 1951, is a highly versatile work with respect to both genre and style. It represents a hymn to heroism, resistance, and the fearlessness of Soviet man. D. was proclaimed a Hero of the Soviet Union in 1956.

Editions: Izbrannoye [Selected Works] Moscow, 1955; *Izbrannoye* [Selected Works], Kazan, 1959; *Sochineniya* [Works], Kazan, 1963

DZHALIL, RAKHIM
Born June 3, 1909, Khodshand (now Leninabad). Tadzhik Soviet poet, novelist, and short-story writer.

D.'s first work was in the field of poetry, but he later turned to prose writing. Following the publication of his volume of poems *The Wave of Victory* in 1933, there appeared, among other works, the volume of short stories *The Dream* (1935), *Stories from the Time of War* (1944), and *The Second Life* (1949).

D. frequently employed a humorous, satirical style to depict the fight against the vestiges of the old life in Tadzhikstan as well as war and postwar problems. His most important works are the novels *Immortal People* (2 vols., 1949, 1956)—about the fight of the Tadzhik workers for the establishment of Soviet power—and *Miners* (1957).

Editions: Pulat and Gulru [Vol. I of *Immortal People*] (in Russian), Moscow, 1949; *Rasskazy* [Stories] (in Russian), Dushanbe, 1958
Further Works: Sana vbor (1938)

DZHAMBUL, DZHABAYEV
Born February 28, 1846, Semirechye; died June 22, 1945, Alma-Ata. Most important modern Kazakh folksinger (*akyne*) and poet.

In his prerevolutionary improvisations D. exposed the exploiters and brought about a rebirth of the *aitys* or folksinging contests. After the revolution D.'s work expressed the new feeling of so-

cialist life. Using newly improvised forms, he earned the approbation of the public with his patriotic poetic work of the war
period. D. was awarded the State Prize in 1941.

Editions: Ysh tomdyk shygharmalar shyinaghy [Selected Works], 3
vols., Alma-Ata, 1955; *Izbrannyye proizvedenii* [Selected Works] (in
Russian), Alma-Ata, 1958

DZHAMI, ABDUR-RAHMAN NURUD-DIN BIN AHMAD

Born November 7, 1414, Dzhami; died November 8, 1492,
Herat. The last important poet of classic Tadzhik and Persian
literature.

D. was a philosopher; a man "equal to anything that had happened before him and that was happening around him" (Goethe).
Despite the fact that he was a favorite at court, D. led the life
of a poor man of God. His numerous poetic works exhibit humanist, antidespotic attitudes, as well as some social, utopian
tendencies.

Further Works: Baharistan; Haft aurang

DZHANGAR

Kalmuck heroic epic of the fifteenth century.

This song extols the wondrous country Bumba, where eternal
happiness, contentment, and well-being prevail. It tells of the
deeds of the hero Dzhangar and his twelve noble companions,
who protect the land from the attacks of foreign armies.

This work has been transmitted by narrators in verbal form in
a number of variations. Two chapters were published in Russian
in 1854, and translated into German in 1857; the first complete
Russian edition appeared in 1940.

Editions: Dzhangar (in Russian), Moscow, 1958

DZHANSUGUROV, ILYAS

Born May 1, 1894, Aul No. 4 near Aksuisk; died 1938, Alma-
Ata. Kazakh poet, playwright, and novelist.

D., the son of a peasant, studied journalism between 1925–28.

His published verses and poems include *Dala* [The Steppe, 1930]; *Kyuishi* [The Musician, 1935]; and *Kulager* (1936), a legendary historic poem based on the life of the prerevolutionary singer Alcan. D. was also the author of one of the first Kazakh Soviet novels, *Goldastar* [Comrades, 1933]. He has also written plays and translated a number of the Russian classics.

Editions: Shyghamalar [Works], 4 vols., Alma-Ata, 1960–63; *Stikhi i poemy* [Verses and Poems], Moscow, 1962

DZHAVAKHISHVILI (Pseud. of *Mikhail Adamashvili*)
Born November 20, 1880, Zerakvi; died 1937. Georgian Soviet novelist and short-story writer.

D. came from a peasant family. He studied horticulture and viniculture in Yalta. He was active in journalism after 1904. Persecuted by the tsarist government, D. fled to Paris in 1907, where he studied literature and art. He traveled in Western Europe, North America, and Turkey before returning to his homeland in 1909.

D.'s short stories, novels, and romances exhibit the social conflicts existing in the declining old world, and the mentality of its representatives. These works include *Kvachi Kvachan tiradze* (1924), *Dshago's Refugees* (1924), and *The White Collar* (1926). The revolutionary events that took place in Tbilisi in 1905 are reflected in his novel *The Fate of a Woman* (1936). The novel *Arsen from Marabda* (1926–32), about the revolutionary peasant movement in Georgia in the first half of the nineteenth century, is of literary significance.

Editions: Rcheuli chsulebani [Selected Works], Tbilisi, 1958–59

EHRENBURG, ILYA GRIGORYEVICH
Born January 27, 1891, Kiev; died September 1, 1967, Moscow. Soviet Russian novelist and political writer.

E. was arrested at the age of sixteen for taking part in school strikes, but thanks to the intervention of his father was released on bail. He emigrated to Paris in 1908, returning to Russia in 1917. Between 1921 and 1928 he was a newspaper correspondent abroad, and in 1934 was a member of the Soviet delegation to the World Congress of Writers held in Paris. E. was a member of the Secretariat of the World Peace Council, and received the Lenin Peace Prize in 1952.

E. started to write in high school. His first collection of poems —*Stikhi* (1910)—chiefly contained verses written in Paris. These clearly showed the influence of Bohemianism. The experience of World War I, during which E. worked as a frontline correspondent, and of the October revolution, brought political and social problems into the foreground of his work.

In the 1920s E. published a series of novels on the inhuman nature of capitalism. Among these were *Neobyknovennyye pokhozhdeniya Khulio Khurenito . . .* (1922; The Extraordinary Adventures of Julio Jurenito . . . 1930); *Trest, D. E.* (1923); *Khronika nashevo vremeni* [A Chronicle of Our Times, 1929–30]; and *Yedninyi front* (1930). In these gripping novels which earned the immediate approbation of progressive readers in many countries, E. unmasked the hypocrisy of capitalist civilization and exposed the shameful greed of the capitalists. These early novels are distinguished by E.'s engrossing narrative style, by his masterly use of the grotesque and of hyperbole, and by his peculiar "telegraphic" style. This is particularly evident in *Khronika nashevo vremeni*.

In the 1930s E. concentrated on depicting Soviet life. His visit to the builders of Kusnetzk, among other things, helped him to overcome his previously rather one-sided view of the Bolshevists. His novels *Den vtoroi*, (1933–34; Out of Chaos, 1934) and *Ne perevodya dykhaniya* [Without Respite, 1935] vividly reflect the atmosphere of reconstruction current during the first Five-Year Plan.

Toward the end of the 1930s E., faced with the threat of war, again began to take as his subject themes from Western European politics, as is evident in his sketches *Ispanski sakal* (Tempered

Spain, 1938). His militant, rousing articles written during World War II earned the approbation of the public despite occasional exaggerations.

In the series of novels *Padeniye Parizha* (1941; The Fall of Paris, 1943), *Burya* [The Storm, 1949], and *Devyati val* (2 vols., 1952; The Ninth Wave, 1955), E. has given a panoramic view of the background and causes of World War II. In the short novel *Ottepel* (1954–56; The Thaw, 1955), E., in a polemic and highly pointed manner, treated the problems of overcoming the cult of personality. This novel is very controversial and, from the artistic point of view, far below the level of his other works.

In 1960 E. began to publish his memoirs *Lyudi, gody, zhizn* (1941–44; Memoirs: Childhood and Youth, 1891–1917 [1962]; First Years of Revolution, 1917–18 [1962]; Truce, 1921–33 [1963]; Eve of War, 1933–41 [1963]; The War, 1941–45 [1964]; Post-War Years, 1945–54 [1966]).

Editions: Sochineniyii [Works], 5 vols., Moscow, 1952–54
Further Works: Lyubov Zhanny Nei (1923; The Love of Jeanne Ney, 1930); *Lev na ploshchadi* [Lion in the Square] (1947)

ELLYAI (Pseud. of *Serafim Romanovich Kulachikov*)
Born November 29, 1904, Nizhne-Amginski (District of Tatta). Yakut Soviet poet and journalist.

In his poems, most of which are lyrically expressive, E. has treated actual problems arising from the development of the Yakut ASSR. These poems include his collection *Ahal sotzialismy* [Establish Socialism, 1934] and *Kyn sirin komyskeliger* [For the Defense of the Country of the Sun, 1943]. Many of his poems have become folksongs. E. has further developed the folklorist traditions of Yakut literature. His collection *Ayar y lehe aykhal* [The Glory of Work] appeared in 1959. E. also has prepared significant translations from the Russian of Pushkin, Mayakovski, and other authors.

Editions: Kihi-kihiekhe [Poems and Verses], Yakutsk, 1962

EMIN, FIODOR ALEKSANDROVICH
  Born in 1735, probably in the Ukraine; died in 1770. Russian novelist and publisher.
  E. spent many years abroad in Europe, Asia, and Africa. After 1761 he lived in St. Petersburg, working as a teacher, translator of adventure novels, publisher of the satirical magazine *Adskaya pochta* [Mail from Hell], and writer. His most important work is the epistolary novel *Pisma Ernesta i Doravry* [The Letters of Ernest and Doravra, 1766], which is based on the tragic love affair between the poor Ernest and the rich Doravra; it exhibits marked features of Russian sentimentalism.

FADEYEV, ALEKSANDR ALEKSANDROVICH
  Born December 24, 1901, Minry (Tver Province); died May 13, 1956, Moscow. Soviet Russian novelist.
  F. was the son of a teacher. He spent his childhood in a remote village in the Far East. He attended a commercial college in Vladivostok, and between 1921 and 1924 studied at the Moscow Mining Academy.
  From his early youth E.'s life was linked with the fight of the party and of the people. He joined the illegal Communist Party in Vladivostok in 1918, and between 1919 and 1921 fought with the partisans. In 1921 he participated in the Tenth Party Congress. He took part in the defeat of the Kronstadt mutineers and was severely wounded during these fights. As a student he was an active worker for the party, and from 1924 to 1926 took over responsible party functions in Krasnodar and Rostov.
  F. became known as a writer following the publication of his short stories *Protiv techeniya* [Against the Current, 1923] and *Razliv* [High Water]. With his novel *Razgrom* (1927; The Nineteen, 1929), he acquired the reputation of an important representative of Soviet literature. F. utilized his own Far Eastern experiences in this work, together with some of the best aspects of classical Russian literature. Tolstoi's psychological character analysis, Gorki's socio-realist style, and the traits of the youthful revolutionary Soviet literature all found their way into this modern

literary classic. *Razgrom* has as its subject the life and struggle of a small group of partisans. Their proving, their heroism, and their spirit of sacrifice are vividly shown in the individual fates of F.'s heroes. The leading role of the proletariat and of the party in both revolution and civil war, together with the development of the new personality within the collective are demonstrated in this novel. In it F. shows that bourgeois individualism and socialism are incompatible.

In his unfinished long novel *Posledni iz Udege* [The Last of the Udehes, 1930–40], the most complete edition of which appeared in 1957, F. continued the theme of the civil war in the Far East.

During World War II, F. exposed the unscrupulous nature of German fascism, and in appeals, sketches, and stories called on his countrymen to defend the socialist fatherland. His book *Leningrad v dni blokady* (1944; Leningrad during the Days of the Blockade, 1946) is dedicated to the heroism of the people of Leningrad, to their high moral qualities, and to Soviet patriotism in general. F.'s novel *Molodaya gvardiya* (1945; second version, 1951; The Young Guard, 1959) represents a permanent literary monument to the heroic fight of the Komsomol organization *Molodaya gvardiya*, and to the illegal work of the Bolsheviks in Krasnodar. F. here showed the great sacrifices the Soviet people had made in order to achieve victory over fascism, and "which qualities people must possess in order to win victory in such a war" (Simonov). F. first started this novel in 1943, but the discovery of new documentary material, together with certain criticisms that had been voiced against the first published version (1945), necessitated a total revision. The second version was published in 1951. The harmonious combination of tender lyricism, sensitive characterization, and calm, reportorial prose presents a convincing picture of the seemingly contradictory natures of the young guardsmen.

F. occupied a leading position in RAPP and later was President of the Soviet Writers' Union. In his capacity as creative artist, theoretician, organizer, editor and publisher, critic and adviser of young writers he greatly aided the development of this literature. F. was Deputy of the Supreme Soviet of the USSR., and a member of the Central Committee of the Communist Party of the Soviet Union. After the war F. was deeply involved in the work of the World Peace Movement. In his book *Za tridtzat let* [In Thirty Years, 1957], he has left a rich literary estate consisting of articles, essays, speeches, and letters on literature and art.

Editions: Sobraniye sochinenii [Collected Works], 8 vols., Moscow, 1958–60

FEDIN, KONSTANTIN ALEKSANDROVICH

Born February 24, 1892, Saratov. Soviet Russian novelist.

F. was interned in Germany during World War I. He lived mainly in Zittau, where he has also appeared as an actor. After the October revolution he edited various magazines, including *Kniga i revolyutziya* [The Book and the Revolution]. During the 1920s F. was close friends with Gorki, whose influence inspired his first literary activities. In his early stories, which are collected in *Pustyr* [Wasteland, 1923], F. dealt, above all, with the bourgeoisie, but in certain instances he himself slipped back into bourgeois, abstract-humanist sentiments.

F.'s first novel, *Goroda i gody* (1924; Cities and Years, 1960), made him known abroad. Here, in an individual and expressive form, he depicted the World War I period and the time of revolution. He was one of the first writers to expose the inhuman nature of German militarism, and to draw an eloquent picture of the people's wish for peace. At the same time he has also dealt with the question of humanism in the revolution. In *Bratya* [Brothers, 1928] he discussed the problems of art in revolution, and showed in the fate of the musician Karev the true perspective of a people-related, national art.

In the 1930s, in the face of the increasing dangers of war, F. took the various political storm centers in Western Europe as the background for his works. In *Pokhishcheniye Yevropy* [The Rape of Europe, 1933–35] F. compared the aggressive policies of Western European industrialists with the heroism of workers on

Soviet construction sites. His short novels *Ya byl aktiorom* [I Was an Actor, 1937] and *Sanatori Arktur* (Sanatorium Arktur, 1957) demonstrate the moral decline of capitalism.

The fate of Russia from the eve of the October revolution to the present time is treated in F.'s trilogy *Pervyye radosti* (1945; Early Joys, 1950), *Neobyknovennoye leto* (1948; No Ordinary Summer, 1950), and *Kostior* [Part One: The Flame, 1961]. In these works F. demonstrates in a masterful manner the complex and partly contradictory development of representatives of the different classes of the Soviet people, and gives an impressive picture of the great road traversed by them. At the same time, F. discusses, in a philosophical, generalized way, the question of the position of man in history as well as the mission of art in revolution.

In this trilogy, which is one of the most significant works of Soviet postwar literature, the revolution is characterized as an absolutely inevitable process, which without fail involves and determines the fate of the intelligentsia and that of each individual. The arts were given a new function by the revolution, which the representatives of the artistic intelligentsia had to work out for themselves.

F. is President of the Society for Soviet–German Friendship and since 1959 has been President of the Writers' Union of the USSR. He was awarded the State Prize in 1949, and the German Democratic Republic awarded him the Order of Merit in Gold in 1965.

Editions: Sobraniye sochinenii [Collected Works], 9 vols., Moscow, 1959
Further Works: Gorki sredi nas [2 vols., Gorki Among Us] (1941–44)

FET-SHENSHIN, AFANASII AFANASYEVICH
Born December 18, 1820, Novosyolki (District of Orel); died December 16, 1892, Moscow. Russian poet.

F. was influenced by Schopenhauer's philosophical ideas, and championed the theories of "pure art." Although F. restricted his work to the so-called eternal themes, he created nature poems and love lyrics of permanent value. These poems combined the realistic side of nature, down to her smallest details, with the depiction of true feelings and emotions.

The peculiar harmony and rising melody F. gave to his verses have inspired numerous composers, including Tchaikovsky, to set them to music. F. has translated many of the classic Roman writers as well as Goethe's *Faust*.

Editions: Polnoye sobraniye stikhotvorenii [Collected Poems], Leningrad, 1959

FIGNER, VERA NIKOLAYEVNA

Born July 7, 1852, District of Kazan; died June 15, 1942. Russian revolutionary and writer.

F. dedicated her life to the populist movement and to the secret revolutionary society *Narodnaya volya* [The People's Will]. She made various attempts to do away with tsarist autocracy by means of individual acts of terrorization, including one attempt to assassinate the tsar. Her memoirs *Zapechatlionnyi trud* [Stamped Labor, 1922] is one of the best biographies in Soviet literature. Here F. recounts in a deeply moving manner the history of the Russian revolutionary movement from 1875 to 1883. The work is also of F.'s twenty-year imprisonment in the fortress of Schüsselburg (1884–1904), and of her experiences during her first two years of liberty.

FIODORV, VASILI DMITRIYEVICH

Born February 23, 1918, Kemerovo. Soviet Russian poet.

F. studied at a school for aircraft engineering. His first volume of poetry, *Liricheskaya triogiya* [Lyric Trilogy], appeared in 1947. His poems are about love and nature as well as the new ideal of interhuman relationships.

Editions: Lesnyye rodniki. Poemy i stikhi [Forest Sources: Poems and Verses], Moscow, 1955; *Maryevskiye zwiozdy. Stikhi i poemy* [Daisy Stars: Verses and Poems], Novosibirsk, 1955

FIRDAUSI, ABDUL-QASIM MANSUR

Born 934 (?), near Tus (now Ferdous); died there 1020 (or 1025–26?). The most important epic poet of Persian-Tadzhik literature.

Using fragments from the *Daqiqi* and other written and verbal sources (national poetry), F. wrote the *Shah-Nameh* (The Epic of the Kings; Shah-nama, 1907), an immense heroic lay consisting of approximately 60,000 couplets. It describes the history of Persia—beginning in the mythological period (third century B.C.) and including the seventh century—in fifty poetic episodes of varying length.

Each of these poetic episodes deals with an individual hero or ruling dynasty. The epic achieves unity by its leading ideas. These are (1) the ultimate victory over the forces of evil (in mythology, history, and the present time), and (2) the belief in a strong and legitimate ruler who will reestablish the unity of all Persian tribes, thus doing justice to the great past of the country. The wars of conquest of these tribes represent the basic reason for the later division into Persian and Tadzhik branches.

The nucleus of the *Shah-Nameh* is formed by the sagas about the Persian national hero Rustam, who demonstrated his superhuman powers in war, hunting, and during gigantic feasts. Love scenes and lyric passages complement this national epic, which has few equals in world literature.

F. dedicated his work to Sultan Mahmud of Gasna, but it appears that the reward promised him for it was not forthcoming, possibly because by 1010 the Sultan's thinking had become Arabic-oriented. According to legend, harsh words were exchanged between F. and the sultan. F. is also said to have written a satire for which he lost favor at court. After many years of want and wandering, F. was pardoned shortly before his death, and returned to Tus. The poem *Jusuf and Suleikha*, which has been attributed to F., was in fact written only after 1083 by Amani.

Editions: Book of the Kings, tr. J. Atkinson (1832); metrical trans. A. G. Warner and E. Warner (9 vols., 1905–24)

FISULI, MOHAMMED SULEIMAN-OGLY
Born in 1498, Kerbela near Baghdad; died 1556. Most important Azerbaidzhani poet of the sixteenth century.

F. was born in Iraq, to which country his father had emigrated, and lived for the most part in Baghdad. He enjoyed an excellent and encyclopedic education. F. witnessed many bloody and rapacious attacks by the Turks on his people, and saw the most severe feudal oppression. F. sided with the simple Azerbaidzhani people, and already during his lifetime, as a result of his poetry, had earned their love and devotion.

F.'s lyric writings remain unsurpassed in the western Orient, and his ghazals and kassides, written in Azerbaidzhani, Persian, and Arabic, for a long time served as models for the Oriental lyric. Their popularity is due to the impressive way in which they present the sufferings of unselfish love, a love that is combined with a marked spirit of protest against the hardheartedness and cruelty of feudalism and the oppression of the free, human individual.

The climax of F.'s poetic work is the romantic poem *Leila and Madshnun*, a song in praise of worldly, optimistic love that is regarded as one of the most important works of Oriental poetry. Using a traditional subject—already treated earlier by Nisami—F. presented in this poem the tragedy of two lovers who cannot find happiness because of class distinction and prejudices. Keis, a talented poet, is made to suffer for his love for Leila, the daughter of a rich feudal ruler. But Leila remains true to her lover despite a forced marriage.

Profound sorrow, frankness, and the honesty of his accusations against autocracy and injustice at the court of the Turkish conqueror Suleiman characterize F.'s autobiographical work *Shikayet-name* (The Book of Indictment). This book represents the first work of Azerbaidzhani prose.

F. has enlarged and perfected both the content and the form of Azerbaidzhani poetry. His literary work represents a contribution to the development of the written Azerbaidzhani language.

Editions: Asarlary [Works], 2 vols., Baku, 1945–49
Further Works: Beng-u-bade, n.d.

FOMENKO, VLADIMIR DMITRIYEVICH
Born September 29, 1911, Chernigov. Soviet Russian short-story writer and novelist.

F. studied mechanical engineering, and graduated from a writers' school after taking correspondence courses. During the war F. was an officer in the armed forces; after the war he worked as teacher in a trade school.

F. has written sketches and stories about the kolkhoz farmers of the Don region, including *Obyknovenniye lyudi* [Unusual People, 1949]. His novel *Pamyat zemli* [(Vol. I, The Earth's Recollection, 1961] deals with the building of the Volga-Don canal as well as with the difficulties encountered by the farmers who settled in the steppes after leaving their old fertile fields.

Editions: Rasskazy [Stories], Moscow, 1954

FONVIZIN, DENIS IVANOVICH
Born April 4, 1749, Moscow; died December 12, 1792, St. Petersburg. Russian journalist and playwright; founder of realistic comedy and prose styles in Russia.

F., together with Novikov, became the ideologist and leading literary representative of Russian liberalism toward the end of the 1760s. The attention of the reading public was already caught by the accusatory tones of F.'s first literary works, the fable *Lisitza-Kosnodei* [The Fox as Preacher, 1762] and the *Poslaniye slugam moim Shumilovu: Vanke i Petrushke* [An Open Letter to My Servants Shumilov, Vanka, and Petrushka, 1763].

In 1769 F. wrote his first original comedy of manners, *Brigadir* [The Brigadier], about the Francophilia and lack of culture among the Russian nobility. Political essays, including *Rasuzhdeniye o nepremennykh gosudarstvennykh zakonakh* [Pamphlet on State Laws Required], begun in 1778, and the significant *Zapiski pervovo puteshestviya* [Notes on the First Voyage, 1777–78], about his voyage to France, consolidated F.'s position as an intelligent and fundamental opponent of absolutistic monarchism, and prepared the road to the climax of his work in the 1780s. F.'s greatest work, the immortal comedy *Nedorosl* [The Country Squire], appeared in 1782. It is a biting indictment of the basic evil of those times—serfdom. In this play Prostakova and Skotinin, two realistically presented Russian estate owners, are forced by Starodum, Pravdin, Sofya and Milon, the opponents of the serfdom order, to realize the limits of their powers.

In a series of intelligent articles—the well-known *Voprosy* [Questions, 1783], *Vseobshchaya pridvornaya grammatica* [A General Court Grammar, 1788; 2nd ed., 1830]—F. exposed the decadence at court, and opposed Catherine II in a manner that eventually forced her to show her true face as a despot. F. was prohibited from publishing both a satirical magazine, *Drug chestnykh lyudei, ili Starodum* [The Friend of Honest People, or Starodum, 1787–88], and his collected works (1788).

F. reformed the Russian literary language, and was a pioneer on the road to nineteenth-century realism in poetry, drama, and prose.

Editions: Sobraniye sochinenii [Collected Works], 2 vols., Moscow–Leningrad, 1959

FORSH, OLGA DMITRIYEVNA
Born May 28, 1873, in the Fortress of Gumi (Dagestan); died July 17, 1961, Leningrad. Soviet Russian novelist.

F.'s work of the 1920s and early 1930s showed some influences of symbolism. She deserves particular praise for her efforts in the development of the Soviet historical novel.

F.'s novel *Odetyye kamnem* [Palace and Prison, 1925] describes the tragic fate of the revolutionary Beideman. The trilogy *Radishchev*, written between 1934 and 1939, is dedicated to the eighteenth-century poet and to contemporary society. It also discusses the way in which Radishchev wrote his most famous work (*Journey from Petersburg to Moscow*). The Decembrist movement is treated in her novel *Perventzy svobody* (1953; Pioneers of Freedom, 1954).

Editions: Sochineniya [Works], 5 vols., Moscow, 1956
Further Works: Mikhailovski zamok [The Mikhailovski Castle] (1946)

FRANKO, IVAN YAKOVLYCH

Born August 27, 1856, Nahuyevychi (Galicia); died May 28, 1916, Lvov. Classic Ukrainian literary writer, literary historian, and critic; translator, and revolutionary democratic politician.

F., the son of a village blacksmith, attended high school in Drogobych; he then studied at the Faculty of Philosophy at the University of Lvov, but was forced to leave because of revolutionary activities as a result of which he was repeatedly arrested. F. subsequently went to Vienna where he studied under the well-known Slavic scholar Jagitsch, receiving a Ph.D. in 1893. He was, however, prevented from following a research career.

Under the influence of the Russian revolutionary democrats and of Shevchenko, F. developed from romanticist to critical realist. His extensive and thematically very versatile poetic work, which encompasses all literary genres, reflects an encyclopedic picture of the difficult life of the Ukrainian working people during the epoch of capitalism. F.'s love for his homeland and his socialist poetic ideals, which give a revolutionary perspective to his poetic statements, are fused in his collection of poems Z *vershyn i nyzyn* [Mountains and Valleys, 1887].

In his historical, philosophical poems, F. has given an optimistic answer to the question: In what direction are the Ukrainian people going? His poem *Ivan Vyshenskyi* (1900), which focuses on the figure of the famous Ukrainian poet of that name, has the idea of selfless service for one's homeland as its main theme. In the verse epic *Moisei* (1905; Moses, 1938) he took the biblical story as a symbol for the fate of his people.

F.'s prose works chiefly describe capitalistic exploitation and the beginnings of the organized proletarian class battles (*Boa Constrictor*, 1878; *Boryslav smiyetsya* [Boryslav Smiles], 1882). Numerous stories written by him deal with the fates of Ukrainian peasants forced to leave their native soil to become city proletariats. In his satirical short stories and fairy tales, F. exposed the parasitic life of the propertied upper classes. His peasant drama *Ukradene shchastya* [Stolen Happiness, 1894] is prominent among his dramatic works. His stories for children still enjoy great popularity.

F.'s literary work is one of the most mature cultural achievements of the Ukrainian people. It has decisively influenced the subsequent development of Ukrainian literature. F.'s translations of works from other national literatures (Shakespeare, Shelley, Byron, Calderón, Dante, Hugo, Goethe, Schiller, and other authors), as well as his translation of the works of Ukrainian poets, including Shevchenko, are of permanent literary value. F. prepared the first translations into the Ukrainian of the works of both Marx and Engels.

Editions: Tvoryi [Complete Works], 20 vols., Kiev, 1955–58
Selected English translations: Poems and Stories, Toronto, 1956

FURKAT (Pseud. *of Sakirdshan*)
Born 1858, Kokand; died 1909, Yarkand. Uzbekistanian democratic poet.

F. was educated in Kokand. From 1889 he lived in Tashkent, where he searched for links with Russian culture. F. became famous after the publication of his optimistic and gripping love lyrics, chiefly written in the form of the ghazal. F. was active in the development of a progressive Uzbek intelligentsia. After 1891 he undertook extensive travels through Turkey, the Balkans, India, and China, which he has described in travelogues.

FURMANOV, DMITRI ANDREYEVICH
Born November 7, 1891, Sereda (District of Kostroma, now Furmanov); died March 15, 1926, Moscow. Soviet Russian short-story writer and novelist.

F. studied in Moscow; during World War I he served as a medical corpsman. Between 1917 and 1918 he worked in the Soviet and, later, as party functionary in Ivanovo-Vosnesensk. In 1919 he joined the Red Army as volunteer, and was a political commissar in the famous Chapayev division. F. has made a significant contribution to the realization of the cultural policies of the party through his activities as secretary of the Moscow Union of Proletarian Writers (MAPP) and in the State Publishing House.

F. started writing while still young, but his actual literary career began only after the civil war. His works, which are largely based on diary notes, exhibit a historic, documentary, and, in part, autobiographical character; they reflect the various stages of the battles against the White Guards and interventionists. F.'s story *Krasny desant* [The Red Landing Party, 1921], tells of a successful raid against Wrangel. His novel *Chapayev* (1923; Chapayev, 1956) which is considered his most important work, is dedicated to the legendary national hero of that name and to the campaign of his division. *Myatezh* [Mutiny, 1925] deals with the defeat of the armed counterrevolutionary uprising in Verny (Alma-Ata).

F.'s works, in particular his novel *Chapayev*, have had a pioneering effect on Soviet Russian literature. F. was the first author who succeeded in presenting a popular hero in such a way as to show his characteristic complexity as well as his intellectual development in a convincing and unusual manner. He also was able to demonstrate the role of the party, in the figure of the commissar Klychkov, on a literary level previously not attained. F. also offered a versatile picture of the fight of the masses, and he accurately demonstrated the different degrees of maturity in the individual social groups and classes, as well the interactions of both spontaneous and conscious forces.

Editions: Sobraniye sochinenii [Collected Works], 4 vols., Moscow, 1960–61
Further Works: V vosemnadtzatom godu [In the Eighteenth Year] (1923)

GAFUR GULYAM (Pseud.: *Gafur Gulyamov*)
Born May 11, 1903, Tashkent; died July 10, 1966. Uzbekistanian Soviet poet and prose writer; member of the Uzbekistanian Academy of Sciences.

G. came from a poor peasant family. With his poem *Hamsa*, G. became the creator of a new Uzbek poetic and metric style. In his verses and prose writings, G. has commented on the social changes taking place in his homeland. His poem *Kukan* [Kukan the Farm Laborer, 1930] showed the development and influence of socialist man on the land. During World War II, G. became famous for his patriotic poems.

Editions: Izbrannyye stikhi [Selected Poems], Moscow, 1958

GAFURI, GABDULMASHIT

Born August 1, 1880, Yelem-Karamovo; died October 28, 1934. Bashkir-Tatar Soviet poet, novelist, and playwright; from 1923 People's Poet of the Bashkir ASSR.

B. was born into the family of a village schoolmaster; both his parents died when he was quite young. His literary activities commenced in 1902, when he began to write in the Tatar language. In 1906–07, he published collections of poems describing the oppression of his people and calling for the overthrow of autocracy. G.'s works were prohibited and in 1911 he was put under police surveillance. He nevertheless remained faithful to his views even after the defeat of the revolutionary movement in 1905–07.

During World War I G. in his poems appealed to the soldiers to fight for their liberty. His lyrics written during the times of the October revolution and the civil war became the foundation of Bashkir Soviet poetry. His collection of poems *Red Grapes* (1925) tells of the pride of the working man liberated from capitalist exploitation. His poems *The Workers* (1921), his autobiographical novel *In the Goldmines of the Poet* (1931), and his novel *Degraded Men* (1927) vividly reflect the hard life of the Bashkir and Tatar peoples before the revolution.

In addition to fables, G. wrote the play *Red Star* (1926). He was one of the founders of Bashkir children's literature.

Editions: Sochineniya [Works] (in Russian), 6 vols., Ufa, 1954–57

GAFUROV, ABUTALIB

Born November 21, 1882, Aul Shuni. Lakh Soviet poet.

G. comes from a peasant family. During the civil war he was a member of a partisan unit. His first poems appeared in 1932 in the magazine *Steps of the Revolution*. G.'s writing, which is

K. A. Fedin

A. Q. M. Firdausi

M. S. Fisuli

I. Y. Franko

D. A. Furmanov

Gaidar

V. M. Garshin

F. V. Gladkov

N. V. Gogol

I. A. Goncharov

closely connected with the life of the people, reflects the work of the kolkhoz farmers and their new life in their homeland. G.'s poetic talents became evident most clearly in his lyric poems *Lenin* (1932); *I Dedicate My Heart to My Friends* (1940); and *The Sun Follows Only One Road on This Earth* (1958). G. has enriched Lakh verses by the introduction of rhyme.

Editions: Inttu gava [Homeland Mountains], Makhachkala, 1960; *Svetly put* [The Light Road] (in Russian), Makhachkala, 1952

GAIDAR (Pseud. of *Arkadi Petrovich Golikov*)

Born January 22, 1904, Lgov (District of Kursk); killed in action on October 26, 1941, near Leplyava, and interred in Kanev (Ukraine). Soviet Russian writer of children's books.

G. was the son of a teacher. At the age of fourteen he fought in the Red Army; at sixteen he was a regimental commander. During World War II he was the frontline correspondent for *Komsomolskaya Pravda*. He volunteered to stay on as a machine-gunner with the partisans, and sacrificed his life in order to save a comrade. A monument in his honor has been erected on his tomb in Kanev on the banks of the Dnieper.

In his partly autobiographical prose work *Shkola* [The School of Life, 1930], G. described the difficult existence and the tests children had to go through during the years of the revolution. G. has had especially great success with difficult themes and genres —in particular novels portraying the development of character. He achieved his greatest success with his story *Timur i yevo komanda* (1940; Timur and His Squad, 1948), which has been adapted for the stage and screen. In this story, which delighted millions of children, the young hero Timur and his friends unobtrusively come to the aid of the family of a frontline soldier. G., who was able to enter into the imaginative world of children, and to inspire them with the life he presented, has greatly influenced the development of the entire Soviet children's literature.

Editions: Sobraniye sochinenii [Collected Works], 4 vols., Moscow, 1959–60

Further Works: RWS [RWS] (1926); *Dalnyye strany* [Far-Away Places] (1932); *Voyennaya taina* [War Secret] (1935); *Chuk i Gek* [Ghuk and Gek] (1939); *Sudba barabanshchika* [Fate of the Drummer Boy] (1939)

GALIN (Pseud. of *Boris Abramovich Rogalin*)

Born September 7, 1904, Nikopol. Soviet Russian journalist and short-story writer.

G. has been publishing short stories since 1925. In the 1920s and 1930s, he worked as special correspondent for *Pravda*; during World War II he was a correspondent for the magazine *Krasnaya Zvezda* [Red Star].

G.'s collection *V. Donbase* [In the Donbas Region] appeared in 1946, and in 1967 he was awarded the State Prize for his collection of sketches *V odnom naselionnom punkte* [In a Settlement]. In his sketches contained in the collections *Sim pobedishi* [With This You Shall Be Victorious, 1957] and *Stritel novovo mira* [Architect of a New World, 1960], G. described the fate of people who met Lenin and then patterned their lives after him.

Editions: Vsegda za mechtoi, Ocherki [Always Following a Dream. Sketches], Moscow, 1964

GAMSAKHURDIA, KONSTANTIN

Born May 15, 1891, Abasha. Georgian Soviet novelist.

The son of a nobleman, G. attended high school in Kutaisi and later studied in Königsberg, Munich, and Berlin, where he took a Ph.D. degree in 1919. After his return to Russia, G. guided the literary "academic association." The modernistic tendencies still evident in his first works, including his collection of short stories *The Land* was overcome by G. in his three-part novel on the problems of collectivization, *Abduction of the Moon* (1935–36). G. also described developments taking place in the country during the 1930s and 1940s in his novel *The Flowering of the Vine* (1956). G. also wrote historical novels on medieval Georgia, including the tetralogy *Davit IV the Founder* (1946–58) which is about the eleventh-century battles for national unification.

GAMZATOV, RASUL

Born September 8, 1923, Zada (District of Khunsakh); Avar. Soviet poet; People's Poet of Dagestan since 1959; son of the poet Gamzat Zadasa.

G. worked as a teacher; between 1945 and 1950 he studied at the Gorki Institute of Literature in Moscow. G. began his literary activities in 1937, and his first collection of poems appeared in 1943. His war poems tell of the heroic deeds of Dagestan soldiers. After the war, G. published a number of poems and verses reflecting life in socialist Dagestan.

G.'s work has reflected the changes in the psychology of the mountain dwellers in the northeastern parts of the Caucasus. He shows how the new generation breaks old customs, and how the young people fight for their right for love and for the equality of women. G. extolls the beauty of his people and their development under the new socialist conditions, depicting with great and vivid talent the life, the people, and the nature of his homeland.

G., one of the most important representatives of multinational Soviet poetry, was awarded the State Prize in 1952 for the poems and verses collected in *My Year of Birth* (1950); he received the Lenin Prize in 1963 for his collection of poems *High Stars* (1962).

Editions: Lirika [Lyric Writings], Moscow, 1954; *Stikhotvoreniya* [Poems], Moscow, 1956; *Stikhotvoreniya* [Poems], Moscow, 1958; *Poemy* [Poems], Moscow, 1960; *Goryanka* [The Mountain Woman], Moscow, 1963

GARSHIN, VSEVOLD MIKHAILOVICH

Born February 14, 1855, Priyatnaya dolina (District of Yekaterinoslav); died April 5, 1888, St. Petersburg. Russian realistic novelist.

G., who came from an impoverished noble family, attended high school in St. Petersburg. In 1874 he began to study at the Mining Academy; he left, however, in order to volunteer for the Russo-Turkish war (1877–78). He was wounded during the war, and after his return dedicated himself entirely to his literary activities.

His first writing was done in the 1870s in the circle of democratic writers around Saltykov-Shchedrin.

The life of this sensitive poet was overshadowed by a severe nervous disorder. In the 1880s, aggravated by the atmosphere of tsarist repression against progressive writers, this illness became more pronounced, and finally led to G.'s suicide.

G.'s literary work includes a few short stories and fairy tales. The dominating themes of these works are the social contradictions existing in the Russia of his time and their effects on the intellectual and psychological state of the simple person. Among his best-known works are the autobiographical antiwar stories *Chetyre dnya* [Four Days, 1877], and *Is vospominanii ryadovogo Ivanova* [From the Reminiscences of Private Ivanov, 1883], *Khudozhniki* [Artists, 1879], and the socially critical story *Krasnyi tzvetok* (1883; The Scarlet Flower, 1959), which has been justly regarded by G.'s contemporaries as a song in praise of the unselfishness and heroism of the revolutionaries.

Laconic conciseness and allegoric and symbolic forms of expression are the particular characteristics of G.'s individualistic prose, which has enriched the novel of critical realism with numerous new ideas.

Editions: Sochineniya [Works], Moscow–Leningrad, 1960

GARTNY, TISHKA (Pseud. of *Smitzer Khedaravich Shylunovich*)
Born November 4, 1887, Kopyl; died April 11, 1937. Byelorussian Soviet poet, dramatist, and novelist.

G. was the son of a poor peasant; he took part in the revolution of 1905–07. In 1919 he headed the new Soviet government of Byelorussia; he later became a leading editor and cultural educator. G. has written lyrics, prose, and dramas, and has also been prominent as a political writer and literary critic. His first collection of poems was published in 1913. His novel *Soki tzaliny* [Sap of the Virgin Lands, 1914–29], which has as its theme the development of revolutionary awareness in the Byelorussian people, is regarded as his main work. G.'s stories written during the 1920s describe civil war events and the development of new aspects of Byelorussian man under Soviet power.

Editions: Sbor tvorav [Collected Works], 4 vols., Minsk, 1929–32; *Vybranyye apavyadanni* [Selected Works], Minsk, 1962

GASTEV (Pseud. of *Aleksei Kapitonovich Dosorov*)

Born October 8, 1882, Susdal; died 1944. Soviet Russian poet and scientist.

G. was the son of a teacher. Because of his revolutionary activities he was repeatedly arrested and exiled; he fled abroad to Paris a number of times. G.'s literary activities commenced around 1900 with poems and short prose pieces. *Poeziya rabochevo udara* [Poetry from the World of the Worker], extolling the world of work and machines in both poetry and rhythmic, hymnic prose, appeared in 1918. After the revolution G. was chiefly occupied with the scientific study of labor methods and problems.

Editions: Poeziya rabochevo udara [Poetry from the World of the Worker], Moscow, 1964

GERASIMOV, MIKHAIL PROKOFYEVICH

Born October 12, 1889, Buguruslan; died 1939. Soviet Russian poet.

G. was the son of a railroad worker; at the age of sixteen he was a member of the Russian Social Democratic Workers' Party. After having been arrested several times he fled to western Europe where he lived as an emigrant for nine years. His first poems appeared in 1913. A period of intense literary activity began in 1918.

G. wrote poems and stories in which he attempted to transpose the ideas of the socialist revolution—which he extolled in hymnic verses—into cosmic terms. G. was a leading representative of the Russian Proletcult and organizer of the Moscow writers' association *Kuznitza* [The Forge]. He dealt with the theme of socialist reconstruction in his volumes of poems *Zemnoye siyaniye* [Earthly

Lustre, 1927], *Bodroye utro* [A Fresh Morning, 1928], and *K sorevnovaniyu* [Come on to the Contest! 1930].

Editions: Stikhotvoreniya [Poems], Moscow, 1959

GERMAN, YURII PAVLOVICH
   Born April 4, 1910, Riga; died January 16, 1967, Leningrad. Soviet Russian novelist.
   G.'s literary activity began in 1926. His novel *Vstupleniye* [The Beginning, 1931] describes the fate of a bourgeois scientist who develops into a fighter for social justice. His novel *Bednyi Genrikh* [Poor Henry, 1934] deals with the Germany of the 1920s. The novel *Nashi-znakomyye* [Our Acquaintances] was written in 1934–36; it considers the problems of overcoming bourgeois individualism. Similar themes have been dealt with in G.'s short stories *Lapshin* and *Aleksei Shmakin* (1937–38), which were later adapted to become the novel *Odin god* [One Year, 1960]. G.'s novels *Delo, kotoromu ty sluzhish* [The Cause You Are Serving, 1957] and *Dorogoi moi chelovek* [My Beloved One, 1961] demonstrate the process of intellectual and moral development of complex characters.

Further Works: Syn naroda [Son of the People] (1934); *Rossiya molodaya* [Young Russia] (1952)

GESERIAD (THE GESER SAGA)
   A saga known all over Central and Eastern Asia (Buryatia, China, Mongolia, Tibet) that has come down to us in written form with many variations.
   This great saga developed between the tenth and the seventeenth centuries. It relates the heroic deeds of Geser-Khan, a just ruler close to his people, who was sent to earth in order to make an end to the oppression of the weak, and who fought against natural and supernatural powers hostile to man. Different variations of the Buryat G. contain up to 30,000 verses, and they all are distinguished by their natural color and wealth of form.

Editions: Arban Züg-ün ezen Geser cha'an-u tu'udshi oroshiba [The Story of Geser-Khan, the Ruler of the Ten Regions], Peking, 1956

GIRA, LIUDAS

Born August 27, 1884, Vilnius; died there July 1, 1946. Lithuanian Soviet poet.

G. came from the family of a minor civil servant. During the first years of his literary activity, he worked with the liberal bourgeoisie. In the 1930s he became interested in Soviet Russia, and, with the establishment of Soviet power in Lithuania, soon followed the road of the socialist artist.

G. takes the heroic fight against the fascist invaders as his theme in his collections of poems *Zalgirio Lietuva* [Greenwood Lithuania, 1942] and *Smurtas ir ryztas* [Force and Determination, 1942]. G. was People's Poet of the Lithuanian SSR.

Editions: Rinktine [Selected Works], Vilnius, 1958; *Raštai* [Works], Vols. 1–5, Vilnius, 1960–62

GLADKOV, FIODOR VASILYEVICH

Born June 21, 1883, Chernavka (District of Saratov); died December 20, 1958, Moscow. One of the first important Soviet novelists.

G. was born of peasant stock. He was an apprentice in various trades and for a number of years held a teaching position. In 1906 he became a member of the Russian Social Democratic Party. G. was exiled for three years because of his revolutionary activities. He fought in the Red Army during the civil war.

His first short story *K svetu* [Toward the Light] was published in 1900. G.'s prerevolutionary works mostly portray—in a somewhat naturalistic manner—the miserable life in the villages and the life of "the barefooted ones" and of the exiled. His novel *Tzement* (1924; Cement, 1929) made him world famous. It was the first important novel to deal with the building up of heavy industry in the Soviet Union under incredibly difficult conditions. G.'s hero Gleb Chumalov reflects the fervor, the heroism, and the romanticism of free creative work.

The novel *Energiya* [Energy, Vol. I, 1933; Vol. II, 1939] demonstrates the movements of the people during the first Soviet Five-Year Plan. G.'s final work is a four-part autobiographical novel on poverty in the old Russian village and in the fisheries: *Povest o detstve* (1949; Restless Youth, 1955); *Volnitza* [The Day Laborer, 1950]; *Likhaya godina* [Bad Times, 1954]; and the incomplete *Myatezhnaya yunost* [Stormy Youth]. Following in the Gorki tradition, G. created a grandiose painting of the life of the Russian people before the revolution.

Editions: Sobraniye sochinenii. [Collected Works], 8 vols., Moscow, 1958–59
Further Works: Novaya zemlya [New Land] (1932)

GLEBKA, PYATRO FYODARAVICH
Born July 6, 1905, Vyalikaya Usa (District of Minsk). Byelorussian Soviet lyric poet.

G. was born into a peasant family. He has been a member of the Academy of Sciences of the Byelorussian SSR since 1956, and is Director of the Institute of the Science of Art, Ethnography, and Folklore.

G.'s literary activities commenced in 1925 with the writing of poems and verses, which have been collected in the volume *Shypshyna* [The Rose Bush, 1927]. The poem dedicated to Lenin, *Muzhnastz* [Courage, 1934], and the poem *U tyya dni* [In Those Days, 1937], which is about the October revolution, represent G.'s most important works. During World War II, G. wrote moving poems and ballads with themes drawn from wartime events. He has also translated Pushkin, Shevchenko, Gorki, and other Russian authors into Byelorussian.

Editions: Sbor tvorav [Collected Works], 2 vols., Minsk, 1958

GNEDICH, NIKOLAI IVANOVICH
Born February 13, 1784, Poltava; died February 15, 1833, St. Petersburg. Russian poet and translator of Homer.

G. came from the family of a poor Ukrainian Cossack. Against the wishes of his parents, G. went to study in Moscow; in 1802 he moved to St. Petersburg, where his literary activities began. G. continued the political and patriotic traditions of eighteenth-century humanist literature in his early drama translations (Schiller's *Verschwörung des Fiesko*, 1803; Voltaire's *Tancrède*, 1807) and in poems such as *Obshchezhitiye* [The Community, 1804], and *Peruanetz k ispantzu* [A Peruvian to a Spaniard, 1805].

G. became the teacher of the Decembrist poets with his stylistically more interesting poem *Rozhdeniye Gomera* [The Birth of Homer, 1816], the idyll *Rybaki* [The Fisherman, 1821], and, in particular, with his passionate *Rech o naznachenii poeta* [A Speech on the Poet's Mission]. His most important work, however, was his translation of Homer's *Iliad* (1807–32), the "spirit, divine simplicity and plastic beauty" (Belinski) of which G. captured in a masterful manner.

Editions: Stikhotvoreniya [Poems], Leningrad, 1856

GOGOL, NIKOLAI VASILYEVICH

Born April 1, 1809, Velikiye Sorochintzy (District of Poltava); died March 4, 1852, Moscow. Classic writer of Russian literature; cofounder of critical realism.

G. came from an art-loving Ukrainian family of estate owners; he attended school in the governmental city of Poltava between 1818–19; in 1821–28 he studied at the high school in Neshin, where he already attracted notice because of his marked literary tendencies. Planning to enter government service, G. went to St. Petersburg toward the end of 1828; despite temporary employment as a government clerk he failed to gain a permanent appointment, and his literary debut with the romantic, idyllic poem *Hans Kuchelgarten* (1829) met with little success. During the following years of want and privation, G. learned at first hand of the misery of the poorer classes. Occasional work as a teacher or actor did little to alleviate his difficult position, which changed only slightly when he was appointed assistant lecturer in general history at the University of St. Petersburg. G. first came to the attention of the reading public in 1832 with his volume of short stories about the life of the Ukrainian people. By 1835 he had dedicated himself completely to the pursuit of his literacy activities.

Strongly supported by both Pushkin and Belinski, G. finally gained recognition as a critical, realistic writer during the second half of the 1830s. The progressive forces in Russian society in particular saw in G.'s poetic works the model of social accusatory literature.

From 1836 on G. lived mostly abroad, in Italy, France, and Switzerland, where he increased his contacts with conservative writers from Slavophile circles. These writers greatly influenced G.'s ideologic development, and finally alienated him from the democratic movement centered around Belinski. The reactionary ideas in G.'s works increased in the 1840s. He attempted to solve the intellectual crisis this development produced in his thinking by turning more and more toward religious mysticism. To the same extent in which G. professed the ideal of a patriarchal Russia —the foundations of which, of course, were autocracy, serfdom, and the Orthodox Church—he became reconciled with the feudal society he had previously criticized in such an unmerciful manner.

G.'s reactionary social utopias are clearly evident in his book *Vybrannyye mesta is perepiski s druzyami* [Selected Passages from Correspondence with Friends, 1847], which was read with indignation by the progressive Russian public. Belinski's appeal to G. to give up his disastrous flight into the past (*Letter to Gogol*, 1847) had no noticeable effect.

After first undertaking a pilgrimage to Jerusalem, G. finally returned to Russia in 1848, where he came even more definitely under the influence of religious, mystic sentiments. In a state of emotional depression, G. destroyed the manuscript of the second volume of his great novel *Miortvyye dushi* (Dead Souls), and only a few chapters were accidentally saved. G. died in complete poverty, alone and mentally deranged.

G.'s early work was romantic in nature. In *Vechera na khutore bliz Dikanki* (1831–32; Evenings on a Farm Near Dikanka, 1926), a volume of stories from his Ukrainian homeland, G. portrayed the lighthearted, untroubled world of the Ukrainian village, and described the beauty and poetry to be found in the life of the simple people. *Mirgorod*, also a volume of Ukrainian village stories, appeared in 1835 at approximately the same time as *Taras Bulba* (Taras Bulba, 1957), a historical story about the fight of the Ukrainian people for liberation from Polish rule. The latter work demonstrates a new phase in G.'s *œuvre*, since he then began to view his social environment in a critical and realistic manner. G.'s so-called St. Petersburg stories contain marked social criticism; these particular stories appear in the volume *Arabeski* [Arabesques, 1835], which also includes a number of essays on history and the theory of art.

In *Nevski Prospekt* and *Zapiski sumashedshevo* (The Diary of a Madman, 1945), G.—following Pushkin—treated the theme of the "little man," a theme he had also used in his novel *Shinel* (1842; The Overcoat, 1957), in a highly artistic manner. Showing great sympathy for his literary hero, G. in the latter novel portrayed the tragic fate of a hardworking minor official who founders on the social contradictions of the aristocratic, bureaucratic order. This work became a biting indictment of the heartless, antisocial tsarist system.

G. continued his realistic, critical exposure of aristocratic society in the comedy *Revizor* (The Inspector General, 1956), which he wrote in 1836 in response to a suggestion made by Pushkin. The play made all the apparatus of tsarist autocracy appear destructively ridiculous. The staging of this comedy became a memorable event in the social life of the Russian public.

G.'s greatest work, the epic novel *Miortvyye dushi* (Vol. I, 1842; Dead Souls, 1951), presents a picture of Russian everyday life in which feudal Russia appears as a land of putrefaction and disintegration. In this novel G. contrasted the satirically drawn estate owners and civil servants—impressive members of the parasitic, declining system—and the profiteer Chichikov—the representative of rising capitalism—with the industrious and freedom-loving Russian people. The poet, who sides with the simple people, with their inexhaustible but slumbering energies, endows the novel with permanent national significance.

G.'s aggressive satire, which is based on an individual linking of comic and tragic elements, his outstanding presentations of character, and his extraordinarily strong linguistic means of expression have made this poet's work a classic in the history of world literature.

G.'s work has affected the subsequent development of Russian realism in a decisive manner. The Natural School came into being in the 1840s under the direct influence of his critical realistic principles of creative writing. G.'s works have been translated into all modern languages.

Editions: Polnoye sobraniye sochinenii [Complete Works], 14 vols., Moscow–Leningrad, 1940–52; *Sobraniye sochinenii* [Collected Works], 6 vols., Moscow, 1959

GOLODNY, MIKHAIL (Pseud. of *Mikhail Semyonovich Epstein*)
  Born December 24, 1903, Bakhmut (now Artyomovsk); died January 20, 1949, Moscow. Soviet Russian poet.

G. studied at the Bryusov Institute of Literature and Art in Moscow. In the 1930s G. wrote ballads and songs permeated by revolutionary and romantic fervor. These, including *Kazn kommunista v Berline* [The Execution of a Communist in Berlin], had as their themes the heroes of the civil war and the communist resistance in Germany. Some of G.'s works have been set to music. His collection of songs, *Pesni i ballady Velikoi Otechestvennoi voiny* [Songs and Ballads on World War II, 1942], is dedicated to the heroism of the Soviet people during the war.

Editions: Izbrannoye [Selected Works], Moscow, 1956; *Stikhotvoreniya, Ballady, Pesni* [Poems, Ballads, Songs], Moscow, 1959

GONCHAROV, IVAN ALEKSANDROVICH
  Born June 18, 1812, Simbirsk (now Ulyanovsk); died September 27, 1891, St. Petersburg. Russian realistic novelist.

G. came from the family of a rich merchant with noble connections. He studied philology in Moscow (1831–34) and then became a civil servant in St. Petersburg (1835–67). His quiet life as a civil servant was interrupted only by a number of voyages to his homeland and to western Europe. In 1852–55, G. participated in a circumnavigation of the globe, which he has described in his travelogue *Fregat Pallada* (1858; The Voyage of the Frigate *Pallada*, 1965). This journey around the world was undertaken by him in an enlightened, liberal, and democratic spirit. Toward the end of his life G.'s conservative tendencies, especially in his social and political views, became more marked.

G.'s literary activities commenced in the 1830s under the influence of Pushkin and Gogol, and in response to the stimulation he received in the St. Petersburg salon of the painter N. A. Maikov. His early stories—*Likhaya bolest* [A Bad Illness, 1838] and *Shchastlivaya oshibka* [A Happy Error, 1839]—dealt with the unworldliness and weaknesses of the epigones of Russian romanticism. With his physiological sketch *Ivan Savvich Podshabrin* (1842, published in 1848), G. formed a link with realism, and he contributed to the formation of the Natural School. In his first novel, *Obyknovennaya istorya* (1847; The Same Old Story, 1957), G. showed the transformation of a romantically idealistic young noble from the provinces into a practical, cold profiteer under the influence of advancing capitalism.

G. published his most important novel, *Oblomov* (1859; Oblomov, 1953), in 1859. The title figure, Ilya Oblomov, is a masterful social-psychological study of a characteristic representative of the declining Russian nobility. G. contrasted the weak-willed, idle Oblomov with the venturesome, energetically proud Olga, filled with efficiency and unselfish love. In Oblomov G. created the prototype of an intelligent, sympathetic person who develops into a useless idler because of the complete inability of his class to function. Both Dobrolyubov and Lenin have drawn attention to the general significance of this figure.

In his last novel, *Obryv* (1869; The Precipice, 1916), G. depicted, in the painter and writer Raiski and in the figure of Vera, the conflicts existing between the old truths of the patriarchal noble society and the new truths of the socialist revolutionary movement. In the character of Volokhov, G. gave a highly distorted picture of revolutionary youth, for which he was sharply criticized by progressive circles.

The value of G.'s work lies in his realistic descriptions of Russian rural conditions and of the characteristic nature of the Russian people. The three novels mentioned have been regarded by G. as representing a trilogy in which he presented the social development of Russia in the period of transition from feudalism to capitalism. As a result of the divided reception given his novel *Obryv*, by the 1870s G. had largely retired from literary life. He did, however, write a number of valuable critical essays on literary subjects, as well as his memoirs. Prominence may be given to the following works: *Milion terzanii* [A Million Agonies, 1872], an excellent analysis of Griboyedov's comedy *Gore ot uma* [Intelligence Causes Sufferings]; *Literaturnyi vecher* [A Literary Evening, 1877]; and *Luchshe pozdno, chem nikogda* [Better Late than Never, 1879]. An important discussion of his realistic views on art is given in *Zametki o lichnosti Belinskovo* [Remarks on Belinski's Personality, 1881].

Editions: Polnoye sobraniye sochinenii [Complete Works], 9 vols., St. Petersburg, 1886–89; *Sobraniye sochinenii* [Collected Works], 8 vols., Moscow, 1952–55
Further Works: Vospominaniya [Memoirs] (1887–88); *Slugi starovo veka* [Servants of the Old Age] (1888)

GORBATOV, BORIS LEONTYEVICH
Born July 15, 1908, in the Donbas region; died January 20, 1954, Moscow. Soviet Russian novelist.

G. began his literary activities in 1922. Most of his work was concerned with the life of the working youth, including *Yacheika* [The Cell, 1928] and the autobiographical novel *Moyo pokoleniye* [My Generation, 1933]. His cycles of stories *Komintern* (1932) and *Mastera* [The Masters, 1933] deal with the same theme. The action of his novel *Nepokorionnye* [The Inflexible Ones, 1943], for which he received the State Prize in 1946, takes place during the fascist occupation of the Donbas, and G.—using in some instances forms close to folklore—describes in it the life of a worker family and the general fate of the Soviet people during the war. *Nepokorionnye* was translated into twenty-six languages. The unfinished novel *Donbas* (Part I, 1951) describes the formation of the innovator movement of the 1930s. G. also wrote a book on his adventures in the Arctic, *Obyknovennaya Arktika* (The Usual Arctic, 1937–38).

Further Works: Nash gorod [Our City] (1930); *Donetzki shakhtiory* [The Don Miners] (1950)

GORKI, MAKSIM (Pseud. of *Aleksei Maksimovich Peshkov*)

Born March 28, 1868, Nizhni Novgorod (now Gorki); died June 18, 1936, Gorki, near Moscow. Leading Soviet Russian novelist, dramatist, and essayist; founder of the literature of socialist realism.

G. was the son of a carpenter; he was early orphaned and spent his childhood in a depressingly bourgeois environment. At the age of ten, following a brief period of schooling, G. was forced to gain his own living working among strangers.

G. came into contact with progressive forces in Kazan, and began to develop into a revolutionary. In 1891 he started an extensive trip across Russia, the Ukraine, the Crimea, and the Caucasus in order to learn more about the Russian people. In 1892 in Tbilisi he published his first short story, *Makar Chudra*, using the pseudonym M. Gorki (The Bitter One). In the course of the next few years, G., aided by V. G. Korolenko (1853–1921), wrote numerous sketches and short stories.

Seen from the point of view of the developing working class, G.'s early work presents a true picture of Russian society during the last decades of the nineteenth century. He indicated the inhumanity of the existing order in *Na Soli* [Salt, 1893], *Suprigi Orlovy* (1897; The Orloff Couple, 1901), *Byvshiye lyudi* (1897; Creatures That Once Were Men, 1901), and *Ozornik* [The Lout, 1897]. In these and other works G., drawing his characters from the ranks of the common people, depicted their moral qualities, their awakening sense of protest, and their striving for a better life. In other stories he wrote of the intellectual discontent and the decline of representatives of the ruling classes—*Kolokol* [The Bell, 1895] and *Toska* [Loneliness, 1896]. G.'s revolutionary, romantic stories, songs and legends extol the self-confident, strong figure fighting for his own liberty and for that of his people. *Pesnya o sokole* [The Song of the Falcon, 1895], *Starukha Izergil* [The Old Woman Izergil, 1895], and *Pesnya o burevestnike* [The Song of the Story Petrel, 1901] are notable among his other songs and stories.

Chelkash (1894; Tchelkache, 1902), *Malva* (1897; Eng., 1901), and *Konovalov* (1897; Eng., 1901) are a series of stories about the barefoot, wandering Russian tramps, and the hopelessness of their occasional spontaneous attempts to change their circumstances. Here G. compared these uprooted people, who still clung to their desire for freedom, with the greedy, profit-seeking bourgeoisie.

In his first novel, *Foma Gordeyev* (1897–99; Eng., 1901), G. described the tragic road of a merchant's son who wished to retain his humanity and was thus doomed to failure in his own environment. At the same time G. presented a panoramic view of the way in which representatives of contemporary capitalism were striving to take over political power. His novel *Troye* (1901; Three of Them, 1902) portrays the process of dehumanization in a member of the lower classes of the city population who acquires property; his antagonist, Pavel Grachov, finds a perspective for his own personality in his contact with the working class.

In the early 1900s G. became more closely connected with the labor movement. He was constantly watched and persecuted by the police. At the same time he became acquainted with both L. N. Tolstoi and A. P. Chekhov. The latter supported G. when he turned his attention toward the drama. G.'s first play, *Meshchane* [The Petit Bourgeois], was staged in 1902 by the Moscow Artists' Theater. It was in this play that the figure of a conscious proletarian was depicted on the stage for the first time. G.'s drama *Na dne* (1902; The Lower Depths, 1922) became an especially great success both in Russia and abroad. The drama, which shows the fate of the barefoot Russian tramps, demonstrates both the inhumanity of the exploitative order and the lies that serve to justify it.

G. took part in both the preparations for and the execution of the revolution of 1905; he was subsequently arrested by the tsarist authorities, but was released following worldwide protests by the people. In the summer of 1905 G. joined the Bolshevik Party; in the fall of that year he worked with V. I. Lenin on the illegal Bolshevist newspaper *Novaya zhizn* [New Life]. His encounter with Lenin in December of 1905 developed into a friendship that was to greatly influence G.'s formation as a revolutionary artist. At the suggestion of the Bolshevik Party G. left Russia in 1906, and traveled across Europe and the U.S.A., where he spoke in support of the revolution and agitated against the alliance between international reaction and tsarism. From 1906 to 1913 G. lived in Capri.

These reactionary forces were exposed by G. in a series of pamphlets and satires, including *Moi intervyu* [My Interviews, 1906] and *V Amerike* [In America, 1906]. While in the U.S.A. he wrote the drama *Vragi* [The Enemies, 1906] and his famous novel *Mat* (1906; Mother, 1907). It was in *Mat* that G.'s aesthetic principles of socialist realism were fully applied for the first time. In a concrete, historical manner, G. has demonstrated the ordered character of the labor movement and its leading role in the process of history. He invested the revolutionaries with the features of the positive hero of socialist literature. In the development of Nilovna from intimidated working-class woman to revolutionary, G. has convincingly shown the humanizing force of socialism and its victory in accordance with an ordered pattern.

In dramas such as *Posledniye* [The Last Ones, 1908], and in a number of epic works, G. dealt with the general decline of the ruling classes. The awakening of progressive forces in the village after the revolution of 1905 has been shown by G. in his novel *Leto* [The Summer, 1909]. In 1909, with the aid of Lenin, G. overcame certain ideologic deviations evident in his postrevolutionary work, which had been brought about by a temporary association with the Otsovists and their "deification of the people" theory. Influences of that theory are evident in his novel *Ispoved* (1908; Confession, 1916).

In the year 1910 G. published his long novel *Zhizn Matveya*

Kozhemyakina [The Life of Matvey Kozhemyakin, 1959]. In it he offered a versatile picture of the social processes, the intellectual arguments, and the growth of the progressive forces in the Russian provinces between 1861 and 1906. G. continued his presentation of the life of the people in *Skazki ob Italii* [Italian Fairy Tales, 1910–13], and in the novel cycle *Po Rusi* (1915; In Old Russia, 1921). In 1913 G. published the first volume of his autobiographical trilogy *Detstvo* (My Childhood, 1961). Volume Two, *V lyudyakh*, appeared in 1915 (My Apprenticeship, 1962), and Volume Three, *Moï universitety*, in 1923 (My Universities, 1952).

During World War I, G. spoke and wrote against chauvinism and war. In the early 1920s G., with the support of Lenin, overcame his doubts, voiced in 1917–18, as to whether the great socialist October revolution may not have been carried out prematurely, and became deeply involved in the cultural aspects of socialist reconstruction in Russia. At Lenin's suggestion, G. went abroad in 1921 for reasons of health; he first lived in Germany and later in Italy. During this period G. wrote numerous literary portraits of his contemporaries, the most important being those on *Lev Tolstoi* (1919; Reminiscences of Lev Nikolaevich Tolstoi, 1920) and *V. I. Lenin* (1924; reissued 1931).

In his novel *Delo Artamonovykh* (1925; The Artamanovs, 1955) G. depicted the periods of rising and declining capitalism, and how they affected the fate and eventual disintegration of three generations of a Russian merchant family. His unfinished epic novel *Zhizn Klima Samgina* (1927–36; The Bystander, 1930; The Magnet, 1931; Other Fires, 1933; The Specter, 1938) portrays the history of Russia and the most important events between 1870 and 1917 as the basis for the ideologic and political differences of those times. G.'s protagonist in this work exposed the type of bourgeois individualist alienated from the people and everything human. The latter figure is contrasted with the Communist Kutosov, the representative of true humanity.

In his later plays, especially *Yegor Bulychov i drugiye* [Yegor Bulychov and the Others, 1932], G. combined the presentation of the revolutionary events of 1917 with a deep understanding of the aspects of various representatives of the bourgeoisie.

After his return to Russia in 1928, G. in his cycle of sketches *Po Soyuzu Sovyetov* [Through the Soviet Union, 1929–30], as well as in various short stories, described the socialist reconstruction and the qualities of the rulers of the country. G. also published and edited a number of magazines including *Nashi dostizheniya* [Our Achievements], *S.S.S.R. v stroike* [The USSR under Reconstruction], and *Literaturnaya uchoba* [The Teachings of Literature]. Through his correspondence with numerous Soviet writers, G. was deeply involved with the development of socialist and world literature. His literary essays, as well as his work in connection with the First Writers' Congress, were also of great importance.

Editions: Sobraniye sochinenii [Collected Works], 30 vols., Moscow, 1948–56; *O literature* [On Literature], Moscow, 1955

GRANIN (Pseud. of *Daniil Aleksandrovich German*)

Born January 1, 1918, Volyn (District of Kursk). Soviet Russian novelist.

G. studied electrical engineering and worked as an engineer. In 1941 he volunteered for services at the front. His first work appeared in print in 1949.

The main themes of G.'s works are the life and work of scientists and technologists. Following a number of short stories, G. portrayed the difficulties of responsible technologists in his first novel *Iskateli* (1954; Those Who Seek, 1950). G.'s works are concerned with actual problems of Soviet society, and the scientific and technological questions treated by him are closely connected with the moral and ideological development of the people involved in the solution of the problems under consideration.

The more individual problems considered in G.'s novels *Posle svadby* [After the Wedding, 1958], and in particular in *Idu na grozu* [Toward the Thunderstorm, 1962], have been treated in a similar manner. In the latter novel, G., in the interactions between many differentiated figures, elucidated significant aspects of the communist ethos of work, and demonstrated that the social responsibility of the scientist represents the decisive precondition for successful work.

Further Works: Pobeda inzhenera Korsakova [The Victory of Engineer Korsakov] (1949); *Vtoroi variant* [The Second Version] (1949); *Novyye druzya* [New Friends] (1951)

GREK, MAKSIM   See MAKSIM GREK

GRIBACHOV, NIKOLAI MATVEYEVICH
   Born December 19, 1910, Lopush (District of Bryansk). Soviet Russian poet and short-story writer.
   G. is the son of a peasant. He began his journalistic activities in 1932; during World War II he was a frontline correspondent. In 1950–54 and again from 1956 G. was editor-in-chief of the magazine *Sovetski Soyuz* [Soviet Union]. G. is a member of the Central Committee of the Communist Party of the USSR. In his poems, his lyric verses—which frequently are dedicated to the country people—and in his stories, G. deals with actual social problems; he demonstrates the development of the ideology and morality of communist man. G. was awarded State Prizes in 1948 and 1949.

Editions: Izbrannyye proizvedeniya [Selected Works], 3 vols., Moscow, 1960

GRIBOYEDOV, ALEKSANDR SERGEYEVICH
   Born January 15, 1795, Moscow; died February 11, 1829, Teheran. Russian dramatist and diplomat.
   G. came from an old noble family, and enjoyed a versatile education. In 1812–15 he served in the imperial army in Byelorussia. In 1815 he went to St. Petersburg, where he began his literary career. G., like Pushkin, was closely connected with the Decembrists. In 1817 he entered the Russian diplomatic service.

He served as Russian minister in Persia, where he was assassinated.

G.'s ideology and work developed under the influence of both the Decembrist movement and the liberal ideas of enlightenment. G.'s early works were mostly descriptions of military life, comedies (*Molodyye suprugi*, The Young Couple, 1815) and vaudeville-type plays (*Student*, The Student, 1817). Some of these were written in cooperation with Katenin, Vyazemski, and other young writers. They appear weak in comparison with G.'s great comedy of social criticism *Gore ot uma* (1823; The Mischief of Being Clever, 1925).

In this comedy G. continued the traditions established by Fonvizin and Kapnist. He gives a realistic picture of Russian society split into two camps on the eve of the Decembrist uprising: the Famusovs and Skalozubs—Russian career officials, empty-headed military men and members of the obtuse world of court nobility —are confronted by the passionate accuser Chatzki, a representative of the revolutionary nobility. Many phrases from this work, which was written in the popular vernacular, became proverbs and maxims, while G.'s characters themselves have come to represent actual concepts.

G., together with Krylov and Pushkin, was one of the founders of nineteenth-century Russian realism.

Editions: Polnoye sobraniye sochinenii [Complete Works], 2 vols., St. Petersburg, 1911–17; *Sochineniya* [Works], Moscow, 1956
Further Works: 1812 god [The Year 1812] (1824–25); *Zagorodnaya poyezdka* [A Trip out of Town] (1826); *Gruzinskaya noch* [A Georgian Night] (n.d.)

GRIGOROVICH, DMITRI VASILYEVICH
Born March 31, 1822, Simbirsk; died January 3, 1900, St. Petersburg. Russian short-story writer and novelist.

G. came from the nobility; as a young man, he became a member of the democratic intelligentsia. He was a cofounder of the Natural School. In his long, compassionate stories *Derevnya* [The

Village, 1846] and *Anton-Goremyka* [Hapless Anton, 1847], G. described the misery and growing feelings of protest among the serfs.

In his novel *Prosiolotshnyye dorogi* [Country Lanes, 1852], G. has given a critical presentation of the life of the estate owners. The novel *Rybaki* (1853; Fishermen, 1916) reflects the life of the simple fishermen and peasants as well as of that of the first Russian factory workers. G. was in sympathy with the patriarchal peasant order and refused to see the historical role of the proletariat. He remained a supporter of Russian realistic literature until his death.

Editions: Izbrannyye sochineniya [Selected Works], Moscow, 1955
Further Works: Pereselentzy [Migrants] (1855–56)

GRIGULIS, ARVĪDS
Born October 12, 1906, Jumpraimuiza. Latvian Soviet short-story writer, poet, and playwright.

G. is the son of a peasant. In 1937 he graduated with a law degree from the University of Riga. He participated in World War II as a correspondent for the Latvian army newspaper, and since 1945 has held a chair at the Faculty of Philology of the Latvian State University.

G.'s literary activities began in 1927 with poems reflecting his rejection of existing social conditions. In 1943–45 G. began to publish poems and short stories on wartime themes. Since 1945 most of his work has been in the field of the drama. G. was awarded the State Prize in 1947 for his play *Māls un porcelāns* [Clay and Porcelain]. G. holds the title of Meritorious Artist of the Latvian SSR.

GRIN, ALEKSANDR
Born August 23, 1880, Slobodskoi (District of Vyatka); died July 8, 1932, Staryi Krym. Soviet Russian novelist.

G. was the son of a Pole exiled to Siberia because of his participation in the revolution of 1863. From the age of sixteen G.

M. Gorki

A. S. Griboyedov

O. T. Honchar

A. I. Herzen

V. V. Ivanov

led an adventurous life as a sailor, gold prospector, and soldier. Under the influence of the socialist revolutionaries, G. became involved in propagating revolutionary ideas, an activity for which he was jailed and later exiled.

G.'s literary career began in 1906. The most significant characteristic of his work is his romantic imagination, out of which he created noble men who fought in imaginary countries for the realization of their humanistic aims. G. is one of the best stylists in Soviet literature.

Editions: Sobraniye pisatelya [Collected Writings], 1948
Further Works: Vetr z yuga [Wind from the South] (1946)

GRISHASHVILI (Pseud. of *Iosif Mamulaishvili*)
    Born April 24, 1889, Tbilisi; died there August 3, 1965. Georgian Soviet poet and literary critic.

G. was the son of an artisan. Some of his poems had already become popular during the revolutionary years of 1905–07. In his early, intensely intimate lyric poems G. formed a link with several different literary traditions, including modern ones. The problems treated in his works became more extensive after the establishment of Soviet power. He extolled the new Georgia and the defenders of the Soviet Union, and drew portraits of socialist man in poems such as *Farewell to the Old Tbilisi* (1925); *Fatherland* (1935); *Homeland and Victory* (1941); *The Light* (1947); and *There Comes a Georgian Car* (1950). G. was awarded the State Prize in 1950. He has also published essays on literary history.

Editions: Rcheuli [Selected Works], Tbilisi, 1959

GROSMAN, VASILII SEMIONOVICH
    Born December 12, 1905, Berdichev; died September 14, 1964, Moscow. Soviet Russian novelist.

G. graduated in 1929 from the Faculty of Physics and Mathematics of the University of Moscow; he then worked as a chemist in the Donbas region.

The themes of G.'s early stories are set in the period of the civil war, and describe the illegal struggles against tsarism and the building of the new society. His novel *Stepan Kolchugin* (1937–40; Kolchugin's Youth, 1948) describes how a young miner sees his way to accepting the revolution. G. was a frontline correspondent during World War II. His first major work, the short story *Narod bessmertem* [People Immortal, 1945], appeared in 1942. It tells of the resistance of the Soviet peoples during the war, but in an artistically generalized form. In his novel *Za pravoye delo* [For the Right Cause, 1952–54], G. offered an epic portrait of the fight against fascism, showing the moral superiority of the Soviet peoples.

Editions: Staryi uchitel. Povesti i rasskazy [The Old Teacher: Short Stories], Moscow, 1962

GUDZENKO, SEMION PETROVICH

Born March 5, 1922, Kiev; died February 12, 1953, Moscow. Soviet Russian poet and journalist.

G. volunteered in 1941 for service at the front while still a student. He took part in the battles around Moscow, and later was a correspondent for a number of army newspapers. His first publications were inspired by wartime events at the front, and similar themes characterized his work until his early death in action.

G.'s verses are convincing because of their restrained passion, harsh realism, and laconic emphatic style.

Editions: Stikhi i poemy, 1942–52 [Poems and Verses, 1942–52], Moscow, 1956
Further Works: Dalni garnizon [The Distant Garrison] (1950)

GULIA, DMITRI IOSIFOVICH

Born February 21, 1871, Uarcha, near Sukhumi; died April 7, 1960, Agudsera, near Sukhumi. Abkhazian Soviet poet and scholar; founder of Abkhaz literature; People's Poet of the Abkhaz ASSR from 1937 until his death.

G., the son of a poor peasant, attended a teachers college in Gori, and later worked as a teacher. Between 1924–26 G. was Professor of Abkhaz language at the University of Tbilisi. In 1892, in cooperation with K. D. Machavariani, G. created the second Abkhaz language alphabet, which is used today in modified form.

In his early poems and verses, published in 1912, G. used themes from Abkhaz folklore, and depicted representatives of the ruling classes in a critically realistic manner. In 1919–20 he published the first Abkhaz newspaper, *Apsny* [Abkhazia]. In 1921, after the establishment of Soviet power, G. was active in the field of culture and education as a collector and publisher of Abkhaz folklore, a translator and the author of essays on Abkhaz history and language. His lyric writings—which continued to use the tonal verse form of Abkhaz folklore as well as introducing the syllabo-tonal verse form—attained their peak in the 1940s and 1950s.

G.'s main themes include socialist reconstruction, creativity, Abkhaz nature, patriotism, and friendship between the peoples. His works frequently reflect strong action with a tendency toward epic generalization. They include the volumes of poetry *Damei* (1949) and *New Year Verses* (1951), the cycle of poems entitled *Sara sykalaky* [My City, 1952], and the poem *Tagalan akytan* [Autumn in the Village, 1952].

G. was the founder of Abkhaz epic and dramatic writing. His novel *Kamachych* (1933–40) describes the social conditions in the prerevolutionary Abkhaz village. While the latter work still reveals strong ethnographic elements, his drama *Anaurkua* [Phantoms, 1946–50], which shows the influence of M. Gorki, exhibits social, psychological forms in its presentation of the social and intellectual differences in prerevolutionary Abkhazia.

Editions: Ieymtakua [Works], 4 vols., Akua, 1956–62; *Izbrannyye proizvedeniya* [Selected Works] (in Russian), Moscow, 1953, 1958

GULYAM, GAFUR See GAFUR GULYAM

GULYAM, HAMID See HAMID GULYAM

GURAMISHVILI, DAVID

Born in 1705, in Saguramo, near Mzkheta; died August 1, 1792, Mirgorod. Georgian poet.

G. came from an old noble family. In 1729–30 he lived in Moscow in the service of the Georgian king Vakhtang VI; he became a Russian citizen in 1737. A member of the Russian army, he was taken prisoner by the Prussians during the Seven Years' War in 1758, and held in the fortress of Magdeburg. He escaped in 1759, and retired from the army.

A series of G.'s writings of an autobiographical character have come down to us under the title *Davitiani* [Davidovo], dated 1787. The two long poems and the lyric verses contained in this collection tell of the poet's love for his homeland, of his sorrow for its fate, and of his sympathy with the fate of the Ukrainian peasant. G.'s simple, songlike poetry has influenced N. Baratashvili and Vasha-Pshavela.

Editions: Davitiani [Davidovo], Tbilisi, 1955

GUSEV, VIKTOR MIKHAILOVICH

Born January 30, 1909, Moscow; died there January 23, 1944. Soviet Russian poet and dramatist.

G.'s first collection of poems, *Pokhod veshchei* [March of Objects], appeared in 1929. He praised the work of Soviet men in his tender, lyrical poems. A number of his songs have become folksongs, including *Polyushko-pole* [Field, My Little Field] and *Pesnya o Moskve* [Song about Moscow]. G.'s most important work is the verse drama *Slava* (1935), which deals with the different aspects of glory. G. was awarded the State Prize in 1942.

Editions: Izbrannyye Proizvedeniya [Selected Works], Moscow, 1948

HAMID GULYAM

Born in 1919, Tashkent. Uzbekistanian Soviet poet; Secretary of the Writers' Union of the Uzbek SSR.

From 1938–41 H. G. studied Russian language and literature at the Institute of Pedagogy in Tashkent, and later worked as a teacher. His first volume of poetry, *I Shall Be the Avenger*, appeared in 1942. In the collections of poems entitled *My Songs, On the Road to Victory*, and *Poems on Love*, H. G. praises the liberated life of the Uzbek woman and her participation in the social life of the region, as well as the friendship, grown stronger during the war years, between the peoples of the Soviet Union.

A number of H. G.'s stories, such as *The Girl from Almas*, are dedicated to the heroic work of the Soviet people. At present H. G. is working on *The Torch*, a trilogy about the revolution in Uzbekistan. He has also written a series of travel sketches and articles inspired by his impressions of Western Europe, entitled *European Impressions*.

HAMZA, HAKIM-ZADE (Writing under the pseud. *Niyasi*)

Born 1889, in Kokand; assassinated March 18, 1929, Shakhimardan (now Hamsaabad), by reactionary forces. Uzbekistanian Soviet author, playwright, and composer; founder of Uzbekistanian Soviet literature; one of the creators of the modern Uzbekistanian theater.

H. had been prominent as a democratic poet and revolutionary fighter after 1905. In 1911–12 in Kokand he directed a school for children of the people. In 1912–14 he traveled through Turkey, Arabia, India, and Afghanistan. In his early poems H. continued the democratic traditions of Uzbekistanian literature, writing intimate and social lyrics in an emphatically simple, folklike manner. As a revolutionary journalist, H. supported the interests of the poor masses. He supported the Bolshevists and took an active part in the organization of the October revolution in Uzbekistan. After the revolution he set up the first Uzbekistanian theater group, which performed before the soldiers of the revolutionary army. For this group, H. wrote a series of didactic plays including *Who Is Right?* (1920), *The Bey and the Servant* (1918), and *The Tragedy of the Mobilized Men* (1920).

During 1917–20 H. created a body of predominantly lyrical heroic poetry, which may be regarded as the beginning of Uzbekistanian socialist verse. After 1920 H. dedicated himself to various educational, propagandistic, and literary tasks. He organized a number of theaters and defended the achievements of the revolution in the plays *The Revolution in Khoresm* (1922) and *The Tragedy of Fergana*. In his masterly dramas *The Secrets of Parandshe* (1926) and *The Pranks of Maisara* (1926), H. treated events in the life of the Uzbekistanian people from the point of view of the revolution. In these works he unmasked the administration of justice in prerevolutionary Uzbekistan, and stood up for equal rights for Uzbekistanian women; he treated the latter theme also in a great number of his postrevolutionary poems.

H. also deserves credit as a composer for having created a new body of Uzbekistanian songs, into which he brought elements from both the Uzbekistanian folksong and the revolutionary hymn. H. has exerted great influence on the entire development of Uzbekistanian socialist literature as well as on other literatures of Soviet Central Asia.

HERZEN, ALEKSANDR IVANOVICH (Pseud.: *Iskander*)
Born April 6, 1812, Moscow; died January 21, 1870, Paris. Russian revolutionary, philosopher, essayist, and journalist.

H. was the illegitimate son of the Russian general I. A. Yakovlev and the German woman L. Haag. The events of the Decembrist uprising impressed him and drew him to liberal ideas while he was still a youth; together with his friend Ogariov he took an oath to fight against autocracy and for the emancipation of the serfs. During his scientific studies at the University of Moscow (1829–33), H. familiarized himself with the ideas of materialistic philosophy and of Saint-Simon's utopian socialism. He and Ogariov together organized a revolutionary circle. H. was arrested and spent the years 1834–49 and 1841–42 respectively in exile and under police surveillance. In the 1840s H., with Belinski, became the leader of the revolutionary intelligentsia.

In his philosophical writings *Diletsantism v nauke* [Dilettantism in Science, 1842–43] and *Pisma ob isuchenii prirody* [Letters on the Study of Nature, 1845–46], H. developed a philosophical system of his own that came close to dialectic materialism (Lenin).

H. emigrated to Western Europe in 1847. He witnessed the events of the French revolution in Paris in 1848, but, not understanding its bourgeois, democratic character, he regarded it as the death of his hopes for a victory of socialist ideas. The intellectual crisis that resulted is reflected in *S tovo berega* [From the Other Shore, 1850], a masterpiece of artistic journalism. H. acquainted Western Europe with progressive Russian intellectual life in his essay "The Russian People and Socialism," which appeared first in German in 1851 under the title "Russlands soziale zustände," then in French, and later in Russian under the title *O razvitii revolyu- tzionykh idei v Rossi* [On the Development of Revolutionary Ideas in Russia]. In 1852, H. emigrated to London and there founded the "free Russian press." Between 1855–62 and in 1896 he pub- lished the almanac *Polyarnaya zvezda* [The Pole Star], which contained literary works prohibited in Russia. Between 1857 and 1868 (from 1865 in Geneva), he was co-publisher with Ogariov of the newspaper *Kolokol* [The Bell], which exposed and attacked the abuses existing in tsarist Russia. The newspaper reached Rus- sia through illegal channels, and there exerted a lasting influence. In the 1860s H. supported the revolutionary democrats. In the last years of his life he recognized the importance of the proletariat: in his *Pisma k staromu tovarishchu* [Letters to an Old Friend, 1869], H. broke with Bakunin, taking a position directed more closely toward Marx's First International.

In his belletristic writings H. proved himself a realistic narrator of the first order. In his social philosophical novel *Kto vinovat?* [Who Is Guilty?], he used the example of a family tragedy to make it clear how much guilt the tsarist order bore in the destruc- tion of worthy Russian people. In Beltov, a main figure in the work, H. continued the tradition of the "superfluous man." In his story *Sorokavorovka* [The Thieving Magpie, 1846] H. again ex- posed the guilt of noble society in the tragic fate of a serf actress. In his story *Doktor Krupov* (1847), he used the subject of a physician's psychiatric studies to call attention to the contradic- tion between autocracy and serfdom. The memoirs *Byloye i dumy* (1852–68; My Past and Thoughts, 1924–27) may be regarded as H.'s most important belletristic achievement. In it he created an artistically developed chronicle of his own life and of social development in Russia and Western Europe as seen from the point of view of the revolutionary movement. The work also contains a number of impressive portraits of important personalities of his time.

Editions: Sobraniye sochinenii [Collected Works], 30 vols., Moscow, 1954–64
Further Works: Zapiski odnovo molodovo cheloveka [Notes of a Certain Young Man] (1838–41); *Dolg prezhde vsevo* [Debt Above All] (1851)

HOLOVKO, ANDRII VASYLOVYCH
Born December 4, 1897, Yurki (District of Poltava). Ukrainian Soviet novelist. One of the founders of Ukrainian Soviet literature.

G., who comes from peasant stock, took an active part in the civil war. G. was one of the first Ukrainian prose writers to take as his theme the complex beginnings of socialist collectivization and its effect on the country (*Zeleni serdtzem* [People Born Young, 1924] and *Pasynky stepu* [The Stepsons of the Steppe, 1925]). His most important work to date is the epic novel *Buryan* [Steppe Grass, 1927], which describes the bitter class battles in the Ukrainian villages during the civil war.

Editions: Tvory [Works], Kiev, 1957
Further Works: Maty [Mother] (1932); *Artem Harmash* [Artem Harmash] (1951–60)

HONCHAR, OLES (OLEKSANDER) TERENTIIOVYCH
Born April 3, 1918, Sukha near Poltava. Ukrainian Soviet prose writer.

G. comes from the village proletariat; he studied journalism in Kharkov, and, after his discharge from active military service in 1946, graduated from the University in Dnepropetrovsk. He has been president of the Ukrainian Writers' Union since 1959.

G.'s extensive, chiefly epic writings have been appearing in print since 1938. They include the novel trilogy on World War II, *Praporonostzi* (1946–48; Standard Bearers, 1948), consisting of the novel *Alpy* [The Alps, 1946], *Holubyi Dunai* [The Blue Danube, 1947], and *Zlata Praha* [Prague, The Golden City, 1948]. In the civil-war novel *Perekop* [Perekop, 1957], and in his present-day novel *Tronka* (1963) G. depicts the face of the simple, moral, communist man as influenced by his direct environment.

G.'s writing is distinguished by a poetically romantic style which endows his realistic epics with a markedly lyrical character. G. received State Prizes in 1948 and 1949, and was awarded the Lenin Prize in 1964.

Editions: Tvory [Works], 4 vols., Kiev, 1959–60
Further Works: Zemlya Hudyt [The Earth] (1947); *Tavriya* (1952); *Lyudyna i zbroya* [Man and Arms] (1960); *Sobor* [The Cathedral] (1968)

IBRAGIMOV, GALIMDZHAN

Born March 12, 1887; died January 21, 1938. Tatar Soviet novelist, philologist, and historian.

In his early work I. wrote of the Tatar village and the problem of the emancipation of women. In 1914–21 he wrote *Our Days*, a historical novel about the revolution. The years of Soviet power were fruitful ones for I.; he became one of the founders of socialist realism in Tatar literature. I. has gained importance as an historian with his work *The Tatars in the Revolution of 1905* (1925).

Editions: Izbrannoye [Selected Works], Kazan, 1957
Further Works: Glubokiye korni [Deep Roots] (1931); *Doch stepi* [Daughter of the Steppes] (1934)

IBRAGIMOV, MIRZA ASHDAR-OGLY

Born October 15, 1911, Eve. Azerbaidzhani Soviet novelist and playwright; President of the Writers' Union of the Azerbaidzhani SSR; Chairman of the Supreme Soviet of the Azerbaidzhan SSR.

From the beginning of his literary activities in 1930 until 1937, I. was prominent primarily as a delineator of the socialist reconstruction of the Azerbaidzhani village, in which he had participated as both party functionary and writer. He wrote stories about the Azerbaidzhani village, as well as his drama *Khayat* (1935).

The heroic battles fought by the Republican Spanish forces inspired him to write his drama *Madrid* (1937–39). This was followed soon after the invasion of the Soviet Union by his play *Makhabbet* (1942), which deals with the heroic activities of the Soviet people in the hinterland. The war led I. to southern Azerbaidzhan and to Iran, where he collected material for his *Southern Stories* (1941–47), and for his best-known novel *The Time Will Come* (1948) on the social struggles in Iran on the eve of World War II. The greater prosperity of the Azerbaidzhani village after the September plenary session of 1953 is treated in his novel *The Great Support* (1957); *The Lighthouse* (1958–60) is about the life of the oil workers.

IKRAMI, DZHALOL

Born September 20, 1909, Bukhara. Tadzhik novelist and playwright.

Since his thirtieth year, I. has been, after Aini, the most important Tadzhik prose writer. His first stories, for example, including *Du hafta* [Two Weeks, 1933], tell of the hard class struggle in Central Asia. The first part of the novel *Shodi*, on the conflicts in Tadzhik agriculture, appeared in 1940. In the postwar years, I. strove especially to give a convincing psychological presentation of his heroes. This led him to write the novels *Man gunahgoram* [I Am Guilty, 1957] and *Duhtari otash* [The Daughter of the Fire, 1962], about the world of women in prerevolutionary Bukhara.

Further Works: Dili modar [Mother's Heart] (1942); *Ocherki mardi tanksikan* [Stories about a Tank Driver] (1944)

ILF, ILYA (Pseud. of *Ilya Arnoldovich Fainsilberg*)

Born October 5, 1897, Odessa; died April 13, 1937. Soviet Russian novelist.

I., the son of a bank clerk, held various positions in industry after graduation from a technical college. He began his literary and journalistic activities in Odessa, and continued them after moving to Moscow in 1923. In 1926 he began working in the editorial department of the newspaper *Gudok* [The Factory Siren] in close cooperation with his countryman J. P. Petrov. Their masterful short stories and essays, some of which are still of contemporary significance, appeared regularly in *Pravda* and other newspapers and magazines.

The climax of the literary partnership of I. and Petrov may be found in the satirical novels *Dvenadtzat stulyev* (1927; The Twelve Chairs, 1961) and *Zolotoi telionok* (1931; The Golden Calf, 1962); these two novels, the main figure of which is the swindler Ostap Bender, form an integrated whole. The extension of the frame evident in the second part, however, leads to a certain shift in emphasis. In the first part, Bender's enterprising resourcefulness depicts him in a more favorable light than the narrow and commonplace representatives of the petit bourgeoisie; in the second part of the novel, on the other hand, Bender is confronted by the gradually increasing strength of the representatives of the new order, and in that encounter is exposed in all his wretchedness.

In 1935, I. and Petrov went to visit America, and in 1936 published a volume of sketches, *Odnoetazhnaya Amerika* (Little Golden America, 1946), in which they showed the life of the average American. I. died of consumption while his work was still at its peak.

Editions: Sobraniye sochinenii [The Collected Works of Ilya Ilf and Yevgenii Petrov], 5 vols., 1961

ILYIN, M. (Pseud. of *Ilya Yakovlevich Marshak*)

Born January 10, 1896, Ostrogoshsk (District of Voronezh); died November 15, 1953. Soviet Russian writer of children's books.

I. studied physics and mathematics, and then worked as an engineer. He is one of the founders of the Soviet movement toward the publication of children's books in the scientific and artistic field. Among his early works are *Solntze na stole* [The Sun on the Table, 1927] and *Kak avtomobil uchilsya khodit* (1930; How the Automobile Learned to Run, 1945). In *Rasskaz o velikom plane* [The Story of the Great Plan, 1930], I. tells his young readers about the first Five-Year Plan. In *Chelovek i stikhiya* [Man and the Elements, 1947], *Pokoreniye prirody* [Conquered Nature, 1950], and *Preobrazovaniye planety* [The Transformation of Our Planet, 1951] I. discusses the theme of transforming and utilizing nature.

Further Works: Rasskazy o veshchakh [Stories about Things] (1936)

INBER, VERA MIKHAILOVNA

Born July 10, 1890, Odessa. Soviet Russian poet and novelist.

I. has been writing since 1911. Her first works showed certain precious, formal tendencies, as may be seen in her volume of poems *Pechalnoye vino* [The Wine of Sorrow, 1914]. In the 1920s her work took a more realistic form. Her main theme was the success of reconstruction in the Soviet Union (*Soyuz materei* [The Union of Mothers, 1938]). *Putevoi dnevnik* [Travelogue, 1938], is a lyric poem about a voyage through Soviet Georgia.

I. has also written a novel on the development of the old intelligentsia, *Mesto na solntse* [A Place in the Sun, 1928]. Her experiences during the siege of Leningrad are reflected in the poem *Pulkovski meridian* [The Pulkovo Meridian, 1942] for which she received the State Prize in 1946.

Editions: Izbrannyye proizvedeniya [Selected Works], 3 vols., Moscow, 1958
Further Works: Aprel. Stikhi o Lenine [April: Poems about Lenin] (1960)

IOANISIAN (OVANNESIAN), IOANNES

Born April 26, 1864, Vagarshapat; died September 29, 1929, Yerevan. Armenian democratic poet and translator of classical Russian literature.

I. employed themes from folklore in his work. He extolled the fight of the Armenian people for liberation from the yoke of the Turkish oppressors. He also has written love lyrics.

Editions: Stikhotvoreniya [Poems] (in Russian), Yerevan, 1940; *Izbrannoye* [Selected Works] (in Russian), Moscow, 1949

ISAAKIAN, AVETIK

Born October 30, 1875, Kasarapat, near Aleksandropol (now Leninakan); died October 17, 1957, Yerevan. Armenian Soviet poet and short-story writer.

I. studied at the University of Leipzig, Germany. His work consisted chiefly of poems, many of which have been set to music, together with some prose. He frequently used themes from folklore and national poetry, and extolled the picturesque beauty of the Armenian landscape and the life of the inhabitants. The struggle for national liberation from Turkish and, later, tsarist oppression, and the battles against the German fascist invaders represent additional themes in I.'s poetic work. I. was awarded the State Prize in 1946.

Editions: Izbrannoye [Selected Works] (in Russian), Yerevan, 1952; *Izbrannyye stikhi* [Selected Poems] (in Russian), Moscow, 1945; *Izbrannaya proza* [Selected Prose Writings] (in Russian), Yerevan, 1947; *Znamya nadezhdy* [The Flag of Liberty: Short Stories] (in Russian), Moscow, 1948; *Mger is Sasuna* [Mger from Sasun: Poems] (in Russian), Moscow, 1939

ISAKOVSKI, MIKHAIL VASILYEVICH

Born January 19, 1900, Glotovka (District of Smolensk). Soviet Russian poet and critic.

Since the early 1920s, I.'s work has been closely connected with the changes taking place in the Russian village, the characteristic features of which are reflected in his popular and simple poems. His collection *Provoda v solome* [Electric Light under the Thatched Roof, 1927]—in contrast to S. A. Yesenin's elegant village poetry—represents a turning point and a truly new beginning in the lyric writings on this theme. I.'s work in the 1930s grew constantly artistically richer as he described the new life in the Soviet village, and the solidarity existing between farmers and workers. The sincerity and the warmth evidenced in his work, his *joie de vivre* and his humor, together with the lyrical musicality of his writings, have made I. one of the most important and popular poets. Songs like *Katyusha, I kto yevo znayet* . . . (Katyusha, Who Can Tell Me . . .) and many other similar songs are frequently heard in the Soviet Union. In sensitive and deeply felt songs dealing with contemporary themes, I. responded to the difficulties of the war period.

I.'s work has influenced and stimulated many Soviet poets. After World War II he wrote relatively little. He has, however, put considerable effort into supporting talented young poets, and his essay *O poetishcheskom masterstve* [On the Poet's Skill, 1952] is directed toward them. I. has also translated poems from the Byelorussian and the Ukrainian.

Editions: Sochineniya [Works], 2 vols., Moscow, 1956

ISAYEV, YEGOR ALEKSANDROVICH
Born May 2, 1926, Korshevo (District of Voronezh). Soviet Russian poet.

Since the end of the war, I. has been working as a journalist and editor; his first literary publications appeared in 1945. I.'s preferred literary form is the poem. In 1958 he wrote *Nad volnami Dunaya* [Over the Waves of the Danube]; his poem *Sud pamyati* [A Passage from Memory], his most important work so far, followed in 1962. In the latter work, I. treats the problem of individual moral and political responsibility. The focal point of the poem is occupied by the figure of a German who, as the symbol of the common philistine unwilling to accept responsibility, is compared with German patriots.

IVANOV, KONSTANTIN VASILYEVICH
Born May 27, 1890, Slakbash (Bashkiria); died there March 26, 1915. Chuvashian poet.

I. was greatly influenced by classical Russian literature. He utilized material from Chuvashian folklore, and in his chiefly lyric writings (fairy tales written in verse form), told of the oppression and misery of his people. Works on these themes include his poem *Vysa aptaranisem* [Hungry People, 1907] and the fairy tale in verse *Talakh aram* [The Widow, 1907].

I.'s most important poem is *Narspi* (1908), which, in realistic images—utilizing themes taken from folklore—tells of the demoralizing effects of early capitalistic development.

Editions: Sobraniye sochinenii [Selected Works] (in Russian), Cheboksary, 1940

IVANOV, VSEVOLD VYACHESLAVOVICH

Born February 24, 1895, Lebyashye (District of Semipalatinsk); died August 15, 1963, Moscow. Soviet Russian novelist.

I. was the son of a village schoolteacher from the region of Semipalatinsk. His first literary writings appeared in 1915. I. participated in the civil war battles in Siberia. In 1920 in Petrograd he joined the literary group known as "The Serapion Brothers." His cycle of partisan stories *Partizany* [Partisans, 1922], *Bronepoyezd 14–69* (1922; Armored Train No. 14–69, 1933), and *Tzvetnyye vetra* [Colorful Winds, 1922] showed I. to be a talented poet who created a highly individual literary portrait of the battles of the Siberian partisans and of the spontaneous rising of the peasants against Kolchak and the interventionists. The stage version of *Bronepoyezd 14–69* (1927) is one of the most important achievements in Soviet drama about the civil war.

The present time, socialist reconstruction, the proletariat, and the Communist Party are treated in I.'s novel *Puteshestviye v stranu, kotoroi yeschcho net* [A Journey into a Country Which Does Not Yet Exist]. I.'s roving life beyond the Urals and the unusual dreams of his youth are reflected in the autobiographical novel *Pokhozhdeniya fakira* (1934–35; The Adventures of a Fakir, 1935). *Parkhomenko* (1937–38) was a comprehensive novel based on the life and battles of the heroic Red Army commander Aleksandr Parkhomenko. I. was a frontline war correspondent during World War II; he took part in the liberation of Berlin from fascism, and was present during the Nuremberg war crime trials. He has written patriotic appeals, short stories, dramas, and a novel on the capture of Berlin, which, however, has not met with great success. After the war, I. published essays on themes taken from literary history; his reminiscences *Vstrechi z Maksimom Gorkim* [Encounters with Maksim Gorki, 1953] may be counted as one of his most noteworthy achievements.

Editions: Sobraniye sochinenii [Collected Works], 8 vols., Moscow, 1958–60

JAKOBSON, AUGUST

Born September 2, 1904, Pärnu; died May 23, 1963, Tallinn. Estonian Soviet novelist, dramatist, and statesman; Chairman of the Supreme Soviet of the Estonian SSR, 1950–58.

J., the son of a factory worker succeeded in graduating from the university despite his strained economic situation. He published his first very successful novel, *Vaeste patuste alev* [The Settlement of the Poor Sinners, 1927], while still a student. After the fall of the bourgeois dictatorship, J. was active both in the reconstruction of the new society and in literature. He published two collections of short stories during the war.

After the liberation of his country from the fascist invaders, drama came to occupy the most important position in J.'s work. Among his important dramas are *Elu tsitadellis* [Life in the Citadel, 1946], *Võitlus rindejooneta* [The Fight without the Front Line, 1947], and *Vana tamm* [The Old Oak Tree, 1954]. J. was People's Writer of the Estonian SSR, and was awarded State Prizes in 1947 and 1948.

JANONIS, JULIUS

Born April 5, 1896, Beržiniai, near Beržai; died May 30, 1917, Petrograd. Founder of Lithuanian proletarian literature.

J., the son of a poor peasant, found his way early to the worker movement. In 1916, J. was a member of the Lithuanian Russian Social Democrat Party (Bolehevik Factor) in Petrograd. J. applied the method of socialist realism to his poems, verses, prose, and political writings. In the years between 1914 and 1917 he wrote the poems *Kalvis* [The Blacksmith], *Bedarbis* [Jobless], and *Kumecio daina* [The Song of the Day Laborer], in which he lashed out at social injustice and asked for constitutional rights for the laborer. In other poetic writings including *Naujas Rytas* [A New Morning], J. spoke up against tsarism and the imperialistic war, thus becoming the herald of the approaching revolution.

Editions: Raštai [Works], 2 vols., Vilnius, 1957

KAKHKHAR, ABDULLA

Born March 10, 1907, Kokand; died May, 1968. Uzbekistanian Soviet short-story writer and playwright.

K. is regarded as the master of the Uzbekistanian short story. In his early stories and sketches, including his collection of short stories *The World Is Becoming Young* (1932), K. realistically described the social conflicts in prerevolutionary Uzbekistan—the struggles against antiquated customs and traditions as well as the formation of socialist life after 1917.

In 1946 K. became well known following the publication of his novel on the collectivization of the Uzbekistanian village, *The Lights of Koshshchinar*. In 1949 his play *On New Soil*, which deals with the reclamation and cultivation of the Central Asian virgin lands, met with great success. K. was awarded the State Prize of 1952 for the latter play.

KAMAL (Pseud. of *Sharif Baigildeyev*)

Born March 28, 1884, Pishlya (District of Penza); died December 22, 1942, Kazan. Tatar Soviet novelist and playwright.

K., who was influenced by Gorki, introduced the genre of the novel into Tatar literature. His novel *At Sunrise* (1927), the first Tatar Soviet novel, is dedicated to the theme of the October revolution. K. depicted the effect of socialist reconstruction on the towns and on the country itself in a series of dramas. In 1934,

K. translated M. Sholokhov's *Podnyataya tzelina* (Seeds of Tomorrow) into Tatar. K. himself became the most important
novelist of the agricultural socialist reconstruction period in Tatar
literature with the publication of his novels *When Beauty Is
Born* (1938) and *With Firm Steps* (1940). K. was awarded the
Order of Lenin for his contribution to the development of Tatar
Soviet literature.

KAMAL HUDZHANDI
Born early in the fourteenth century, in Khodzhent (now
Leninabad); died circa 1400, Tabriz. Best-known lyric writer of
classical Tadzhik and Persian literatures.

K. H.'s short ghazals showed him to be independent of the
courts and of religious asceticism; his poems, in fact, show that
he was a rather rebellious man, who praised love and the joys
of life.

Editions: Divan, Tabriz, 1958

KANTEMIR, ANTIOKH DMITRIYEVICH
Born September 21, 1708, Constantinople; died April 11, 1744,
Paris. Russian poet, essayist, and diplomat.

K., who came from a Moldavian dynasty of princes, was given
an excellent education. He was a friend of the literary group centered around Archbishop Prokopovich of Novgorod (1681–1736),
and was the Russian envoy (1732–38) to London and later to
Paris.

K. was the first Russian writer to show strong tendencies toward
classicism and humanism. These tendencies are reflected, in particular, in his nine satires, which were rewritten a number of times
(French edition, 1794; German edition, 1752; Russian edition,
1762). K. is regarded as the founder of the didactic satire in
Russian literature. He translated in 1730, and published in 1740,
Fontenelle's *Entretiens sur la pluralité des mondes* [Dialogues on
the Plurality of the World], which is about the Copernican system. He also wrote the deistic *Pisma o prirode i cheloveke* [Letters

on Nature and on Man, 1742] and an essay on the theory of versification.

Editions: Sobraniye stikhotvernii [Collected Poems], Leningrad, 1956

KAPNIST, VASILII VASILYEVICH
Born February 23, 1757 (or 1758), Obukhova (District of Poltava); died November 9, 1823, Kibintzy. Russian poet and dramatist.

K. came from a noble Ukrainian family. His development as an artist took place in the anticlassicist circle of poets around Derzhavin (1743–1861). His *Satira I* [First Satire, 1780] pilloried the subservience of court poetry, and his *Oda na rabstvo* [Ode on Slavery, 1783], with all its forthright, outspoken boldness, is one of the most important works of political lyrical writing of the eighteenth century. K.'s poetic mastery is reflected very convincingly in his most important work, the comedy *Yabeda* [A Sneak, 1796], a biting satire on feudal justice.

Editions: Sochineniya [Works], Moscow, 1959; *Sobraniye sochinenii* [Collected Works], Moscow–Leningrad, 1960

KARAMZIN, NIKOLAI MIKHAILOVICH
Born December 12, 1766, Mikhailovka (District of Simbirsk); died June 3, 1826, Tzarskoe Selo. Leading representative of Russian sentimentalism; political writer, critic and historian; publisher of the magazines *Moskovski zhurnal* [Moscow Journal, 1791–92] and *Vestnik Yevropy* [Messenger from Europe, 1802 ff.], and of various literary collections.

Despite the fact that the events of the French revolution had strengthened his noble, monarchistic views and beliefs, K. always remained true to his liberal convictions, and attempted to influence Aleksandr I in this direction. The attention of K., who was something of a sentimentalist, was focused on the wealth of feelings present in man as he faces a hostile world. K.'s early literary activities consisted of translations of Lessing and Shakespeare. His short stories, which first appeared in print in 1789, exerted a marked influence on the development of Russian literature, and he became the founder of the Karamzin School.

K. became famous following the publication of his *Pisma ruskovo puteshestvennika* (1791–92; Letters of a Russian Traveler, 1957) which described his journey through Germany, France, and England in the years 1789 and 1790, and of his sensitive, tragic love story, *Bednaya Liza* [Poor Lisa, 1792]. His "purely sentimental" phase ended with the story *Yuliya* (1796; Julia, 1803). K. then turned his attention to the depiction of the contemporary nobility and psychological phenomena. This period reached a climax with the collection of stories entitled *Chuvstvitelnyi i kholodny* [The Sentimentalist and the Coldhearted, 1803], a masterful, satirical study, and in the historical story *Marfa Posadnitza* [Marfa the Governor, 1803]. From 1802, K. concentrated on the preparation of his extensive *Istoriya Gosudarstva Rossiskovo* [History of Ancient and Modern Russia, 1816 ff.].

K. is one of the founders of Russian aesthetic criticism. His light, flowing style contributed greatly to the development of Russian linguistics, and his later stories paved the way for Bestuzhev, Pushkin, and Lermontov.

Editions: Izbrannyye sochineniya [Selected Works], 2 vols., Moscow–Leningrad, 1964

KARAVAYEVA, ANNA ALEKSANDROVNA

Born December 27, 1893, Perm. Soviet Russian short-story writer and novelist.

During the 1920s K.'s short stories and novels told of the changes that were taking place among the country folk after the revolution. These works included *Fligel* [The Wing, 1923], *Dvor* [The Yard, 1926], and *Lesozavod* [The Factory in the Forest, 1928], among others. In the latter work, through which she first became well known, K. demonstrated the changes brought to the villages by industrialization and the worker collective.

K.'s striving for broad generalizations is at times impaired by naturalistic tendencies. The trilogy *Rodina* [Homeland], consisting of *Ogni* [Fires, 1943], *Razbeg* [The Beginning, 2 vols., 1946–48], and *Rodnoi dom* [The Home, 1950], is dedicated to the heroism of the Soviet people fighting in the interior of the country during World War II. K. was awarded the State Prize in 1951.

Editions: Sobraniye sochinenii [Collected Works], 5 vols., Moscow, 1957

KARIM, MUSTAI (Pseud. of *Mustafa Safich Karimov*)

Born October 20, 1919, Klyashevo. Bashkir Soviet poet and dramatist.

K.'s literary activities commenced in the 1930s. In 1938 he published a collection of poems entitled *The Section Is on the March*. These poems are dominated by the poet's love for his homeland and his hope for friendship among peoples. During World War II K. wrote several poems, including *Ulmasbai*, which were later to become very popular. K. himself was a soldier, and was severely wounded in 1942. In 1948, he published *Flowers on the Stone*—the poem of the same title included in this volume is considered to be K.'s best poetic achievement. The collection of poems *Europe-Asia* (1954) earned the approbation of the public; the critics have stressed the philosophical profundity and original imagery exhibited by these poems. In the well-known poem *I Am a Russian* (1958) K., in the name of his people, speaks of the long friendship existing between the Bashkir and the Russian peoples. His later volume of poetry *The River Speaks* (1964) has been well received in the Soviet Union. K.'s verses are closely linked with nature, the people, and the customs of his homeland.

K.'s plays *The Lonely Birch* (1951), *The Abduction of the Girl* (1958), and *A Song None Sings* (1961) are among the great successes of Bashkir national drama. K. has written children's books, including *The Happiness is Our Home* (1952). He is also a literary historian and critic.

K.'s lyric writings are passionate, but they also contain profound philosophical generalizations. K. has been People's Poet of the Bashkir ASSR since 1963.

N. M. Karamzin

Y. Kolas

M. Karim

A. V. Koltzov

O. Y. Korniichuk

KARPENKO-KARYI (Pseud. of *Ivan Karpovych Tobilevych*)

Born September 29, 1845, Arsenyevka (District of Kirovograd); died September 15, 1907, Berlin. Ukrainian dramatist, actor and director.

K., the son of a country estate manager, worked for many years as a clerk. In 1882 he was discharged because of his progressive views.

K.'s ideology was greatly influenced by the Russian revolutionary democrats. The following peasant dramas and satirical comedies are particularly important among his plays based on popular themes: *Rozumnyi i duren* [The Wise Man and the Fool, 1885], *Sto tysyach* [One Hundred Thousand, 1890], and *Khazyayin* [The Lord, 1900]. These works describe the beginning of capitalism in the Ukrainian village, the misery of the peasants, and the formation of the village bourgeoisie.

Editions: Tvory [Works], 3 vols., Kiev, 1960
Further Works: Sava Chalyi (1899)

KASSIL, LEV ABRAMOVICH

Born July 10, 1905, Pokrovskaya (now Engels). Soviet Russian writer of children's books.

K. has been publishing books for children and young people since 1930. These books tell of life in the old schools—*Konduit* (1930), *Shrambraniya* (1933; The Land of Shrambania, 1935)—and of life in the new ones—*Cheriomysh, brat geroya* [The Big Brother, 1938]. In cooperation with M. L. Polyanovski K. has written two books that have earned the approbation of the reading public. These are *Velikove protivostoyaniye* [The Great Opposition, 1942–47] and *Ulitza mladshevo syna* [The Road of the Youngest Son, 1949]. K. has also gained prominence as a literary critic, specializing in the work of Mayakovski. He was awarded the State Prize in 1950.

Editions: Sobraniye sochinenii [Collected Works], 5 vols., Moscow, 1965 ff.

Further Works: Khod beloi korolevy (1956; The Queen of the Snows, 1956)

KATAYEV, IVAN IVANOVICH

Born May 27, 1902, Moscow; died there May 2, 1939. Soviet Russian short-story writer.

In his stories K. depicted scenes drawn from Soviet life, although for a long time he was guided by abstract, humanist considerations. His belief in humanity frequently developed into a kind of passive compassion, even for the enemy. The figures of his communists appear as victims of their duty, as may be seen in *Serdtze* [The Heart, 1928] and *Zhena* [The Wife, 1928]. His best-known work is *Moloko* [Milk, 1930].

KATAYEV, VALENTIN PETROVICH

Born January 28, 1897. Odessa. Soviet Russian novelist and playwright.

K. was a soldier and frontline correspondent during World War I. In 1918–20, as a Red Army soldier, he participated in the civil war in the Ukraine.

K. is, for the most part, a prose writer, but he has also written a number of plays. Most of his early works, written during the 1920s, are further removed from reality than is his later novel *Vremya vperiod* (1932; Time, Forward, 1933) or his tetralogy *Volny Chornovo Morya* [Waves of the Black Sea] which has become known as his "Odessa cycle." This work, which is of a semiautobiographical and documentary nature, is linked together by the main figures, who appear in each successive volume. The tetralogy is concerned with the development of three generations of revolutionaries. *Beleyet parus odinoki* (1936; A White Sail Gleams, 1954), the first volume, opens the series with the tumultuous events of 1905. The second volume, *Khutorok v stepi* (1956; Cottage in the Steppe, 1957), is about the October revolution; the third and fourth volumes in the series, which carry the reader from the beginning of World War II to the liberation of Odessa in 1944, are *Simni veter* [Winter Winds, 1960] and *Katakomby* [The Catacombs of Odessa, 1941–51]. This last volume was originally entitled *Za vlast sovetov* [For Soviet Power]; it was reissued in a new Russian version in 1961.

Editions: Sobraniye sochinenii [Collected Works], 5 vols., Moscow, 1956
Further Works: Doroga tsvetov (1934; The Path of Flowers, 1936); *Povesti i rasskazy* (2 vols., 1947–49); *Gorokh v stenku* [Throwing Peas against the Wall] (1963)

KATENIN, PAVEL ALEKSANDROVICH

Born December 22, 1792, Shaiovo (District of Kostroma); died there June 4, 1853. Russian poet, dramatist, and critic of the progressive, romantic movement.

K. was a leading member of the early Decembrist movement; he was exiled from St. Petersburg as an undesirable person.

K. was one of the first writers to declare war on Zhukovski's elegant romanticism. In his ballads *Natasha* (1814) and *Ubiitza* [The Murderer, 1815], and in *Olga* (1816), which was aimed as an attack on Zhukovski's ballad *Lyudmila*, K. opposed the latter's polished style with the full force and, occasionally, with the vulgar crudeness of the vernacular. K.'s attacks gave rise to stormy literary controversies. Pushkin valued him as "one of the first apostles of the new romanticism." The presentation of ancient heroism in the tragedy *Andromakha* [Andromache, 1818] served the aims of the Decembrists.

Editions: Stikhotvoreniya [Poems], Leningrad, 1954
Further Works: Leschi [Beams] (1816); *Zhenikh* [Fiancé] (1827); *Utoplennik* [The Drowned Man] (1829)

KAUSHUTOV, ATA

Born 1903, Besmein (District of Ashkhabad); died November 15, 1953, Ashkhabad. Turkmenian Soviet novelist.

In 1929 K. wrote the civil war play *On the Kaspi Front*. In 1944–46 he dealt with the problems of internationalism in his novel *Mekhri and Vepa*. The novel *At the Foot of the Kopet-Dag* (1951) is about kolkhoz life in Turkmenia.

KAVERIN (Pseud. of *Veniamin Aleksandrovich Silber*)

Born April 19, 1902, Pskov. Soviet Russian novelist.

In the 1920s, at a time when his views were influenced by "The Serapion Brothers' " literary group and by formalistic concepts of literary theory, K. had already taken some of his themes from real life, as is evident in his novel *Devyat desyatykh sudby* [Nine-Tenths of a Fate, 1926]. His realistic leanings became even more evident in his novel *Ispolneniye Zhelanii* [Fulfillment of Wishes, 2 vols., 1935–38].

K.'s best-known work is the novel *Dva kapitana* (2 vols., 1940–45; Two Captains, 1942), for which he was awarded the State Prize in 1946. Written in the first person, the novel offers a realistic picture of the years 1915–44. It is written on two different thematic levels—it relates the fate of Aleksandr Grigorev and the figures connected with him on the one hand, and on the other tells the story of Tatarinov, the leader of the expedition.

The main theme of the trilogy *Otkrytaya kniga* (1949–57; The Open Book, 1955), which is also written in the first person, is the contrast between true scientific work and political intrigue. The trilogy is composed of *Yunost* [Youth, 1949], *Doktor Vlassenkova* [Doctor Tatyana Vlassenkova, 1952], and *Poiski i nadezshdy* [Search and Hopes, 1956].

Editions: Sobraniye sochinenii [Collected Works], 6 vols., Moscow, 1963
Further Works: Khudozhnik neizvesten [The Unknown Artist] (1931)

KAZAKEVICH, EMMANUIL GENRIKHOVICH

Born February 24, 1913, Kremenchug; died September 22, 1962, Moscow. Soviet Russian prose writer.

K., the son of a teacher, participated in World War II as a scout. He quickly became known following the publication of his novel *Zvezda* [The Star, 1947], which tells of the exploits of the Soviet scouting forces during the war. The novel *Vesna na Odere* (1949; Spring on the Oder, 1953) tells of the battles of the Soviet armies in the last months of the war against Germany. In the sequel to this novel, *Dom na ploshchadi* (1956; The House on the Square, 1960), K. shows the officers of the Soviet army working with the German antifascists in the first hours of building a new democratic Germany in a small town in the Hartz Mountains. K.'s novel *Sinyaya tetrad* [The Blue Notebook, 1961] is about Lenin's underground activities shortly before the October revolution. K. was awarded State Prizes in 1948 and 1950.

Further Works: Dvoye v stepi [Two in the Steppe] (1948); *Serdtze druga* [The Heart of a Friend] (1953)

KAZAKOV, YURII PAVLOVICH
    Born August 8, 1925, Moscow. Soviet Russian short-story writer.
    Following his graduation from the Gorki Institute of Literature in Moscow, K. has been publishing short stories since 1952. He is among the most popular representatives of the so-called lyric prose. His concise, highly concentrated short stories deal with moral and philosophical problems for the most part. They also depict the life of the simple man and his relationship to nature. K.'s impressive, frequently austere prose exhibits the influences of Chekhov and Paustovski.

Further Works: Na polustanke [At the Station] (1958); *Po doroge* [Along the Road] (1961); *Goluboye i zelionoye* [The Blue and the Green] (1963)

KAZBEGI (Pseud. of *Aleksander Mochkhubaridze*)
    Born January 20, 1848, Stepantzminda (now Kazbegi); died December 22, 1893, Tbilisi. Georgian novelist and playwright.
    After attending school in Tbilisi, K., who came from a noble family, studied at the School of Forest Economics and Agriculture in Moscow. Among his first works, written after 1870, were a

number of ethnographic papers on the life of the freedom-loving Georgian mountain tribes. He later described their struggle for freedom in versatile social novels and stories, including *Elisso* (1882), *The Parricide* (1882), *The Pastor* (1885), *Elgudsha* (1881), and *Khevis beri gocha* (1887), among other similar stories. He also wrote numerous dramas. K.'s heroes are strong, romantic characters. His works reflect a certain idealization of patriarchal conditions.

Editions: Krebuli [Collected Works], 5 vols., Tbilisi, 1948–50; *Chsulebani* [Works], 4 vols., Tbilisi, 1948–50

KEDRIN, DMITRII BORISOVICH

Born February 17, 1907, Bagudokhovski (now Ilyich), in the Donetzk region; died September 18, 1945, Tarasovka, near Moscow. Soviet Russian poet.

K.'s versatile lyric talents, which had been recognized by Gorki in 1932, developed in the 1930s. In sensitive and impressive verses, K. sang of work and nature, and, above all, adapted themes from Russian history. These poems, which were frequently in ballad form, occupy a special position in the lyric writings of the 1930s.

Among K.'s most important works are the poem *Zodchiye* [Builders, 1938] and the dramatic poem *Rembrandt* (1938). His first collection of lyric writings, *Svideteli* [Witnesses], appeared in 1940. During World War II K. worked for an army newspaper.

Editions: Izbrannoye [Selected Works], Moscow, 1957

KEKILOV, AMAN

Born 1912, Keshi, near Ashkhabad. Turkmenian Soviet poet and literary historian.

K. studied at the Institute of History, Philosophy, and Literature in Moscow, and later did postgraduate work at the Institute of Pedagogy in Ashkhabad. His poem *Forward* (1935) is dedicated to the class battles taking place during collectivization in the Turkmenian village.

Following World War II, K. depicted the new Turkmenian intelligentsia and the life of Turkmenian students in his poem *Love*. He is also the author of the national anthem of the Turkmenian SSR. As a literary historian, K. has produced important essays on literary theory and on the various periods of Turkmenian Soviet literature.

KERBABAYEV, BERDY

Born March 15, 1894, Aul Amansha-Kapan. Turkmenian Soviet lyric poet and novelist.

K.'s first poems and verses were about the revolutionary changes taking place in the life of Turkmenia. In 1943, K. wrote the libretto for the first Turkmenian opera, *Abadan*.

K. became known following the publication of his two-part novel *The Decisive Step* (1940–47), in which he described the development of Turkmenia during the revolution.

K. is a Meritorious Artist of the Turkmenian SSR. He was awarded State Prizes in 1948 and 1951.

Further Works: Kurban Durdy (1942)

KETLINSKAYA, VERA KAZIMIROVNA

Born May 11, 1906, Sevastopol. Soviet Russian novelist.

K. has become known following the publication of her novel *Muzhestvo* [Courage, 1938], dedicated to the heroic efforts of Soviet youth in the building of Komsomolsk. The central idea of this work is the realization that human happiness depends chiefly on one's own uncompromising attitudes in social as well as in personal life. The novel *Inache zhit ne stoit* [To Live Any Other Way Is Not Worth While, 1961] also takes place in the 1930s in the Soviet Union. The heroic defense of Leningrad is the subject of K.'s novel *V osade*, [The Siege, 1947], for which she received the State Prize in 1948.

Further Works: Natka Michurina (1939); *Rost* [Growth] (1934)

KHEMNITZER, IVAN IVANOVICH

Born January 15, 1745, District of Astrakhan; died March 31, 1784, Smyrna. Russian fabulist.

K. was the son of a doctor of German extraction. In his fables, K., who took a moderate, democratic point of view, but nonetheless was filled with the spirit of true indignation, criticized the abuses of the feudal orders. Some of his best known fables include *Volchye rassuzhdeniye* [Wolfish Deliberations]; *Pauk i mukhi* [The Spider and the Flies]; *Stryapchi i vory* [The Lawyer and the Thief]; *Privilegiya* [The Privilege]; *Kon verkhovy* [The Riding Horse].

In his later work, however, K. frequently replaced accusatory satire with lessons on humility, filled with a hopeful confidence in a better future. Among his later fables are *Privyazannaya sobaka* [The Tied-up Dog] and *Durak i ten* [The Fool and the Shadow]. K.'s best fable is *Metafizik* [The Metaphysician].

Editions: Basni i skaski [Fables and Fairy Tales], St. Petersburg, 1799; *Sochineniya i pisma* [Works and Letters], St. Petersburg, 1873

KHERASKOV, MIKHAIL MATVEYEVICH

Born November 5, 1733, Pereyaslavl; died October 9, 1807, Moscow. Versatile Russian poet and pseudo-classicist; monarchist.

K. prepared the way for sentimentalism—for Karamzin's "new style"—with his poems and his plays, which included *Venetziyanskaya monakhinya* [The Venetian Nun: A Tragedy, 1745]; *Borislav* (1774); *Bezbozhnik* [The Atheist: A Comedy, 1761], as well as with his prose writings—*Numa, ili protzvetayushchi Rim* [Numa, or Flowering Rome, 1768]; *Kadm i Garmoniya* [Cadmus and Harmony, 1786]; *Polidor, syn Kadma i Garmonii* [Polidor, the Son of Cadmus and Harmony, 1794]. K.'s best known work is the long heroic poem *Rosiyada* [Rossiiad, 1771–79], in which he extolled the capture of Kazan by Ivan IV in 1552.

Editions: Tvoreniya [Works], Moscow, 1796–1802
Further Works: Vladimir (1785)

KHETAGUROV, KOSTA (KONSTANTIN)

Born October 15, 1859, Bergdorf Nar (now North Ossetian ASSR); died April 1, 1906, Georgiyevo-Ossetinskoye (now Khetagurov). Founder of Ossetian literature.

K., whose ideology was formed under the influence of the Russian revolutionary democrats, formulated the standards for the Ossetian literary language. K.'s works reflect the fight of his people for liberation from nationalists and bourgeois liberals. His collections of poems, *Stikhotvoreniya* [Poems] (in Russian) and *Iron fendr* [The Ossetian Lyre] (in Ossetian), appeared in 1895 and 1899 respectively. K. also wrote children's stories, fables, and a series of political essays.

Editions: Sobraniye sochinenii [Collected Works], 3 vols., Moscow, 1951; *Izbrannoye* [Selected Works], Dsaudshikau, 1953

KHLEBNIKOV, VELEMIR (VIKTOR) VLADIMIROVICH

Born November 9, 1885, Tundutov (District of Astrakhan); died June 28, 1922, Santalovo (District of Novgorod). Soviet Russian poet.

K.'s great linguistic talent—which has been stressed by Mayakovski, who was stimulated by it—began to develop in 1908 under the influence of both symbolism and futurism. In his search for a new means of representation, K., in poems on Russia and her history, arrived at an individualistic but frequently formalized stylization of Russian folklore. After the October revolution K. wrote poems from a subjectively honest but nevertheless bourgeois, anarchistic point of view, reflecting the fervor of the times in a contradictory manner.

Editions: Sobraniye proizvodenii [Selected Works], 5 vols., Leningrad, 1929–33

KIACHELI, LEO (Pseud. of *Leon Mikhailovich Shengelaya*)

Born February 19, 1884, Obudshi; died December 19, 1963, Tbilisi. Georgian Soviet novelist.

K. came from a noble family. He attended the high school in

Kutaisi and then studied law in Kharkov; in 1906 he was persecuted for his revolutionary activities. In 1907 he escaped from prison and lived illegally in Moscow till 1911; he then emigrated to Switzerland. He returned home in 1917.

K.'s work formed a link with the traditions of critical realism. He described the revolutionary times of 1905–07 in his novel *Tariel Golua* (1915), while in the novel *Blood* (1927) he told of the struggle of the Georgian people during the years of reaction. With *Gvadi Bigva* (1938), for which he was awarded the State Prize in 1941, K. created the first great novel in Georgian literature. This work told of the class struggles during the socialist reconstruction of the country. The fight of the Soviet people in World War II is the subject of his novel *A Man from the Mountains* (1950)

Editions: Krebuli [Collected Works], 3 vols., Tbilisi, 1946–50; *Chsulebani khut tomad* [Works], 5 vols., Tbilisi, 1960–64

KIRILLOV, VLADIMIR TIMOFEYEVICH

Born October 14, 1890, Kharino (near Smolensk); died December 18, 1943. Soviet Russian poet.

K. joined the revolutionary movement at an early age. He was sentenced to three years in exile for participating in a sailors' strike in 1905–06. From 1918 on, K. was active in the Proletcult organization. K. published little in the 1930s, and spent the years between 1929 and 1937 traveling widely in the Soviet Union.

K. praised the struggles of the Russian working class, which was then changing the course of world history, in passionate verse, including *My nezmetnyye, groznyye milliony truda* [We Are Uncounted, Threatening Millions of Labor, 1917], *Zhelesznyi mesyats* [The Iron Moon, 1918], *Ya podslushal eti pesni bliskikh, radostnykh vekov* [I Have Heard the Songs of the Coming, Joyous Centuries, 1918]. In these works, K. frequently used stressed accents and employed abstract symbols which, when used in combination, produced fervent, triumphant effects.

Editions: Stikhotvoreniya [Poems], Moscow, 1958

KIRSANOV, SEMION ISAAKOVICH
Born September 18, 1906, Odessa. Soviet Russian poet.

K.'s early poems exhibit a markedly militant character, with some tendencies toward formalistic experimentation. During World War II his writings—permeated by profound patriotic feelings—were frequently distributed as leaflets. The themes of his postwar poems and verses are versatile, and deal with actual problems, as can be seen in *Aleksandr Matrosov* (1946) and *Nebo nad Rodinoi* [The Sky over the Homeland, 1947]. These works are characterized by their philosophical overtones and their symbolic, fairy-tale imagery.

K. has translated poems by Neruda, Brecht, Aragon, and other foreign poets. He was awarded the State Prize in 1951.

Editions: Izbrannyye stikhotvoreniya [Selected Poems], Moscow, 1956; *Poemy* [Poems], Moscow, 1956

KIRSHON, VLADIMIR MIKHAILOVICH
Born August 19, 1902, Nalchik (in the northern Caucasus); died July 28, 1938. Soviet Russian journalist and dramatist.

Among K.'s earliest works was the play *Konstantin Terekhin* (1926), which he wrote in cooperation with A. Uspenski, and the drama *Relsy gudyat* [The Rails Are Humming, 1927]. In his historical play *Gorod vetrov* [The City of Winds] written in 1929 and dedicated to the heroic death of the Baku commissars, K. overcame a certain illustrative schematism evident in his early works.

In *Khleb* [Bread, 1930], K. dealt with the class struggles in the Soviet villages. His dramas *Sud* [The Judgment, 1932] and *Bolshoi den* [The Big Day, 1936] are concerned with such important political subjects as the class struggles in Germany and Soviet patriotism. K.'s best work is the comedy *Chudesnyi splav* [A Wonderful Alloy, 1933], about the life of Soviet youth. A leading functionary of RAPP (Russian Association of Proletarian Writers) and, later, of the Soviet Writers' Union, K. also wrote important essays and speeches on cultural and literary themes.

Editions: Dramaticheskiye proizvedeniya [Dramatic Works], Moscow, 1957

KLDIASHVILI, DAVID

Born September 11, 1862, Simoneti (District of Kutaisi); died there April 24, 1931. Georgian Soviet novelist and playwright.

K., the son of an impoverished nobleman, became an officer in the army but was discharged on account of his revolutionary activities. His novels, stories, and comedies described the declining feudal order.

In his novels *Solomon Morbeladze* (1894) and *Samanishvili's Stepmother* (1897), as well as in his comedies *Irina's Happiness* (1897) and *Misfortune* (1914), K. created the figure of the "autumnal nobleman," the impoverished young nobleman unable to find his position in life. In novels such as *The Curse* and *The Sacrifice*, both written in 1894, and in *At the Arrival* (1897), K. depicted the depressing life of the Georgian peasants. From 1930 until his death K. held the title of People's Artist of the Georgian SSR.

Editions: Krebuli [Collected Works], 2 vols. Tbilisi, 1950–52

KLDIASHVILI, SERGO

Born October 18, 1895, Simoneti (District of Kutaisi). Georgian Soviet dramatist and novelist; son of David Kldiashvili.

K. became known in 1932, following the publication of his novel *Ashes*, one of the best works on World War I in Georgian literature. Conflicts arising during socialist reconstruction occupy the focal point in his drama *A Generation of Heroes* (1937). In his novel *The Quiet Defile*, K. gave extensive coverage to the difficulties encountered in the establishment of Soviet power in Georgia.

Further Works: The Silent Hermitage (1958)

KNYAZHNIN, YAKOV BORISOVICH

Born October 14, 1742, Pskov; died January 25, 1791, St. Petersburg. Most popular dramatist of Russian classicism.

Influenced by the progressiveness of his time, K. came to oppose Catherine II. He employed the stage for propagating his views on virtue and justice, and for fighting against the abuses of the times. K. used a highly emotional language in his presentation of the interplay of human passions.

K. also wrote four masterful comedies, including *Khvastun* [The Show-Off, 1786], five comic operas, including *Neshchastye ot karety* [Misfortune through a Carriage, 1779], and eight tragedies, of which *Vadim Novgorodski* [Vadim of Novgorod, 1789], a glorification of the republic and republican virtues, has become K.'s most important work.

Editions: Sobraniye sochinenii [Collected Works], St. Petersburg, 1787; *Izbrannyye proizvedeniya* [Selected Works], Leningrad, 1961

KOCHERHA, IVAN ANTONOVYCH
Born October 6, 1881, Nosivka; died December 29, 1952, Kiev. Ukrainian Soviet dramatist.

K., who came from a peasant family, graduated from the Law Faculty of the University of Kiev after having suffered great privations as a student. After 1917 he occupied leading administrative positions during the socialist cultural revolution in the Ukraine.

K.'s most important literary achievements may be found in the dramatization of historical subjects, chiefly those taken from Ukrainian history. Among his more mature works are the historical dramas *Svichynne vesillya* [Svichka's Wedding, 1931] and *Yaroslav Mudryi* [Yaroslav the Wise, 1946]. His comedy *Hodynnykar i kurka* [The Watchmaker and the Chicken, 1934] became a great success.

Editions: Tvory [Works], 3 vols., Kiev, 1956
Further Works: Marko v pekli [Mark in Hell] (1928); *Istyna* [The Truth] (1947); *Prorok* [The Prophet] (1948)

KOCHETOV, VSEVOLOD ANISIMOVICH
Born February 4, 1912, Novgorod. Soviet Russian narrator and novelist.

K. graduated in 1931 from an agricultural college. From 1938 to the outbreak of World War II he has worked as a journalist; he was a frontline correspondent during the war. He has been editor-in-chief of the magazine *Oktyabr* [October] since 1961.

K. first became known following the publication of his novel *Zhurbiny* (1952; The Zhurbins, 1953), which deals with the relationships and conflicts of a worker family following the war. In this novel K. has depicted problems existing in work and personal life, and has opened new avenues for Soviet postwar literature.

Questions of morality, the responsibility of the individual with respect to society, and the relations between party and people in connection with the discussions before and after the Twentieth Party Congress of the Communist Party of the Soviet Union have been dealt with by K. in his novels *Molodost z nami* [Youth Is With Us, 1954], *Bratya Yerzhovy* [The Brothers Yerzhov], and *Sekretar Obkoma* [The Regional Party Secretary, 1962].

Editions: Izbrannyye sochineniya [Selected Works], 3 vols., Moscow, 1962
Further Works: Ulitzi i transhei. Zapisi voyennykh let [Streets and Trenches: Notes on the War Years] (1965)

KOIDULA, LYDIA (Pseud. of *Lidia Emilie Florentine Jannsen*)
Born December 24, 1843, Vändra; died August 11, 1886, Kronstadt. The most popular and important Estonian poet and dramatist of the nineteenth century.

K.'s passionately patriotic poems exerted a great influence on the people. She was also the author of a number of studies and plays, including *Saaremaa onupoeg* [The Cousin from Saaremaa, 1840] and *Säärane ehk Sada vakka tangusoola* [One Hundred Measures of Salt, 1872].

Editions: Teosed [Works], 2 vols., Tallinn, 1957
Further Works: Vainulilled [Field Flower] (1866); *Emajõe ööbik* [The Nightingale from Emajõe] (1867)

KOLAS, YAKUB (Pseud. of *Kanstantin Mikhailavich Mitzkevich*)
Born November 3, 1882, Akinchytzy (District of Minsk); died August 13, 1956, Minsk. Byelorussian Soviet poet and prose

writer, from 1928 a member of the Academy of Sciences in Minsk.

K., the son of a poor peasant and woodsman, became a village teacher. He was arrested in 1908 for revolutionary activities and remained in prison for three years. K.'s early poems and fables, written between 1906 and 1910, describe the harsh lot of the working peasant; his early stories are permeated by revolutionary protests against the national and social oppression of the Byelorussian people. K. at first found it hard to understand the progressive character of the October revolution, but soon found his way to socialist realism.

In his poems, stories, and plays K. depicted life before the revolution and the development of the socialist village in Byelorussia —his poems *Novaya zyamlya* [New Earth, 1923] and *Symonmuzyka* [Simon the Musician, 1925] are representative of this period. In his war lyrics, for which he was awarded the State Prize of 1946, K. called for battle against the fascist invaders. After the war K. became particularly well known for his poem *Rybakova khata* [The Fisherman's Hut, 1947]. In this poem, for which he was awarded the State Prize of 1948, K. treated the theme of reunification of all the Byelorussian people within the Socialist Soviet state.

K. has made an important contribution to the development of Byelorussian prose writing. Of particular importance is his autobiographical novel trilogy—consisting of the volumes *U Paleskai glushy* [In the Solitude of the Polesye, 1923], *U glybi Palesya* [Deep in the Polesye, 1927], and *Na rostanyakh* [At the Crossroads, 1954–55]—in which K. described the development of the Byelorussian village and that of the national intelligentsia. His novel on the partisans, *Ded Talash* [Old Man Talash], appeared in 1944.

K., together with Y. Kupala (1882–1942), is regarded as the classic writer of Byelorussian literature. From 1926 until his death K. held the title of People's Poet of the Byelorussian SSR.

Editions: Sbor tvorav [Collected Works], 7 vols., Minsk, 1952

KOLLONTAI, ALEKSANDRA MIKHAILOVNA
Born March 31, 1872, St. Petersburg; died March 9, 1952, Moscow. Soviet Russian essayist and diplomat.
K. first became a member of the revolutionary movement in the 1890s. In 1920 she became the director of the women's section of the Central Committee of the Russian Communist Party, and between 1921–22 was secretary of the international women's secretariat of the Comintern. K. entered the diplomatic service of her country in 1923, and was Soviet Russian minister in Sweden from 1930 to 1945.

K. published a series of papers on problems concerning women, and developed a naïve sociology of love in presocialist society, the results of which gave the erroneous impression that proletarian morals strive for polygamous companionships. This theory of "new" kinds of relationships—a theory incompatible with proletarian morals—has also been propagated by K. in *Lyubov pchel trudovykh* [Love of the Laboring Bees, 1923] and similar essays, all of which exhibit a certain straining after sentimental effects. K. has offered a clear picture of the German Social Democrats during the first months of World War I in excerpts from her 1914 diary, which was published in 1924.

KOLTZOV, ALEKSEI VASILYEVICH
Born October 15, 1809, Voronezh; died there November 10, 1842. Russian poet.
K.'s father, a butcher and cattle-dealer, thought little of education, and K. was forced to acquire his knowledge secretly by self-study. In 1835 Stankevich and Belinski (1811–48) aided him in the publication of his first collection of poems. In these poems, which included *Pesnya pakharya* [The Song of the Ploughman, 1831], *Ne shumi ty, rozh* [Do Not Rustle, Rye, 1834], and *Razdumye selyanina* [Thoughts of a Peasant, 1837], the peasant theme was treated for the first time in Russian literature from the point of view of the peasants themselves. It was this aspect of K.'s poems that was to have a considerable influence on Russian literature, especially on the work of Nekrasov (1821–78).

The wide range of emotions and themes in K.'s poems is surprising. He never depicted peasant life as merely an idyll, but presented it with all its daily struggles and difficulties. Occasionally his poems exhibit elements of social protest, and they frequently treat religious ideas. In his later work, however, including *Is Goratziya* [From Horace, 1841], K. gradually overcame his religious sentiments and themes.

In the course of the years K.'s material situation deteriorated but, wishing to remain independent, he refused aid from his friends. The poems of these later years exhibit in their creative sentiments a greater depth than did his earlier works. These later poems tell of the tragedy inherent in the lives of simple people (*Ya lyubila yevo* [I Once Loved Him, 1841]).

KOLTZOV, MIKHAIL YEFIMOVICH

Born June 12, 1898, Kiev; died April 4, 1942. Soviet Russian novelist and journalist.

K. studied for a short period at the Institute of Psychoneurology in Petrograd, where he came into contact with revolutionary-minded students. K. began his political and journalistic activities after the February revolution. In 1918 he became a member of the Communist Party, and during the civil war worked on army newspapers; he was subsequently for many years associated with *Pravda*. In the field of cultural education and politics, K. worked in close cooperation with Gorki.

K.'s chief work lay in the field of essays and sketches distinguished for their high literary quality. K. satirically exposed the representatives of imperialism and the White Guard elements abroad, and attacked all phenomena in Soviet society detrimental to the growth of socialism. He also created impressive pictures of the creative work of Soviet man.

K.'s book *Ispanski dnevnik* [Spanish Diary, 1938], based on personal experiences, unfortunately remained unfinished. It nonetheless offers impressive portraits of the first antifascist fighters, and contains masterful views of the men fighting in Spain. This book, because of its profoundly humanist content, which is powerfully and realistically presented, ranks as one of the most important publications of Soviet literature in the 1930s.

Editions: Izbrannyye proizvedeniya [Selected Works], 3 vols., 1957

KONETZKI, VIKTOR VIKTOROVICH

Born June 6, 1929, Leningrad. Soviet Russian short-story writer.

K.'s first short stories appeared in print in 1956; since then, he has published a number of collections of stories which have earned the approbation of a large circle of readers. His concise and laconic tales, which frequently treat themes from the lives of sailors, give a versatile picture of Soviet everyday life. K. here endeavors to present characteristic, usually complex destinies, and to show how people react in times of crisis.

Further Works: Kamni pod voidoi [Stones under the Water: Short Stories], 1959; *Zavtrashnyye zaboty* [Future Problems: Short Stories], 1961; *V kontze nedeli* [On the Weekend], 1965

KOPTYAYEVA, ANTONINA DMITRIYEVNA

Born November 7, 1909, Priisk Yuzhny (in the Amur region). Soviet Russian novelist.

Following World War II, K. wrote a series of novels about the ethics of the Soviet physician; she frequently deals with the complex conflicts between duty and private life. Her novels *Ivan Ivanovich* (1949; Eng., 1952), for which she received the State Prize in 1950, and *Derzaniye* [Daring, 1958], in which she dealt with problems encountered by the working woman who holds a responsible position, have also been well received by foreign readers. Her novel *Dar zemli* [Gift of the Soil, 1963] tells of the life of Tatar oilworkers who are taking part in the building of a new chemical industrial complex.

KORNIICHUK, OLEKSANDER YEVDOKYMOVYCH

Born May 25, 1905, Khrystynovka (District of Kiev). Ukrainian Soviet dramatist; member of the Academy of Sciences of the USSR and the RSFSR.

K., the son of a mechanic, attended the Faculty of Literature at the Kiev Institute for Adult Education in 1929. During World War II he worked for various newspapers. K. has occupied several extremely high government positions, and since 1959 has been Chairman of the Supreme Soviet of the Ukrainian SSR; he was President of the Writers' Union of the Ukrainian SSR for many years. K. has been active in the World Peace Movement since 1935, and was awarded the Lenin Peace Prize in 1959.

K.'s literary activities began in the mid-1920s with the publication of his short stories. His dramas deal with the complex formation processes of socialist awareness in Soviet man. During the prewar period K. wrote a number of plays that are particularly important. The civil war drama *Zagibel eskadry* [The Sinking of the Fleet, 1933] deals with the controversial decision by revolutionary sailors to sink the Russian Black Sea fleet in order to prevent its capture by the German interventionists. *Platon Krechet* (1934) tells of the socialist and humanistic activities of Soviet intellectuals. The hero of the historical drama *Bogdan Khmelnitzki* (1938) is Khmelnitzki, the Cossack hetman who led the Ukrainian people in their national fight for liberation from Polish foreign rule in the seventeenth century.

K.'s war play *Front* (1942) was very well received when it was published in *Pravda*.

K.'s most successful postwar works include the lyrical comedy *Kalynovi hai* [The Snow-Ball Tree Park, 1950], which, in witty, satirical dialogue and impressive scenes, deals with outmoded ideas about work, and *Kryla* [Wings, 1954], which demonstrates the profound solidarity of both the people and the Soviet Communists in their struggle against bureaucracy and pettiness.

In one of his most recent plays, *Nad Dniprom* [On the Dnieper, 1960], K. depicts the new processes in the awareness of the Ukrainian kolkhoz farmers, and demonstrates the growth of their intellectual and cultural demands. K.'s dramatic work is characterized by pointed actions, effective stage figures, polished dialogue, and accurate, popular language.

K. has also written numerous articles on the theory of literature, in which he discusses the work of Shevchenko, Franko, Lesya Ukrainka, and Gorki, among others. K. was awarded State Prizes in 1941, 1942, 1943, 1949, and 1951.

Editions: Sochineniya [Works], 3 vols., Moscow, 1956
Further Works: Kamennyi ostriv [The Rocky Island] (1929); *V stepakh Ukrayiny* [In the Steppes of the Ukraine] (1940); *Makar Dibrova* (1947); *Stranitza dnevnika* [A Page from a Diary] (1963)

KOROLENKO, VLADIMIR GALAKTIONOVICH
    Born July 27, 1853, Zhitomir; died December 12, 1921, Poltava. Russian realistic short-story writer and novelist.
    The son of a judge, K. was early aware of problems of social injustice. He became a member of the populist movement while studying at the Technical Colleges in St. Petersburg and Moscow.
    Following his participation in student protests, he was arrested in 1879 and exiled to Siberia (1882–84). In the years 1885–99 K. lived in Nizhni Novgorod, working as a prose writer and a political journalist. In 1891–92, K. helped organize the movement for the relief of the famine-stricken Volga region. In the Multansk ritual trial of 1896, K. denounced nationalist and racist persecution. During his stay in Poltava (1900–21), K. courageously supported social justice and human rights, and fought against anti-Semitism. In 1902 he refused to become an honorary member of the Imperial Academy of Sciences as a protest after the tsar had intervened to withdraw Gorki's nomination.
    As a narrator, K. combined both realistic and symbolic presentations in order to enhance the expressiveness of his humanistic and democratic ideals. In his first important story, *Son Makara* (1885; Makar's Dream, 1916), K. described the awakening of social protest in a Russian peasant who joined the nomadic Yakut tribe. K. used dramatic motifs taken from national life in his stories *Les shumit* (1886; In the Murmuring Forest, and Other Stories, 1916), *Sokolinetz* [The People from Sakhalin, 1885], and *Reka igrayet* [The River Moves, 1892].
    K.'s sympathies for the revolutionary struggle for liberation are reflected in such stories as *Chudnaya* [The Wonderful Girl,

1880] and *Skazaniye o Flore, Agrippe i Menakheme, syne Ye-gudy* [The Story of Flor, Agrippa, and Menakhem, the Son of Yehuda, 1886]. In his famous story *Slepoi Muzykant* (1886; The Blind Musician, 1952), K. demonstrated both his optimistic view of life and his ability to present a psychological portrait. The story *V durnom obshchestve* (1885; Bad Company, 1892), as well as his important belletristic work *Istoriya moyevo sovremen-nika* [History of My Contemporaries, 4 vols., 1906–22], is of great autobiographical and critical value. In the latter work, K., in vividly drawn word paintings, described the social development in Russia and in the Ukraine during the second half of the nineteenth century, as well as the intellectual development of a typical revolutionary and democrat.

Editions: Sobraniye sochinenii [Collected Works], 10 vols., Moscow 1953–56
Further Works: Yashka (1880); *Ubivetz* [The Murderer] (1882); *Paradoks* [A Paradox] (1894); *Bez yazyka* [Speechless] (1895); *Marusina zayimka* [Mary's Cottage] (1899); *Ogonki* [Lights] (1900); *Mgnoveniye* [A Moment] (1900)
Selected English translations: The Vagrant, and Other Tales (1887)

KOSTOMAROV, MYKOLA IVANOVICH (Pseud. of *Yeremiya Halka*)
    Born May 16, 1817, Yurasivka; died April 19, 1885, St. Petersburg. Ukrainian romantic poet and liberal historian.
    K., the son of an estate owner, graduated in 1837 from the University of Kharkov with a degree in philology and history. He later became well-known in scientific circles for his numerous historical and ethnographical studies. He was repeatedly persecuted by the tsarist government. K.'s literary work dealt chiefly with themes from Ukrainian history, related from the conservative, romantic point of view. His translations of the freedom songs of the Greek revolutionaries against their Turkish oppressors, and of works by Byron, Shakespeare, and other Western European poets are of great artistic value.

Further Works: Sava Chalyi (1838); *Pereyaslawska nich* [A Night in Pereyaslav] (1841); *Kudeyar* [Kudeyar] (1875)

KOTLYAREVSKYI, IVAN PETROVYCH

Born September 9, 1769, Poltava; died there November 10, 1838. Father of the new Ukrainian literature; author of numerous lyric and dramatic works.

K., the son of a minor official, studied at the Poltava Seminary from 1780 to 1789 and then worked as a clerk and a private tutor. In 1806–07 he participated in the Russo-Turkish war, and in 1812 took part in the campaign against Napoleon. In 1816 he became director of the Poltava theater. K. was a member of numerous literary associations, and was connected with the Decembrist movement.

K. first became known in 1798 following the publication of his parody of Vergil's *Aeneid*. (A complete edition of this work was published posthumously in 1842.) This parody forms a link with both the Russian "satire of enlightenment" and the verse parody. K.'s satirical presentation of the propertied classes in Ukrainian society, together with his impressive characterization of simple people, can also be found in the drama *Natalka-Poltavka* [Natalka from Poltava, 1813], and in the realistic vaudeville-like sketch *Moskal-charivnik* [The Moscovian Magician, 1819].

K.'s poetry has exerted a permanent influence on the literary development of Russian writers (Gogol) and those of the Ukraine (Shevchenko).

Editions: Povne zibrannya tvoriv [Collected Works], 2 vols., Kiev, 1952–53; *Tvory* [Works], Kiev, 1960

KOTZYUBNYSKYI, MIKHAILO MYKHAILOVYCH

Born September 17, 1864, Vynnytzya; died April 25, 1913, Chernyghiov. Ukrainian revolutionary, democratic novelist, critic, and translator.

K., the son of a minor civil servant, taught at the high school in Vynnytzya from 1891 to 1900. From 1900 on he worked as a statistician for the Zemstvo government in Chernyghiov. He had been an active member of the revolutionary movement against tsarism since 1880, and was friends with both I. Franko and

M. Gorki. The social and national oppression of the Ukrainian people by tsarist officials, clergymen, and foreign estate owners, as well as the revolutionary activities of the people, occupies the focal point in K.'s critical, realistic writings.

Much of K.'s work was produced in creative competition with the best writers of both Russian and Ukrainian literatures—Nekrasov, Saltykov-Shchedrin, Shevchenko, Franko, and Vovchok, among others. The quality of his work may be seen in the stories *Lyalechka* (1901); *V putakh shaitana* [In Satan's Clutches, 1899]; *Persona grata* (1907); *Intermezzo* (1908); and *Tini zabytykh predkiv* [Shadows of Our Forgotten Ancestors, 1911]. His best work, the two-part novel *Fata morgana* (1903–10), deals with the social patterns of the Ukrainian village in the epoch of imperialism. It also describes the rise of revolutionary sentiments in the peasant masses on the eve of the 1905 revolution.

K.'s work, because of its treatment of themes of social importance, its characteristic figures, and its lyrically melodic and direct, popular language, occupies a special place in world literature. His works have been translated into many foreign languages.

Editions: Tvory [Works], 3 vols., Kiev, 1955–56

KOZHEVNIKOV, ALEKSEI BENEDIKTOVICH
Born March 18, 1891, Khabasy (District of Vyatka). Soviet Russian novelist.

K. took part in the civil war, and in 1923 commenced his studies at the Bryusov Institute for Literature and Art; he was a member of the literary association *Kuznitza.*

K.'s literary career commenced in 1924. His works are based on his own impressions of socialist reconstruction and of the transformation that followed the revolution in the various regions of the Soviet Union. His novel *Zolotaya golytba* [Golden Have-nots, 1927] and his short story *Pervyi priz* [The First Prize] both take place in the Urals of the 1920s. His short story *Tansky* (1930) and his novel *Z dravstvui, put!* [Welcome, Railroad! 1934] are about the builders of the Turkmenian-Siberian railroad. K. was awarded the State Prize of 1951 for his novel on the agricultural innovations, *Zhivaya voda* (1950; Living Water, 1954).

Further Works: Turmalin-kamen [The Stone Tourmaline] (1927); *Brat okeana* [The Ocean's Brother] (1939)

KOZHEVNIKOV, VADIM MIKHAILOVICH
  Born April 22, 1909, Narym (Siberia). Soviet Russian short-story writer and novelist.
  K.'s parents were exiled to Siberia for their revolutionary activities. K. completed his studies of literature and ethnology at the University of Moscow in 1933. He wrote numerous sketches, travelogues, and short stories based on his frequent travels.
  K.'s cycle of short stories *Truzheniki voiny* [Workers of the War, 1945] describe the character of Soviet man as seen in the course of World War II. His partly autobiographical novel *Zare navstrechu* [Toward Dawn, 1956–57] shows the development of a boy during the years of the October revolution. *Znakomtes Baluyev!* [May I Present: Mr. Baluyev, 1960] and other later works deal with the problem of directing people; they reflect the author's attempts to depict the versatile face of the contemporary Soviet people. K.'s work shows strong journalistic tendencies.

Further Works: Den letyashchi [The Flying Day] (1962); *Shchit i mech* [The Shield and the Sword] (1965)

KRAPIVA, KANDRAT (Pseud. of *Kandrat Kandratavich Atrakhavich*)
  Born March 5, 1896, Nisok (District of Minsk). Byelorussian Soviet novelist and playwright; Vice President of the Byelorussian Academy of Sciences and People's Writer of the Byelorussian SSR since 1956.
  K., the son of a peasant, became a village schoolteacher. Early in the 1920s he attempted to write poems in the style of Lermontov (1814–41); he later criticized contemporary abuses in prose and poetry. In his satirical fables K. followed the traditions of Krylov (1769–1844). K. later gained prominence as a dramatist. He wrote numerous plays including *Partyzany* [The Partisans,

1937], *Khto smyayetztza apozhnim* [He Who Laughs Last, 1939], and *Pyayutaz shavaranki* [The Larks are Singing, 1950]. Many of these are frequently staged in the Soviet Union, and are popular because of their genial good humor. K. was awarded State Prizes in 1941 and 1951.

Editions: Sbor tvorov [Collected Works], 4 vols., Minsk, 1963

KREUTZWALD, FRIEDRICH REINHOLD

Born December 26, 1803, Jõepere, near Rakvere; died August 25, 1882, Tartu. Estonian writer, poet, and scholar.

K., the son of a serf shoemaker, was a schoolteacher for a short time and then began studying medicine (1826) in Tartu; he started practicing medicine in Voru in 1833. K. has taken his place among the Estonian people as an important, enlightened philosopher and democrat. His poems have greatly influenced the development of both Estonian literature and the Estonian literary language. His best-known work is the national epic *Kalevipoeg* [The Son of Kalev, 1857–61]; it is based on numerous folksongs and sagas. Because its hero exhibited all the most favorable features of the national character it contributed greatly to the enhancement of the national image.

KRĖVĖ-MICKEVIČIUS, VINCAS

Born October 19, 1882, Subartony; died July 7, 1954, Marple Township, near Philadelphia, Pa. Lithuanian historical novelist and playwright; folklorist and university professor.

K.'s *Dainavos šalies zmoniu padavimai* [Legends Told by the Old People from the Region around Dainava] appeared in 1912. Among his most important works are the historical dramas *Šarūnas* (1911) and *Skirgaila* (1925), as well as *Žentas* [The Son-in-law], a drama based on a theme taken from village life in bourgeois Lithuania, and *Mindaugo mirtis* [Mindaugas' Death, 1935], a drama about the invasion of the Teutonic knights, the theme of which incorporates certain features of Hitlerism.

K. has written a great number of masterful short stories, most of which have been collected in volumes such as *Šiaudinėj pastogėj* [Under the Thatched Roof, 1928], *Raganius* [The Magician, 1930], and *Miglose* [In the Fog, 1937–40]. Characteristic of K.'s work is the tightly knit combination of romanticism and realism, of stylization and the use of folklore. These characteristics are frequently put together in epic form.

As an ideologic idealist, K. was frequently able to enrich realistic art in an objective manner by his profound psychological understanding. K.'s work can truly be said to belong to the classics of Lithuanian literature. In the last decade of his life, however, K. failed to evaluate social developments correctly (he made anti-Soviet declarations during World War II). He left Lithuania in 1944 with the retreating German armies, and, after a three-year stay in Austria, emigrated to the U.S.A. in 1947.

Editions: Rinktine [Works], Kaunas, 1958

KRON (KREIN), ALEKSANDR ALEKSANDROVICH

Born July 13, 1909, Moscow. Soviet Russian playwright.

K.'s first play, published in 1929, was *Vintovka 492 116* [Rifle No. 492 116], which deals with the fate of a group of neglected children adopted by a Red Army unit. The theme of his tragedy *Trus* [The Coward, 1935] is concerned with the development of the new man under the changing conditions of the revolution. His play *Ofitzer flota* [The Fleet Officer] appeared in 1945. The comedy *Vtoroye dykhaniye* [The Second Breath, 1946] tells of the high moral qualities of Soviet officers, and rejects cynicism and degeneracy. The play *Kandidat partii* [The Candidate of the Party, 1950; rev., 1953] is distinguished by ideas of true humanity and ethical ideals. Conflicts between socialist and egotistical modes of behavior are handled in a psychologically impressive manner in K.'s drama *Glubokaya razvedka* [Secret Service].

Editions: Dramaticheskiye proizvedeniya [Dramatic Works], Moscow, 1958

KRYLOV, IVAN ANDREYEVICH

Born February 13, 1769, Moscow; died November 21, 1844, St. Petersburg. One of the greatest Russian fabulists; dramatist and journalist.

K. entered the civil service in St. Petersburg in 1782, but, persecuted by censorship, he left the capital in 1793. K. returned to St. Petersburg in 1806, and from 1812 until his death continued to work there as a librarian.

In his first literary attempts—comedies and comic operas, including *Beshenaya semya* [The Crazy Family, 1786], *Sochinitel v prikhozhei* [The Author in the Antechamber, 1786], and *Prokazniki* [The Knaves]—K. depicted the moral decline evident in the nobility and exposed the lack of talent among the contemporary literati.

K. produced his best comic works—the biting political satire on the Prussomania of Paul I, *Podschipa* [Trumps, 1800], and the comedies *Modnaya lavka* [The Fashionable Salon, 1806] and *Urok dochkam* [Instructions for Daughters, 1807] (in which he derided the Francophilia of the nobility)—during the period of his final transition to the genre of the fable.

K. was noteworthy as a journalist, and became the successor to Novikov (1744–1818) on the satirical magazine *Pochta dukhov* [Ghost-mail, January–August 1789]. K.'s criticism of the favoritism shown by Catherine II and the plundering of the people by nobility and civil servants caused this magazine to be prohibited. In another magazine, *Srital* [The Observer, 1792], K. continued to expose the inhumanity of the estate owners (*Pokhvalnaya rech v pamyat moyemu dedushke*, Panegyric to the Memory of My Little Grandfather) and of the despotic government (*Kaib*). Following the publication of his magazine *Sankt-Petersburgski Merkuri* [St. Petersburg Mercury, 1793], K. was forced to leave the country.

Early in the nineteenth century K. turned toward writing fables; he raised this form of art from mere moralizing to realistic social satire. K. showed his mastery in this genre in both the adaptation of traditional fable themes—*Vorona i lisitza* [The Crow and the

Fox, 1807]—and in the creation of new fables. As early as 1806–12, K.'s fables sided with the weaker classes and with the working people, as can be seen in *Volk i yagnionok* [The Wolf and the Little Lamb, 1808] and *Listy i korni* [Leaves and Roots, 1811]. The fables K. produced during the War of 1812 reflected his democratic patriotism— *Razdel* [The Division], *Oboz* [The Cartload], *Vorona i kuritza* [The Crow and the Chicken], and *Volk ba osarne* [The Wolf in the Doghouse]. These works were very popular and were widely circulated among the soldiers and the militant peasants.

With the growing influence of the Decembrist movement, K.'s fables gained in their power to expose and accuse. Among his best fables written at this time are *Krestyane i reka* [The Peasants and the River, 1814], *Mirskaya shodka* [The Village Meeting, 1816], *Ovtzy i sobaki* [The Sheep and the Dogs, 1818], *Piostryye ovtzy* [Colored Sheep, 1824], and *Rybya plyaska* [The Dance of the Fishes, 1824]. Other prominent fables written during the 1830s and included in K.'s eighth and ninth books of fables are *Lev* [The Lion, 1830], *Pastukh* [The Shepherd, 1832], and *Velmozh* [The Dignitary, 1834].

The appearance of K.'s first book of fables represented a victory for realism in Russian literature. The common wit of the people, the simple, vivid language used, the democratic content of the themes, and the realism of the conflicts and of the characters presented have made K. one of the first Russian national poets and the teacher of Pushkin and Griboyedov.

Editions: Sobraniye sochinenii [Collected Works], 3 vols., Moscow, 1946; *Basni* [Fables], Moscow–Leningrad, 1956

KRYMOV (Pseud. of *Yuri Solomonovich Beklemishev*)
Born January 19, 1908, St. Petersburg; died (killed in action) September 20, 1941, near Poltava. Soviet Russian novelist.

K. worked as a radio technician and engineer with the oil fleet in the Caspian Sea from 1930. He participated in the Stakhanov movement for increase of production.

K.'s literary works belong to the 1930s; it was at this time that a new development had been reached in depicting manual labor and the socialist relationships existing between people involved in that labor.

K.'s novel *Tanker "Derbent"* (1938; The Tanker "Derbent," 1944) demonstrates these concepts. It also shows that the formation of the socialist collective on a ship is a process rich in conflicts. At the focal point of *Tanker* is the technician Basov—one of the most successful presentations of the hero as socialist innovator. The novel *Inzhener* [The Girl Engineer, 1941] continued this theme, but never attained the artistic unity of design K. achieved in the former work.

Editions: Povesti [Short Stories], Moscow, 1953

KUDASH (Pseud. of *Saifi Kudashev*)
Born October 3, 1894, Klyashevo, near Ufa. Bashkir Soviet poet and novelist.

K., the son of a peasant, commenced his literary activities before the beginning of the October revolution; his early writing was done in the Tatar language. K. became widely known after 1917 for his poetry, poems, fables, short stories, novels, and literary sketches. His poems on themes from Red Army life appeared in 1919. In his collection of poems *Songs of the Plow* (1926), he tried to express the sentiments of a people delivered from exploitation. Many of the poems K. wrote in the 1920s reflect images of the "'new man" in the socialist Republic of Bashkir, while the poem *The Letter* (1930) and the verse-novel *Kushkayyn* (1936), as well as the volume of poetry *The Republic Sings* (1940), reflect the development of the kolkhoz village. Numerous poems written during the 1930s are dominated by the theme of Soviet patriotism.

During the war K.'s poems were among the most popular works of Bashkir literature. After the war K. published his novel *Toward Spring* (1954), which tells of the friendship between the two poets Tukai and Gafuri, as well as *Unforgettable Moments*, a series of reminiscences about Gafuri and his contemporaries. K.'s greatest achievement—which continued the tradition established by Gafuri—lies in the field of the lyric poem. His work in this genre is distinguished by original forms and the masterful use of stylistic elements taken from Bashkir national poetry.

Editions: Izbrannaya lirika [Selected Lyric Writings] (in Russian), Moscow, 1964

KUEKHELBECKER, VILHELM KARLOVICH

Born June 21, 1797, St. Petersburg; died August 23, 1846, in Tobolsk. Russian lyric poet, dramatist, and critic.

K., who came from the impoverished Baltic-German nobility, was a college friend of Pushkin. In 1820 he traveled to Germany, where he visited Goethe, and then on to France. Because of his revolutionary writings K. was exiled to the Caucasus, where he became the friend of Griboyedov. In 1825 Ryleyev admitted K. into the Decembrist Northern Society. He took an active part in the uprising against Nicholas I which took place on December 14, 1825. He was first sentenced to death, but this sentence was later commuted and K. was exiled to Siberia for life.

Within the sphere of revolutionary romanticism, K. favored a popular vernacular style, as is indicated in his *O napravlenii nashei poezii preimushchestvenno liricheskoi, za posledneye desyatiletive* [On the Direction of Our Poetry—in Particular of Our Lyric Poetry—Within the Last Decade, 1824]. He extolled in ardent verses the struggle of the people for liberation—*Grecheskaya pesnya* [Greek Song, 1821]—and praised the theme of the heroic poet—*Smert Bairona* [The Death of Byron]; *Prorochestvo* [The Prophecy]; *A. P. Yermolovu* [To A. P. Yermolov]; *Ten Ryleyeva* [Ryleyev's Shadow]. The pattern of Decembrist tragedy is reflected in *Argivyane* [The Argonauts, 1822]. Despite the arduous conditions of his exile, K. continued his poetic work, which remained imbued with the spirit of the Decembrist movement.

Editions: Stikhotvoreniya [Poems], Leningrad, 1959
Further Works: Ivan-kupecheski syn [Ivan, The Merchant's Son] (1832-42); *Prokofii Lyapunov* [Prokofii Lyapunov] (1834); *Izhorski* [Izhorski] (1835–41)

KULAKOVSKI, ALEKSEI YELISEYEVICH (Pseud. of *Oloksoi Oksukuleekh*)

Born March 16, 1877, Shekhsogonski nasleg, District of Tatta; died June 6, 1926, Moscow. Yakut poet and cultural educator; founder of Yakut literature.

K. was a teacher after 1897. His first poem, *Bayanay algyha* [The Malediction of Bayanay], appeared in 1900; this represented the first step in the development of Yakut artistic poetry. Using a national poetic style occasionally mingled with folkloric themes, K. exposed the backward feudal and patriarchal conditions in Yakutia; at the same time he pilloried the greed of the rising bourgeoisie. K. was also known as a prominent Yakut folklorist and ethnographer. After the October revolution K. took an active part in the cultural reconstruction of his homeland.

Editions: Yryalar-khohoonnor [Poems and Songs], Yakutsk, 1957

KULESHOV, ARKADZ ALYAKSANDRAVICH

Born February 6, 1914, Samatzeyevichy (District of Mogilyov). Byelorussian Soviet poet.

K., the son of a teacher, received a university education and then worked as a journalist. He wrote his first poems in 1926, but it was only after the publication of *Roskvit syamli* [The Soil Is Flowering, 1930], *Pa pesnyu-pa sontza* [Following the Song and the Sun, 1932], and *My zhivyom na granitzy* [We Are Living at the Border, 1923] that he became widely known. At first he was inclined to be overly rhetorical; under the influence of Kupala and Kolas, however, his work began to approach Byelorussian national poetry in feeling.

K. was awarded the State Prize of 1946 for his poem *Stzyag brigady* [The Banner of the Brigade, 1942], about an episode that occurred during the struggle against the fascist invaders. He received the same high award for his poem *Novaye rechyshcha* [The New River Bed, 1948], in which he described developments after the war. K.'s most recent poems, sensitive and rich in ideas, have earned the particular approbation of the public; these poems appeared in Russian under the title *Novaya kniga* [A New Book, 1964].

Editions: Vybranyya tvory [Selected Works], 2 vols., Minsk, 1964

KULISH, PANTELEIMON OLEKSANDROVYCH (Pseud. of *Panko Kasyuka, Danilo Yus,* among others)
Born August 8, 1819, Voronezh; died February 14, 1897, Motronivka. Ukrainian bourgeois writer, liberal historian, and critic.

K. came from the lower nobility; he studied at the University of Kiev, and became known as a scholar; he is credited with numerous important historical and folkloristic studies, including the collection *Zapiski o Yuzhnoi Rusi* [Notes on Southern Russia, 1856–57].

K. was for the most part a conservative romanticist. His work dealt chiefly with themes from Ukrainian history; these writings exhibited strong nationalistic overtones and idealized existing conditions. His poem *Ukrayina* (1843) and his historical novel *Chorna rada* [The Cossack Council, 1857] are prominent among his epic works.

K.'s translations of Goethe, Schiller, Heine, Byron, Shakespeare, Mickiewicz, and Pushkin are of great artistic value.

Editions: Sochineniya i pisma [Works and Letters], 5 vols., Kiev, 1908–10

KUPALA, YANKA (Pseud. of *Ivan Daminikavich Lutzevich*)
Born July 7, 1882, Vyasynka (near Minsk); died June 28, 1942, Moscow. Byelorussian Soviet poet and playwright. People's Poet of the Byelorussian SSR after 1925; member of the Academies of Sciences of the Byelorussian and the Ukrainian SSR after 1928.

K. was the son of a small landowner; his literary activities commenced in 1905, during the period of revolutionary uprising. He wrote many poems distinguished by the intensity of their emotions and the musicality of their language. *Shaleika* [The Shaleika,

1908], *Guslyar* [The Gusli Player, 1910], and *Shlyakham zhy-tztzya* [On the Road to Life, 1913] have as their theme the dreams of the Byelorussian peasants for a free life and a call to battle against the oppressors. In these collections of poems K. championed the needs of the Byelorussian people for their own national literature. His poems are usually closely linked with national, folkloristic poetry. In *Advechnaya pesnya* [The Old Song, 1910] and *Son na kurgane* [The Dream on the Grave-Mound, 1913], K. again expressed the hopes of his people for a happier life. His plays *Pavlinka* (1912) and *Raskidanaye gnyazdo* [The Abandoned Nest, 1913] represent important landmarks in the development of the Byelorussian national theater.

K. welcomed the October revolution with great enthusiasm. His close association with the life of the people enabled him to overcome certain ideologic confusions evidenced in his work of the civil war years and during the brief interlude of bourgeois, nationalistic reaction. In numerous poems and verses written in the 1930s, K. skillfully presented the socialist development in Byelorussia, as can be seen in his poems *Nad rakoi Aresai* [On the Oresa River, 1933] and *Barysav* [Borisov, 1934]; and in his volume of poems *Ad sertza* [From the Heart, 1960] for which he received the State Prize of 1941. K., together with Y. Kolas, may be regarded as the creator of the new Byelorussian literature.

Editions: Sbor tvorav [Collected Works], 6 vols., Minsk, 1961–63

KUPRIN, ALEKSANDR IVANOVICH

Born September 7, 1870, Narovchat (District of Penza); died August 25, 1938, Leningrad. Russian novelist and short-story writer.

K.'s first stories were written while he was serving in the army as an officer. At the beginning of the twentieth century, supported in his literary efforts by both Bunin and Korolenko, K. developed into one of the most popular Russian writers. Although sometimes bourgeois and anarchistic, his progressive views are already clearly reflected in his great story *Molokh* [Moloch, 1896], a passionate indictment of capitalistic exploitation.

V. G. Korolenko

M. M. Kotzyubnyskyi

I. A. Krylov

Y. Kupala

V. Lācis

L. M. Leonov

M. Y. Lermontov

N. S. Leskov

K.'s talents matured under Gorki's political and artistic influence. His novel *Poyedinok* (1905; The Duel, 1916) offers a merciless picture of the inhuman militaristic system existing in the Russian army; it represents the climax of K.'s work.

During the 1905–07 revolution, K was on the side of the progressive forces. Although many of his stories show that he was sympathetic toward the revolutionary struggle, he was unable to realize both the aims of that struggle and the driving social and political forces behind it. Because of his close association with the people, K. did, however, succeed in giving emotionally impressive portraits of their lives.

K.'s political firmness began to waver after 1910, and his work began to exhibit philanthropic, liberal elements. He failed to understand the importance of the October revolution, and emigrated to France, a move which led to a marked decline in his work. After many difficult years spent abroad K. returned to the Soviet Union in 1937.

Editions: Sobraniye sochinenii [Collected Works], 6 vols., Moscow, 1957

KURATOV, IVAN ALEKSEYEVICH

Born July 19, 1839, Kebra (District of Vologodsk); died November 29, 1875, Verny (Alma-Ata). Leading poet of the Komi people; founder of the literary language of the Komi.

K., whose ideology was materialistic in nature, was active as a teacher. His work, which was greatly influenced by classical Russian literature, was published in its original language only after the October revolution. In his poems K. depicted the miserable existence of his people (*The Beggar*), and praised their high moral standards (*The Blind Old Man*). He championed the right of the Komi people for education and freedom. K. has also translated Krylov, Heine, Pushkin, and other writers into the Komi language.

Editions: Boryom gishodyas, Syktyvkar, 1951

KUROCHKIN, VASILII STEPANOVICH
Born August 9, 1831, St. Petersburg; died there August 27, 1875. Russian revolutionary, democratic lyric poet, and journalist.

K. created excellent adaptations of Béranger's satirical songs. Between 1859–73 K., together with the caricaturist Stepanov, published the magazine *Iskra* [The Spark], which contained satirical poems, parodies, and essays. In 1861 he joined the revolutionary secret society *Zemlya i Volya* [Land and Freedom]; from that time on he suffered continuous persecution. K.'s work included philosophical and political poems reflecting his belief in social progress.

Editions: Stikhotvoreniya, Stati, Feletony [Poems, Essays, Feuilletons], Moscow, 1957

KUZNETZOV, ANATOLII VASILYEVICH
Born August 18, 1929, Kiev. Soviet Russian novelist.

As a twelve-year-old boy, K. witnessed the fascist occupation of Kiev. In 1952 he volunteered to work as a laborer on the large building site in Novaya Kakhovka. The experiences he gained there are reflected in his first book, *Prodolzheniye legendy* (1957; Sequel to a Legend, 1963), in which he describes the moral growth of a young man through manual labor. The latter novel was the first in a series of similar books for young people. The documentary autobiographical novel *Babi yar* appeared in 1966, and was published in English the same year. During a trip to London in 1969, V. decided not to return to the Soviet Union.

Further Works: U sebya doma [In Your Own House] (1964)

KVITKA (KVITKA-OSNOVYANENKO), HRYHORYI FEDOROVYCH
Born November 29, 1778, Osnova, near Kharkov; died August 20, 1843, Kharkov. First important prose writer of Ukrainian literature.

K. attended a monastery school and became the tutor of several young noblemen. He wrote a number of comedies in which he derided the habits of the provincial nobility from the bourgeois, democratic point of view. His satirical humoristic *Malorossiskiye povesti* [Ukrainian Stories, 1834–37], the satirical novels *Pan Khalyavskyi* [Mr. Khalyavskyi] and *Ukrayinski dyplomatyi* [Ukrainian Diplomats, 1840], among other works, have greatly influenced the subsequent development of Ukrainian literature, and of Russian-Ukrainian cultural relations.

Editions: Sochineniya [Works], 6 vols., Kharkov, 1887–94; *Tvory* [Works], 6 vols., Kiev, 1956–57

LĀCIS, VILIS

Born May 12, 1904, Vecmilgrāvis, near Riga; died February 6, 1966, Riga. Latvian Soviet novelist and statesman.

L.'s father was a dock worker; his mother was the daughter of a fisherman. In 1917 the family were evacuated to the Altai region, where they witnessed the civil war and the establishment of Soviet power. It was in Altai that L. first became interested in journalism. In 1921 L. returned to Latvia, where he held various jobs—as a dock worker, fisherman, stoker on merchant ships, and woodcutter, and in 1928 he became a member of the illegal Communist Party. He constantly tried to improve his education by self-study, putting his observations on paper; it was not until the 1930s, however, that his work began to be published.

The trilogy *Putni bez spārniem* [Birds without Wings, 1929–31] and the novel *Zvejnieka dēls* (1933; The Fisherman's Son, 1959) occupy a special place among the numerous stories and novels he wrote during this period. The author's strong sense of commitment and his use of hero-figures taken from the ranks of the dock workers and sailors caused these works to be greatly appreciated by the people.

L. has occupied important state and party positions in Soviet Latvia. He was President of the Council of Ministers of the Latvian SSR for a considerable time, during which he published some of his most important works. These include the three-volume novel *Vētra* [Stormy Years, 1945–48], which describes the situation in Latvia before the establishment of Soviet power, the

Second World War, and the beginning of socialist reconstruction. The historical development leading to the victory of socialism is the subject of L.'s novel *Uz jauno krastu* [To New Shores, 1951]. The novel *Pazudušā dzimtene* [Lost Homeland] was written between 1940 and 1952. From 1947 L. held the title of People's Writer of the Latvian SSR. He was awarded State Prizes in 1949 and 1952.

LAHUTI, ABULQASIM

Born October 12, 1887, Kermanshah (Iran); died March 16, 1957, Moscow. Tadzhik Soviet poet.

L. was the son of a Persian artisan and a folksinger. He participated in the Persian revolution of 1905–11 and in 1920 in the uprisings in Tabriz; in 1922 he was forced to flee first to Turkey and then to the Soviet Union. His work, which had had its beginnings in symbolism, had up until this time dealt chiefly with the problems of fighting a reactionary political system. From 1920 on, however, L.'s main concern was the battle of the Tadzhik people to achieve supremacy. Poems on this subject include *Kreml* [Kremlin, 1923], *Mo zafar khohem kard* [We Shall Be Victorious, 1930], and *Dostoni Galabayi Tanya* [Doston on Tanya's Victory, 1943].

LAICENS, LINARDS

Born November 15, 1883, Jaunroze; died December 14, 1938. Latvian revolutionary politician, poet, and journalist.

L. was the son of a smallholder; he acquired his knowledge mainly by self-study. He took an active part in the revolution of 1905, and as a result was imprisoned for two years. L. was active in bourgeois Latvia on behalf of the Communist Party, and was constantly persecuted. In 1928 he was elected to the Latvian parliament (Saeima), and became the leader of the Worker-and-Farmer group. In 1932 L. found it politic to emigrate to the Soviet Union.

L. had already begun to write by 1904, but he created his most important works after the October revolution, following his adoption of socialist realism. A number of works written at that time, however, still show certain constructivist theories. The collection of stories *Attaisnotie* [Righteous People, 1921] sharply attacked the bourgeoisie, while the cycle *Skaistā Italijā* [Italy the Beautiful, 1925] gave a realistic picture of the misery of Italian workers. L. pilloried the treachery of the social-democratic leaders in bourgeois Latvia in his story *Augusts uz stalažām* [August on the Building Scaffold, 1933]. In his militant poetry, L. continued the traditions established by Mayakovski. In 1922 he published the collection of love lyrics entitled *Ho-Tai*.

Further Works: Berline [Berlin] (1924); *Mītiņš ballē* [A Meeting at the Ball] (1925); *Emigrants* [The Immigrant] (1926); *Kompromiss* [The Comprise] (1926); *Limitrofija* [Limitrophy] (1935)

LAVRENEOV, BORIS ANDREYEVICH
Born July 17, 1891, Kherson; died January 7, 1959, Moscow. Soviet Russian dramatist, poet, and novelist.

As a young man, L. led a colorful sailor's life. During World War I he was an officer; during the civil war he fought in the ranks of the Red Army. Before the revolution, L. wrote symbolist, futuristic verses; in the 1920s he published revolutionary and civil-war stories, including *Sorok pervyi* (1926; The Forty-First, 1959). L.'s most important drama, *Razlom* [The Breach, 1928–44], deals with the human conflicts existing during the preparation for the armed uprising that resulted in the October revolution. The plot of this drama is based on an incident that occurred in 1917, when the crew of the cruiser "Aurora" defected to the side of the revolutionaries. L. has frequently used the life of the Russian sailors as a theme, including *Za tekh, kto v more* [To Those on the High Seas, 1945]. L. received the State Prize in 1950.

Further Works: Krusheniye respubliki Itl [The Fall of the Itl Republic] (1926); *Golos Ameriki* [The Voice of America] (1949)

LAY OF THE HOST OF IGOR, THE   See SLOVO O POLKU IGOREVE

LEBEDEV-KUMACH, VASILII IVANOVICH

Born August 8, 1898, Moscow; died there February 20, 1949.
Russian Soviet poet.

L.'s satirical poems started to appear in 1918 in various newspapers and magazines published by the Red Army. L. later worked
in the editorial department of the magazine *Krokodil*. His songs
Shiroka strana moya rodnaya [My Great Homeland, 1935],
Moskva maiskaya [Moscow in May, 1937], and *Pesnya o Volge*
[Song of the Volga, 1937] gained wide popularity. His well-
known song *Svyashchennaya voina* [Holy War] was written
during L.'s service in the Soviet Navy. He received the State Prize
in 1941.

Editions: Pesni [Songs], Moscow, 1953

LEBERECHT, HANS

Born December 1, 1910, St. Petersburg; died November 10,
1960, Tallinn. Estonian Soviet short-story writer and journalist.

L. wrote in the Russian language. He was the son of a proletarian from Tallinn; after graduation from high school, L.
worked for the Elektrosila Company, taking evening courses at
the Gorki Institute of Literature.

L.'s first literary works were in the field of the short story. During World War II, he was a soldier and a correspondent for the
frontline newspaper *Punaväelene* [The Red Guard]. He continued to work as a journalist after the war. His important story
Svet v Koordi [Light over Koordi] appeared in 1948; L. received
the State Prize for this story, which is about collectivization in
Estonia. L. held the title of Meritorious Writer of the Estonian
SSR.

Further Works: Kapitany [The Captains] (1954); *Soldaty idut domoi*
[The Soldiers Are Going Home] (1956); *Vodnom dome* [In One
Home] (1957); *Dvortzy Vasarov* [The Palaces of the Vasarovs]
(1960)

LIFE OF ALEKSANDR NEVSKI, THE   See ZHITIYE ALEKSANDRA
NEVSKOVO

LENIN (Pseud. of *Vladimir Ilyich Ulyanov*)

Born April 22, 1870, Simbirsk; died January 21, 1924, Gorki, near Moscow.

L. was the most important theoretician of revolutionary Marxism; founder and leader of the Communist Party of the Soviet Union, and of the Comintern; organizer of the great socialist October revolution, and founder of the Soviet State; leader and teacher of the working people throughout the entire world. He has indicated new avenues to creative, humanitarian thinkers in many fields. L. has also enriched Marxist aesthetics with many new ideas and concepts. Already in the 1890s, L., basing his thinking on the principle of partiality in literature, destroyed the theories of the bourgeois objectivists and those of the followers of subjective sociology; in doing so, he demonstrated the social and class importance of the theories evident in the literature of the time.

L.'s essay *Partinaya organisatziya i partinaya literatura* [Party Organization and Party Literature, 1905] led to a revolutionary change in aesthetics; in this essay L. stressed the organic unity of Bolshevik aesthetics with Marxist-Leninist philosophy, economics, politics, and sociology. He described the literature of the proletariat as an "element of the general proletarian state of affairs," subordinate to the struggle of the proletariat for liberation. On the other hand, L. demonstrated the direct material dependence of bourgeois artists on the ruling classes; he subjected their aesthetic views and, in particular, the idea of "freedom of art" to strong critical comment. In this essay, L. solved a series of other basic aesthetic problems: he drew attention to the difficult questions of artistic popularity, of tradition, and of innovation, and stressed the specific characteristics of literature in general.

In his philosophical work *Materializm i empiriokrititsizm* (1908; Materialism and Empirio-criticism, 1927), which represented a profound analysis of the new achievements of science in the light of dialectic materialism, L. developed certain basic principles of Marxist philosophy and the theory of cognition. This work became the foundation of the Marxist theory that everything should reflect the general ideology, and demonstrated the significance of that theory as it related to the realistic trend in art.

L. sharply criticized the theoreticians of decadent aesthetics, and demonstrated their connections with different subjectivist and idealist philosophical systems. L.'s "reflection" theory and his principle of partiality represent important contributions to the philosophical foundation of the artistic method of socialist realism. In determining the relationship of socialist realism to the cultural inheritance of the past, L. always opposed the bourgeois theory of a uniform trend in the development of culture.

In his essay *Kriticheskiye zametki po natzionalnomu voprosu* [Critical Remarks on the Problem of Nationality, 1911], L. discussed the doctrine of the two cultures in a society split into antagonistic classes. In contrast to the Russian decadents, L. always had a high regard for the representatives of Russian revolutionary democracy and for the Russian realistic writers, although he did not idealize them. L. regarded the history of literature as a series of tense class struggles. In his essay *Lev Tolstoi, kak zerkalo ruskoi revolyutzii* (1908; Articles on Tolstoi, 1951) L. has offered a magnificent, scholarly analysis of Tolstoi, one of the greatest, most contradictory, and complex artists of the world; L. has written similar essays on other great Russian writers.

L. early discovered the social importance of Gorki's work; he loved Gorki both as man and as artist, and saw great political value in Gorki's novel *The Mother*. In the years following the 1905–07 revolution, and again after the October revolution, L. helped Gorki overcome a temporary political defection. Until his death L. and Gorki remained close friends. This friendship is reflected in numerous documents as "the great classical example of the relationship between a statesman and an artist" (Becher).

On the basis of the prerevolutionary achievements of Marxist aesthetics, after the October revolution L. gave valuable directives on the development of the new Soviet culture. These directives were filled with the spirit of revolutionary belief in the power of the people, and had the effect of orientating Soviet artists toward a study of the new Soviet reality. L. realized that the strength of Soviet art lay in its popularity, and he rejected narrowness and sectarianism. L. subjected the policies of the Proletcult to devastating critical comment, and indicated the road to a free, versatile, and creative development for Soviet art and literature.

Editions: O literature i iskusstve [On Literature and Art], Moscow, 1957; O literature [On Literature], Moscow, 1957

LEONOV, LEONID MAKSIMOVICH
Born May 31, 1899, Moscow. Soviet Russian novelist.

L. graduated from high school in 1918; he participated in the civil war and worked for a frontline newspaper. During this period he wrote short stories, poems, and articles concerning the construction of the new social order. L. followed the literary traditions established by Gogol, Dostoyevski, and Gorki. Tendencies toward stylization and abstractionism shown in his early work were soon replaced for the most part by a more concrete method of social presentation, as may be seen in his novel Barsuki (1924; The Badgers, 1947). The action of this novel is focused on the conflict between two brothers, resulting from their different political views on the revolution. A certain overestimation of the bourgeois forces in the Soviet Union in the 1920s is reflected in his novel Vor (1927; second version, 1959; The Thief, 1931), and also in his drama Untilovsk (1928).

In his subsequent work—dealing with new themes—L. succeeded in presenting the figures of communist functionaries and their struggles with outdated views most convincingly; among the works written during that period is his novel Sot (1930; Soviet River, 1931), which is about the building of a paper combine in Siberia. In 1932 L. published his novel Skutarevski (Eng., 1936), which deals with the problem of the postrevolutionary development of the older members of the technical intelligentsia after the revolution. The growth of a new awareness and the decline of the old world have been treated by L. in his novel Doroga na okean (1936; Road to the Ocean, 1944).

During World War II, L. published a series of articles permeated by humanist and patriotic ideas. The drama *Nashestviye* (1942; Invasion, 1945) shows the growing resistance of the people to the fascist invaders. The long novel *Russkii les* (1953; The Russian Forest, 1966) represents a climax in L.'s work. In the conflict of opinions between the two rival professors Vikhrov and Gratzianski, L. demonstrates their basically different views of life and behavior. L., who openly takes sides, shows that the negative forces in socialism are without perspective. Truth will in due course conform to social laws. In *Russkii les* L.—following Gorki's idea of man—succeeded in combining both a psychological and a social analysis of his heroes.

In 1961 L. wrote the film script *Begstvo mistera Mak-Kinli* (The Flight of Mr. McKinley), in which he both satirized and devastatingly criticized the imperialist system of the Western world. In 1963 he published his short story *Yevgeniya Ivanovna*, of which the author has said that it "deals with an important, natural theme—our attitude toward and our love for our homeland, for Russia." L. was awarded the State Prize in 1943, and the Lenin Prize in 1957.

Editions: Sobraniye sochinenii [Collected Works], 9 vols., Moscow, 1960–62

LERMONTOV, MIKHAIL YURYEVICH

Born October 15, 1814, Moscow; died July 7, 1841, Pyatigorsk. Russian poet and novelist.

L. came from a noble family and grew up in the house of his rich grandmother Arsenyeva. In 1830–32 he studied at the University of Moscow; he was expelled from the university because of his rebellious attitude and entered the St. Petersburg Officers' School, from which he graduated in 1834 as a Guards officer.

L.'s early work, which from 1828 on consisted chiefly of poems, verses, and dramas including *Ispantzy* (The Spaniards), reflected the traditions of Russian romanticism. It showed the influence of Ryleyev and, even more, of Pushkin and Byron. L.'s work also showed a strong link with German culture; he was stimulated by

German intellectual life through his knowledge of the works of both Schiller, Goethe, and, later, of H. Heine. L. translated poems by all three authors. More important than these influences was L.'s early and extremely emotional involvement with problems of decisive importance to the Russia of his time. He responded negatively to the increasing pressure of tsarism on the intellectual life in the 1830s. These sentiments are reflected in his diarylike poems. In *Predskazaniye* [The Prophecy, 1830], L. predicted a new people's uprising and the fall of tsarism. *Parus* [Soil, 1832] tells of a happiness that can be found only in battle. His poem *Posledni syn volnostoi* [The Last Son of Liberty, 1831] touched on the democratic and fighting traditions of Russian history. The theme of unhappy love was predominant in his work at this period.

After a hiatus of twelve years, in 1835 L. published the tragedy *Maskarad* [Masquerade], which reflected his sharp opposition to court society. L.'s anti-aristocratic tendencies are even more strongly evident in his poem *Smert poeta* [The Poet's Death, 1837], written after Pushkin had been killed in a duel. L. was exiled to the Caucasus for one year following the publication of this poem. There L. became acquainted with soldiers, peasants, and members of the mountain tribes. The fact that these new acquaintances made a deep impression on him is reflected in his work by the fact that figures representative of the people and their intellectual world are treated more frequently, as can be seen in *Borodino* (1837) and *Pesnya pro tzarya Ivana* (1837; The Song about Tsar Ivan, 1929). L. began to view the current problems from the point of view of the peasants, as may be seen in his poem *Rodina* [My Homeland, 1841]. In this way he came to regard the progressive representatives of the nobility in a critical light. *Duma* [Consideration, 1838] and the final version of his poem *Demon* (1829–41) are evidence of this.

The absence of friends, the realization of the impossibility of achieving an individual victory over tsarism, and the difficulties encountered in the search for new poetic attitudes caused the rise of pessimistic sentiments in L.'s work. These were frequently combined with militant themes, as in *Vykhozhu odin ya* [Lonely I Am Walking On] and *Prorok* [The Prophet], both written in 1841. L.'s poems exhibit rare lyrical power, new rhythms, and emotional images, and have paved the way for the lyric writings of our times. L. was also an innovator in his method of depicting natural experiences—*Tuchi* [The Clouds, 1840] *Mtzyrii* [The Mtzyri, 1840], and *Demon* (1930).

L.'s novel *Geroi nashevo vremeni* (1840; A Hero of Our Times, 1951) may be regarded as a synthesis of his most significant creative tendencies; in the figure of Pechorin (which is only to a limited extent biographical in character) L.'s novel reflects the problems mentioned above. L.'s psychological mastery, which had already been evident in his earlier works, including the poems *June 11* (1831) and *Mtzyrii*, among others, reached a climax in this novel. It can be said that the psychological novels of both Dostoyevski and Tolstoi are based on L.'s literary achievements.

In 1840 L. was again exiled to the Caucasus, and the tsar himself ordered him assigned to the most dangerous sectors. Applications for leave of absence or retirement and requests submitted by his superiors for decorations were refused. Like Pushkin L. was killed when he was forced into a duel by the nobility.

Editions: Sobraniye sochinenii [Collected Works], 4 vols., Moscow, 1957–58

LESKOV, NIKOLAI SEMIONOVICH

Born February 18, 1831, Gorokhovo (District of Orel); died March 15, 1895, St. Petersburg. Russian journalist and novelist.

L. was the son of an ennobled civil servant. He attended the high school in Orel until the early death of his parents. He later acquired more knowledge by self-study; as a civil servant in Orel and Kiev and between 1857–60 as the sales representative of a British firm, L. learned much about the different aspects of Russian life. From 1861 on, L. worked as a journalist and writer in St. Petersburg. He also occasionally worked for the government.

L. underwent a complex intellectual development. He first

wrote articles and stories on the question of serfdom, the exploitation of the workers, and the oppression of the Old Believers (*Raskolniki*). L.'s *Ovtzebyk* [Musk-Ox, 1862] tells of a political dreamer who unsuccessfully tries to agitate the peasants against the estate owner. L. wrote an article in 1862 following the May burnings in St. Petersburg, in which he appealed to the government for a detailed investigation of this catastrophe. This article, which could be regarded as a denunciation of revolutionary circles, aroused a storm of indignation among the progressive forces, a conflict that increased after L. published a number of novels directed against the revolutionary movement—*Nekuda* [No Way Out, 1864] and *Na noshakh* [To the End, 1870].

In the 1870s, however, L. again joined forces with the democratic and progressive movements of his time. He wrote a great number of realistic prose pieces distinguished by their use of the vernacular and their characteristically Russian color. L. was the first author to write of the Russian clergy in realistic terms. In his later stories and legends, including *Na krayu sveta* [At the End of the World, 1875], *Nekreshchionny pop* [The Unbaptized Priest, 1877], *Melochi arkhiyereiskoi zhizni* [Trivialities in the Life of a Bishop, 1878–80], and *Skomorokh Pamfalon* [Pamphalon the Buffoon, 1877], L. overcame a certain tendency toward idealization still evident in his novel *Soboryane* (1872; The Cathedral Folk, 1924).

In L.'s narrative work considerable space is devoted to the critical description of the merchant class, as can be seen in *Ledi Makbet Mtzenskovo uyezda* [Lady MacBeth of Mtzensk, 1865] and *Voitelnitza* [Fighting Nature, 1866]. His drama *Rastochitel* [The Spendthrift, 1867] is dedicated to a similar theme. L.'s positive moral and social ideals are embodied in his character studies of so-called just persons (*pravedniki*), who stand for truth, justice, and humanity—*Nesmertelny Golovan* [Golovan the Immortal, 1880], *Pavlin* (1874), *Pigmei* [The Pigmy, 1879], *Kadetski monastyr* [The Cadet Monastery, 1880], *Pugalo* [The Bogeyman, 1884], and *Figura* (1889).

L.'s narrative work is at its most noteworthy in the stories that reflect the vitality, dexterity, and magnanimity of simple Russian people—*Ocharovanni strannik* (1873; The Enchanted Wanderer, 1956), *Zapechatlienny angel* [The Sealed Angel, 1873], *Skaz o tulskom Kosom Levshe i o stalnoi blokhe* (1881; The Steel Flea, 1943), and *Tupeiny khudozhnik* [The Artist with the Toupée, 1883]. L.'s criticism of the tsarist system turned into biting satire in his best tales: *Zagon* [The Sheep Wattle, 1893] and *Zayachi remis* [The Rabbit's Fire, 1894].

Editions: Sobraniye sochinenii [Collected Works], 11 vols., Moscow, 1956–58
Further Works: Zheleznaya volya [The Iron Will] (1876); *Chelovek na chasakh* [A Man on Guard] (1877); *Zver* [An Animal] (1883); *Prekrasnaya Asya* [The Beautiful Asya] (1888); *Improvizatory* [Improvisors] (1892); *Yudol* [Vale] (1892); *Zimnii den* [A Cold Day] (1894); *Askalonski zlodei* [The Thief from Askalon] (1889)

LEVADA (Pseud. of *Oleksander Stepanovych Kosyak*)
Born November 26, 1909, Krivchuntzy, near Cherkasy. Ukrainian Soviet dramatist.

L. is the son of a teacher; in 1930–32, he studied philology at the Institute of Pedagogy in Vynnytzya. He worked for some time as a journalist, and as a frontline correspondent during World War II. L. began his literary career in 1925 as people's correspondent; he published numerous poems and sketches in the daily press, but soon found his way to the drama, which is now his preferred genre.

Among L.'s most important plays, which are distinguished by a profound philosophical analysis of the problems being treated, are *Kamo* (1940), about the well-known Bolshevist revolutionary Tar-Petrosyan; *Shlyakh na Ukrayinu* [The Road to the Ukraine, 1946]; *Ostannya zustrich*, [The Last Meeting, 1956]; and the philosophical drama *Faust i smert* [Faust and Death, 1960]. L. has also written a number of film scripts and opera libretti. He has been awarded the State Prize.

Editions: Vybrani pyesi [Selected Dramas], Kiev, 1959

LEVITOV, ALEKSANDR IVANOVICH

Born July 2, 1835, Dobroye (District of Tambov); died January 16, 1877, Moscow. Russian revolutionary democratic short-story writer.

L.'s first book, which appeared in 1861, was *Tipy i stzeny selskoi yarmarki* [Characters and Scenes from the Village Fair]. This was followed in 1865–67 by *Stepnyye ocherki* [Sketches from the Steppes]. In these stories L. presented peasant life with loving warmth and realism, without, however, being uncritical. His impressions, obtained in the course of a restless life of wandering, are reflected in two other volumes of critical, realistic stories and sketches, in which he described the miserable existence in the city slums—*Moskovskiye nory i trushchoby* [Moscow Hovels and Holes, 1869] and the hopeless conditions in the villages *Gore siyol, dorog i gorodov* [The Misery in the Villages, on the Highways, and in the Cities, 1874].

Editions: Sobraniye sochinenii [Collected Works], 8 vols., St. Petersburg, 1911; *Sochinenii* [Works], Moscow, 1956

LIBEDINSKI, YURII NIKOLAYEVICH

Born December 10, 1898, Odessa; died November 24, 1959, Moscow. Soviet Russian novelist.

L., the son of a physician, spent his childhood in the Urals; he attended high school in Chelyabinsk. In 1920 he became a member of the Communist Party; he did extensive political work while enlisted in the Red Army, and from 1922 was active in the proletarian literary movement. He was one of the founders of the Oktyabr (October) group and between 1923–32 occupied leading positions in RAPP, the proletarian writers' group that initiated the concept of workers writing about labor.

L.'s first novel, *Nedelya* [A Week, 1922], offers an objective picture of the early struggles of the Communist Party in the 1920s. At the time of its publication this novel was one of the most widely read works of early Soviet prose. L.'s story *Komisary* [Commissars, 1925], the play *Vysoty* [Heights, 1928], and the novel *Rozhdeniye geroya* [The Birth of a Hero, 1930] also earned the attention of RAPP. During World War II L. wrote stories and sketches based on his own experiences in the battles of Moscow, Stalingrad, and Kursk. In the postwar years he completed his novel trilogy on the October revolution, which he had already started in the 1930s—*Gory i lyudi* [Mountains and People, 1947], *Zharevo* [Blaze of Fire, 1952], and *Utro sovetov* [The Morning of the Soviets, 1957]. In 1958 L. published a volume of interesting reminiscences of his meetings with various writers (Furmanov, Yesenin, Mayakovski, N. Ostrovski, A. N. Tolstoi, and others) under the title *Sovremenniki* [Contemporaries].

LIDIN (Pseud. of *Vladimir Germanovich Gomberg*)
Born February 15, 1894. Soviet Russian novelist.

L., the son of a merchant, studied Oriental languages in Moscow; he fought as a Red Guard in Siberia and Mongolia. During World War II, L. was the frontline correspondent for *Izvestiya*. L. has written numerous stories and novels, some of which have been criticized for such artistic defects as disorganization and an overly fragmented presentation of characters. His main works are the novels *Idut korabli* [The Ships Pass, 1926], *Otstupnik* [The Renegade, 1926], *Veliki ili Tikii* [The Great or Silent Ocean, 1933], *Dve zhizni* [Two Lives, 1950], *Dalioki drug* [The Distant Friend, 1957], and his war story *Zima 1941* [Winter, 1941, 1942]. L. is also the author of *Lyudi i vstrechi* [People and Encounters, 1957], which occupies an important position in Soviet belles lettres.

Editions: Sobraniye sochinenii [Collected Works], 6 vols., Moscow, 1928–30; *Povesti i rasskazy* [Short Stories], Moscow, 1958

LIPATOV, VIL VLADIMIROVICH
Born April 10, 1927, Chita. Soviet Russian short-story writer and novelist.

L. studied pedagogy in Tomsk. Between 1952 and 1960 he worked as a journalist; he is now living in Chita. L. has been writing short stories and novellas since 1956. His most common theme is the proving of young people—*Strezhen* [Deep Stream,

1961], *Zub mudrosti* [The Wisdom Tooth, 1962]—and the fight against philistinism—*Chornyi var* [The Black Ravine, 1963], *Chuzhoi* [The Foreigner, 1964].

Further Works: Glukhaya myata (1960); *Smert Yegora Susuna* [The Death of Yegor Susun] (1963)

LOMONOSOV, MIKHAIL VASILYEVICH

Born November 19, 1711, Mishchaninskaya, near Arkhangelsk; died April 15, 1765, St. Petersburg. Russian philosopher, poet, dramatist, and scientist.

L. came from a fisherman's family; from 1731 he studied in Moscow and St. Petersburg. He was stimulated by studies he undertook in Marburg and Freiberg in 1736–41. In 1745 he was appointed professor of chemistry at the St. Petersburg Academy of Sciences, where he was active in many fields.

L. was, perhaps, one of the most universal Russian philosophers and thinkers of the eighteenth century—a true "Renaissance man." He paved the way for many pioneering discoveries and inventions in the fields of natural science, history, and economics. In his scientific work L. took a materialist point of view. Both patriot and explorer, L. was involved in the exploration of Siberia; he was the driving force behind the founding of the University of Moscow in 1755. L.'s "theory of the three styles" (1757) paved the way for extensive linguistic reforms. This theory, together with the Russian grammar he published in 1757, his work on rhetoric (1748), and his other linguistic papers became the foundation for the modern Russian literary language. He restricted the use of Church Slavonic, thus making the colloquial language of the time more available for literary use.

L., who may be considered as one of the first modern Russian writers, was a classicist. In addition to two tragedies, *Tamira i Selim* [Tamira and Selim, 1750] and *Demofont* (1752), and the unfinished epic *Piotr Veliki* [Peter the Great], L. wrote 280 odes and poems; the basic ideas expressed in these works are his positive attitude toward the Petrian reforms, his passionate love for his homeland, and the enlightened concept of a peaceful development of science. The following works may be considered among his most important: the didactic poem *Pismo o polzke stekla* [A Letter on the Uses of Glass, 1752], his theological work *Vecherneye razmyshleniye o bozhiyem velicheste* [Evening Meditations on the Greatness of God, 1743; published in 1747], *Utrenneye razamyshleniye* . . . [Morning Meditations on . . . 1751], and the satirical *Gimn borode* [Hymn to the Beard, 1756–57]. L. sanctioned and improved Trediakovski's efforts to reform Russian verse in his *Pismo o pravilakh rossiiskovo stikhotvorstva* [Letter on the Rules of Russian Poetry, 1739], which paid special attention to the theoretical aspects of verse. His *Oda . . . na vzyative Khotina* [Ode . . . on the Capture of Khotin, 1739] discussed the practical aspects of the poetic art.

Editions: Sobraniye sochinenii [Collected Works], 10 vols., Moscow–Leningrad, 1950–57. *Sochineniya* [Works], Moscow, 1957

LUGOVSKOI, VLADIMIR ALEKSANDROVICH
    Born July 1, 1901, Moscow; died June 5, 1957, Yalta; Soviet Russian poet.
    In the years 1919–24, L. served in the Red Army. His first volume of poems, *Spolokhi* [Summer Lightning, 1926], deals with themes from the civil war. L. was at first under the influence of the constructivists; in 1930 he joined RAPP. A voyage to Turkestan in the spring of 1930, organized by RAPP, yielded artistic ideas that decisively influenced L.'s entire work. In a cycle of four books entitled *Bolshevikam pustyni i vesny* [To the Bolsheviks of the Wasteland and of the Spring, 1931–52], he described how certain problems of the Orient have been changed by socialism.
    After overcoming certain schematic tendencies and, subsequently, a somewhat forced use of metaphor, L. reached a high artistic level with his volume of poetry *Novyye stikhi* [New Poems, 1941]. L.'s postwar work reached a climax in his mature works on contemporary socialist man, which were published posthumously—*Seredina veka* [Halfway through the Century,

1958], *Solntze-vorot* [Solstice, 1961], and *Sinyaya vesna* [Blue Spring, 1961]. With their romantic accents and stressed emotions, L.'s lyric writings occupy a prominent place in Soviet poetry.

Editions: Izbrannyye proizvedeniya [Selected Works], 2 vols., Moscow, 1956

LUKONIN, MIKHAIL KUZMICH

Born October 29, 1918, Tzaritzyn. Soviet Russian poet.

L. participated in World War II as a correspondent for army newspapers. His first literary work appeared in 1940. L.'s numerous poems, most of which are permeated by a fighting spirit, have been a noteworthy contribution to Soviet verse of the last decades. For some time his war experiences have determined the themes of his work. His poem *Rabochii den* [Work Day, 1948] is one of the most important works of the early postwar years; here L. describes the life of a young worker in the Stalingrad Tractor Works. In his poem *Priznaniye v lyubvi* [Declaration of Love, 1959] L. has attempted to give an interpretation of our epoch by engaging in a direct dialogue with the reader. L. received the State Prize in 1949.

Editions: Stikhotvoreniya i poemy [Poems and Verses], Moscow, 1952

LUNACHARSKI, ANATOLII VASILYEVICH

Born December 6, 1875, Poltava; died December 26, 1933, Mentone (Southern France). Soviet Russian cultural educator, theoretician of the philosophy of art, critic, and writer.

L., the son of a civil servant with radical views, joined the Social-Democratic organization in 1892; he became a member of the Bolshevik faction after the Second Party Congress of the Social-Democratic Workers' Party of Russia. During the revolution of 1905 L. cooperated closely with Lenin in various revolutionary and propagandist activities; L. emigrated in the years between 1906 and 1917. He joined the group led by A. Bogdanov and V. Bazarov; during the Fourth Party Congress he was admitted into the Bolshevik Party. In 1917–29, L. was People's

Commissar for Education; in 1933 he became the first official representative of the USSR in Spain.

L. has greatly contributed to the building of a socialist culture in the Soviet Union. In his prerevolutionary works, L. defended Lenin's principle of partiality in literature and the possibilities of building a proletarian culture (*Dialog ob iskustve* [Dialogue on Art, 1905]; *Zadachi sotzial-demokraticheskovo khudoshestvennovo tvorchestva* [Tasks for Artistic Work in Social Democracy, 1906]; *Pisma o proletarskoi kulture* [Letters on Proletarian Culture, 1914]). His activities as People's Commissar were chiefly concerned with the development and execution of Lenin's cultural policies, with the general assimilation of the classical inheritance, and with the promotion of socialist cadres in literature and art. In his articles *Lenin i literaturovedeniye* [Lenin and Literary Scholarship, 1932], *Marks ob iskustve* [Marks on Art, 1933], and other essays, L. demonstrated the achievements of Marxist classics in the field of aesthetics. He developed significant elements of the theory of socialist realism, and his numerous essays on artists have led to the realization of certain patterns in the development of art.

L. gave particular attention to literature and the theater, to which he himself contributed a series of plays. In his historical dramas *Oliver Kromvell* [Oliver Cromwell, 1920], *Foma Kampanella* [Thomas Campanella, 1920], and *Osvobozhdionnyi Don Kikhot* [The Liberated Don Quixote, 1923], L. gave new interpretations of historical and literary figures. L. also co-authored film scripts, and was prominent as a translator of Lenau, Petöfi, and C. F. Meyer.

Editions: Sobraniye sochinenii [Collected Works], 8 vols., Moscow, 1963 ff.

LUPAN, ANDREI
    Born February 2, 1912, Mikhuleny (in the Resinsk district). Moldavian Soviet lyric and dramatic writer.
    L. began his literary career as a student; in 1935 he joined the Communist Party of Rumania, and supported the revolutionary

struggles of his party. L. took his themes chiefly from the life of the peasants. After the liberation of Bessarabia, he overcame certain modernist tendencies.

In his poetic works he developed the traditions of Eminescu and Alecsandris, and was strongly influenced by Moldavian folklore. In the years 1941–45, his themes were for the most part determined by the battle against fascism; after the war he dealt with the social reconstruction of his homeland. His most important works are the poem *The Forgotten Village* (1940) and the drama *Light* (1948). L.'s work after 1968, once he overcame certain superficial tendencies, exhibited a marked increase in satirical elements. L. has also become important as a translator of Shakespeare, Nekrasov, and Mayakovski, and as a literary critic.

LYNKOW, MIKHAS (MIKHAIL TIKHANAVICH)
Born November 30, 1899, Sasby (District of Vitebsk). Member of the Academy of Sciences of the Byelorussian SSR since 1952.

L. is the son of a railroad worker; he became a teacher. He first wrote short stories on the civil war and on the life of the workers (*Nad Bugam* [On the River Bug, 1928] and *Andrei Lyatun* [1930]). His novel *Na chyrvonykh lyadakh* [On the Red Virgin Lands, 1934] tells of the class struggles in the Byelorussian village and of the role of the proletariat in winning the peasants over to the ideals of the revolution and to the collectivization of agriculture. Some of his short stories and the four-volume novel *Vekapomnyya dni* [Unforgettable Days, 1951–57] deal with the fight of the Byelorussian people against the fascist invaders; a number of these works are artistically impressive memorials to the partisans. L. has also written a number of popular children's books.

Editions: Vybranyye apavyadanni [Selected Short Stories], Minsk, 1947

LYASHKO (Pseud. of *Nikolai Nikolayevich Lyashchenko*)
Born November 24, 1884, Lebedino (District of Kharkov); died August 26, 1953, Moscow. Soviet Russian novelist.

L. came from a working-class family; from 1902 he was involved in revolutionary activities. His first stories appeared in 1904. In 1992, L. organized an association of young writers drawn from the people; he was a member of the Proletcult, and cofounder of the *Kuznitza* group (The Forge). In his volume *Rasskazy o kandalakh* [Stories about the Shackles, 1920], L. described the revolutionary problems in the Russian village after the revolution. In his novel *Domennaya pech* [The Blast Furnace, 1926], L., emulating the style of Gladkov, discussed the educational effects of work during the transition from the time of the civil war to peaceful reconstruction. His two-volume novel *Sladkaya katorga* [Sweet Prison, 1934–36] is of considerable significance; this book deals with the life and struggles of the Russian workers early in the twentieth century.

Editions: Sobraniye sochinenii [Collected Works], 3 vols., Moscow, 1955
Further Works: Minuvshaya smert [Death Passed By] (1928); *Kamen u morya* [A Stone near the Sea] (1939)

MADARIK, JUHAN (Pseud. of *Johannes Lauristin*)
Born October 29, 1899, Tallinn; died there August 28, 1941. Estonian revolutionary, statesman, and novelist.

M. joined the revolutionary movement as a young man, and became a member of the Communist Party in 1917. He carried out various party assignments, and was active in both the legal and the illegal press. In the years 1923–38, he was imprisoned for political reasons; after his release, he immediately continued the revolutionary struggle. After the fall of the bourgeoisie, M. became Chairman of the Council of People's Commissars. He was killed in action in 1941, during the defense of Tallinn.

M.'s novel *Riigikukutajad* [The Revolutionaries, 1929], written in prison, and the unfinished epic novel *Vabariik* [The Republic, 1941] are dedicated to the revolutionary worker movement.

MAIKOV, APOLLON NIKOLAYEVICH
Born June 4, 1821, Moscow; died March 20, 1897, St. Petersburg. Russian poet.
M. came from a family of artists. He worked as a civil servant in the Moscow Rymyantzev library, in the St. Petersburg censorship office, and in various other positions. His first literary works showed democratic tendencies (as may be seen in the collection of poems published in 1842, and in his poem *Mashenka*, 1846), but these were soon replaced by an antibourgeois idealization of both classical antiquity—*Ocherki Rima* [Roman Sketches, 1847] —and early Russian history. He also wrote perfectly formed poems expressing an aesthetic appreciation of nature.

Editions: Izbrannyye proizvedeniya [Selected Works], Leningrad, 1957

MAIKOV, VASILII IVANOVICH
Born 1728, Yaroslavl; died July 28, 1778. Russian classicist.
M. grew up on the estate of his father, and later entered government service. His literary activities commenced in Moscow in 1761; he translated and wrote odes, fables, poems, epigrams, and plays. M. was one of the most important representatives of Russian enlightenment. His main work is the poem *Yelisei ili razdrazhonny Wakkh* [Yelisei, or The Enraged Bacchus, 1771], which reflects certain elements indicating the attempt to overcome the narrowness of classicism and to use realistic, popular images.

Editions: Sochineniya i perevody [Works and Translations], St. Petersburg, 1867

MAILIN, REIMBET (BIMAGANBET)
Born November 15, 1894, Aktynbinsk; died November 10, 1938, Alma-Ata. One of the founders of Kazakh Soviet literature.
M. was a teacher. He had been writing poems and short stories (*Shuga's Hill*, 1915) from 1912. After 1917 he described the class struggles, the emancipation of women, and, in his novel

Asamat Asamatovich (1934), socialist reconstruction. His work consists mostly of novels, short stories, poems, and plays.

MAIRONIS (Pseud. of *Jonas Maciulis*)
Born November 2, 1862, Pasandravys, near Siluva; died June 28, 1932, Kaunas. The greatest poet of Lithuanian literature.
M., the son of a peasant, became a clergyman and later a professor of theology. His literary works show his profound love for Lithuania; they tell of that country's struggles against the oppressors. M. is considered the founder of the positive tradition in Lithuanian romanticism.
The themes of M.'s poetry were frequently taken from the great past of Lithuania; in these works he occasionally gave a somewhat idealized picture of feudal times. As he grew older, nationalist, bourgeois ideas became more prominent in his writings. His main work is the collection of poems *Pavasario balsai* [The Voices of Spring, 1895]. M. has also written a number of outstanding ballads, as well as plays and epic poems.
Editions: Pavasario balsai [The Voices of Spring], Vilnius, 1958

MAKARENKO, SANTON SEMIONOVICH
Born March 1, 1888, Belopole (District of Kharkov); died April 1, 1939, Moscow. Soviet Russian novelist and educator.
M. came from a worker family. In 1914–17 he attended the teachers college in Poltava; in 1920 he became director of the Gorki camp near Poltava, a colony for young delinquents. In 1927 he became director of the Dzerzhinski people's commune near Kharkov. From 1936 M. was a fulltime writer.
On the basis of his rich experience in the field of youth education, M.—as one of the first Soviet writers—has been able to describe the growth of socialist man in a psychologically and poetically beautiful manner. He was directly supported in these efforts by Gorki, who, in 1928, visited the camp named after him.
M.'s literary works reflect his own educational principles—the belief that the formation of the young person in the collective,

including training and education for the responsibilities of citizen-
ship, is of considerable importance. These works also demonstrate M.'s ability to describe the dramatic struggle to rehabilitate
these young people. This is especially true for his most important
work, the *Pedagogicheskaya poema* (1933–35; The Road to Life,
1936), which shows the development of the collective and the
conflict-filled road of a number of young people in the Gorki
camp.

In *Flagi na bashnyakh* [Flags on the Towers, 1938], M., using
the Dzerzhinski camp as an example, describes the beauty of
work and of life in a socialist collective that has become settled.
M. also wrote a number of short stories, including *Marsh tridtza-
tovo goda* [The March of the Year Nineteen-thirty, 1930], works
of a literary, pedagogic character, including *Kniga dlya roditelei*
(1937; The Collective Family, 1967), dramas, and film scripts as
well as critical essays on literary themes.

Editions: Sochineniya [Works], 7 vols., Moscow, 1950–52, 1957, 1959

MAKHTUM-KULI (Surnamed *Fragi*)

Born circa 1730; died between 1780 and 1790. Turkmenian
poet; founder of classical Turkmen literature.

M. was an agriculturalist as well as a silversmith and a leather
worker. The main theme of his work was the unification of all
Turkmenian tribes against external enemies (*Appeal, The Bird
of Good Omen*). M. also expressed the protest of the impoverished
masses against their feudal rulers, and described vivid scenes
from national life. He exposed the greed and despotism of the
feudal upper classes, as well as the obscurantism of the Mussul-
man fanatics. He described the best human characteristics of the
working people.

M.'s poems reformed the Turkmenian literary language by
introducing the vernacular into literature. His poetry is rich in
images and very melodic. Many of his poems have become folksongs, and certain lines from his verses have become proverbs.

M.'s ideology, including his views on revolution, was very controversial, and these conflicts led to temporary feelings of desperation. Bourgeois nationalists have declared M. to have been a mystic.

Editions: Sailanan goshgylar, Ashkhabad, 1940

MAKSIM GREK (Secular name, *Mikhael Tribolis*)
Born 1480; died 1556. Russian theologian and political writer.
M. G. became acquainted with humanist ideas while staying in Italy; he later became a monk in the Athos monastery in Greece. In 1518 he came to Moscow to work as a translator. He supported the Boyar opposition, and as a result was exiled several times. In addition to traditional epistles he wrote various philosophical and critical works in a style that at that time was considered modern.

Editions: Sochineniya [Works], 3 vols., 1859–60, 1910–11

MALASHKIN, SERGEI IVANOVICH
Born 1890. Soviet Russian novelist.
N. was born into a peasant family and as a young child was already familiar with poverty. In 1908–14 he traveled across Russia in search of work.
M.'s literary works deal with the new life after the revolution; his writing frequently exhibits both bourgeois and humanistic concepts, as is the case in his impressive novel *Zapiski Ananiya Shmurkina* [Notes of Anani Shmurkin, 1947], in which he handled the problems of war from a point of view opposite to that of E. M. Remarque. In *Luna s pravoi* [Moon from the Right, 1927] M. described the wild sexual life of a young Komsomol girl without, however, showing the background and social roots that were the cause of this life. In *Pokhod kolonn* [The March of the Columns, 1930], M. has shown the Soviet village during collectivization, and discussed the problem of the class struggle evident during those times.

MALTZEV (Pseud. of *Yelizar Yuryevich Pupko*)
Born January 4, 1917, Khan-khaloi. Soviet Russian novelist. M. comes from a peasant family in the Buryat ASSR; he studied at the Gorki Institute of Literature. His novel *Goryachiye klyuchi* [Hot Springs, 1945] describes the heroic deeds of the Siberian kolkhoz farmers during World War II. *Ot vsevo serdtza* [From the Bottom of the Heart, 1948] also deals with the theme of socialist work; this novel, for which M. received the State Prize, shows the life of a simple peasant woman who becomes a famous and acknowledged agriculturalist.

Developments in the Soviet villages after the Plenary Meeting of the Central Committee of the Communist Party of the SSSR in September of 1953 are the theme of the novel *Voidi v kazshdy dom* [Enter Into Any House, 1961].

MALYSHKIN, ALEKSANDR GEORGIYEVICH
Born March 21, 1892, Bogorodskoye, near Mokshany (District of Penza); died August 3, 1938, Moscow. Soviet Russian novelist.

M. graduated from the Faculty of Philology of the University of St. Petersburg. He began his literary career in 1912. He took part in the October revolution, and in the civil war was a commander in the Red Army; in 1920 he aided in the defeat of Wrangel's army on the Crimea. These battles, especially the Bolshevist victory of Perekop, have been described by M. in his novel *Padeniye Daira* [The Fall of Dair, 1923]. This novel, which is permeated by romantic fervor, represents a permanent memorial to the heroic fight of the people—it is essentially the people who determine the composition of the work.

M. has captured impressive episodes from the year 1917 in his novel *Sevastopol* (1929–30), which shows the progressive forces of the bourgeois intelligentsia going over to the side of the socialist revolution. In his unfinished novel *Lyudi iz zakholustya* [People from the Back Country, 1937–38], M. dealt with contemporary themes. He showed how the socialist reconstruction of the 1930s involved even the most remote corner of the country, and how it promoted the development of a proud Soviet people.

Editions: Sobraniye sochinenii [Collected Works], 3 vols., Moscow, 1940–47

MALYSHKO, ANDRII SAMIILOVYCH
Born November 19, 1912, Obukhov. Ukrainian Soviet lyric poet.

M., the son of a village shoemaker, graduated in 1932 from the Kiev Institute for Adult Education. He then worked as a teacher and occupied responsible positions in the field of journalism.

Although M. first started writing poetry in 1930, it was not until the publication of his first collection of poems in 1936 that his impressive lyrical talents became noticeable. Vivid artistic generalizations, a timely sense of relevance, and numerous stylistic and thematic borrowings from Ukrainian folklore characterize M.'s versatile and melodious lyrics. It is the lyric poem that has become his preferred genre. M. was awarded State Prizes in 1947 and 1951.

Editions: Tvory [Works], 3 vols., Kiev, 1956–57

MAMIN-SIBIRYAK, DMITRI NARKISOVICH
Born November 6, 1852, Visimo-Shaitansk (Urals); died November 15, 1912, St. Petersburg. Russian novelist of the naturalist school.

M., who came from the family of a poor priest, attended the theological seminary in Perm (1868–71); he subsequently studied veterinary medicine and, later, was a law student at the University of St. Petersburg. He was forced to interrupt his studies for health reasons, and returned to the Urals in 1877. In 1891 he moved to St. Petersburg, where he was closely associated with Gorki, Chekhov, and Stanislavski, who greatly influenced his ideology. M. stood by his democratic convictions and ideals even during the period of Stolypinian reaction.

M.'s *oeuvre*, which had its beginnings in 1875, is very extensive.

It includes novels, short stories, and sketches, dealing for the most part with social development in the Urals region during the early period of capitalism. M.'s themes are concerned chiefly with the life of simple people in the Urals, who, after emancipation from serfdom, experienced the arrival of capitalism. These people see how the old patriarchal conditions are destroyed only to be replaced by new and even crueller conditions.

M.'s epic work, which in many respects is indebted to that of Émile Zola, is almost a chronicle of the first phase of capitalist development in Russia. Among his best-known works are the novels *Privalovskiye milliony* (1883; The Privalov Fortune, 1958), *Zoloto* [Gold, 1892], *Khleb* [Bread, 1895], and the cycle of sketches *Ot Urala do Moskvy* [From the Urals to Moscow, 1881–82].

Editions: Sobraniye sochinenii [Collected Works], 8 vols., Moscow, 1953–55

MANAS

The greatest Kirghiz national epic.

The legends of Manas, his son Semetei, and his grandson Seitek reflect the battles of the Kirghiz people against outside enemies during the twelfth and fifteenth to eighteenth centuries, and other historical events from prefeudal times. This work also contains many ethnographic details, proverbs, and elements of national poetry. The different variations that have come down to us exhibit features of either pan-Islam or nationalist ideologies. V. V. Radlov was the first author (1862) to put these legends and sagas on paper; the version written down by the folksinger Sayakbai Karalayev in 1948–49 has approximately 200,000 verses.

MANDELSTAM, OSIP EMILYEVICH

Born January 15, 1891, Warsaw; died 1939. Russian Soviet poet.

M., one of the chief representatives of Acmeism, first started publishing poems in 1909. His first volume *Kamen* [The Stone] appeared in 1913. M., in highly formal, neoclassic verses, exhibited an aristocratic individualism; he declared himself indifferent to the historical events of his time. After the October revolution, to which he had a negative attitude, M. continued to hold his *l'art pour l'art* views. His themes dealt only with the isolated individual; he was not concerned with the problems of a socialist society. His lyric writings as such are of a high formal level.

Further Works: Tristia [Tristia] (1922); *Shum vremeni* [Noise of the Times] (1925); *Yegipetskaya marka* [Egyptian Postage Stamp] (1928)

MARKOV, GEORGI MOKEYEVICH

Born April 19, 1911, Novo-Kushkovo (District of Tomsk). Soviet Russian novelist.

M. comes from a family of peasants and hunters; he has been active as a leader in youth groups and as an editor of various newspapers.

M. wrote his first essays and sketches as a village newspaper correspondent. His novel *Strogovy* [The Strogovs], a description of three generations in the life of a beekeeper's family in Eastern Siberia, appeared in 1939. M. took part in World War II as a frontline correspondent. In his novel *Sol semli* [The Salt of the Earth, 1956], which is permeated by fresh enthusiasm and love for his Siberian homeland, M. demonstrated the human conflicts that arose during the reconstruction of that rich country.

Further Works: Otetz i syn [Father and Son] (1965)

MARSHAK, SAMUIL YAKOVLEVICH

Born November 4, 1887, Voronesh; died July 4, 1964, Moscow. Russian Soviet poet and writer for children.

M. met Gorki while still a high-school student. His first poems and translations appeared in 1907. In 1912–14, he studied in England. After the October revolution, M. became one of the founders of Soviet children's literature. His melodic, comprehensive poems have become very popular both in Russia and abroad. These poems and verses are extraordinarily versatile with respect to both themes and genres; they deal with all the aspects of nature and society a child could understand.

Among M.'s best-known works are the stories in verse *Bagazh* (1926; The Baggage, 1938), *Mister Twister* (1933; Mister Twister, 1936), *Byl-nebylitza* (1947; Cock-and-Bull Story, 1956), and the plays *Dvenadtzat mesyatzev* [Twelve Months, 1943] and *Umnyye veschi* [Intelligent Things, 1964]. Toward the end of the 1930s M. began to write poetry and satire.

M. was one of the most important Soviet translators. In addition to many translations from the English that have become classics (Shakespeare, Burns, Keats, Byron, Blake, Kipling), M. has translated Heine, Petöfi, and Smaj into Russian. M. was awarded State Prizes in 1942, 1946, 1949, and 1951; he received the Lenin Prize in 1963.

Editions: Sochineniya [Works], 4 vols., Moscow, 1958–60

MARTYNOV, LEONID NIKOLAYEVICH
Born May 22, 1905, Omsk. Soviet Russian poet.

M. grew up in Siberia; he traveled across wide regions of the Soviet Union working at various jobs before his first volume of poetry, *Gruby korm* [Rough Food], appeared in 1930. The intense social contradictions existing in Northern Russia, the intermingling of past and future, and the restless search for happiness are the main themes of M.'s prewar poems, including *Tobolski letopisetz* [The Chronicle from Tobolsk].

M. became very popular in the middle fifties for his concise philosophical examinations of everyday phenomena—*Voda* [The Water, 1946]; *Royal* [The Grand Piano, 1964]—for his demanding appeals—*Kto sleduyushchi?* [Who Is the Next One?]; *Sled* [The Trail, 1948], and his philosophical, aesthetic poetry—*Ekho* [Echo, 1955]; *Grozsa* [The Thunderstorm, 1962]. M. frequently uses complex language and classical symbols (*Mne kazhetsya . . .* [Waking Up, 1955]; *Dvenadtzat tzesarei* [Twelve Caesars, 1964]).

Editions: Stikhi [Poems], Moscow, 1955; *Lirika* [Lyric Writings], Moscow, 1958; *Stikhotvoreniya* [Poetry], Moscow, 1961

MAYAKOVSKI, VLADIMIR VLADIMIROVICH

Born July 19, 1893, Bagdadi (now called Mayakovski, Georgian SSR); died April 14, 1930, Moscow. Soviet Russian poet.

M., the son of a forest ranger, grew up in a democratic home. As a high-school student in Kutaisi he read Marxist literature, and took part in demonstrations in 1905. M.'s contacts with the revolutionary worker movement became more intense following the death of his father and his subsequent move to Moscow. In 1908 he became a member of the Social Democratic Workers' Party of Russia; he left high school and worked as a propagandist; he was arrested three times. M.'s first poems, which have been lost, were written in prison. In 1910 he interrupted his work for the party, and in 1911 entered the Moscow School of Painting, Sculpture, and Architecture. He published his first poems in the futurist collection *Poshchochina obshchestvennomu vkusa* [A Fig for Public Taste, 1912].

M.'s early work (1912–17) was from the beginning democratic and antibourgeois in nature, and its themes were determined by M.'s passionate hatred for the existing order and by his need to protest against the alienation of man. M.'s friends included several representatives of futurism, including Burlyuk, Khlebnikov, and Kamenski, but the aesthetic platform of that movement in art—which was concerned only with formal innovations—soon became too small for him. In his early works, some of which are still characterized by the use of complex metaphors, M. arrived at a decisive rejection of both bourgeois morals and imperialist war. This may be seen in various works written by him at that time, including the tragedy *Vladimir Mayakovski* (1913), the poems *Oblako v shtanakh* [The Cloud in Trousers, 1915] and *Voina i mir* [War and Peace, 1916]. The note of tragic solitude and resignation evident in some of these works may be ascribed to M.'s relative isolation from the revolutionary worker movement. Only the October revolution reunited both his work and his feelings with that movement.

M., who still called himself a futurist, aimed at attaining mass effects with the poems he wrote about the revolution. In poems such as *Levy marsh* [Left March!, 1918], he presented appeals for action. His drama *Misteriya-buff* (1918; second version, 1921; Mystery Bouffe, 1933), written in an allegoric, parabolic form, showed the road of the proletariat to revolution. In his poem *150.000.000* (1921), M. attempted to demonstrate the worldwide struggle between capitalism and socialism by using folklorist forms of representation.

M. was an active agitator with the central press agency in 1919–21, creating signs carrying easily understood verses commenting on actual political events. In this work and in daily practice, M.'s artistic methods gradually changed. His search for novel forms and for new ways to attain different content is directly connected with his examination of his relationship with reality. The lyrical, strongly autobiographical poems *Lyublyu* [I Love, 1922] and *Pro eto* [About It, 1923] overcome the conflict between individual happiness and the needs of society; it carries love beyond its narrow petit-bourgeois concept to serve the high ideals of socialist morals of the future.

M.'s poem *Vladimir Ilyich Lenin* (1924) indicates the beginning of his most mature period. In an extensive synthesis of historical events and lyric commentary, M. here traced the development of the revolutionary worker movement to the time of Lenin's death. To this day, M.'s Lenin poem has remained the model for the poems of a similar nature. M.'s poem *Khorosho!* [Well and Good, 1927] is one of the most moving descriptions of the first decade of Soviet power; it offers a convincing picture of the new socialist feeling of life.

M. related the development of the Soviet state between 1917 and 1927 to his development as artist, feeling that such a development could only be possible within socialist society. The posthumously published (1930) prologue to his poem *Vo ves golos* [With Full Voice, 1930] is a passionate summary of M.'s desire to be a standardbearer, and to participate in the building of socialism. This concern is evident in many of M.'s sublime poems, including *Yubeleinoye* [Jubilee Verses, 1924] and *Razgovor s fininspektorom o poezii* [A Discourse with the Tax Inspector on the Art of Poetry, 1926].

M.'s universality is also reflected in his extensive satirical work, which in its aggressive polemicism is directed against the remnants of capitalism in the Soviet Union; it also deals with the signs of decline exhibited by the bourgeois world. M.'s only extensive prose work, *Moyo otkrytiye Ameriki* [My Discovery of America, 1926], like many of his sketches and poems about foreign countries, is a sarcastic squaring of accounts with an antiquated world. His satirical comedies *Klop* (1928; The Bedbug, 1960) and *Banya* [The Sauna, 1929] are directed against philistinism and bureaucratism; their fragmented form and aggressive wit make them masterpieces of the comic genre. During his last years M. disengaged himself from the aesthetic confines of *Lef*, the futurist magazine of which he was editor, and began to examine the effect of his work, developing what appeared to be a constant dialogue with his reading public.

M.'s poetry attained world rank; it influences today's socialist world literature to an ever-increasing extent. M.'s innovations were based on the new position of the artist in a socialist society. These innovations include the development of new themes and new artistic images, new rhymes, and new verbal and rhythmic possibilities. Seen as a whole, they represent the synthesis of a genial linguistic talent with an indefatigable endeavor to do justice to the demands made by socialism on poetry.

Editions: Polnoye sobraniye sochinenii [Complete Works], 13 vols., Moscow, 1955–61
Further Works: Kak delat stikhi [How Verses Are Made] (1926)

MEKHTI HUSSEIN (Pseud. of *Mekhti Ali-ogly Huseinov*)
Born April 4, 1909, Shishly; died March 10, 1965. Azerbaidzhani Soviet novelist.

M. H.'s versatile work is dedicated to the new Azerbaidzhan. His first stories about the Azerbaidzhani village were written during the 1920s and 1930s. The theme of his gripping novel

M. V. Lomonosov

A. V. Lunacharski

S. S. Makarenko

Makhtum-Kuli

V. V. Mayakovski

E. Mieželaitis

N. A. Navoi

N. A. Nekrasov

I. Y. Nizami Gandzhevi

Tarlan (1940) is based on the heroic fight of the first Azerbaidzhani people's commune—the Chailin commune—against counterrevolutionary bands.

M. H.'s most important novel, *Apsheron* (1949), deals with the Azerbaidzhani workers and the intelligentsia. The development of these groups toward the acceptance of communism is shown in M. H.'s novel *Black Rocks* (1958). The struggles of the Baku proletariat between 1909–18 have been described by him in the trilogy *Morning* (1954–55).

Further Works: Nizami [Nisami]; *Komissar* [Commissar] (1942)

MELEZH, IVAN PAVLAVICH
Born February 8, 1921, Glinishchi (District of Gomel). Byelorussian Soviet novelist and playwright.

M., the son of a farmer, has been writing poetry since 1939. He has recently been writing stories about World War II. His novella *Garachy zhniven* [Hot August] on village life was written in 1946; the novel *Minski napramak* [In the Direction of Minsk], which deals with the liberation of Byelorussia from fascist occupation, was published in 1953. In addition to numerous stories and plays, M. has written the novel *Lyudi na bolote* [People in the Swamps, 1956–60], representing the first part of a planned novel cycle about the changes in the life and thinking of the Polesye farmers after the October revolution.

MELNIKOV-PECHERSKI, PAVEL IVANOVICH
Born November 6, 1818, Nizhni Novgorod; died there February 13, 1883. Russian novelist of the realist school.

M., the son of a small estate owner, studied in Kazan, and then worked as a teacher and civil servant. His work first became known in the 1850s, when he published stories containing criticism of socialism. His main works are the novels *V lesakh* [In the Forests, 1868–74] and *Na gorakh* [On the Mountains, 1875–81]. In these two novels M. has given a detailed description of the merchants and the peasants in the Volga region belonging to the *Raskolniki* (a sect formed following a schism or *raskol* within the Orthodox Church in the seventeenth century; these Old Believers found themselves exposed to persecutions by both the official church and the government). M. P.'s two novels are distinguished by the versatile ethnographic material they contain (folksongs, spirituals, local tales and legends, and proverbs), and they offer a socially differentiated language rich in popular turns of speech.

Editions: Polnoye sobraniye sochinenii [Complete Works], 7 vols., St. Petersburg, 1909

MEREZHKOVSKI, DMITRI SERGEYEVICH

Born August 14, 1865, St. Petersburg; died December 9, 1941, Paris. Russian philosophical writer and novelist.

M. was one of the founders of Russian symbolism; he expounded the theories of the symbolist movement in his book *O prichinakh upadka i o novykh tendentziyakh sovremennoi ruskoi literatury* [On the Reasons for the Decline and on the New Movements in Contemporary Russian Literature, 1895]. M. demanded a withdrawal from the traditions of revolutionary democratic art, from reality, and from realism. Under the influence of Nietzsche and the reactionary Russian philosophers Solovyov and Rosanov, M. constructed an antithetical world picture in which the forces of the spirit oppose those of the flesh. His historical novels are based on this principle; they expound on M.'s religious, mystical ideas more than they do justice to historical truth. They include the trilogy *Khristos i Antikhrist* [Christ and Antichrist], Part I, *Smert bogov. Yulian-Otstupnik* (1894; The Death of the Gods: Julian Apostate, 1929); Part II, *Voskreseniya bogov. Leonardo da Vinchi* (1901; The Resurrection of the Gods: Leonardo da Vinci, 1953); Part III, *Antikhrist: Piotr i Aleksei* (1905; Antichrist: Peter and Alexis, 1937). M.'s religious philosophy influenced Western European bourgeois views of Russia in an extremely negative manner; this philosophy was discussed by M. Gorki. M. emigrated to Paris in 1919 and was active against the Soviet. During World War II he collaborated with the Germans.

MEYERHOLD, VSEVOLOD EMILYEVICH
Born February 9, 1874, Penza; died March 17, 1942, Moscow. Soviet Russian theater director and actor; People's Artist of the RSFSR after 1923.

After completing his law studies, M. was trained by Nemirovich-Danchenko; from 1898 to 1902 he was an actor at the Moscow Artists' Theater. He later worked as a director at different theaters, continually seeking for new forms derived from the national theater. After the revolution, in which he took an active part, M. continued his experiments aimed at the establishment of a revolutionary theater. As an official active in the field of culture, M. was involved in the reorganization of the Soviet theater. Between 1920–38 he was director of the theater that had been named after him in 1923.

M.'s striving for a valid, politically oriented theater of the people was hindered by the influence of both futurist and constructivist elements. His greatest achievements in the 1920s included his productions of works by Ostrovski, Gogol, and Mayakovski, whose grotesque, biting styles were characterized by elements of aggressiveness. M. was also searching for a richer and deeper method of presentation in his realistic productions; after the closing of his theater, he worked closely with Stanislavski. Much of M.'s work continues to influence both the Soviet and the progressive world theater.

MIEŽELAITIS, EDUARDAS
Born October 3, 1919, Kareiviškiai. Lithuanian poet; President of the Lithuanian Writers' Union since 1959.

M. grew up in a proletarian environment, and fought against the fascists in bourgeois Lithuania. He later occupied many high government positions.

The climax of M.'s literary work is the volume of poetry *Žmogus* [Man, 1961], which in the 1940s and 1950s was preceded by numerous collections of poems, including *Lyrika* (1943); *Teviškes vejas* [Homeland Winds, 1946]; *Broliška poema* [Brotherly Poem, 1954]; and *Mano lakštingala* [My Nightingale, 1956].

M.'s lyrics are distinguished by a profound conception of man; they are permeated by socialist ideals, philosophical concentration, and true innovations in form. M. was awarded the Lenin Prize in 1962.

Editions: Žmogus [Man], Vilnius, 1962
Further Works: Autoportretas. Aviaeskizai [Self Portraits] (1962); Lyriniai etiudai [Lyric Studies] (1964)

MIKHALKOV, SERGEI VLADIMIROVICH
Born March 12, 1913, Moscow. Soviet Russian poet and dramatist.

M.'s first political poems were written in the 1930s. After graduating from the Gorki Institute of Literature, M., following in the steps of Mayakovski and Marshak, wrote songs and verses for children and young people. Some of these, including *A chto u vas?* [And What Do You Have?, 1935] and *Dyada Stiopa* [Uncle Styopa, 1936], became very popular. M.'s rhythmically versatile poems, rich in ideas, unobtrusively combine socialist education, instruction, and humorous entertainment. They belong to the heritage of Soviet children's literature.

M.'s plays for children—*Krasnyi galstuk* [The Red Scarf, 1946] and *Sombrero* (1957)—have also been great successes. His plays, which are frequently very satirical (*Raki* [The Crabs, 1959] and *Zeliony Kuznechik* [The Green Cricket, 1964]), like his fables—which follow the traditions established by Krylov and Demyan Bedny—deal for the most part with the traces of the bourgeois attitudes remaining in Soviet life. M. was awarded State Prizes in 1941, 1942, and 1950.

Editions: Sochineniya [Works], 2 vols., Moscow, 1954

MIRSHKAR (Pseud. of Mirzaid Mirshakarov)
Born May 5, 1912, Sindev. Tadzhik Soviet poet.

M. has become known through his poems (in particular, through those for children) and dramas. His best-known works are the poems *Livoyi zafar* [The Banner of Victory, 1933]; *Qisloqi tolloji* [The Golden Village, 1942]; *Pangi noorom* (The Vehement Pyandsh, 1949), and *Lenin dar Pomir* [Lenin on the Pamir, 1955]. M. was awarded the State Prize in 1950.

Editions: Se'rho va poemaho [Poems and Verses], 1945; *Mo az Pomir omadem* [We are Coming from the Pamir], 1954

MOLENIYE DANIILA ZATOCHNIKA (Petition of Daniil the Exile)
An anonymous pamphlet addressed to a Russian prince of the twelfth or thirteenth century, which has come down to us in a number of different versions. This request for aid and acceptance into the service of the prince contains strong attacks against the Boyars and the clergy, and is written in a highly rhetorical and aphoristic form.

Editions: Slovo Daniila Zatochnika [Petition of Daniil the Exile], Leningrad, 1932

MOLLANEPES
Born ca. 1810; died ca. 1862. Turkmenian poet.
M. has written many *destanes* (cf. Turkmenian literature), in which he described the contradictions existing in the feudal system. They include *Zokhre i Takhir*. He also was a master of the love lyric. His works were collected and recorded on paper only after the revolution.

MONTVILA, VYTAUTAS
Born March 4, 1902, Chicago; died July, 1941 (murdered by German fascists). Lithuanian revolutionary poet.
M., who came from a worker family, lived through a very difficult childhood and youth in bourgeois Lithuania. He joined the revolutionary worker movement, and was an active participant in the antifascist struggle. His first collection of poems, *Naktys be nakvynes* [Nights without Quarters], appeared in 1931. His work reached its climax in 1940, following the establishment of Soviet power, with *I plačia žeme* [Into the Far Country, 1940]. M. continued the work of Julius Janonis, and was one of the most

important representatives of revolutionary poetry of socialist realism in Lithuania.

Editions: Rastai [Works], 2 vols., Vilnius, 1956

MORDINOV, NIKOLAI YEGOROVICH (Pseud.: *Amma Achchygyya*)
Born January 6, 1906, Nizhne-Aginski Nasleg (District of Tatta). Yakut Soviet short-story writer and novelist.

M. has sensitively described the changes in character and awareness of the simple Yakut people after the revolution (*Byhakh ugun kystymmat* [The Knife Does Not Cut the Lever, and Other Short Stories, 1927]). Together with Oyunski and Kyunde, M. was involved in the development of Yakut prose writing. His novel *Saasky* [Springtime, 1944–51] represents an important landmark in the development of the Yakut novel; it contains a portrait of the historical rebirth of the Yakut people. M. has also written a play on the collectivization in Yakutia, *Sitim bystyyta* [Breakthrough, 1937]. He is also known for his translations in the field of Russian literature. M. is a Meritorious Artist of the Yakut ASSR.

MUKANOV, SABIT
Born April 13, 1900, Aul No. 2, near Tuasarsk. One of the founders of Kazakh Soviet literature.

M. came from a very poor family; he became a teacher. After the revolution he studied in Orensburg, Leningrad, and Moscow, later becoming a member of the Kazakh Academy of Sciences. He has directed the Kazakh Writers' Union since 1935. M.'s poems and verses, which have been influenced by Mayakovski, have greatly enlarged the expressivity of Kazakh poetry. In addition to other prose works, M. has written the naturalistic autobiography *The School of Life*, and the historical novel *Botagos* (1948–53)

MUKIMI, MOHAMMED AMIN-HODZHA
Born 1851; died May 25, 1903. Uzbekistanian democratic poet.

M. was the son of a poor baker in Kokand; he studied at schools in Kokand, Bukhara, and Tashkent. His home in Kokand became the center of the democratic movement in nineteenth-century Uzbek literature. M. acted as a social accuser. His satirical poems on the feudal rulers and capitalist profiteers—*The Bill of Exchange, The New Estate-Owner*—and *The Surveyor, The Holy Man, The Erring Son*—poems on the corrupt officials and the Islam clergy—were also popular. M. has also written lyrics in both the Uzbek and the Tadzik languages.

MUSTAFIN, GABIDEN

Born November 26, 1902, Sartobe. Kazakh Soviet novelist and dramatist.

M. first worked as a journalist; he has been publishing short prose pieces since 1927. His most important achievements came after 1945, with his novels *Shiganak* (1945 and 1951) on collectivization and *Karaganda* (1952) on the industrialization of Kazakhstan. His best-known novel is *The Millionaire* (1948), based on the life of the kolkhoz farmers. M.'s works have given a new force to Kazakh prose writings.

MYKOLAITIS, VINCAS

Born January 13, 1893, Piliotiškes; died June, 1967, Kachergin. Lithuanian poet, narrative writer, and dramatist.

M. came from peasant stock; he first studied theology, and later, in Germany, philosophy, art history and literary history. He first sided with the clerics; as an artist he was closely connected with the representatives of romanticism and symbolism. In the mid-1930s he left the clerical ranks and joined the ranks of the anti-fascist writers. One of his most important works is the novel *Altoriu šešely* [In the Shadow of the Altars, 1933], which, despite its idealistic conception, is of great importance because of its anticlerical outlook.

After World War II M. took an active part in the cultural and scientific life of his homeland. He created new poetic masterpieces, and produced important essays in the fields of literary criticism and history. He received the State Prize of the Republic for his historical novel *Sukileliai* [Vol. I, The Rebels, 1937].

M. was a Meritorious Writer of the People of the Lithuanian SSR, a university professor, and a member of the Academy of Sciences.

Editions: Rastai [Works], 8 vols., Vilnius, 1959–62

MYRNYI, PANAS (Pseud. of *Afanasii Yakovlevich Rudchenko*)
Born May 13, 1849, Mirgorod; died January 28, 1920, Poltava. Ukrainian novelist; founder of the Ukrainian realistic social novel.

M. came from the petit bourgeoisie, and, after graduation from a county school, worked for forty years as a civil servant. His ideological development continued under the strong influences of Russian revolutionary democratic ideas and of Taras Shevchenko. In his broadly based novels *Khiba voly revut, yak yasla poveri* [Do Oxen Bellow When Their Manger Is Full? 1880], *Poviya* [The Whore, 1883–1919], and *Lykho davnye i sohochasne* [The Old and the New Miseries, 1903], M. described the social conflicts in the post-emancipation period (1861–1905). In these descriptions he demonstrated the process of class differentiation as well as the consolidation of the capitalistic order. M. succeeded in creating literary characters who exhibited profound psychological motivation.

Editions: Vibrani tvory [Selected Works], 2 vols., Kiev, 1949
Further Works: Lykhi lyudy [Evil People] (1876)

NADSON, SEMION YAKOVLEVICH
Born December 26, 1862, St. Petersburg; died January 31, 1887, Yalta. Russian poet.

N.'s work expressed the contradictory sentiments felt by the Russian intelligentsia during the period of transition from the revolutionary movement to the proletarian phase of the liberation movement. N, whose work formed a link with that of Nekrasov, wrote emotional, noble-minded philosophical lyrics, in which he called for the preservation of revolutionary ideals. In the 1880s N.'s poetry began to reflect tones of pessimism and doubt, which, however, did not destroy his faith in the ultimate victory of social progress.

Editions: Polnoye sobraniye sochninii [Complete Works], Moscow–Leningrad, 1962

NAGIBIN, YURII MARKOVICH

Born April 3, 1920, Moscow. Soviet Russian short-story writer. N. has been working as a reporter and journalist. Since 1943 he has been writing war stories, including the collection *Chelovek na fronte* [Man up Front, 1963], *Bolshoye serdtze* [The Great Heart, 1944], and *Zerno zhisni* [A Grain of Life, 1948]. His heroes are simple people whose experiences N. has depicted in a lyrical and emotional manner.

Editions: Trudnoye schchastye [Hard-Won Happiness], Moscow, 1956; *Rasskasy* [Stories], Moscow, 1953–55

NALBANDIAN, MIKAEL

Born November 14, 1829, Novaya Nakhichevan, near Rostov-on-Don; died May 11, 1866, Kamyshin (District of Saratov). Armenian revolutionary democrat; materialistic philosopher; poet and literary critic.

N.'s views were greatly influenced by Herzen and Chernyshevski. In 1853 he graduated from the Faculty of Oriental Studies of the University of St. Petersburg. He later studied medicine and natural sciences, and became involved with philosophy, literature, and history. His poem *The Song of Liberty* became the creed of the progressive Armenians of his time. Among N.'s most important works are his *Narration on Armenian Literature*, completed in 1854, and his *Introduction to the Grammar of the Armenian Language*. As a critic, N. analyzed contemporary Armenian literature.

Editions: Izbrannyye proizvedeniya [Selected Works], Yerevan, 1941

NAMSARAYEV, KHOTZA

Born May 9, 1889, District of Kishinga; died July 28, 1959. Founder and most important representative of Buryat Mongol literature.

N., who came from a poor village family, was a short-story writer and novelist. Numerous impressive poetic works on factual themes, including the drama *Darkness*, written in 1919, and popular short stories (*One Night*, 1938) characterize N.'s development in the 1920s and 1930s.

N.'s work reached a climax during World War II. In his dramas and stories he created permanent memorials to the patriots of Buryat Mongolia—*The Light of Victory* (1942); *The Golden Arrow* (1944). In addition to a number of other postwar poems, stories (*Young Men*, 1949) and plays (*The Key to Happiness*, 1947), in 1950 N. wrote his well-received novel on prerevolutionary Buryatia, *At Dawn*.

NAREZHNI, VASILII TROFIMOVICH

Born 1780, Ustivitz; died July 3, 1825. Russian short-story writer and novelist; founder of the Russian novel of manners.

N.'s two first novels *Rossiski Shilblas, ili pokhozhdeniya knyazya Gavrily Simonovicha Chistyakova* (1814; first complete edition, 1938) [The Russian Gil Blas, or The Adventures of Prince Gavrila Simonovich Chistyakov] and *Chorny god, ili Gorskiye Knyazya*, (1817; first complete edition, 1829) [The Black Year, or The Mountain Princes] are characterized by sharp criticism of the social conditions in Russia, and of the robberies committed by Russian officers and Caucasian princes. N.'s striving for realism is particularly evident in his last and best novel, *Dva Ivana, ili Strast k tyazhbam* [Two Ivans, or The Passion for Lawsuits, 1825]. N.'s realistic descriptions of the parasitic life of the small Ukrainian estate owners and his vivid, simple language make him a direct precursor of Gogol.

Editions: Izbrannyye romany [Selected Novels], Moscow–Leningrad, 1933; *Rossiski Shilbas*, knigi 1 & 2 [A Russian Gil Blas, Books One and Two], Moscow, 1938; *Dva Ivana, ili Strast k tyazhbam* [Two Ivans, or the Passion for Lawsuits], Moscow, 1956

NARIMANOV, NARIMAN

Born April 14, 1817, Tbilisi; died March 19, 1925, Moscow. Azerbaidzhani novelist, playwright, and political writer; important functionary of the Communist Party.

Under Lenin's direction, N. participated in the revolution and execution of Lenin's plans for federating the nationalities of the Soviet Union. In 1921 he became Chairman of the Council of People's Commissars of the Azerbaidzhani SSR. In his drama *Nadir shah* [Shah Nadir, 1899], N. showed the tragic portrait of a revolutionary leader defeated in the battle against reaction. N.'s most important novel *Bakhadur and Sona* (1896) is a song in praise of friendship between peoples; it is dedicated to exposing the artificially created distrust between the Azerbaidzhan people and the Armenians.

Editions: Bakhadur i Sona [Bakhadur and Sona] (in Russian), Moscow, 1958

NARODNIKI See POPULISTS

NASIR-I-KHUSRAU, ABU MU'IN

Born 1004, Qubadiyan (Province of Merv); died between 1072 and 1077, Yumgan. Persian philosopher and poet.

N.'s didactic, philosophical prose works *Zad'ul-musafirin* [The Livelihood of Travelers, 1061] and *Gami'u'l-hikmatain* [Amalgamation of the Two Wisdoms, 1070], his *Safar-name* [Book of Travels], and his lyrics show him to have been a well-educated and widely traveled man who was persecuted because of his sympathies for the Ismaelite sect.

Editions: Divan, Teheran, 1925–28

NASYRI, KAYUM

Born 1825; died 1902. Tatar writer and teacher; cofounder of critical realism in Tatar prose writings.

N.'s linguistic and literary essays have greatly influenced the Tatar language. N. championed the friendship between the Tatars and the Russian people, and propagated progressive Russian culture among the Tatars.

NATURAL SCHOOL

The most important group in Russian literature of the 1840s, the Natural School led to a new phase in the development of critical realism. A great number of young writers belonged to the School, and created works that were openly critical, following the tradition established by N. Gogol. Their manifesto consisted of the almanacs *Fisiologiya Peterburga* [The Physiology of Petersburg, 1844–45] and the *Peterburgski sbornik* [Petersburg Collection, 1846], both published by N. Nekrasov. The acknowledged theoretical leader of the group was V. Belinski.

The N. S. produced a great number of prominent Russian writers, including A. Herzen, N. Nekrasov, I. Turgenev, M. Saltykov-Shchedrin, F. Dostoyevski, I. Goncharov, D. Grigorovich, and A. Pisemski. Their most important themes were the indictment of serfdom, the sympathetic presentation of "the little man," and the espousal of free development and the emancipation of Russian women. The psychological sketch, the milieu-accented story, and the subject-directed poem were their favorite genres. The writers of the N. S. realized that man is formed by his environment and that each individual is the product of his social milieu. The N. S. exerted a decisive influence on the entire development of nineteenth-century Russian literature.

NAVOI, NISAMADDIN ALISHER

Born 1441, Herat; died there January 3, 1501. Ancient Uzbekistanian poet, scholar, and statesman.

N. grew up in the house of his rich father, who was interested in the arts. At the age of fifteen, N. had already won acclaim for his poems. He was forced to flee to Samarkand because of feudal struggles, returning to Herat in 1469, where he worked as a writer at the court of the sultan Hussein Baikara. Later made court vizier, N. opposed the despotism of the khans, and supported reforms in the fields of education, health, and irrigation. A patron of the arts, he influenced the development of Uzbekian art.

In his philosophical writings, N. fought against medieval scholasticism. In his essay *Mukhakamat al-lugatain* [The Controversy about the Two Languages], N. showed that the Uzbekian language was as pure and flexible as Persian, which at that time was regarded as the chosen literary language of Central Asia; he demanded that the ancient Uzbekian language should be revived. Defamed by court cabals, N. was exiled by the sultan in 1487. He later returned to Herat and made great efforts to stop the feudal struggles that were ruining the country.

N. left a very extensive *œuvre* written in ancient Uzbek. He wrote deeply felt love lyrics and philosophical poems (in the form of ghazals); these were collected in four volumes of the *Divan Fani* [The Enchanted Divan]. The climax of his poetic work is *Khamse* [Five Poems, 1483–85], consisting of *The Confusion of the Just, Leili and Medshunun, Farhad and Shirin, The Seven Planets,* and *Alexander's Wall.* The basic themes of these works—as is the case in the *khamse* written by the famous twelfth-century poet Nisami—are love for the homeland, respect for work, striving for moral perfection and freedom and an understanding of true humanity. With its abundant ideas and figures, N.'s *khamse* are among the most important poetic works of world literature. The philosophical, allegoric poem *Lisanat-tair* [The Language of the Birds] and his collection of aphorisms *Makhbub al-kulub* [The Loved One of the Heart] belong to the late work of the poet, which exhibits great philosophical wisdom. N. has greatly influenced the entire literature of Central Asia, and to this day is one of the most popular poets of his people.

NEDOGONOV, ALEKSEI IVANOVICH
Born October 19, 1914, Shakhty (near Rostov); died March 12, 1948. Soviet Russian poet.

N. came from a working-class family. He worked in a manufacturing plant before publishing his first poems in 1934. N. served in the Soviet Army between 1939–46, and numerous poems written by him are dedicated to the heroism of the Soviet soldier. His poem *Flag nad selsovetom* [The Flag over the Village Soviet, 1947], which is among the most important works of the postwar period, tells of the conflicts and difficulties encountered in the rebirth of the kolkhoz village after the war.

Editions: Stikhi i poemy [Poems and Verses], Moscow, 1957; *Lirika* [Lyrics], Moscow, 1964

NEKRASOV, NIKOLAI ALEKSEYEVICH

Born December 10, 1821, Nemirovo (District of Kamenetz-Podolsk); died January 8, 1878, St. Petersburg. Russian revolutionary democrat, poet, and journalist.

N. came from a noble family; he attended high school in Yaroslavl, and in 1838 went to St. Petersburg, where he joined the democratic forces. In 1842, N. formed a close and lasting friendship with V. Belinski. N. became the organizer of the Natural School in the 1840s, publishing the periodicals *Fisiologiya Peterburga* [The Physiology of Petersburg, 1844–45] and *Petersburgski sbornik* [Petersburg Collection, 1846]. Between 1847–66 N. also published the leading Russian literary magazine *Sovremennik* [The Contemporary], and in 1868–78 *Otechestvennyye Zapiski* [Patriotic Leaves]. N. greatly influenced the realistic and democratic character of the Russian literature of his times through these publications.

As a poet, N. raised the level of social criticism and increased the popularity of Russian lyric writing. The first collection of N.'s poems (1856) represented a true turning point in the development of Russian poetry. In these works N. showed that he was a supporter of critical, realistic, and social revolutionary poetry (*Poet i grazhdanin*, Poet and Citizen). The basic themes of his lyrics are the loving depiction of the village, protest against oppression (*V doroge* On the Way, 1845; *Zabytaya derevnya*, The Forgotten Village, 1855), as well as the indictment of both the nobility and the bourgeoisie (*Rodina*, Homeland, 1846; *Zheleznaya doroga*, The Railroad, 1864).

N. introduced the theme of the great city into Russian poetry with *Yedu li nochyu po ulitze tiomnoi* [At Night I pass through the Silent Streets, 1867]. The revolutionary climax of his work was reached in the poems *Pesnya Yeriomushke* [Song of Yeryomushka, 1859] and *Razymyshleniya u paradnovo podyezda* [Thoughts at the Palace Staircase, 1858]. These, and others of a similar nature, were written during the revolutionary situations existing before and after the emancipation of the serfs in 1858–62.

N. also wrote a number of masterful poems modeled on the style of the folksong—*Zeliony shum* [The Green Rustling, 1862], *Orina, mat-soldatskaya* [Orina, the Mother of the Soldiers, 1863]. The collection of poems entitled *Posledniye pesni* [The Last Songs, 1877] forms the basis of N.'s artistic and ideological legacy. N. was the most important Russian poet after Pushkin and Lermontov. His works dealt with the major social problems of his time. In his poem *Sasha* (1855) he presented for the first time the new hero of Russian democratic literature, a hero who combined words with action and deeds.

The poems *Korobeiniki* [The Basket-Carriers, 1861] and *Moroz, Krasny nos* (1863; Red-Nosed Frost, 1887), written in a popular style, are dedicated to rural life. From the artistic point of view, the latter poem, which tells of the tragic fate, the beauty and the human greatness of a Russian peasant woman, may be regarded as N.'s most important poem. During the rise of the populist movement N. wrote poems about the Decembrists, so as to provide contemporary youth with revolutionary models. In 1870 N. wrote *Dedushka* [Little Grandfather], the hero of which is a revolutionary nobleman who has returned after thirty years in exile in Siberia. In the course of the next two years he wrote *Knyaginya Trubetzkaya* [The Princess Trubetzkaya] and *Knyaginya M. N. Volkonskaya* [The Princess M. N. Volkonskaya]; these two poems have been combined into one volume under the title *Russkiye zhenshchiny* [Russian Women]. In them, N. describes the noble deeds of the wives of the Decembrists who followed their husbands into exile in Siberia.

Among N.'s numerous satirical poems, which were directed against tzarist censorship, the following stand out: *Pesni o svobodnom slove* [Songs of the Free World, 1865]; *Balet* [The Ballet, 1866]; and *Sud* [The Judgment, 1867]. *Sovremenniki* [Contemporaries, 1875] exposes the wealthy *nouveau riche* during the period of feverish speculation in Russia.

N.'s most important work is the verse epic *Komu na Rusi zhit khorosho?* (1863–77; Who Can Be Happy and Free in Russia?, 1917), which combines elements of artistic and national poetry. Using as his frame the travels of seven peasants across Russia seeking for truth, N. presents a very vivid and versatile picture of rural Russia, of the social conflicts existing there, of the human values of the people, and of the Russian landscape. The action of the story takes place during the period of change following the agricultural reforms of 1861. It reflects the desire of the Russian people for freedom. As in the poems dedicated to Belinski, Dobrolyubov, and Chernyshevski, N., in the figure of Grisha Dobrosklonov, glorified the unselfish dedication of the Russian revolutionaries. This work has become a true popular romance.

N. also has left a number of important critical essays, short stories, novels, and lyric dramas.

Editions: Polnoye sobraniye sochinenii i pisem [Complete Works and Letters], 12 vols., Moscow, 1948–53; *Sochineniya* [Works], 3 vols., Moscow, 1959
Further Works: Neschastnyye [Without Luck] (1856); *Nedavneye vremya* [Recent Times] (1871); *Peterburgskiye ugly* [The Corners of Petersburg] (1845)

NEKRASOV, VIKTOR PLATONOVICH

Born June 17, 1911, Kiev. Soviet Russian short-story writer and novelist.

N. demonstrates the moral face of the Soviet people as observed in the setting of unpretentious, everyday situations. His most important story so far is *Sudak* [The Pike-Perch, 1960]. In his novel *V okopakh Stalingrada* [In the Trenches of Stalingrad, 1946], N., who himself participated in World War II, tells of the daily worries and difficulties of a small group of soldiers, demonstrating their high fighting morale. In 1954 N. published the novel *V rodnom gorode* [In the Home Town], which deals with the problems confronting soldiers returning to peacetime work. N.'s newest book, *That Damn Number Seven* (1967), has been well received in the Soviet Union.

Further Works: Pervoye znakomstvo [The First Acquaintance] (1958); *Kira Georgivevna* [Kira Georgievna] (1961)

NERIS (Pseud. of *Saloméja Bačinskaite-Bučiene*)
Born November 17, 1904, Kiršai; died July 7, 1945, Moscow. Lithuanian Soviet poet; member of the Supreme Soviet of the USSR.

N. came from rural stock. In her first period of creative work, which extended into the 1930s, N. wrote poems in the romantic style that did not deal with social questions. She later turned toward Marxist revolutionary ideology, and her art become realistic. This fact is evident in the poems published in the years 1931–33 in the illegal communist press, as well as in her *Per lužtanti leda* [On Weak Ice, 1935] and *Diemedžiu žydesiu* [I Shall Flower As Pink Hawthorn, 1938].

In these works N. has combined the best elements of Lithuanian national poetry with the presentation of the great social problems of the prewar period. The year 1940 saw a considerable rise in the importance of N.'s work, and a transition to socialist realism. The poem *Bolseviko kelias* [The Road of a Bolshevik, 1940] tells of Lenin and the Soviet people.

The climax of N.'s work may be found in the poems created during World War II. These works, which are characterized both by profound ideas and by perfect artistic form, have greatly influenced Lithuanian Soviet poetry. N. was posthumously awarded

the State Prize of 1947; she was named People's Poetess of the
Lithuanian SSR in 1954.

Editions: Raštai [Works], Vols. 1–3, Vilnius, 1957
Further Works: Mama! Kur tu?, 1941 [Mother! Where Are You?]
(1941); *Grisiu* [I Will Return] (1944–45); *Marija Melnikaite*
[Maria Melnikaite] (1944)

NESTOR, CHRONICLE OF   See POVEST VREMENNYKH LET

NEVEROV (Pseud. of *Aleksander Sergeyevich Skobelev*)
   Born December 20, 1886, Nivikhovka (District of Samara);
died December 24, 1923, Moscow. Soviet Russian novelist.
   N., the son of a peasant, graduated in 1906 from the teachers
college in Samara, and then worked as a village teacher. He was
active in the establishment of Soviet power in Samara.
   In a number of stories published since 1906, N. depicted the
cheerless life and the class struggles taking place in the prerevolutionary Russian village. He continued to follow the development of the village after 1917. He was one of the first authors
to describe realistically the extent of the changes taking place
in the country, the harshness of the conflicts, the growing social
role played by the farmers, the gradual emancipation of the
women, and the work of the Communists. These stories include
Ya zhit khochu! [I Want to Live!, 1920] and *Litzo zhizni* [The
Face of Life, 1925], as well as the unfinished novel *Gusi-Lebedi*
[Geese and Swans, 1923]. N.'s novel *Tashkent—gorod khlebny*
(1923; Tashkent, the City of Bread, 1930) is also well-known;
this novel—in which N. offers a versatile picture of the people—
tells the story of a boy seeking to find a new life.

Editions: Sobraniye sochinenii [Collected Works], 7 vols., Moscow–
Leningrad, 1926–27; *Sobraniye sochinenii* [Collected Works], 4 vols.,
Kuibyshev, 1957–58

NIKITIN, AFANASH (ATHANASIUS)
   Died 1472, near Tver.
   N., Russian merchant from Tver, traveled through Persia and

India in 1466–72. His very individualistic, diarylike travelogue *Khozheniye za tri morya* [Journey Beyond the Three Seas, 1475] is a high point in medieval Russian literature.

Editions: Knozheniye za tri morya Afanasiya Nikitina [The Journey of Athanasius Nikitin Beyond the Three Seas], Moscow–Leningrad, 1948

NIKITIN, IVAN SAVVICH
Born October 3, 1824, Voronezh; died there October 28, 1861. Russian democratic poet.

N., who came from a bourgeois family, continued to write popular poetry in a vein similar to that of Koltzov. His poems of social criticism on the life of the Russian peasant and the petit bourgeoisie are related to the work of Nekrasov. In addition to impressive poems about the southern Russian steppe, N.'s poem *Kulak* [The Kulak, 1858] tells of the dark, dirty struggle for existence of a man belonging to the Russian bourgeoisie. In *Dnevnik seminarista* [Dairy of a Seminarian, 1860] N. disclosed certain conditions existing in the theological seminaries of his time.

Editions: Sochineniya [Works], Moscow, 1955

NIKOLAYEVA (Pseud. of *Galina Yevgenyevna Volyanskaya*)
Born February 18, 1911, Usmanska (District of Tomsk); died October 18, 1963, Moscow. Soviet Russian novelist.

N. took part in World War II as an army physician. Her literary activities began in 1945 with poems, sketches and stories. Her novel *Zhatva* (1950; Harvest, 1953) tells of the struggles of the Soviet kolkhoz to overcome the devastating effects of war.

Her most important novel, *Bitva v puti* (1957; Battle along the Road, 1958), depicts impressively and realistically the human problems faced by Bakhirev, a true Soviet innovator and activist, in the establishment of new work and life standards. N.'s discussion of problems of work production and of love and marriage, treated with harmonious unity and attention to form, shows the spiritual and moral wealth of the Soviet people during the period of change occurring in the 1950s. Because of its general applicability, this novel (which has also been made into a film) has been used in other communist countries as the basis for a discussion of production problems. The novel may, in fact, be regarded as a true handbook of socialist life and counseling. N. received the State Prize in 1951.

Further Works: Gibel komandarma [Death of the Commander] (1945); *Povest o direktore MTS i glavnom agronome* [The Story of the Director and the Chief Agronomist] (1954); *Rasskazy babki Vasilisy pro chudesa* [Grandmother Vasilisa's Tales about Miracles] (1962)

NIKULIN, LEV VENIAMINOVICH (Pseud. of *Lev Vladimirovich Olkonitzki*)

Born May 20, 1891, Shitomir; died March 9, 1967. Soviet Russian novelist.

N. studied economics; in 1921–22 he was a member of the Soviet diplomatic service in Afghanistan; later he was a correspondent for Soviet newspapers. N. first published poems (1918–1919), but he became known through his partly autobiographical, partly historical novels. His most important works were written during the 1950s: the autobiographical short novel *Vremya, prostrantstvo, dvizheniye* [Time, Distance, Movement, 1931–32] and the historical novel *Rossii vernyye syny* [Russia's Faithful Sons, 1950], on the battles of the Russian armies in Europe in 1813–14, as well as *Moskovskiye zori* [Moscow Dawn, 1954], the second part of which is entitled *Dorogi slavy* [The Roads of Glory, 1958], on the life of a Russian artist during the historical events that took place early in the twentieth century. N. also published a number of travel sketches including *Pisma ob Ispanii* [Letters about Spain, 1931] and *Vo Frantzii* [In France, 1959–60]. N. was also a prominent literary scholar. He was awarded the State Prize in 1952.

Editions: Sochineniya [Works], 3 vols., Moscow, 1965

NILIN, PAVEL FILIPOVICH
Born January 16, 1908, Irkutsk. Soviet Russian novelist.

N. was a journalist during the war. In his most important work, *Zhestokost*, (1956; Cruelty, 1958), which deals with the battle against the counterrevolutionaries during the time of the civil war, N.'s hero shows the tragic conflict between unfeeling bureaucratic treatment and the socialist views of human rights and justice. In his novel *Cheres kladbische* [Through the Cemetery, 1962], N. treated the fight of Soviet peoples in the regions occupied by the fascists.

Further Works: Blizhaischchii rodstvennik [The Closest Relative] (1937); *Ispytatelnyi srok* [A Trial Term] (1956)

NIZAMI GANDZHEVI, ILYAS YUSSUF-OGLY
Born circa 1141, Gandzha (Kirovabad); died there March 12, 1209. Azerbaidzhani poet and philosopher.

N. G., the son of an artisan, acquired an extensive education. Refusing tempting offers to serve the feudal lords, he instead linked his life with the fate of the people and lived in poverty. All of N. G.'s work was dedicated to the liberation of the human personality from feudal oppression, and to the liberation of the intellect from the confines of medieval scholasticism. In his lyric works, ghazals and *kassides*, N. G. lamented the sad fate of the people. He also praised the beauty of his loved one, a slave girl who later became his wife.

N. G. became known throughout the world for his romantic *Khamze* [Five Epics]. The first of these epics, *Sirrlar khasinassi* [The Treasury of Secrets, 1179], is directed against the injustice and despotism of the land owners. In the name of humanity and justice, N. G. here appealed to the powerful leaders in the country to become aware of their misdeeds and to serve God. The focal point of the second epic, *Khosrau va Shirin* [Khosrau and Shirin, 1180], is the story of the love of a young princess for the talented architect Farhad. The third epic of this cycle, *Leili va Medshnun* [Leila and Madzhnun], which has been imitated numerous times, appeared in 1188. In the fate of his characters N. G. skillfully demonstrated the people's desire for love, freedom, and happiness —a wish doomed to be unfulfilled because of the conditions existing at that time. The fourth epic, *Eddi Kysal* [The Seven Beauties, 1197], contains seven stories about the adventures of a legendary ruler; these stories are filled with excellent characterizations of simple people from the masses. *Eddi Kysal* gave Schiller the material for his drama *Turandot*. The *Iskander-name* [The Alexander Book], written sometime after 1200, concludes the cycle, and is also N. G.'s last work. His desire for a free and happy society found its clearest expression in the figure of the mighty and just ruler Alexander and in the *Iqbal-name* [The Book of Happiness].

Editions: Lirik sheirlar [Lyric Works], Baku, 1947; *Izbrannyye proizvedeniya* [Selected Works] (in Russian), Moscow, 1947; *Pyat poemy* [Five Poems] (in Russian), Moscow, 1946; *Sirlar khasinassi* [Treasury of Secrets], Baku, 1947

NOSOV, NIKOLAI

Born 1908, Kiev. Soviet Russian writer of children's books.

N.'s first story appeared in 1938. Since World War II, N.'s works, which frequently are written from the point of view of ten- to eleven-year-old boys, are among the standard works of Soviet children's literature. His numerous stories are distinguished by a capacity for projecting himself into the mind of the child; these stories are aimed at awakening in the child love for work, honesty, fearlessness, and thirst for knowledge. His story *Vitya Maleyev v shkole i doma* (1952; Vitya Maleyev at School and at Home, 1952) convincingly describes the development of a schoolboy. *Dunno on the Moon* tells how the little hero Dunno proved all the astronomers, geologists, and meteorologists of the Academy of Astronomical Sciences to be very wrong indeed concerning their views and ideas about outer space.

Further Works: Tuk-tuk-tuk! [Knock-knock-knock] (1945); *Priklyucheniya neznaiki i yevo druzei* [The Adventures of a Know-nothing and his Friends] (1954); *Neznaika v solnechnom gorode* [The Know-nothing in a Sunny City] (1960)

NOVIKOV, NIKOLAI IVANOVICH
Born May 8, 1744, Tikhvinskoye, near Moscow; died there
July 30, 1818. Russian political and satirical writer and publisher;
founder of Russian eighteenth-century liberalism.
After 1760, N. published a number of satirical magazines
(*Truten* [The Drones, 1769–70]; *Zhivopisetz* [The Painter,
1772–73]; *Kosheliok* [The Change Purse, 1774]). The antifeudal
tendencies developed in these magazines were in sharp contrast
to the policies of Catherine II, and gave impetus to the development of a broad literature independent of the government. Because of their intense liberal fervor, N.'s satires—*Pisma Falaleyu*
[Letters to Phalalei] published in *Zhivopisetz*, and his *Otryvok
puteshestviya Vxxx.* I.T. [Fragments of a Voyage to Vxxx. I.T.]
—are among the outstanding monuments of eighteenth-century
democratic literature. N. also deserves praise for his widespread
propagation of the ideas of enlightenment, and for the publication
of numerous works of Russian and Western European liberalism.
In 1792, N. was sentenced to fifteen years' imprisonment; in
1796, however, he was pardoned by Paul I.

Editions: Satiricheskiye zhurnaly N.I. Novikova [The Satirical Magazines of N.I. Novikov], Moscow–Leningrad, 1951

NOVIKOV-PRIBOI, ALEKSEI SILYCH
Born March 26, 1877, Aleksandrovskoye (District of Tambov);
died April 29, 1944. Soviet Russian novelist.
N., the son of a peasant, was a sailor in the Baltic fleet (1899–
1906). In 1903 he was arrested for distributing revolutionary
literature. In 1905 N. participated in the sea battle of Tsushima,
and was taken prisoner by the Japanese. He emigrated in 1907,
and between 1912–13 lived with Gorki on Capri. His literary
activities began while he was a POW of the Japanese, but it was
only after the October revolution that he was fully able to develop
his talents.
N.'s works are chiefly dedicated to the sea and to sailors; he
was one of the first Soviet authors to treat these themes from
the socialist point of view. A number of his prerevolutionary

stories, such as *Lishni* [Superfluous, 1913] and *Porcheny* [The Depraved, 1917], treat the harsh life of the peasants in tsarist Russia. The life of the sailor—N.'s main theme—is the subject of the stories *Podvodniki* [Submarine Sailors, 1923], *Zhenshchina i more* [The Woman and the Sea, 1928], and *Solionaya kupel* [Saltwater Baptism, 1929], while the stories *Zub za zub* [Tooth for Tooth, 1922] and *Vekovaya tyazhba* [The Century-old Lawsuit, 1922] tell of the participation of the peasants in the revolution and in the civil war.

N.'s main work is the two-part historical documentary novel *Tzusima* (1932–35; enlarged edition, 1940; Tsushima, 1937), in which he demonstrated the reasons for the defeat of the tsarist fleet in the Russo-Japanese war of 1904–05, at the same time erecting a memorial to the heroism of the simple Russian sailors. N. received the State Prize in 1941.

Editions: Sochineniya [Works], 5 vols., Moscow, 1945–50

ODOYEVSKI, ALEKSANDR IVANOVICH
Born December 8, 1802, St. Petersburg; died October 22, 1839, in the Caucasus. Russian poet.

O., then an army officer, took part in the Decembrist uprising of 1825. He was sentenced to eight years' hard labor and degraded to the rank of private. With his poems and songs, he became the voice of the exiled Decembrists. His reply to Pushkin's *V Sibir* [A Letter to Siberia, 1827] contains the line: "A flame shall arise from this spark." This sentence clearly reflects the historic significance of the Decembrists, as well as their confidence in the future even after their defeat. Lenin chose these words as the motto for the newspaper *Iskra* [The Spark].

Editions: Poety pushkinskoi pory [Anthology: Poets of the Time of Pushkin], Leningrad, 1954

OGARIOV, NIKOLAI PLATONOVICH
Born December 6, 1813, St. Petersburg; died June 12, 1877, Greenwich. Russian revolutionary, poet, and journalist.

In the 1840s, O., under the influence of his friend, A. Herzen, became a follower of philosophical materialism and upheld revolutionary, democratic views. It was at this time that he created his romantically exaggerated philosophical poetry—*Kniga lyuboi* [The Book of Love, 1841–44], *Yumor* [Humor, 1841] and *Monologi* [Monologs, 1847]—as well as works depicting the enserfed village and the decadent noble families. In 1856, he followed Herzen into emigration in London, where he wrote his most prominent revolutionary poems: *Svoboda* [Liberty, 1858] and *Pamyati Ryleyeva* [In Memory of Ryleyev, 1859]. In London, O., in cooperation with Herzen, organized the free Russian press, and supported and encouraged publication of the magazine *Kolokol* [The Bell, 1857–68]. O. was one of the organizers of the secret society *Zemlya i volya* (1861–62).

Editions: Izbrannyye proizvedeniya, 2 vols., Moscow, 1956

OGNOIOV, NIKOLAI (Pseud. of *Rozanov, Mikhail Grigoryevich*)
Born 1880; died 1938. Soviet Russian novelist.
O.'s great contribution to the Soviet literature of the 1920s was the figure of the student Kostya Ryabtzev, whose story he told in the form of a diary in *Dnevnik Kosti Ryabtzeva* [The Diary of Kostya Ryabtzev, 1926] and *Iskhod Nikpetocha* [Student Years, 1927]. In these books O. offers an interesting and vivid picture of life in Soviet schools and universities in the first half of the 1920s.

OIUNSKI (Pseud. of *Sleptzov, Platon Alekseyevich*)
Born November 11, 1893, in the Third Zhekhsogonski nasleg, Rayon Tatta; died October 29, 1939. Yakut Soviet writer; founder of Yakut Soviet literature; revolutionary and cultural philosopher.
In his revolutionary, romantic works, O., using the vivid images of Yakut national poetry, re-created the heroic fervor of the revolution. He was of invaluable assistance in the researching and publication of the *Olonkho* (Yakut national epic). He was the first poet to introduce a distinct verse system into Yakut poetry.

Among his most important works are the verse drama *Kysyl Oyun* [The Red Shaman, 1925], the drama *Basabyyk* [The Bolshevik, 1928], and the story *Dyeberetten takhshyy* [Escape from the Mire, 1936].

O. also translated many works, including those of Pushkin, Gorki, Goethe, and Petofi, into the Yaku language.

Editions: Ayymnyylar, 7 vols., Yakutsk, 1958

OLESHA, YURII KARLOVICH

Born March 4, 1899, Yelisavetgrad (Ukraine); died May 10, 1960, Moscow. Soviet Russian novelist and short-story writer.

O. became known soon after the publication of his novel *Zavist* [Jealousy, 1927], which became a play in 1929 under the title *Zagovor chuvstv* [Conspiracy of Emotions]. This novel aroused much stormy discussion because in it O. viewed Soviet life from the point of view of a misunderstood personal freedom. The novel has been used repeatedly to slander the Soviet. In the closing years of the 1920s and the beginning 1930s, O. published a series of stories including *Lyubov* [Love], *Tzep* [The Chain], and *Chelovecheski kharakter* [The Human Character].

Since the mid-1930s O. has been concentrating on filmmaking: he wrote the screen play *Strogi yunosha* [The Severe Youth, 1934], and after World War II produced Dostoyevski's *The Idiot*. During the war, while living in Ashkhabad, he translated numerous works of Turkmenian literature into Russian. O. also wrote the children's novel *Tri tolstyaka* [The Three Fat Fellows, 1924].

Editions: Povesti i rasskasy; Moscow, 1955

OMAR KHAYYAM

Born circa 1021, Nishapur; died there, 1123. Persian poet, mathematician, and astronomer.

O.K. became widely known during the years 1074–79 for his leading role in the reform of the ancient Persian calendar. In the East O.K. is esteemed chiefly as a mathematician and philosopher (his views were influenced by Avicenna). In the Western world, however, he has become known chiefly for his quatrains. Edward Fitzgerald's translation of the *Rubaiyat* into English (1859) had an extraordinary success. (See also *Omar Khayyam, A New Version Based Upon Recent Discoveries*, tr. A. J. Arberry, 1952, and *The Original Rubaiyat of Omar Kayaam*, tr. Robert Graves, with Omar Ali Shah, 1968.) In these verses we frequently find a rebellious, frivolous, antireligious insouciance side by side with religious piety. A common theme in his work, however, is his sharp distaste for sanctimoniousness and obscurantism. O.K.'s view of existing social conditions resulted in a certain amount of pessimism. The determinating factor in his work, however, is his cheerful type of philosophy: live and enjoy today and its worldly pleasures, and think little about tomorrow.

ORDUBADY, MAMED SAID

Born March 24, 1872, Ordubade; died 1950. Azerbaidzhani Soviet author and journalist; founder of the historical novel form in Azerbaidzhani literature.

O.'s first work, *The Unhappy Millionaire* (1914), which was directed against Iranian reaction, was based on his personal experiences gained during the days of the Iranian revolution of 1907–11. The Baku proletariat appears as the hero in his novels *The Battling Town* (1938) and *Illegal Baku* (1940). O.'s best work is the novel *Fog over Tabriz*, (4 vols., 1933–48). Here, in an epic, realistic style, he describes the fight of South Azerbaidzhan for liberation from Iranian oppression. O.'s historical novel *The Sword and the Pen* (1946–48) is a memorial to the poet Nisami.

Editions: Sechilmish sheilar va hekayalar, Baku, 1951

ORLOV, SERGEI SERGEYEVICH

Born August 22, 1921, Megra (Gouv. Vologda). Soviet Russian poet.

O.'s studies at the university in Petrosavodsk were interrupted by World War II. He graduated from the Gorki Institute of Literature in 1954. O. based his poems on small incidents occurring at the front and in Soviet everyday life, as in *Ya v sorok tretyem byl komsorgom roty* [In 1943 I Was the Komsomol Secretary of the Regiment], *Shura Kaparulina,* and others. His poems reflect joy in the beauty of Soviet life and Soviet man.

Editions: Stikhotvoreniya 1938–1958 [Poems], Moscow–Leningrad, 1959

OSMONOV, ALYKUL
Born in 1915, Kaptal-Aryk; died December 12, 1950, Frunze. Kirghiz Soviet poet.

An orphan, O. lived in a children's home between 1925 and 1928. In 1929 he began to study at a teachers college. Seriously ill since 1932, O.'s work reached its peak during the war years with his poems *The Great Canal of Chui* (1941); *My Mother* (1945); and *Love* (1945). In 1946 O. returned to the theme of war with *Dzhenishbek* (1946). In his lyrical poems O. attempted to establish links between man's most intimate thoughts and the important problems touching the country. He used a traditional, image-rich language of exaggerated emotion and extraordinary incident, as can be seen in *When I Arrive at the Lake* (1946); *The Town of Frunze* (1945); *The Gathering of the Grapes* (1946); and *The Song of Rain* (1945). O. also translated the works of Heine, Shakespeare, and other foreign writers.

Editions: Izbrannoye (Russian); Moscow, 1958

OSTROVSKI, ALEKSANDR NIKOLAYEVICH
Born April 12, 1823, Moscow; died June 14, 1866, Shchelykovo. Russian dramatist.

O. was the son of a law official; between 1840 and 1842 he studied law in Moscow and, as a judicial officer, had occasion to become acquainted with the practices of the Moscow merchants. His literary work was to some extent formed under the influence of the Natural School of Gogol and Belinski. This is evident in his first significant work, *Svoi lyudi—soshchtiomsya* [Amongst Our Own Kind of People], which he recited with great success before

Gogol in 1849. The title of this piece indicates that the work, in the form of a comic conflict, presents differences existing among the representatives of one class only. Censorship prevented its presentation on the stage, and its author was put under police surveillance.

O. subsequently attempted to idealize the "national basis" of the life of the merchants, so that his works of that particular period appear to be an expression of the democratic movement among the Slavophiles. One work written at that time is *Ne v svoi sani ne sadis* [Stick to Your Last!, 1852]. His piece *Ne tak zhivi, kak khochetsya* [Do Not Live the Way You Like To, 1854], in which he employed religious symbolism, was a great success on the stage because, despite the fact that it still retained certain false tendencies, overly lifelike presentations of a number of characters and incidents, democratization of themes, and a preoccupation with true conflicts, it nonetheless represented a new kind of dramatic art. These new aspects subsequently led to great changes in the Russian theater.

Around 1860, O. came politically closer to the revolutionary democrats—a fact that is reflected in several of his plays. *Dokhodnoye mesto* [A Paying Position, 1857], a comedy in which O. describes the civil service from a critical point of view, was prohibited by the censors, as was *Vospitanniza* [The Foster-Girl, 1858]. In *Groza* (1859; The Thunderstorm, 1937), his most important work, O. created the tragedy of an idealistically romantic young woman who seeks for a way out from the depressing atmosphere of a small town on the Volga. The merchants, having usurped power, are not receptive to her new ideas. O. presented Katarina's protest as a "ray of light in the realms of darkness" (Dobrolyubov), and showed the possibilities for a protest by the people themselves.

After an interval of one year, during the reactionary period, O. wrote a number of weaker psychological pieces, the "extensive sentimentality" of which was criticized by Lev Tolstoi. At that time O. also wrote a number of historical chronicles and rather effective comedies. In 1868 he returned to the theme of contemporary conflicts, viewing them from a new point of view. In his comedies and dramatic pieces *Beshenyye dengi* (1870; Easy Money, 1944), *Les* (1871; The Forest, 1940), and *Volki i ovtzy* [Wolves and Sheep, 1875], O. depicted the everyday morals of the bourgeoisie, who, allying themselves with the nobility, appeared stronger than the industrialists. Remaining marauders at heart, they devoured their victims and finally attacked each other. The fate of the individual no longer depends on the cruelty or the kindness of the lord and master, but on money. In spite of the "wolves," however, one almost always finds simple people who have kept their love for honest work and thus also their moral strength; the latter individuals, however, are usually the ones vanquished.

A similar clash is shown in *Bespridannitza* [The Girl without a Dowry, 1879]. Larisa, because of her own inner conflicts, is at the mercy of various forces. With the exception of her own hopes, she has no defense against the realization that she is but an object —the object of a trade. O. has thus grouped a whole series of conflicts around one of the great problems of his time. The injustices done to the simple people is also the main theme of *Talanty i poklonniki* [Talents and Admirers, 1881] and *Bez viny vinovatyye* [The Guiltlessly Guilty, 1884].

Among the fifty plays written by O. is *Snegurochka* [The Snowdrop, 1874], "a spring fairy tale," in which the conflict between the spiritual coldness in the Russia of that time and the desire of the people for love is presented in a form readily understood by children.

Editions: Polnoye sobraniye sochinenii, 16 vols., Moscow, 1949–1953

OSTROVSKI, NIKOLAI ALEKSEYEVICH

Born September 29, 1904, Viliya (Volynia); died December 22, 1936, Moscow. Soviet Russian writer.

O., the son of a railroad worker and a cook, was an active member of the Komsomols. He fought in the Red Army against intervention and counterrevolution. In 1920 he was severely injured, and from 1926 until his death was paralyzed. O. regarded his literary activities as a way in which he could continue to participate in the revolutionary battles of the people.

O.'s novel *Kak zakalyalas stal* (1934; How the Steel Was Tempered, 1952) depicted the exemplary fight of the Komsomols for Soviet power. The life of the author is artistically reflected in the central figure of Pavel Korchagin. The characteristics of socialist morals are expressed in his heroic fight against the counterrevolution, in his relation to socialist work, and in his personal life. *Kak zakalyalas stal* was one of the first novels of socialist realism to portray the development of an individual's character; the creation of Pavel Korchagin represents an unique contribution to the formation of the communist image. This novel has played a great part in the education of the young people of the Soviet Union and in the formation of socialist consciousness in the progressive youth of the entire world. Numerous documents recounting the struggles of many who have followed the example set by O. have been collected in the O. museums in Moscow and Sochi. In his unfinished novel *Rozhdionnyye burei*, (Part 1, 1936; Born of the Storm, 1939), O. showed the fight of the revolutionary youth against the counterrevolution in the Ukraine.

Editions: Sobraniye sochinenii, 3 vols., Moscow, 1959

OVECHKIN, VALENTIN VLADIMIROVICH

Born June 22, 1904, Taganrog; died January 29, 1938, Tashkent. Soviet Russian writer.

O. was the leader of an agricultural artel; from 1927 on he worked as a writer. O. became known for his sketches and stories about life in the kolkhozes. His first collection of writings, *Kolkhoznyye rasskazy* [Stories from the Kolkhozes], appeared in 1935. In 1945 he published a long story, *S frontovym privetom* [With Greetings from the Front], about the agricultural problems emerging during the postwar reconstruction period. Part of O.'s fame rests on his collection of sketches entitled *Trudnaya vesna* [Spring Storms, 1956], in which he traced the difficulties existing in agriculture and the way in which they were solved. O. also wrote plays, including *Nastya Kolosova* (1949) and *Vremya pozhinat plody* [The Time for Harvesting, 1961].

Further Works: Upryamyi khutor (1960)

PAEGLE, LEONS
Born June 10, 1890 in the county of Vidrizs (Latvia); died January 28, 1929, Riga. Latvian dramatist, short-story writer, and novelist.
P. was the son of a village blacksmith. He was trained to become a teacher, and taught for a number of years. Between 1914 and 1918 he lived in Moscow, where he took part in various revolutionary battles. In bourgeois Latvia he was constantly persecuted for his political views.
P. had already started to write before World War I. He wrote plays, poems, short stories, and novels based on contemporary themes. Imprisoned between 1922–23, he published a collection of poems in 1923 entitled *Cietumi nelīdz* [Prisons Do Not Help]. In 1924 he published the novel *Nāves cilpa* [The Noose of Death].

PANFIOROV, FIODOR IVANOVICH
Born October 2, 1886, Pavlovka (District of Simbirsk); died September 10, 1960, Moscow. Soviet Russian dramatist and novelist.
P. first wrote plays based on village themes, including *Pakhom* (1920) and *Muzhiki* [Farmers, 1924], and published collections of sketches about village life.
P.'s important novel *Bruski* (4 vols., 1928–34; And Then The Harvest, 1939) occupies a central position in his *œuvre*. This long novel deals with the development of the Soviet village from the time of the revolution to 1937; the first and second volumes cover the development of the entire Soviet country. The plot, particularly that of the first two volumes, is rich in figures and episodes of dramatic, epic character, and, when P. extols nature

and the beauty of the simple man, attains a high degree of lyricism. The main problems treated by the author are connected with the creation of an agricultural system that does justice to both the interests of the farmers and those of society as a whole. Gorki drew attention to certain linguistic deficiencies in P.'s work. The last two volumes of *Bruski* give evidence of a somewhat superficial declarative presentation of reality.

The life, work, and struggles of Ural workers and Soviet scouts and partisans during the war of 1941–45 are described by P. in his novels *Borba sa mir* [The Fight for Peace, 1945–47], for which he received the State Prize in 1948, *V strana povershennykh* [In the Country of the Conquered, 1948], for which he received the State Prize in 1949, and *Bolshoye iskusstvo* [The Great Art, 1949]. The regional secretary of the Communist Party of the Soviet Union, Akim Morev, as depicted in the novel *Razdumye* [Reflections, 1958] exhibits many features of a true leader.

Editions: Sobraniye sochinenii [Collected Works], 6 vols., Moscow, 1958–59
Further Works: Volga matushka reka [Mother Volga] (1952); *Kogda my krasivy* [When Are We Beautiful?] (1952)

PANOVA, VERA FIODOROVNA
Born March 20, 1905, Rostov-on-the-Don. Soviet Russian novelist and playwright.

From 1922 to 1935 P. was a journalist; since the 1930s she has been active in literature. Her first important novel, *Sputniki* (1946; The Train, 1948), for which she was awarded the State Prize in 1947, was based on events taking place during World War II. P. here described the unobtrusive heroism of the personnel of a hospital train, showing, in a psychological perceptive and sensitive manner, the different figures involved who become fused into a collective through their common work.

The novel *Khrushilikha* (1947; Looking Ahead, 1957) describes the unselfish work carried out in a factory in the interior of the country. With the help of small details which seen by themselves are insignificant and commonplace, P. depicts the spiritual and moral development of her hero. A perhaps overly important emphasis is given to the details of everyday life in P.'s novel *Vremena goda* (1953; Span of the Year, 1956), in which she discusses the problems of a teacher.

In the later works P. returned to themes of a more general character, although the problems of Soviet youth still remained her chief concern. Moral behavior and the everyday conflicts found in the lives of young people are discussed by her with psychological empathy in *Sentimentalyni roman* [A Sentimental Romance, 1958] and in the play *Provody belykh noche* [Goodbye to Those White Nights, 1961]. P. was awarded State Prizes in both 1948 and 1950.

Editions: Izbrannyye sochineniya [Selected Works], 2 vols., Leningrad, 1956
Further Works: Ilya Kosogor [Ilya Kosogor] (1939); *Yasnyye berega* [Bright Shores] (1949); *Seriozha* (1955; Times Walked, 1959)

PANTELEYEV, LEONID (Pseud. of *Yeremeyev, Aleksei Ivanovich*)
Born August 22, 1908, St. Petersburg. Soviet Russian juvenile writer.

P. became popular immediately following the publication of his semiautobiographical *Respublika Shkid* [Shkid, The Republic of Vagabonds, 1927], written in cooperation with G. Belykh, a work, incidentally, which was highly regarded by Gorki. P. subsequently became one of the best loved juvenile writers in the USSR. One of his common themes is the arduous life of orphaned children during and after the Civil War.

In his story *Chasy* [The Clock, 1928], he described a neglected boy's victory over egotistical behavior, and his formation of new ideals. *Paket* [The Parcel, 1932] depicts the civil war in a series of alternately dangerous and amusing incidents as seen through the eyes of a small boy. P.'s work of the 1930s and 1940s—the atmosphere of which is similar to that found in Gaidar's stories—

is concerned with the socialist education of children and, in particular, with education that can lead to discipline and self-control.

Further Works: Pervyi podvig [The First Try] (1941); *Chestnoye slovo* [Word of Honor] (1941); *Vesiolyi tramvai* [The Happy Trolley-Bus] (n.d.)

PAPASHKIRI, IVAN GEORGIYEVICH

Born 1902. Abkhazian Soviet novelist.

P.'s novels continued the movement, begun by D. I. Gulia, toward a new Abkhazian prose. In addition to ethnographic elements, social changes and their influences occupy the foreground of P.'s work. In his novel *Temyr* [For a Long Life, 1937], P. described the formation of new social relations in the Abkhazian village of the 1930s. The novel *The Way to Khimur* (1948) focuses on the changes that have taken place in the life of the Abkhazian women since the establishment of Soviet power.

Further Works: U podnozhiya Erzakhu [At the Foot of Erzach] (1953)

PARONIAN, AKOP

Born 1842, Adrianapolis (Turkey); died July 8, 1891. Armenian short-story writer and novelist; one of the founders of Armenian realistic literature.

P.'s work pilloried the foreign colonizers of the economically retarded Turkey and the traitors among the Armenian people. He also depicted the chauvinistic Turkish intelligentsia, civil servants, merchants, and the clergy, as can be seen in his novella *A Promenade Through the Suburbs of Constantinople* (1890).

PASTERNAK, BORIS LEONIDOVICH

Born February 10, 1890, Moscow; died May 31, 1960, Peredelkino, near Moscow. Soviet Russian poet and novelist.

P.'s early poems were written before World War II. In these poems he reflected on natural experiences and universal human problems. In his lyric poetry, in which he expressed his philosophical views, P. saw the individual against a background of glorious, untamed nature.

After the October revolution P. approached contemporary themes, but in a contradictory manner and with mental reservations. The effects of the new social milieu may be seen in his historical poems *Leitenant Shmidt* [Lieutenant Shmidt, 1926] and in *Devyatsot pyatyi god* [The Year 1905, 1927], in which the continuity of the Russian revolutionary movement and its roots in history are clearly presented. His long poem *Vsokaya bolezn* [The Great Illness, 1924] exhibits strong realistic features, including an impressive presentation of Lenin, Mayakovski, and the Lef, to which P. belonged between 1923 and 1928. P., however, continued to occupy the relatively isolated position of an observer, thus limiting his considerable formal talents, which were effective only to a very small extent.

During World War II P.'s distinct, complex, associative, and metonymic style of writing gained in clarity. His novel *Doktor Zhivago* (1956; Doctor Zhivago, 1958), however, was written from a subjectivist position; it must therefore be regarded as an artistic failure despite the fact that it has won praise in capitalistic countries. P. refused the Nobel Prize in 1958 when it was offered to him for this novel.

P.'s translations of works by Goethe and Shakespeare, among other writers, are among the best in the Russian language.

Editions: Izbrannoye [Selected Works], Moscow, 1948. *English: The Collected Prose Works, Part I: Autobiography, Part II: Stories,* London, 1945
Further Works: Bliznetz v tuchakh [A Twin in the Clouds] (1914); *Poverkh baryerov* (1917; republished with new poems, 1929. Trans. "Above the Clouds" in *Poems,* 1959); *Sestra moia zhizn* (1922; Sister: My Life, 1967); *Okhrannaya gramota* (1931; "Safe Conduct" in *Prose and Poems,* 1959); *Vtoroye rozhdeniye* (1932; "Second Birth" in *Prose and Poems,* 1959); *Na rannikh poyezdakh* (1943; "On Early Trains" in *Poems,* 1939)

PAUSTOVSKI, KONSTANTIN GEORGIYEVICH
Born May 31, 1892, Moscow; died there July 15, 1968. Soviet
Russian novelist, biographer, and dramatist.

P., the son of a railroad employee, studied in Kiev and Moscow,
and then worked in various fields as a laborer, journalist, and
sailor. P. was a medical orderly during World War I. After the
revolution he again worked as a journalist; during the civil war
he was a member of the Red Army. After the civil war he traveled
widely throughout Russia.

P. himself rejected his first literary attempts; his literary career
really began in the mid-1920s with abstract, romantic stories, some
of which showed the influence of A. Grins. In the mid-1930s his
work became permanently socialistic and realistic; this was especially evident in his important novels *Kara-Bugas* [Kara-Bugas,
1932] and *Kolchida* [Colchis, 1934]. P. saw the theme of man
and nature within the larger framework of socialist reconstruction.
His simple, reserved, and sensitive narrative art proved effective
in those stories having chiefly historical, biographical, and nature-
related themes, as in *Severnaya povest* [A Northern Story, 1939]
and *Povest o lesakh* [The Song about the Forests, 1948]. In his
collection of essays entitled *Zolotaya roza* (1955; The Golden
Rose, 1959), P. discussed the significant experiences he had gained
through his literary work.

The high point of P.'s work may be found in the autobiographical cycle *Povest o zhizni* (1947, 1955, 1958. In English translation this appeared as The Story of a Life, 1964–69. Vol. I:
Childhood and Schooldays, 1964; Vol. II: Slow Approach of
Thunder, 1956; Vol. III: In That Dawn, 1967; Vol. IV: Years
of Hope, 1969). As a masterful portraitist of the Russian landscape and its people, P. has enriched Soviet literature with works
of permanent value.

Editions: Sobraniye sochinenii [Collected Works], 6 vols., Moscow,
1957–58
Further Works: Morski nabroski [Sea Tales] (1926); *Vstrechniye
korabli* [Passing Ships] (1928); *Chernoye more* [Black Sea] (1936);

Poruchik Lermontov [Lieutenant Lermontov] (1941); *Nash sovremen-nik Pushkin* [Pushkin, Our Contemporary] (1949); *Brosok na yug* [A Jump to the South] (1961); *Zolotoi Lin* [Golden Lin] (1966); *Nayedine s Osenfu* [All Alone with Osenfu] (1967); *Sobraniye sochinenii* [Collected Works] (1967)
Selected English translations: Selected Stories by K. P. (1967)

PAVLENKO, PIOTR ANDREYEVICH

Born July 11, 1899, St. Petersburg; died June 16, 1951, Moscow. Soviet Russian novelist.

P. worked at the Soviet trade agency in Turkey; he later became a Communist Party official and a political journalist. His early writing on the transformation taking place in the Near Eastern Republics of the USSR occasionally still showed certain formalistic tendencies.

The theme of the Paris Commune was employed by P. in his historical novel *Barrikady* [The Barricades, 1932]. P. took part in World War II. In *Shchastye* (1947; Happiness, 1950), P.'s work reached its climax. The role of the Communist Party in the difficult period after the war is embodied here by P. in the figure of Colonel Voropayev, in his belief in the people, and in his optimism. The hero, a wounded and depressed officer, finds inner fulfillment and happiness in working for others. P.'s novel *Tru-zheniki mira* [The Workers of the World, 1952] is dedicated to the international communist movement and its ideals. P. was awarded the State Prize in 1948.

Editions: Sobraniye sochinenii [Collected Works], 6 vols., Moscow, 1953–55
Further Works: Stepnoye solntze [The Sun in the Steppes] (1949); *Kavkazkaya povest* [The Caucasian Tale] (1957)

PERVENTZEV, ARKADII ALEKSEYEVICH

Born May 26, 1905, Nagut. Soviet Russian novelist.

In his novels *Kochubei* (1937) and *Nad Kuanyu* [Across the River Kuban, 1940], P.'s themes were connected with the civil war; he also wrote stories about the legendary commander of the Red Kuban Cossacks. During World War II he wrote *Ispitaniye*

(1942; The Testing, 1944), about the great courage shown by the Soviet people during the rapid evacuation of an aircraft plant from the Ukraine to the Urals. *Ognionnaya zemlya* [The Burning Land, 1945] concerns the heroic frontline battles. The formation and education of a young man during the civil war is the theme of *Chest z molodu* [The Youth as the Hero, 1948], for which P. was awarded the State Prize in 1949.

P. wrote a number of other novels, including *Lyudi odnovo ekipazha* (1954), *Matrossy* [Sailors, 1961], and *Olivkovaya* [An Olive Branch, 1965], as well as dramas and travelogues, including those on Korea (1949), Albania (1951), and India (1954).

PERVOMAISKI, LEONID SOLOMONOVICH (Pseud. of *Gurevich, Ilya Sholyomovich*)
Born May 17, 1908, Konstantinograd. Ukrainian poet and novelist.

P., the son of an artisan, first worked as a librarian and then for some time as a journalist. In his early works, including the collection of sketches entitled *Komsa* (1926), the volume of poems *Terpki yabluka* [Tart Apples, 1929], and the play *Komsomoltzy* (1930), P.—himself a correspondent on a youth newspaper—re-created the heroism of the Komsomols during the civil war and the period of socialist reconstruction.

In his later works, which were predominantly lyrical, P.'s themes remained closely connected with the problem of economic and cultural reconstruction in the Soviet Union. His two volumes of poems *Zemlya* [Earth, 1943] and *Den rozhdeniya* [The Day of the Birth, 1943], for which he received the State Prize, are important examples of his wartime poetry. His war novel *Dikyi med* [Wild Honey, 1964] has gained wide acceptance.

Editions: Tvory [Complete Works], 3 vols., Kiev, 1946–50

PESTRAK, FILIP SYAMYONAVICH
Born November 27, 1903, Sakavtzy (Brest). Byelorussian Soviet poet and novelist.

P., who came from a poor peasant family, has been writing poetry since the end of the 1920s. After World War II he began to write prose. His novel *Zustrenemsya na barykadakh* [Let Us Meet on the Barricades, 1954], which tells of the workers' struggle for liberation in Western Byelorussia, has become well known, as have many of his short stories.

PETITION OF DANIIL THE EXILED See MOLENIYE DANIILA ZATOCHNIKA

PETROV, YEVGENII (Pseud. of *Katayev, Yevgeni Petrovich*)
Born December 13, 1903, Odessa; died July 2, 1942. Soviet Russian prose writer.

After completing high school in 1920, P. worked as a correspondent for the Ukrainian telegraph agency. In 1923 he moved to Moscow, where his brother, the well-known writer Valentin Katayev, introduced him to the editors of the satirical magazine *Krasnyi peretz* [Red Pepper]. In 1926 he met Ilya Ilf, with whom he collaborated until the latter's death in 1937.

P. spent the years between 1937 and 1942 writing the memoirs of his friend Ilf; he also published the satirical comedy *Ostrov mira* [The Island of Peace], sketches, and film scripts. He started to write a utopian novel but was unable to complete it. P. was also a member of the editorial board of both the *Literaturnaya gazeta* and the magazine *Ogoniok*. During World War II he served as a war correspondent, and while returning from the besieged city of Sevastopol he met his death.

PILNYAK (Pseud. of *Vogau, Boris Andreyevich*)
Born September 12, 1894, Mozhaisk; died in 1938. Soviet Russian novelist.

P. welcomed the October revolution, but was unable to understand its socialist meaning and the revolutionary changes taking place in the country. He never acquired a socialist philosophy of life. His stories and novels give only a distorted image of Soviet life; they present the revolution as a natural event and as an anarchistic movement which merely awakened animal instincts in man. This attitude is particularly evident in his civil war novel *Goly god* (1922; The Naked Year, 1928). In his later work P. attempted to capture an image of the new "machinelike" Russia. He re-created certain problems of the period of the Five-Year Plan in his novel *Volga vpadeyet v Kaspiiskoye* (1930; The Volga Falls to the Caspian Sea, 1935). Because of its distortions of Soviet reality, P.'s work has been used as anti-communist propaganda in the capitalist countries, where its worth has generally been over-estimated.

Further Works: Povest o nepogashchennoi lune [Tale about the Shining Moon] (1927); *Krasnoye derevo* [The Red Tree] (1929)

PISAREV, DIMITRI IVANOVICH

Born October 14, 1840, Znamenskoye (Orlov District); died July 16, 1868, Dubbeln, near Riga (Latvia). Russian revolutionary democrat, political writer, and literary critic.

P. came from the wealthy nobility; from 1856–61 he studied history and philology at the University of St. Petersburg. From 1861 he worked for the leading democratic magazine *Russkoye slovo* [The Russian Word] and for *Otechestvennye zapiski* [Patriotic Notes]. He was arrested in 1862 and, accused of circulating revolutionary propaganda, sentenced to four years' imprisonment.

A materialistic thinker and decisive enemy of autocracy, P. continued the revolutionary, democratic activities of Chernyshevski and Dobrolyubov without, however, reaching the level of philosophical and theoretical comprehension attained by his predecessors. His influential theory of realism, which was based on Chernyshevski's anthropologism but contained strong elements of vulgar materialism (C. Vogt, J. Moleschott, L. Büchner), supported materialistic principles. Occupying a democratic position, he criticized capitalism and propagated utopian, socialist ideas. These ideas were particularly evident in his articles *Realisty* [Realist, 1864] and *Myslyashchi proletariat* [The Thinking Proletariat, 1865]. P.'s endeavors to promote the development of realistic art culminated in the demand for a sociocritical, democratic art, which he contrasted in a polemic manner with "pure" art.

P.'s essays *Bazarov* (1862), a sensitive analysis of the revolutionary, democratic content of Turgenev's *Fathers and Sons*, and *Heinrich Heine* (1867) in which P. appears as a passionate advocate of Heine's poetry, may be counted among his best works of literary criticism.

Editions: Sochineniya [Works], 4 vols., Moscow, 1955–56

PISEMSKI, ALEKSEI FEOFILAKTOVICH

Born March 23, 1821, Ramenye (District of Kostroma); died February 2, 1881, Moscow. Russian novelist, short-story writer, and dramatist.

P. came from the lesser aristocracy. His philosophy had much in common with that of the Slavophiles, and was focused on the life of the peasantry and their relationship to the nobility. P. at times was close to the conservative viewpoint, but in his best works evinced democratic and progressive ideas.

P.'s work was characterized by vital, naturalistic descriptions of people and places, but lacked any depth of ideas. In his first novel *Boyarshchina* [The Boyar Order, 1846], and in a number of short stories, he criticized the unjust legal status of Russian women. In his story *Tyufyak* [The Weakling, 1850] he created a satire on the general unfitness of the Russian provincial nobility. *Ocherki iz krestyanskovo byta* [Sketches from Peasant Life, 1852–55] and the famous peasant drama *Gorkaya sudbina* (1895; Bitter Fate, 1933) decribe the severe lot of the enserfed Russian peasants. In these works P. showed the characteristic features of the Russian peasant to be pride, intelligence, and an awareness of the dignity of the individual.

P.'s most important novel, *Tysyacha dush* [A Thousand Souls, 1858], depicted the failure of the *Raznochintzy* intellectuals to improve tsarist society by reforms from above. In the 1860s P. turned against the revolutionary democratic movement in his novel

Vzbalamuchennoye more [The Agitated Sea, 1863]. In his later works, however, P. returned to a democratic philosophy and produced a number of remarkable novels dealing with contemporary problems, including *Lyudi sorokovykh godov* [People of the 'Forties, 1869], *V vodovorote* [In the Maelstrom, 1871], *Meshchane* [The Petit-Bourgeoisie, 1877], and *Masony* [Freemasonry, 1880]. P. also wrote dramas, including *Samoupravtzy* [The High-Handed Ones, 1867], *Poruchnik Gladkov* [Lieutenant Gladkov, 1867], and *Waal* [Baal, 1873].

Editions: *Sobraniye sochinenii* [Collected Works], 9 vols., Moscow, 1959

PLEKHANOV, GEORGI VALENTINOVICH

Born December 11, 1856, Gudalovka (District of Tanbov); died May 30, 1918, Teriyoki (now Zelenogrosk). Russian revolutionary; noted leader of both the Russian and the international workers' movements; philosopher, art historian, and literary critic, whose writings on art and literature have been of great importance to Marxist art theories.

P. applied the Marxist theory of class warfare to the field of aesthetics; he defended the most important principles of materialist aesthetics—as defined by the Russian revolutionary democrats—against reactionary popular and decadent views. He made a considerable contribution to Marxist aesthetics, especially in his *Pisma bez adresa* [Letter without Address, 1899–1900], which contains his historical, materialistic declaration on the origins of art. His essay, written in 1905, *Frantzuskaya dramaticheskaya literatura i frantzuskaya zhipvopis XVIII veka s tochki zreniya sotziologii* [French Dramatic Literature and Paintings of the Eighteenth Century from the Standpoint of Sociology], demonstrates the dependence of art on class warfare and on prevailing conditions of production in class society. *Iskusstvo i obshchestvennaya zhizn* [The Art and Social Life, 1912] draws attention to the social significance of art and the role of progressive ideas as opposed to both idealistic and decadent theories and formalistic and naturalistic art movements. P. stated here that the arts represent a formidable weapon in class warfare, and that "the value of a work of art, ultimately, is determined by the profundity of the idea it expresses." P. thus unremittingly supported the cause of realism in art, which is upheld by great ideas of social significance. In opposition to this he brilliantly demonstrated how reactionary ideas have a restraining effect on the creative potentialities of even the greatest artists.

Among P.'s most important works of literary criticism are his essays on Ibsen and Hamsun. He was sharply critical of the bourgeois art of the imperialistic epoch, as well as of contemporary decadent poetry and painting. He was not, however, a consistent follower of Marxism, as was evident in both his philosophical and aesthetic views. He did not recognize Lenin's principle of partiality, and his association with the Mensheviks resulted in a series of grave philosophical errors. His negation of the active role of socialist ideas in social development was paralleled by his theory that art criticism was not an actively creative genre.

P. himself, however, did not adhere to this principle, and in his various articles on literature he criticized the works of the Russian, Scandinavian, and Western European writers from the point of view of the proletariat. He evaluated these works by deciding to what extent they served the cause of the battle against capitalism or enhanced the victory of the new socialist order. As a literary critic P. was unable to attain a complete Marxist point of view, as postulated by Lenin. This may be seen in his unusual approach to the work of Tolstoi and in his contradictory evaluation of Gorki's novel *The Mother*.

Editions: Iskusstvo i literatura [Art and Literature], Moscow, 1948; *Literatura i estetika* [Literature and Aesthetics], 2 vols., Moscow, 1958

PLESHCHEYEV, ALEKSEI NIKOLAYEVICH
Born December 4, 1825, Kostroma; died October 8, 1893, Paris. Russian poet; forerunner of democratic and utopian socialist ideals.

POGODIN, NIKOLAI-FIODOROVICH 355

As a result of his membership in the Petrashevtzy circle—a radical group to which members of the highest Russian nobility, including Dostoyevski, belonged—P. was exiled to Siberia from 1849 to 1858. Throughout his life he continued to work as a promoter of Russian literature. His collection of poems published in 1846 was accepted as the manifesto of the Petrashevtzy circle. His poem *Vperiod! bez strakha i somnenya* [Forward without Fear or Doubt!, 1846] became a revolutionary battle hymn. P.'s love and nature lyrics were the inspiration for numerous compositions by Tchaikovsky, Rubenstein, and Mussorgski, among other composers.

Editions: Izbrannyye stikhotvoreniya [Prose Writings], Moscow, 1960

POGODIN, NIKOLAI-FIODOROVICH
Born November 16, 1900, Gundurovskaya, near Rostov; died September 19, 1962, Moscow. Soviet Russian dramatist.

Following a period during which he concentrated on journalism, P. began to write plays in 1929. He was one of the first writers to employ the theme of socialist work in his dramatic writings, as is shown in *Temp* [Tempo, 1929], *Poema o topore* [The Poem of the Axe, 1930], and *Moi drug* [My Friend, 1932]. Although his first works were sketchy and episodic, he gradually acquired a more compact style. P.'s permanent achievement lies in the dramatic presentation of the work taking place on the construction sites, manufacturing plants and kolkhozes at the time of the first Five-Year Plan.

Among P.'s other works were the comedies *Sneg* [Snow, 1932], and *Posle bale* [After the Ball, 1934], and the play *Aristokraty* [Aristocrats, 1934]. P.'s most famous work was the trilogy *Chelovek s ruzhiom* [The Man with the Rifle, 1937], the second and third volumes of which are *Kremliovskiye kuranty* [The Bells of the Kremlin, 1940] and *Tretya pateticheskaya* [Final Chord, 1958]. Here P. created a convincing portrait of Lenin as seen before the background of the period between 1917–23. P. received the Lenin Prize for this work. The best plays from his extensive but somewhat uneven *œuvre* form an important part of the repertoire of the Soviet theater.

Editions: Sobraniye proizvedenii [Selected Works], 5 vols., Moscow, 1960
Further Works: Sonet Petrarki [The Sonnet of Petrarch] (1957); *Chornyye ptitzy* [The Black Birds] (1960)

POLATAYEV, NIKOLAI GAVRILOVICH
 Born 1889; died 1935. Soviet Russian poet.
 P., who had been active in literature since 1918, first attended a commercial school and then worked in a railroad office. He was later a member of the Moscow section of the Proletcult. His early poems, based on abstract, symbolistic motifs, are highly emotional. At the time of the revolution P. also wrote a number of markedly pessimistic poems about the poverty-stricken lives of city people in prerevolutionary times. His first important work was the poem *Portretov Lenina ne vidno* [Lenin Portraits Cannot Be Seen, 1927–28], in which he expressed his feeling of kinship with the battling proletariat.
 P.'s poems, which exhibit a profound lyricism, frequently combine symbolistic elements with clear, realistically concrete details. He was also the author of a number of short stories about railroad workers, including the cycle *Zheleznodoroshniki* [Railroad Men, 1925].

Editions: Izbrannyye stikhi [Selected Poems], Moscow, 1935

POLEVOI, BORIS (Pseud. of *Kampov, Boris Nikolaeyvich*)
 Born March 17, 1908, Moscow. Soviet Russian novelist and journalist.
 P. first worked as a technologist in a textile plant. During World War II he was a war correspondent for the newspaper *Pravda*. P., who has been writing since the 1920s, presented the high moral sense of the Soviet man in a versatile manner. His first novel, *Goryachi zekh* [The Crank], appeared in 1939.

In 1947 P. was awarded the State Prize for his novel *Povest o nastoyashchem cheloveka* (1946; A Story about a Real Man, 1959). Basing his story on factual accounts, P. described how Marasyev, a severely wounded pilot, fought through enemy territory to regain his own unit. Despite a leg amputation he was able to continue flying in the antifascist air force. P.'s novel created an extraordinary picture of the firmness and strength of Soviet man and of his confidence in a final victory. The novel was filmed in 1948, and in the same year was used by the composer S. Prokofieff as the basis for an opera. P. has thus become well known in foreign countries.

The tense heroism of female workers during the war was described by P. in his novel *Gluboki tyl* [Deep in the Interior of the Country, 1958]. Here P. described the characteristics and the role of a true collective, and in impressive and convincing scenes showed the relationship of the Soviet people to the German prisoners of war. In his novel *Na dikom brege* [On the Wild Riverbank, 1962] he described the drama connected with the building of a hydro-electric plant in the taiga.

P. also wrote sketches and eyewitness accounts of the Soviet Union and places abroad. These include correspondence from the war fronts—*Ot Belgoroda do Karpat* (1945; From Belgorod to the Carpathians, 1947), and *My, sovyetskiye lyudi* (1948; We Are the Soviet People, 1949), for which he received the State Prize in 1949. He recorded his American experiences in *Amerikanskiye dnevniki* [American Diaries, 1956]. His volume of essays *Sovremenniki* [Contemporaries, 1952] presents portraits of contemporary Soviet figures.

Further Works: Zoloto [Gold] (1950)

POLEZHAYEV, ALEKSANDR IVANOVICH

Born August 30, 1804 (?), Rusayevka; died January 28, 1838, Moscow. Russian poet.

P. was the son of an estate owner and a serf peasant woman.

In 1826, while still a student at Moscow University, he was arrested because of anti-Czarist sentiments shown in his poem *Sashka*. He was exiled to the Caucasus, where he served first as a non-commissioned officer and, after an unsuccessful attempt to escape, as a common soldier. His life as a soldier is reflected in his starkly realistic poems about the Caucasus, including *Erpeli*. His lyric writings—*Pesu plennovo irokeza* [Song of a Captured Iroquois, 1828] and *Opyat nechto* [Again Something, 1835]—exhibit, despite the hopelessness of some of his themes, his faith in the ideals of the Decembrists. His poem *Lozovskomu* [To Lozovski, 1828] shows P.'s acquaintance with the ideas of the French materialists.

Editions: Stikhovoreniya i poemy [Writings and Poems], Leningrad, 1957

POLOTZKI, SIMEON   See SIMEON POLOTZKI

POMYALOVSKI, NIKOLAI GERASIMOVICH

Born April 23, 1835, St. Petersburg; died there October 17, 1863. Russian novelist.

The son of a sexton, F. attended a church seminary or *bursa*. In *Ocherki bursy* [Sketches from the *Bursa*, 1862] he described the conditions existing there. He gave up a career as a priest to work, first as a teacher and later as a writer. Under the influence of Chernyshevski he became a follower of radical democratic ideals.

P.'s main work, the two-volume novel *Meshchanskoye shchastye* [Bourgeois Happiness] and *Molotov*, appeared in 1861 in the magazine *Sovremennik*. Here P., in the character of Molotov, depicted the desire for independence among the *Raznochintzy* intelligentsia, as well as showing how bourgeois ideas of prosperity would eventually cripple mankind. P.'s critical presentations of the bourgeoisie influenced both Chekhov and Gorki.

Editions: Sochinenya [Works], Moscow–Leningrad, 1951

POPULISTS (Also called *Narodniki*, from *narod*)
An influential group of belletrists writing in Russia in the 1870s and 1880s. The populists were closely connected with the Russian bourgeois democratic populist movement. Their interests were concerned almost exclusively with the life of the Russian villages. Writing for the most part in political journals, they described village life under conditions of growing capitalism, indicating the increasing class differences. They demonstrated the process of transition from village poverty to factory proletariat without, however, being able to understand the historic necessity of capitalism in Russia. For this reason they were unable to indicate the truly characteristic features of the Russian peasantry, and their works frequently became sterile documentary descriptions of the peasant environment.

The following popular belletrists were particularly well known: Sergei Mikhailovich Stepnyak-Kravchinski (1851–95); Nikolai Ivanovich Naumov (1838–1901), whose volume of sketches written in 1874, *Sila solomu lomit* [Force Overcomes Everything], belongs to the most important propaganda writings of the populists; Pavel Vladimirovich Zasodimski (1843–1912), whose most important work was the *Chronika sela Smurina* [Chronicle of the Village Smurino, 1874]; Karonin, the pseudonym of Nikolai Yelpidiforovich Petropavlovski (1853–92), who published a cycle of sketches entitled *Z nizu v verkh* [Up from Below, 1886]; and Nikolai Nikolayevich Slatovratzki (1845–1911), who wrote the novel *Ustoi* [The Supports, 1883].

POVEST O GORE-ZLOSHCHASTII (*The Story of Sorrow-Trouble*)
The most important verse story of the seventeenth century, this work relates the fate of a merchant son who falls into bad luck following his revolt against the moral code of the *Domostroi* (a collection of parochial rules). He is pursued by "Trouble," who symbolizes the suffering of the people, until he dies in a monastery.

This work, which still exhibits certain characteristics of national poetry, is a prelude to the secular literature of the eighteenth century. A similar theme is treated in *The Story of Savva Grudtzyn*.

POVEST VREMENNYKH LET (*The Story of Times Past; The Chronicle of Nestor*)
This is probably the most important historical work and literary document of the Middle Ages in Russia. It has come down to us in numerous different manuscript versions.

This work presumably originated in the beginning of the twelfth century, and was based on an extant version of the eleventh century, as well as on other contemporary chronicles. The compiler of *The Chronicle of Nestor*, the monk named Nestor, lived in the Kiev cave cloister. The legends, documents, and factual reports contained in this chronicle, some of which exhibit strong folkloristic features, represent a source of great literary value. The chronicle includes episodes concerning the blinding of Vasilko, the death of Oleg, and the Boris and Gleb legend, among others. Despite its theocentric aspects, this chronicle defends the idea of the greatness of the Russ against feudal separatism under the leadership of Kiev.

PRISHVIN, MIKHAIL MIKHAILOVICH
Born February 4, 1873, Khrushchovo (Oriol); died January 17, 1954, Moscow. Soviet Russian novelist and nature writer.

P. came from a merchant family. He was under arrest between 1897 and 1899 because of his participation in a Marxist circle. After the completion of his agricultural studies in Leipzig in 1902 he worked as an agronomist. He wrote his first book, *V krayu nepuganykh* [In the Country Where the Birds Do Not Show Fear, 1905]—for which he was elected a member of the Russian Geographical Society—as the result of extensive walking tours through northern Russia. His early works exhibit a certain tendency toward an idyllistic view of history and of nature untouched by man.

After the October revolution harmony between man and nature gradually became the main theme of his work. P. was also deeply sensitive to human emotions, especially those of children, as well as a master of poetic language, in which he utilized certain aspects of Russian national poetry. We find various genres represented in P.'s work, including miniatures from nature such as *Kalendar pirody* (1925; Nature's Diary, 1958) and *Okhotnichyi byli* [Hunting Stories, 1920–26]; prose poems such as *Shen-Shen* (1932); autobiographical works, including his novels *Kashcheyeva zep* [The Chain of the Kashchey, 1923–36] and *Korabelnaya chashcha* [The Legend of the Northern Forests, 1954].

Editions: Sobraniye sochinenii [Collected Works], 6 vols., Moscow, 1956–57

PROKOFYEV, ALEKSANDR ANDREYEVICH
Born December 2, 1900, Kobona (St. Petersburg). Soviet Russian poet.

P. took part in the civil war, the Finno-Soviet war, and the two World Wars. He has described the heroism of the revolutionary battle and of liberated work; he created impressive pictures of Russian nature, and sang of the force of love and friendship.

Almost all types of poetic genres may be found in his work, in which he frequently employed motives from the folklore of northern Russia. His poem *Rossiya* [Russia, 1934–44], for which he was awarded the State Prize in 1946, deserves special mention. In this poem, in which he extolled the heroism of the Soviet people during the fight against the German fascists, P. succeeded in creating a synthesis of lyrical and epic elements. A number of P.'s poems appeared in collected editions in the 1950s, but his main work, for which he was awarded the Lenin Prize in 1961, was the cycle of poems entitled *Priglasheniye k puteshestviyu* [Invitation to a Journey, 1959]. His central theme is Russia, which he extols in all her beauty and diversity.

Editions: Stikhotvoreniya [Poems], Moscow–Leningrad, 1950; *Sochineniya* [Works], 2 vols., Leningrad, 1957–58

PROKOPOVICH, FEOFAN

Born in 1681, Kiev; died September 19, 1736, Novgorod. Russian humanist and church reformer; confidant of Peter I.

P. received his theological training in Kiev and Rome. He became Bishop of Pskov in 1717, and later Archbishop of Novgorod. His "Circle of Learned Men" supported the enlightened absolutism of Peter I. In addition to scientific papers he wrote inflammatory sermons; he was also the author of the first Russian historical drama *Vladimir* (1705), which removed Russian literature from the realm of purely religious circles and used it to try and bring about social changes.

P.'s work, which included patriotic poems such as *Epinikion* (1709), formed a link between the seventeenth century (S. Polotzki) and the latter classicists (A. Kantemir).

Editions: Virshi Sillabicheskaya poeziya 17–18 vv [The Syllabic Poetry of the 17th and 18th Century] (1936)

PUMPURS, ANDRĒJS

Born September 22, 1841, Liebyumprave; died July 6, 1902, Riga. Latvian poet.

P. was the son of a farm laborer. In 1876 he took part in the Serbian war of liberation as a volunteer, and later became an officer in the Russian army. His main work, the heroic *Lāčplēsis* [The Bear-Killer, 1888], expresses his belief in the sure future victory of the people. It is based on Latvian sagas and songs and, to some extent, on the epic works of other nations as well as on historical sources.

PUSHKIN, ALEKSANDR SERGEYEVICH

Born June 6, 1799, Moscow; died February 10, 1837, St. Petersburg. Russian poet.

P., the founder of Russian realism, helped Russian literature to attain world rank. P. came from the old landed nobility. His nurse, a countrywoman named Arina Rodionovna, taught him to respect and love the Russian language and the poetry of the people. In the lyceum at Tzarskoye Selo, which P. attended between 1811 and 1817, he was exposed to the ideas of the French liberal philosophers as well as to the works of Russian writers such as Batyushkov, Zhukovski, and Radishchev. The first poems of the young P. already exhibited both his individual point of view and his personal observations made in his own milieu.

In 1817 P. became an official in the Russian State Department, and led the easy life of the St. Petersburg nobility. At the same time, however, he also became involved with members of certain secret societies whose aims included the overthrow of tsarism. P.'s poems *Volnost* [Freedom, 1817], *K. Chaadeyevu* [To Chaadayev, 1818], and *Dervnya* [The Village, 1819] clearly demonstrated his philosophy. These poems called for the downfall of tyrants and thus, by implication, of tsarism. In his poems P. castigated the injustices then existing, although his protests at first touched only the surface of the social situation and its problems. In his lighthearted fairy-tale epic *Ruslan i Ludmilla* (1820; Ruslan and Ludmilla, 1936) he used national poetry as a starting point for a democratic reform of the Russian literary language, a project on which P. continued to work all his life. With the aid of a deft, peasant humor, he succeeded in creating a brilliant parody on romanticism. As a result of some of these early poems P. was exiled to the south of Russia—Odessa and Kishinev.

P.'s encounter with a number of future Decembrists, among them Pestel, led to an even more marked condemnation of tsarism, as is shown in the poems *Kinzhal* [The Dagger, 1821], *Uznik* [1822; The Prisoner, 1948], and others. At the same time P. attempted to present in his work the most progressive ideas of the young and noble intelligentsia. This aspect of his work eventually led to the creation of *Evgeny Onegin* (1831; Eugene Onegin, 1937); it also greatly influenced the entire spectrum of Russian literature, including the writers Lermontov, Herzen, Goncharov, and Turgenev. The young hero of this period also appears in P.'s poem *Kavkzki plennik* [The Prisoner of the Caucasus, 1821], at first as a dark, heroic figure who only later begins to develop as an individualist. In the poem *Tzygany* [The Gypsies, 1826], Aleko, too, rejects the life of the average nobleman, seeking salvation in his closeness to the people. Aleko, however, is unable to overcome the moral standards of the nobility, and an old gypsy man—the representative of the people—passes judgment on him.

His newly won realizations led P. to write the tragedy *Boris Godunov* (1825; Boris Godunov, 1953) while living on the P. estate at Mikhailovskoye, where he had been exiled by the tsar. In *Boris* the people appear as the major, history-determining force, and P. shows that only those individuals who have the support of the people can finally achieve victory. P. is here in opposition to the Decembrists, who, a few months later, in December, 1825, attempted to pull off a coup without the help of the people and, therefore, were doomed to failure. In his poems *Arion* (1827) and *V. Sibir* [An Open Letter to Siberia, 1827] and even in conversations with the tsar P. continued to proclaim his loyalty to his valued friends—with the result that he was placed under strict police surveillance.

Evgeny Onegin, the first great social novel of Russian literature, was created by P. between 1823 and 1830. This verse novel describes how idleness and lack of purpose in the life of the progressive representatives of the nobility make them appear to be "superfluous individuals" (Herzen). In the figure of the educated Tatjana, whose sympathies were with the Russian people, a way out appeared for the intelligentsia which later on did in fact—with the coming of the revolution—materialize.

In 1830 P. wrote five stories, which appeared under a pseudonym as *Povesti Belkina* (The Tales of Ivan Belkin, 1954). One of these stories, *Stantzionny smotritel* (The Postmaster) had as its hero the "little man," with all his problems and worries; for the first time in Russian literature a representative of the lower classes appeared in the work of a major writer. A similar type of characterization, as well as the appearance of the outcast, or "superfluous one" (*lishni chelovek*) as used by P. was to determine the subsequent development of Russian literature, and can be seen in the works of Gogol, Turgenev, Dostoyevski, and Nekrasov.

This "little man"—this time shown in his relationship to Peter I —was again depicted in P.'s masterful poem *Medni vsadnik* (The Bronze Horseman, 1883). This tendency toward democratization also became evident in P.'s prose works. In *Pikovaya dama* (1853; The Queen of Spades, 1929) he criticized the ghoulish, rapidly growing power of capitalism. He was also interested in the theme of the peasant uprising under Pugachev which had taken place in 1773–75 and, following extensive research into archives and investigations in the Volga region, he wrote the historical piece *Istoriya Pugachova* [The Story of Pugachev, 1834]. The novel fragment *Dubrovski* (1833, Dubrovsky, 1958) was also written at this time. P. later used material from national poetic works and from eyewitness accounts by participants in the Pugachev uprising to compose the novel *Kapitanskaya dochka* (1836; The Captain's Daughter, 1954). This novel is constructed in such a way that the reader gradually obtains a true picture of the leader Pugachev as it emerges through the thicket of false accusations and the prejudices existing against this peasant revolutionary.

P. was not a believer in the general uprising of the people which, in his opinion, could bring about no positive results, but he viewed such an uprising as a legitimate and thus justifiable consequence of the brutal exploitation and mistreatment of the peasants by the estate owners and civil servants. These views were not appreciated by the tsar and his court, and P. was refused permission to leave St. Petersburg. In 1834 he was appointed to the position of gentleman-in-waiting—a position for very young noblemen—in order to put him under even closer surveillance. His personal mail was opened and he was finally provoked into a duel with the French emigré d'Anthès, in which he was killed.

P.'s last poems clearly reflect his feelings during those years. *Vnov ya posetil* (1835; I've Visited Once More, 1945) expresses sad memories as well as the hope for future joys which, however, the poet himself will never experience. His syntax and rhythms created the kind of melancholy spectral discourses that, later, were to be characteristic of Lermontov. *Pamyatnik* [The Monument,

1836] may be regarded as P.'s poetic testament. Paraphrasing Horace, he speaks of a monument that he has created for himself in the heart of the peoples of Great Russia.

Editions: Polnoye sobraniye sochinenii [Complete Works], 16 vols., Moscow, 1937–49
Selected English translations: The Captain's Daughter and The Negro of Peter the Great, tr. R. Edmonds, 1958; *Letters,* 3 vols., ed. and tr. J. T. Shaw, 1963; *The Queen of Spades and Other Tales,* tr. Ivy Litvinov, 1962

RADISHCHEV, ALEKSANDR NIKOLAYEVICH
Born August 31, 1749, Moscow; died September 24, 1802, St. Petersburg. Russian poet and journalist; the first Russian nobleman to become a revolutionary.

The son of a nobleman, R. was educated in the Royal Corps of Pages at the court of the tsar. He studied law in Leipzig between 1766 and 1771, and there became acquainted with the ideas of the humanist philosophers, including Mably, Rousseau, and Helvétius, whose work greatly influenced him. Following his return to Russia R. worked in both the civil and the military services, in the judicial system, and in the customs service.

Influenced by actual events in Russia, and greatly affected by the Pugachev uprising in 1773–75, R. gradually acquired more definite revolutionary convictions, and came to reject the demagogic policies of Catherine II (1762–96), the entire tsarist system, and the serfdom order in general.

R. expressed his position in his early literary works—see, for instance, his ode *Volnost* [Freedom, 1783], *Pismo k drugu . . . v Tobolske* [A Letter to a Friend . . . in Tobolsk, 1782, pub. 1790], and, in particular, his *Puteshestviye iz Peterburga v Moskvu* (1790; Journey from St. Petersburg to Moscow, 1958). In the latter work R. created a unique genre picture; in it, on the basis of the philosophical, political, and social conditions then existing in Russia, he concluded that the people would eventually have to free themselves by revolution. This idea became the high point of eighteenth-century Russian thought, and R. thus an-

A. N. Ostrovski

N. A. Ostrovski

B. L. Pasternak

K. G. Paustovski

A. S. Pushkin

A. N. Radishchev

Rainis

S. Rustaveli

K. F. Ryleyev

M. T. Rylskyi

ticipated the thinking of the revolutionaries of the nineteenth century.

R., who had already shown his awareness in his psychologically sensitive, if sentimental, observations in *Dnevnik odnoi nedeli* [Diary of One Week, 1773], was repeatedly able to attain realistic positions in the sentimental *Journey* by his sharp social criticism. His use of language, however, was frequently clumsy. The *Journey* was immediately prohibited, and in 1790 R. was tried and exiled to Siberia. While there he wrote numerous scientific and philosophical pamphlets from the materialist point of view, including *O cheloveke, yevo smertnosti i besmertii* [On Man, his Mortality and his Immortality, 1792; pub. 1809]. R. was pardoned in 1796. In 1801 he cooperated in certain reform projects and wrote a number of popular works, among them the fairy tale *Bova*. In 1802, when he was again suspected of illegal activities, he committed suicide.

Editions: Polnoye sobraniye sochinenii [Complete Works], 3 vols., Moscow–Leningrad, 1938–52

RAFFI (Pseud. of *Melik-Akopian, Akop*)
   Born 1835, Pajadshuk (Iran); died May 6, 1888, Tiflis. Armenian novelist.
   Progressive romanticism attained a high level of development in R.'s work of the 1870s and 1880s. In his historical novel *Samvel* (1885) R. described the liberation movements of the Armenian people against foreign oppressors in the fourth century. His historical novel *David-bek* (1880) was about similar movements in the early eighteenth century.
   R. called for battle against the Turkish oppressors of Armenia in the nineteenth century in his novel *The Madman*. Stylistically most of his prose works are characterized by a blend of romanticism and realism.

RAGIM, MAMED (Pseud. of *Guseinov, Mamed Ragim Abas-ogly*)
   Born April 20, 1907, Baku. Azerbaidzhani Soviet lyric writer.
   The pathos of R.'s lyrical poetry lies in his involvement with

the Soviet people in their battle against the enemies of the revolution and the fascist aggressors (*Poem on Leningrad,* 1948). His collection of lyric poems *Wishes* (1939) and *The Second Book* (1933) depict pride in the liberation of man. R. also extols the achievements of socialism and communism in *On the Shores of the Caspian Sea* (1948) and *Mingechau Poems* (1945–50). The revolutionary activities of S. M. Kirov stimulated R. to write his poem *The Immortal Hero* (1946).

A number of R.'s poems indicate that he was profoundly influenced by Azerbaidzhani folklore—*The Star of My Grandmother* and *The Girl Arsu* (1939) are examples of this influence. The battle for peace, social liberation, and democracy in the capitalist countries is the theme of a number of other poems, including *From My Tabriz Notebook* (1944–50) and *Nazim Hikmet,* among others. R. was awarded the State Prize in 1949.

Editions: Sheirlar va poemlar, Baku, 1951

RAINIS (Pseud. of *Pliekšans, Jānis*)

Born September 11, 1865, near Ilukste; died September 12, 1929, Marjori (near Riga). Latvian national poet, thinker, and revolutionary.

R., the son of a farmer, graduated from the law faculty of St. Petersburg University, but he soon turned to journalism. He was a member of the left wing of the so-called New Movement, and also edited the newspaper *Dienas Lapa* [The Daily News] between 1891 and 1895. In the summer of 1893 R. was in Zurich, where he heard Engels' speech during the closing session of the Second International; he also met Bebel. In 1896 R. lived in Berlin-Charlottenburg, where he worked on a translation of Goethe's *Faust.* He returned to Latvia in 1897, and was soon arrested as dangerous to Imperial Russia. R. continued his literary work in various prisons and places of exile; he concluded his translation of *Faust,* and also translated other works of world literature.

In Slobodskoi, in the Gouv. of Vyatka, his final place of exile

(1899–1903), he established contacts with the Bolsheviks. In 1905 he took part in the revolution and was forced to emigrate to Switzerland with his wife, the poet Aspazija. He returned to his home country in 1920.

R.'s philosophical and aesthetic views were influenced by Marxism and Russian literature, in particular by the work of Gorki. R.'s first collection of poems, *Tālas noskaņas zilâ vakarâ* [Faraway Sounds in a Blue Night, 1903], show that he had found an adequate form in which to express the feelings of the growing proletariat. In his drama *Uguns un nakts* [Fire and Night, 1903–04], R. gave a new philosophical meaning to the Lāčplēsis (bear-slayer) saga. In his later verse poems, R. founded socialist realism in Latvian literature. His collections *Vētras sēja* [The Seed of the Storm, 1905], *Jaunais spēhks* [New Strength, 1906], *Klusā grāmata* [The Quiet Book, 1909], *Tie, kas neaizmirst,* [Those Who Do Not Forget, 1910], and his poem *Ave, sol!* (1910) are among the most important works of Latvian literature. These works, which are permeated by socialist ideas, contain pictures of harsh class battles, philosophical reflections, and sunny scenes from nature.

R. remained true to his ideals in his last works, which he created in bourgeois Latvia. His work in the field of dramatic writing is considered to be excellent.

Further Works: Zelta zirgs [The Golden Horse] (1909); *Pūt, vēgiņi!* [Roads, Wind] (1913); *Jāzeps un viņa brāļi* (1919; The Sons of Jacob, 1924); *Spēlēju, dancoju* [I Play, I Dance] (1915); *Krauklītis* [The Young Raven] (1920); *Daglas skiču burtnīcas* [The Notebooks of Dagda] (1920–25)

REISNER, LARISA MIKHAILOVNA
Born May 13, 1895; Lublin; died February 9, 1962, Moscow. Soviet Russian poet and journalist.

R., who studied in France and Germany, came from a progressive bourgeois family of scholars. Her abstract, symbolist poetry was first published prior to World War I. Her humanist, socialist ideals led her to side with the Bolsheviks; she took part in the civil war as a Red Army commissar, producing several stirring articles about her wartime experiences. In the course of numerous journeys she learned to know the USSR, Afghanistan, and Germany. The sketches created at that time represent significant examples of socio-realist journalism, somewhat dominated by emotion.

The characteristic features of R.'s work are a laconic terseness and vividness, with a tendency toward symbolism. Her last book describes the building of socialism in the manufacturing plants of the Urals.

Editions: Izbrannoye [Selected Works], Moscow, 1965

REKEMCHUK, ALEKSANDR YEVSEYEVICH

Born 1927, Odessa. Soviet Russian short-story writer and novelist.

R. first studied at an artillery school and then at the Literature Institute in Moscow. Between 1947 and 1962 he lived in the Komi ASSR, where he worked as a journalist and writer. He has lived in Moscow since 1963.

R.'s first stories and novellas were written in 1952. His subjects include studies of life and work in the northernmost parts of the country, as in *Vremya letnikh otpuskov* [Summer Holiday, 1959] and *Molodo-zeleno* (1962), which are characterized by an optimistic joyousness.

REMIZOV, ALEKSEI MIKHAILOVICH

Born July 7, 1877, Moscow; died November 28, 1957, Paris. Russian poet and novelist.

R. was educated in the religious tradition, and became the abbot of various monasteries. He later studied natural sciences in Moscow, and emigrated to France in 1921.

R.'s work, which exhibits considerable linguistic mastery, was mostly concerned with religious, ethical problems. He condemned reality as the realm of the devil, and considered life to be nonsensical and pitiful. These views are presented in *Krestovy ya siostry* [Sisters Under the Cross, 1911], *Prud* [The Pond, 1907], and *Chasy* (1904; The Clock, 1924). R.'s descriptions, in which he emphasized the senselessness of the world, frequently took on surrealistically grotesque and fantastic aspects. His ideal was the pre-Petrian, patriarchal life of the Russian merchant class; this view influenced his works to a certain extent—they essentially represent a stylization of precapitalist Russian folklore.

R. never attained great popularity, although Gorki valued him as a "master of the Russian language." R. was strongly opposed to the October revolution; in his pamphlet *Slovo o pogibeli zemli russkoi* [A Word on the Ruin of the Russian Land, 1918] he turned sharply against the growing power of the young Soviet.

Editions: Sochineniya [Works], 8 vols., St. Petersburg, 1910–12

RESHETNIKOV, FIODOR MIKHAILOVICH
Born September 17, 1841, Yekaterinburg; died March 21, 1871, St. Petersburg. Russian novelist.

R., who grew up in great poverty, was influenced by the ideals of the revolutionary democrats. His novel *Podlipovtzy* [The Householders of Podlipnaya, 1864] is considered to be his main work. Here R. described the extreme poverty of the peasants and boatmen on the River Kama. In his novels *Gornorabochiye* [Miners, 1866] and *Glumovy* [The Glumovs, 1866–67] the life of the factory workers was presented in a realistic manner for the first time in Russian literature.

Editions: Polnye sobranye sochinenii [Complete Works], 6 vols., Sverdlovsk, 1936–48

ROMASHOV, BORIS SERGEYEVICH
Born June 30, 1895, St. Petersburg; died May 6, 1958. Soviet Russian dramatic, critical, and political writer.

R.'s artistic work encompasses the drama as well as satirical and lyrical comedies. *Ognenny most* [The Flaming Bridge] which saw its première in 1929, and in which R., as one of the first Soviet dramatists, created the figure of a leading Communist Party worker, was followed by a number of pieces with contemporary themes, including *Velikaya Sila* [The Great Force, 1947]. Since 1949 R. has held the title of Meritorious Artist of the RSFSR; he was awarded the State Prize in 1948.

Editions: Pyesy [Plays], Moscow, 1951; *Dramaturg i teatr* [The Dramatist and the Theater], Moscow, 1953

ROZHDESTVENSKI, ROBERT IVANOVICH
Born June 20, 1932, Kosikha (in the Altai region). Soviet Russian poet.

R. studied at the Faculty of Philology of the University of Petrosavodsky and at the Literature Institute in Moscow. His characteristic style was already revealed in his volume of poems *Flagi vesny* [The Banners of Spring, 1955] and in his poem *Moya lyubov* [My Love, 1956]. His poetic themes include a yearning for faraway places and a forward-looking philosophy, as can be seen in his poem *Pismo v tridsaty wek* [Letter to the 30th Century, 1963].

R. attempted to further develop Mayakovski's poetic reforms; many of his poems are written in the form of a dialogue. His striving for the discovery of new truths permeates his work. His *Requiem* (1961), dedicated to the dead of World War II, may be regarded as one of his most mature works.

Further Works: Ispytaniye [A Trial] (1956); *Neobitayemiye ostrova* [Uninhabited Islands] (1962)

ROZOV, VIKTOR SERGEYEVICH
Born August 21, 1913, Yaroslavl. Soviet Russian actor and playwright.

R.'s career as an actor, which commenced in 1938, was interrupted by World War II. After the war he became involved with the formation of a children's theater in Alma-Ata, and later became a producer at the children's theater in Moscow.

R. has depicted the problems and conflicts of contemporary young people in a very sensitive manner, showing their moral growth in everyday situations. His first play was *Yeo druzya* [Her Friends, 1949]. The film *The Cranes Are Flying* is based on his play *Vechno zhivyye* [The Eternally Living Ones, 1956]. The question of the relationship between intelligence and emotion becomes increasingly important in R.'s later plays, which include *V dobry chas* [Happy Landings!, 1954], *V doroge* [On the Way, 1959], and *V den svadby* [The Wedding Day, 1964]. R. was awarded the State Prize in 1967.

Further Works: V poiskakh radosti [In Search of Happiness] (1957); *Pered uzhinom* [Before Dinner] (1963)

RUCHIOV (Pseud. of *Krivoshchokov, Boris Aleskandrovich*)
Born June 15, 1913, Stanitza Yetkulskaya (near Chelyabinsk). Soviet Russian poet.

R., the son of a teacher, went as a youth to the major building site in Magnitogorsk. It was here that he wrote his first cycle of poems, *Vtoraya rodina* [Second Homeland, 1933], which is dedicated to the heroism of labor and the development of the personality in the socialist collective. In his later works R. frequently returns to the theme of Magnitogorsk, as in his poem *Industrialnaya poema* [A Poem on Industry], but he also treated war themes as in the poem *Nevidimka* [The Invisible, 1958].

RUDAKI, ABU-ABDILLAH DSHAFAR
Born circa October 858, Pandshi Rudak; died there, 941. The founder of Tajik and Persian literatures.

R. was a court poet in Bukhara, but he fell out of favor circa 938 and was blinded, probably because of his sympathy for the democratic ideas of the Karmate sect. Of his extensive work only fragments remain today, although in his own time he was widely known.

R. created the first didactic poem (*Kalila and Dima*, 932), which was based on an older Indian story cycle, numerous kassides (odes or laments), and other works. His total *œuvre* presents R. as a poet fighting injustice, human weakness, and the dogmatic assertion of faith. His hymns on the importance of human knowledge greatly influenced Avicenna and other later thinkers.

RUSTAVELI, SHOTA

Born September 25, 1166; died during the first years of the thirteenth century. Georgian national poet and humanist.

R. created the most important epic of ancient Georgian literature, *Vepkhis-tgaosani* [The Knight in the Tiger's Skin], in 1200. We know nothing of R.'s life or of his other work. By analyzing his work, in which the author refers to himself as "Rustaveli"— "the man from Rustavi"—literary historians have concluded the R. was a member of the nobility. He was supposedly educated in the spirit of the Georgian philosophers of his time, among them Petre Iberieli and Ioanne Petrizi, perhaps at the academy of Gelati. He was close to the court of the Georgian kings, and could possibly have been a court poet. Historians, including S. Nuzubidse, believe that R. was forced to leave Georgia and that he died in a Georgian cloister near Jerusalem. Since his epic is dedicated to the Georgian queen Tamar it is supposed that it was composed sometime between 1198 and 1207.

The Knight in the Tiger's Skin ranks side by side with the most mature achievements of Renaissance poetry. It is free from both religious mysticism and scholasticism, and reflects pantheistic materialism. The story is about the Arab prince Avtandil, who leaves his love Tinatin, the king's daughter, in order to learn the story of Tariel (the hero in the tiger's skin), who is the son of the king of India. He then goes to seek the place where Nestan, Tariel's abducted lover, is imprisoned, finally freeing her with the help of both Tariel and the valiant hero Pridon. The epic has little in common with the Middle Ages' "novel of chivalry." It is based on the idea that evil can win the upper hand for a short time only, while virtue is eternal. Men can attain happiness only by first passing through misery and unhappiness. The friendship of the three warriors represents the friendship between nations.

R. reflects the transition period (H. Huppert), and as well as depicting the knightly milieu also showed the growing strength of the merchant class. His epic, which is written in the Georgian folkloric meter, greatly influenced the development of Georgian literature. It was first printed in 1712.

Translation: The Man in the Panther's Skin, tr. M. Wardrop, 1912; *The Knight in the Tiger's Skin*, 1938

RYBAK, NATAN SAMIILOVYCH
Born June 3, 1913, Ivanivka. Ukrainian Soviet novelist.
R.'s literary career began in the 1930s with the publication of numerous stories about socialist reconstruction. Among his early works were the student novels *Kiev* (1936) and *Dnepr* (1937–38), a trilogy on the life of the Dnieper raftsmen. The historical novel, a literary form considered to be his greatest achievement, became his preferred narrative genre. His life of Balzac, *Pomylka Onore de Balzaka* [The Error of Honoré de Balzac, 1940; 2nd version, 1956], and the two-volume novel *Pereyaslavska rada* [The Pereyaslav Treaty, 1945–54], which is a description of the fight of the Ukrainian people for reunification of the Ukraine with Russia in the seventeenth century, are examples of this literary form. R. was awarded the State Prize in 1950.

Further Works: Zbroya z namy [We Have the Arms] (1943); *Chas spodivan i zavershen* [A Time of Expectations and Conclusions] (1960)

RYBAKOV (Pseud. of Aronov, Anatoli Naumovich)
Born January 14, 1911, Chernigov. Soviet Russian novelist.
R. is a professional engineer, and he has been working in the automobile industry for some years. He became known after the publication of his novel *Voditeli* [Men at the Helm, 1950], for which he was awarded the State Prize in 1951. Here R. describes the daily life of workers in an automobile plant, and shows the growth of the communist personality.
In 1955 R. published his novel *Yekaterina Voronina*, a novel about the life of the Volga boatmen. R. also wrote a series of

exciting stories for children, including *Kortik* (1948; Kortik, 1953) and *Priklyucheniya Krosha* [Fight Your Way Out, Krosh!].

RYCHËU, YURII SERGEYEVICH
   Born May 8, 1903, Uëllen. Chukchi Soviet novelist.
   R. worked as a hunter, porter, and sailor before studying at Leningrad University. His literary career began in 1947; he is the first writer of the Chukchi people. He has described the severe lot of the American Eskimo, comparing it with the changes in thinking and feeling that have taken place among his own people living at the easternmost tip of the Soviet Union.

Further Works: Drusya-tovarishchi [Friends and Comrades] (1953); *Lyudi nashego berega* [People from Our Shore] (1953); *Vremya tayaniya snegov* [Farewell to the Gods] (1958)

RYLENKOV, NIKOLAI IVANOVICH
   Born February 15, 1909, Alekseyevka (Region of Smolensk). Soviet Russian poet.
   R., the son of a peasant, became a village schoolteacher. His literary activities began in 1926, but his first collection of poems, *Moï geroï* [My Hero], did not appear until 1933. R. frequently wrote of the Russian village and its development toward socialism. The earth for him is the good mother to which both the poet and his heroes are closely attached. *Pyatoye vremya goda* [The Fifth Season, 1965] contains poems that are profound reflections on our times and on contemporary man. In his story *Mne 14 let* [I Am Fourteen, 1963–64] the poet shows us his childhood.

Editions: Stikhotvoreniya i poemy [Poems and Verses], Moscow, 1959

RYLEYEV, KONDRATII FIODOROVICH
   Born September 29, 1795, Batovo; died July 25, 1826, St. Petersburg. Revolutionary Russian romanticist and the most important poet of the Decembrist movement.
   R., who was a friend of Pushkin, took part in the War of 1812

and in 1820 moved to St. Petersburg. In 1823 he became a member of the constitutionalist Northern Society, changing its orientation toward a more republican one. R. was hanged as one of the leaders of the Decembrist revolution of December 14, 1825.

R.'s lyric, dramatic writings as well as his works of literary criticism represent the artistic expression of a personality living for the revolution. His satire *K vremenshchiku* [To the Favorite, 1820], in which he severely criticized Arakcheyev, one of the ministers at the court of Alexander I, represented the birth of R. as a political poet. R.'s lyric writings reached their peak in the years just prior to the Decembrist revolution—1823–25. He wrote poems of great emotional impact and strength, including *Grazhdanin* [The Patriot, 1824–25], which saw publication only in 1893, and the popular *Agitazionnyye pesni* (1823–25), which he co-authored with A. Bestuzhev.

R.'s *Dumy* (1821–23) occupies a special position. This work is a collection of historical elegies in which the poet extolled the life of Russian and Ukrainian historical personalities with a view to setting examples the youth of his time could imitate. His romantic poem *Voinarovski* (1825) had a similar aim. Here Mazeppa's nephew Voinarovski, suffering in Siberian exile, appears as the heroic fighter against autocracy and for the liberation of the people. A. von Chamisso used the theme of this poem in the first part of his own poem entitled *The Exiles*. Another of R.'s poems, *Nalivaiko*, remained unfinished, as did his tragedy *Bogdan Khmelnitzki* (1825).

R. laid down his views on the aims of revolutionary romantic writings in his article *Neskolko myslei o poezii* [Some Thoughts on Poetry, 1825]. Between 1823 and 1825 R., together with A. Bestuzhev, published the almanac *Polyarnaya Zvezda* [Polar Star], in which the best works of the contemporary poets appeared.

Editions: Stikhotvoreniya, stati, ocherki, dokladnyye zapiski, pisma [Poems, Essays, Sketches, Notes, and Letters], Moscow, 1956; *Stikhotvoreniya*, Leningrad, 1956

RYLSKYI, MAKSIM TADIEIOVYCH

Born March 19, 1895, Kiev; died there July 24, 1964. Ukrainian Soviet poet, scholar, translator, and literary critic.

R. was the son of a well-known ethnographer and a peasant woman. After studying medicine and philology at the University of Kiev, he worked as a teacher between 1919 and 1929. In 1943 R. was elected a member of the Academy of Sciences of the Russian Soviet Republic and in 1958 became a member of the Academy of Sciences of the USSR.

R.'s debut as a poet came in 1918 with his collection of poems *Pid osinnymy zoryamy* [Under Autumn Stars]. This was soon followed by numerous other collections, including *Synya dalechin* [Blue Distances, 1922], *Trinadtzyata vesna* [The Thirteenth Spring, 1924], and *Kriz buryu i snikh* [Through Storm and Snow, 1925]. The conscious linking to the classical traditions of Ukrainian poetry (Shevchenko; Franko) already characterized R.'s lyric writings. Because of his adherence to the so-called neoclassicists, R.'s stylistically mature poetry exhibited certain aesthetic features that disappeared only in the second half of the 1920s. This period was characterized by a move toward significant social themes, and to a realistic presentation of the new socialist reality, as is evidenced in his collections *De s'khodyatsya dorohy* [Where the Roads Cross, 1929] and *Homin i vidhomin* [The Sound and the Echo, 1929], as well as in his poem *Sashko* (1928) in which R. for the first time presented the figure of a revolutionary proletariat.

Since the 1930s R. has developed into one of the leading lyric poets of Ukrainian Soviet literature. In more than forty volumes of poetry he has expressed the new socialist feelings of Soviet man with incomparable skill. R.'s themes—creative work, patriotism, and friendship among peoples—fully utilized all possibilities of poetic expression, encompassing the heroic, ideological poem, nature songs rich in feeling, and satirical epigrams. These aspects are reflected in his poetry collections *Kiev* (1935), *Lito* [The Summer, 1936], *Ukraina* (1938), and *Zbir vynohradu* [The

Vintage, 1940]. His collection *Slovo pro ridnu matir* [Song of the Mothers at Home, 1943] gained great popularity among the passionate, emotional poems produced during the war years. Philosophical and political ideological poems dominated R.'s work during the postwar years, as may be seen in the cycles *Virnist* [Loyalty, 1946], *Mosty* [Bridges, 1948], *Orlyina simya* [The Eagle's Family, 1951], and *Nasha syla* [Our Strength, 1952]. R.'s lyric work experienced a new rise after the Twentieth Party Congress of the Communist Party of the Soviet Union. This is shown in his collections entitled *Troyandy i vynohrad* [Roses and Grapevines, 1957], *Daleki neboskhyly* [Distant Skies, 1959], and *V zatinku zhaivoronka* [Where the Lark Sings, 1960].

The philosophical profundity and force of emotional expression in R.'s writing, together with its popularity and unusual melody, have made it a yardstick for the work of future writers in the Ukrainian Soviet. R. has written a great number of significant literary essays, and has contributed many ideas on the theory of translation. His own translations of classical works of world literature, including those of Pushkin, Mickiewicz, Shakespeare, Voltaire, Hugo, Heine, and Byron, are of permanent artistic value. He was awarded the Lenin Prize in 1960.

Editions: Tvory [Selected Works], 10 vols., Kiev, 1960–62

SABIR, ALEKPER TAÏRZADE

Born May 29, 1862, Shemakh; died July 25, 1911. Azerbaidzhani poet and revolutionary satiricist.

During the 1905 revolution S. turned away from the intimate lyric poetry of his earlier years to produce political poems and satires. As one of the most active writers contributing to the revolutionary democratic magazine *Molla Nasreddin* he castigated the religious fanaticism in the political life of prerevolutionary Azerbaidzhan. He was sympathetic toward the struggles of the Baku workers and those of the Azerbaidzhani peasants, as well as toward the strivings for liberation of the people of both Iran and Turkey.

S. created unique and impressively realistic pictures of the life of the people. A popular collection of S.'s works appeared in 1912 under the title *Hop-hop-name* [The Hop-hop book].

Editions: Sechilmish sheirlar, Baku, 1946; *Hop-hop-name,* Baku, 1954

SAADI (Pseud. of *Abu-Abdillah Musharrif-uddin ben Muslih-uddin*)

Born between 1213 and 1219, Shiraz; died there between 1291 and 1295. Persian poet.

S. studied in Baghdad. He traveled extensively between 1226 and 1256, visiting Mesopotamia, Asia Minor, Syria, Egypt, and Mecca. In 1257 he wrote the moralizing poem *Bustan* (1257; The Bustan of Sadi, 1911), in which justice, charity, and other virtues were treated in verse form in ten chapters. *Gulistan* (1258; The Gulistan or Rose Garden, 1964) is a collection of anecdotes and prose epigrams interspersed with verses.

S. also wrote many songs, and was famous for his ghazals; these are charged with emotion and almost free from traditional mystic symbolism. "His life and work reflect extensive empirical knowledge; both are rich in anecdotes adorned with epigrams and verses. To inform his readers and his listeners is his main objective" (Goethe).

S. became known in Europe as one of the foremost Persian poets through the translations of the seventeenth-century scholar A. Olearius.

Selected English translations: Immortal Rose, tr. A. J. Arberry, 1948; *Stories from Sa'di's Bustan and Gulistan,* tr. R. Levy, 1928

SA'DI SEE SAADI

SAKSE (Pseud. of *Absalom, Anna*)

Born January 16, 1905, Vidzeme (County of Lejasciems). Latvian Soviet novelist.

S., the daughter of a peasant, studied philology in Riga until

1927, after which she worked as a translator and proofreader. She published her first poems in the same year. A few years later she established contact with the illegal Communist Party organization. Since the re-establishment of Soviet power she has been active in both journalism and literature. Her best-known work is the novel *Pret kalnu* [The Field without Boundary Stones, 1948] in which she describes collectivization. She was awarded the State Prize for this novel in 1949. S. has recently been working on fairy tales for adults. She holds the title of People's Writer of the Latvian ASSR.

Further Works: Darba cilts (1941); *Atgriešanas dzvive* (1945)

SALTYKOV-SHCHEDRIN, MIKHAIL YEVGRAFOVICH
Born January 27, 1826, Spas-Ugol (Tver province); died May 10, 1889, St. Petersburg. Russian satirist of world rank.

S. came from a noble family. Ever since childhood, he was repelled by the serfdom system. Between 1838 and 1844 he attended the lyceum in Tzarskoe Selo, and was subsequently appointed to a position in the war ministry in St. Petersburg. At this time he showed great interest in the revolutionary ideas of Belinski as well as in the French utopian socialism of G. Sand and Fourier. He was a member of the secret circle around Petrashevtzy and propagated utopian socialism in his stories *Protivorechiya* [Contradictions, 1847] and *Zaputannoye delo* [An Entangled Affair, 1848]. These stories caused him to be exiled to Vyatka between 1848 and 1855. He received a pardon in 1855, and continued to work in the civil service in order to be able to continue to do at least a little in the interests of the people. He was appointed vice governor in Ryazan and Tver, but became more and more hated by the tsarist bureaucracy, and in 1868 finally left the civil service.

Between 1863 and 1864 S. was a frequent contributor to *Sovremennik*, and developed into one of the leading revolutionary democratic writers. Between 1868 and 1884—until 1877 in cooperation with N. Nekrasov—he was the publisher of the leading democratic magazine *Otechestvennyye zapiski* [Patriotic Writings]. Until his death in 1889 S. was regarded as the incorruptible guardian of the revolutionary tradition in Russian literature. S. achieved his first literary success with the *Gubernskiye ocherki* [Sketches from the Underground, 1856–57], in which he drew on the experiences gained in Vyatka and in which he depicted the provincial nobility, the estate owners, and the civil servants in a satirical manner. S.'s literary activities reached their peak in the 1870s and 1880s. Between 1869–70 he created *Istoriya odnovo goroda* [The Story of a Town], a work that is counted among the classical satires of world literature. This work, which is in the form of a historical chronicle, exposes the political despotism and pseudoliberalism of tsarism. Using allegorical imagery, S. predicted the victorious outcome of the Russian revolution.

S. next wrote an entire series of masterful political satires, all of which exhibit the characteristic cyclic form used in his portrait and milieu sketches. These satires include *Gospoda Tashkentzy* [The Gentlemen of Tashkent, 1869–72], an indictment of tsarist colonial policies in central Asia, and *Pompadury i pompadurshi* [Pompadour and Lady Pompadour, 1873–74], a satire on the favoritism and two-faced political game of autocracy. *Blagonamerennyye rechi* [Kind Speeches, 1863–76] and *Za rubezhom* [The Journey to Paris, 1880–81] are satirically exaggerated expositions of Russian and Western European capitalism and of the antagonisms existing between them, while *Sovremennaya idilliya* [Contemporary Idylls, 1877–83] and *Melochi zhizni* [Small Matters of Life, 1886–87] are expositions of the political reaction and the intellectual obscurantism of the 1880s.

In his most important novel, *Gospoda Golovliovy* (1875–80; The Golovlov, 1961), S. depicts the gradual decline of a noble Russian family over a period of three generations, demonstrating also the downfall of Russian feudal society. The cycle of sketches entitled *Poshekhonskaya starina* [The Province Poshekhonia, 1887–89] describe the old serfdom order in Russia. A final review of his many-sided poetic themes was presented by S. in his *Skazki* (1869, 1880–86; Tales, 1956), which are counted among his most popular works. In these stories S. castigated the parasitic bureaucracy, the nobility who existed as parasites on the serfdom order, the intimidated bourgeois intelligentsia, and the venal liberals. In these stories he described the misery of the masses and expressed his belief in the ultimate triumph of revolution and humanity.

Editions: Polnoye sobraniye sochinenii [Complete Works], 12 vols., Moscow, 1933–41; *Sobraniye sochinenii* [Collected Works], 12 vols., Moscow, 1951 *Further Works: Smert Pazukhina* (1857; The Death of Pazukhin, 1924); *Nevinnyye rasskazy* [Innocent Tales] (1857–63); *Satiri v proze* [Satires in Prose] (1859–62); *Priznaki vremeni* [Characteristics of the Times] (1863–71); *Nasha osshchestvennaya zhizn* [Our Social Life] (1863–64); *Pisma o provintzii* [Letters about the Provinces] (1868–1870); *Dnevnik provintziala v Peterburg* [Diary of a Provincial in Petersburg] (1872); *Kulturnyye lyudi* [Cultured People] (1876); *Ubezhishche Monrepo* [The Flight of Monrepo] (1878–79); *Krugly god* [The Whole Year] (1879–80); *Pisma k tiotenke* [Letters to Auntie] (1881–82); *Son v letnuyu noch* [A Summernight's Dream] (1881)

SAMUILIONAK, EDUARD LUDWIGAVICH
Born June 25, 1907, St. Petersburg; died February 12, 1939. Byelorussian Soviet short-story writer and novelist.
After 1918 S., the son of a workingman, lived in the country; after 1934 he lived in Minsk. He wrote a total of some thirty stories and novels, as well as a number of plays. In his novel *Buduchynya* [The Future, 1938], which today is regarded as being among the most important works of Byelorussian literature, S. describes the fight of the Georgian workers against the Menshevik government of 1921; the theme of international solidarity among workers dominates this novel.

Editions: Sbor tvorov [Collected Works], 2 vols., Minsk, 1952

SARIAN, GEGAM

Born December 25, 1902, Tabriz (Iran). Armenian Soviet poet. In his poems S. extols the socialist reconstruction of the 1920s and 1930s, as well as friendship among the Soviet peoples. His patriotic ballads and poems are characterized by their dramatic strength and by great psychological understanding. S. also wrote plays and several novels in verse, most of which had the postwar life of the Armenian villages as their theme.

SARYKHANOV, NURMURAD

Born in 1904 in the region of Ashkhabad; died May 4, 1944 (killed in action). Turkmenian Soviet novelist.

S. was greatly influenced by the works of A. Chekhov and M. Gorki. He is regarded as the founder of realism in Turkmenian literature. S.'s works describe the changes that took place in the Turkmenian villages during collectivization and the prewar Five-Year Plans. They include *The Dream* (1938), *The Anger of the Bey* (1940), *The Book* (1941), and other works.

SASUNC'I DAVITH

Armenian heroic epic created between the fourth and tenth centuries, but appearing in written form for the first time in 1873.

This epic consists of four parts, in which four generations of heroes are described. The chief heroes of the first part are Sanasar and Bagdasar, of the second Sanasar's son Mger the Elder. The heroes of the third and fourth parts are Mger's son, David of Sasun, and Mger the Younger. This epic describes the fight of the Armenian people for liberation from the Arabs and other foreign oppressors. It also propagates the ideas of liberty and love of peace, and of friendship and solidarity between peoples. The artistic interweaving of old myths with actual historical events is characteristic of this work. Individual themes and ideas from *Sasunc'i Davith* have been used by both Tumanian and Isaakian writers in modern adaptations.

SAYANOV, VISSARION MIKHAILOVICH
Born June 16, 1903, Ivanushkinsk (Region of Irkutsk); died January 22, 1959. Soviet Russian novelist and journalist.
The first poems written by S. are dedicated to the Soviet Komsomols. S. wrote the novel *Nebo i zemlya* [The Sky and the Earth], which is about the beginnings of aviation in the Soviet Union, between 1935 and 1948. In *V boyakh za Leningrad: Zapiski voyennovo korrespondenta* [The Battles around Leningrad: Notes of a War Correspondent, 1943] S. described the heroic defense of Leningrad in World War II. In 1945 S. covered the Nuremburg war crime trials as a newspaper correspondent; his cycle of poems *Nyurbergski dnevnik* [Nuremburg Diary] appeared in 1948. His novel *Strana rodnaya* [My Homecountry, 1953–55] is about the great changes that have taken place in the consciousness of the people. S. was awarded the State Prize in 1949.

SCHREDRIN   See SALTYKOV-SCHREDRIN, MIKHAIL YEVGRAFOVICH

SCHWARTZ, YEVGENI LVOVICH
Born November 2, 1896, Rostov-on-Don; died January 15, 1958, Leningrad. Soviet Russian playwright and journalist.
In the late 1920s S. began to concentrate on his work as a dramatist. His first play, *Undervud* [Underwood, 1929], already indicated his involvement with an original, fantastic fairy-tale style which he was to develop successfully in his later works. His plays are of particular importance for the Soviet children's theater, although with respect to their significance they go far beyond that particular theater. S. was gifted in his ability to demonstrate political and moral questions of the day in allegorical and figurative form. He occasionally borrowed from well-known fairy tales in order to make his point.
Among S.'s best-known pieces are *Drakon* (1943; The Dragon, 1963), *Goly korol* [The Naked King, 1934], and *Ten* [The Shadow, 1940]. S.'s style is characterized by intellectual, pointed

dialogue and a romantic atmosphere. His clear-cut psychological and moral characterization, together with his use of irony and satire, is taken directly from the fairy tale.

Further Works: Snezhnaya koroleva [Snow Queen] (1938); *Obyknovennoye chudo* [An Ordinary Miracle] (1956); *Povest o molodykh suprugakh* [Story about a Young Married Couple] (1957)

SEIFULLIN, SAKEN (SADVAKAS)

Born July 12, 1894, Aul No. 1 near Nildinsk; died October 9, 1939, Alma Ata. Kazakh Soviet poet and statesman; one of the founders of Kazakh Soviet literature.

S., the son of a stock farmer, attended the teachers college in Omsk. He was one of the founders of Soviet power in Kazakhstan, and between 1920 and 1937 occupied a number of high positions, including that of cabinet council president. S. glorified the revolution, Lenin, and the new socialist life in stirring poems and verses, including *Sovietstan* (1926) and *Sotzialistan* (1935). S. also wrote strongly political poetry as well as the lyric epic *Kokchetau* (1935), the important historical novel *The Hard Road, the Difficult Transition* (1927), and a number of plays, including *Red Falcons* (1920).

SEIFULLINA, LYDIA NIKOLAYEVNA

Born April 3, 1889, Varlamovo (District of Orenburg); died April 25, 1954, Moscow. Soviet Russian novelist.

S. was a teacher. Her novel *Pravonarushiteli* [The Runaway, 1921] was among the first books to discuss the problem of children neglected during the civil war. She became known through her novels *Peregnoi* [Humus, 1922] and *Wirineya* (1925); the latter was dramatized in the same year. *Peregnoi* colorfully described the decisive, basic changes that took place in the villages after the revolution. In *Wirineya* S. showed how women after the revolution freed their minds from traditional bonds. During World War II S. wrote a series of short stories, including *Na svoyei zemle* [On Our Own Soil, 1942].

SELVINSKI, ILYA LVOVICH
Born October 24, 1899, Simferopol; died March 1, 1967. Soviet
Russian poet and dramatist.

S. took part in the civil war as a Red Guard partisan. Between
1924 and 1930 he was one of the foremost members of the Constructivist Party. He wrote his first poems in the early 1930s. S.
wrote a number of stories in verse based on events that took place
during the civil war and during the Antarctic voyage of the
"Chelyuskin," in which he had participated.

S.'s volumes of poetry contain love songs, renderings of Oriental
poetry, antifascist poems (written during his travels across Berlin
and the rest of Western Europe during the 1930s), and war
poems. S. also wrote a number of historical tragedies in verse,
including *Rytzar Ioan* [The Peasant Tsar Joan, 1927], *Orla na
pleche nosyashchi* [The Eagle on Our Shoulder, 1940], *Livon-
skaya voina* [The Livonian War, 1940], *Chitaya "Fausta"* [Read-
ing "Faust," 1947], and *Bolshoi Kiril* [The Great Cyril, 1954].
In 1960 he created the lyric poem *O vremeni o sebe* [On the
Times and On Myself], and in 1966 published the autobiographical novel *O yunost moya* [My Youth].

SERAFIMOVICH (Pseud. of *Aleksandr Serafimovich Popov*)
Born January 19, 1863, Stanitza Nizhne-Kurmoyarskaya (Don);
died January 19, 1949. Soviet Russian novelist; cofounder of
Soviet literature.

In 1887, while still a student in St. Petersburg, S. was exiled
to Mezen, north of Archangel, because of his connections with
the populist movement that was centered around Aleksandr
Ulyanov (Lenin's brother), and because of the publication of a
revolutionary leaflet. In 1902 he moved to Moscow, where he
became a member of the literary circle *Sreda* and later joined
Znaniye, a publishing house and literary organization founded
by M. Gorki. S. was an eyewitness to the December revolution
of 1905. His decisive attitude in the days of the October revolution was exemplary; in 1918 he became a member of the Bol-

shevist party and subsequently worked as a frontline journalist during the civil war. A member of RAPP, he worked actively toward the formation of a proletarian literature. Throughout his life S. remained occupied with numerous social and literary activities.

From the beginning of his literary career S. sided with the working classes. His works, even at this time, contained the essential elements of social realism. In his numerous early sketches and stories—*Na ldine* [On the Ice Floe, 1887] and *Strelochnik* [The Switch Man, 1891]—he described the miserable life and the hellish working conditions of the exploited people. The experiences of the 1905 revolution enabled him to give a realistic portrayal of the fighting proletariat (*Bomby* [Bombs, 1906]).

In the course of the following years S.'s realism became more profound, as is shown in his novels *Peski* (1908; Sand and Other Stories, 1955), which was highly regarded by L. Tolstoi, and *Gorod v stepni* [The Town in the Steppe, 1912]. The latter used the development of a town during the construction of one of the first Russian railroads to show the birth of capitalism and the path taken by the liberal intelligentsia, as well as the growing power of the working class.

The reports brought home by participants in the legendary Taman campaign (1918) stimulated S. to write his most important work, the novel *Zhelezny potok* (1924; The Iron Flood, 1935), which is counted among the classical works of Soviet literature. As was the case with many works written at that time, its heroes were the revolutionary masses. S. did, however, raise a number of characters above the mass—the army leader Kozukh and the peasant woman Gorpina among them—and, by using a concrete, historical method of presentation, explored the formative processes of socialist awareness more deeply than did the other authors of his time.

In his later years S. frequently took the socialist reconstruction of the Soviet land as his subject, as in his unfinished novel *Kolkhoznyye polya* [Kolkhoz Fields, 1933–39] and in several of his stories and sketches. S. considerably influenced many younger writers, including M. Sholokhov. He was awarded the State Prize in 1943.

SEREBRYAKOVA, GALINA IOSIFOVNA
Born December 20, 1905, Kiev. Soviet Russian biographer and novelist.

S. fought in the frontlines of the civil war. After the war she studied at the Worker and Peasant Faculty in Kiev and at the University of Moscow. She traveled extensively in Germany, Holland, Belgium, France, England, Italy, and Switzerland, collecting material for her literary work. It is thanks to S. that the figure of Karl Marx was introduced into the literary language of Russia. Even in her first work, *Zhenshchiny epokhi frantzuskoi revolyutzii* [Women of the Time of the French Revolution, 1929] S. had turned her thoughts toward historical themes.

S.'s efforts in the artistic presentation of significant historical events reached a peak in her trilogy *Prometei* [Prometheus, 1934–62], in which, with great factual knowledge, historical veracity, and artistic power she described the life of Karl Marx. Artistically combining biographical and fictional themes, S. succeeded in giving a broad and convincing picture of European life in the nineteenth century. The first volume of the trilogy, *Yunost Marksa* [Marx as a Youth, 1934–35] introduces the reader to the youth of her hero. The second volume, *Pokhishcheniya ognya* [The Rape of the Flame, 1960], describes Marx's life between 1844 and 1864, while the last volume, *Vershina zhisni* [The Peak of Life, 1962], discusses his last eighteen years.

In 1962 S. published *Svet neugasimy* [The Eternal Flame], which contained seven short stories on Lenin, Nadezhda Krupskaya, Dserzhinski, Furmanov, Dimitroff and other contemporary figures, as well as a scientific biography of Karl Marx.

Further Works: Lyudi iz predmestya Krua-Rus [People from the Suburb Croix Rousse] (1933); *Ochnaya stavka. Kartina angliiskoi zhizhni* [Confrontation: A Picture of English Life] (1933); *Stranstviya po minuvshim godam* [Journey through the Past Years] (1965)

SERGEYEV-TZENSKI, SERGEI NIKOLAYEVICH
Born September 30, 1875, Preoprazhenskoye; died December 3,
1958, Alushta. Soviet Russian novelist.
S. worked as a teacher; he held a doctorate in philology, and
was a member of the Academy of Sciences from 1943 until his
death. In his early stories S. described the decay of the personality in old Russia. Because of its pessimism we must assign this
work to a position close to decadence despite the strongly critical
features it exhibits. After the 1905 revolution we find a decisive
transition to critical realism in S.'s work, as is shown in his novel
Babayev (1907).
In 1913–14 S. began his major work, the multi-volume novel
Preobrazheniye Rosii [The Transformation of Russia]; the first
volume, *Valya*, indicates that the need for a constantly changing
life is to be regarded as a necessary inner change for man.
The October revolution led S. to discuss greater social and historical problems. Among his works at this time is *Obrechonnyye
na gibel* [Those Destined for Destruction, 1923]. His discussions
of Soviet life, especially in his stories about Soviet youth and in
his novel *Iskat, vsegda iska* [Searching, Always Searching, 1934]
led S. on a successful search for the positive hero. In the novels
depicting World War II, including *Brusilovski proryv* (1943–44;
Brusilov's Breakthrough, 1945) he re-created the great patriotic
traditions of the Russian people.
After the war he dealt with the relations between the intelligentsia and the people, as in *Preobrazheniye cheloveka* (1955;
Transfiguration, 1962). S. also wrote a number of other works,
including a long novel about the Crimean War entitled *Sevasto-
polskaya strata* [The Hot Days of Sevastopol, 1936–38], for which
he was awarded the State Prize in 1941. This novel is one of the
most important historical novels in Soviet literature.

Further Works: Ledokhod [Floating Ice] (1923); *Zdrastvui zhizn*
[Hello, Life] (1925)

SESPEL, MISHSHI (Pseud. of *Mikhail Kuzmin*)
Born November 16, 1899, Shugurov (District of Kazan); died
June 15, 1922, Starogorodka (Ukraine). Chuvash Soviet poet.
S. was the founder of Chuvash Soviet poetry. He was influ-
enced by Russian literature, especially by Gorki. In passionate
verses—*The Plowing of the New Day* (1921) and *Far in the
Field* (1921)—he glorified the rebirth of the Chuvash people
during the October revolution and extolled creative work in gen-
eral. The renewal of life is demonstrated by him in his poem
The Chuvash Language.

SHAGINYAN, MARIETTA SERGEYEVNA
Born March 21, 1888, Moscow. Soviet Russian poet and novelist
of Armenian origin.
S., who held a doctoral degree in philosophy, wrote poems,
sketches, and novels. Disassociation from her earlier idealistic
views is already evident in her collection *Orientalia* (1913). She
overcame her formalistic tendencies in her novel *Kik* (1929),
although some of her earlier works—the novels *Permena* [The
Change, 1922–23] and *Proklvucheniye iz obshchestva* [The Adventures of a Lady, 1923]—had already been dedicated to the
theme of revolution. Despite the fact that it is not an entirely
mature work from the artistic point of view, her novel *Gidrotzentral* [The Hydroelectric Plant, 1930–31] is of particular importance since it is one of the first works of Soviet literature in which
the theme of work and its determinant influence is used to present
the development of positive moral qualities.
In the postwar years S. has attained fame with her novel *Semya
Ulyanovykh* [The Family Ulyanov, 1957], with collections of
sketches such as *Puteshestviye po Sovyetskoi Armenii* (1950;
Journey through Soviet Armenia, 1954), for which she was
awarded the State Prize in 1951, and with works on the history
of literature, including an autobiography of Goethe (1952).

Editions: Sobraniye sochinenii [Collected Works], 6 vols., Moscow,
1956

SHAMYAKIN, IVAN PAYATROVICH
  Born January 30, 1921, Karma (Region of Gomel). Byelorussian Soviet novelist.
  S., who came from a poor peasant family, became a village schoolteacher. His literary career started after World War II with a series of short stories. He was awarded the State Prize in 1951 for his novel about the partisans, *Glybokaya plyn* [Deep Currents, 1949]. His novel *U dobry chas* [In Good Time, 1953] describes life in the Byelorussian villages after the war.
  In his novel *Krynitzy* [Sources, 1956], S. tells of the changes in the villages after 1953, while in the novel cycle *Trevozhnoye shchastye* [Disquieted Happiness, 1957–59] he writes of his own youth. His novel *Serdze na ladoni* [The Heart Is Never Alone] has become very popular in the Soviet Union.

SHAROV, ALEKSANDR ALEKSEYEVICH
  Born April 13, 1904, Semionovskaya near Moscow. Soviet Russian poet and journalist.
  Between 1916 and 1918 S., who has been publishing since 1919, occupied a number of positions in the Komsomol movement. Since 1925 he has been working as an editor and journalist. His poems, filled with *joie de vivre* and optimism, sing of work, youth, and love. The theme of spring predominates in his descriptions of nature. His poem *Garmon* [The Harmonica, 1926] has been especially popular.

SHCHIPACHOV, STEPAN PETROVICH
  Born January 7, 1899, Shchipachi (Urals). Soviet Russian poet.
  S. was a farm hand and shop assistant. He joined the Red Army in 1919 and soon became a political functionary. His first volume of poems, *Po kurganam vekov* [Graves of the Century, 1923], was dedicated to the events of the time, although it also contained a number of short poems on love and on the gradually changing ways of our world. During World War II S. was a war correspondent. In 1944 he wrote a poem on Lenin entitled *Domik v Shushenskom* [The Little House in Shushenskoye]. He was

awarded State Prizes in 1949 and 1951 for his *Stikhotvoreniya* [Poems, 1948] and for the poem *Pavlik Morozov* (1951).

SHEFNER, VADIM DERGEYEVICH

Born January 12, 1915, Petrograd. Soviet Russian poet and short-story writer.

S. was an apprentice in the Chemical Training Combine in Leningrad. During World War II he fought at the front near Leningrad. S.'s poems link the great problems of our times with naturalistic pictures of the city, the sky, and of man, as can be seen in his collections of poems entitled *Znaki zemli* [Signs of the Earth, 1961] and *Ryadom z nebom* [Beside the Sky, 1962].

S.'s short stories show the writer's constant effort to rediscover and redefine his own milieu.

SHEININ, LEV ROMANOVICH

Born March 25, 1906, Brusovanka near Smolensk. Soviet Russian novelist.

Between 1923 and 1950 S. occupied leading judicial positions. He was Soviet deputy chief prosecutor in the Nuremburg trials in 1945–46. His first works, most of which were exciting criminal and spy stories, appeared in 1928. The basic theme of many of S.'s books is the rehabilitation under socialism of people who have become politically alienated. S. was awarded a number of State Prizes for his work.

SHESTEV, MIKHAIL (Pseud. of *Mark Ilyich Levinson*)

Born October 19, 1902, Kreslavl (District of Vitebsk). Soviet Russian short-story writer and novelist.

After attending the University of Saratov S. worked in the Leningrad office of *Pravda*. His collections of sketches entitled *Den velikikh rabot* [The Day of the Great Work, 1929] and *Gody i lyudi* [Years and Men, 1932] tell of the growth of industrialization and collectivization during the early 1930s. His *Novelly o ehustvakh* [Short Stories on Emotions] appeared in 1933. After the war S. published sketches about the Soviet village of today, including *Derevenskiye ocherki* [Sketches from the Village, 1947] and *Pod odnoi kryshei* [Under One Roof, 1955]. S.'s best-known work is the novel *Zolotoye koltzo* [The Golden Ring, 1958], in which, using his own experience as the basis for the novel, he describes the situation existing in the Soviet villages. His novel *Tatyana Tarkhanova* (1962) tells of the fate of a peasant family.

SHEVCHENKO, TARAS

Born March 9, 1814, Moryintzy (District of Kïev); died March 10, 1861, St. Petersburg. Ukrainian national poet; founder of critical realism in Ukrainian literature; prominent painter; revolutionary, democratic pioneer in the social and national liberation of the Ukraine.

S., the son of a serf, was orphaned at the age of eleven. He became the servant of a brutal estate owner, who, noticing the boy's artistic talent, arranged that he should undergo training as a court painter in St. Petersburg. In 1838 S. was bought off and freed from his serfdom by friends. He subsequently studied with great success at the St. Petersburg Art School.

In the mid-1840s S. established contact with revolutionary circles and, after his return to the Ukraine, was arrested and sent into exile in Siberia for ten years (1847–57). He was not permitted to undertake any artistic activities while in exile. In the last years of his life in St. Petersburg S. was closely connected with the group of revolutionary democrats led by Chernyshevski.

In his uniquely expressive works S. depicted the profound feelings and hopes of the Ukrainian peasants and their will to fight against the yoke of oppression. His closeness to the nature and traditions of the Ukrainian people, as well as his own close association with nature, resulted in a great number of folksong-like poems, ballads, historical stories in verse form, socio-critical poems, and sensitive lyrics.

The poetic work of S. is based chiefly on three major themes: the everyday life in the Ukrainian village, with its profound conflicts, joys, and sufferings; the heroic past of the Ukraine; and the self-sacrificing fight of the Ukrainian peasantry against both the tsarist oppressors and the traitors among their own people. In his most important work, the collection of poems about one of the nameless Ukrainian bards entitled *Kobzar* (1840; The Kobzor of the Ukraine, 1922), to which he constantly added new poems, S. depicted the many-sided world of the Ukrainian peasant village in all its unique charm and characteristic color.

The nucleus of *Kobzar* is the great historical ballad *Gaidamay* [The Haidamaks, 1841], in which S. drew a colorful picture of the heroic Cossack uprising of 1768. By depicting the revolutionary traditions of Ukrainian history he invited a critical comparison with the traditions of his own time. Other works calling for revolution against the yoke of the estate owners, the civil servants, and the tsar may be found in his poem about Jan Huss entitled *Yeretik* [The Heretic, 1845], the satirical poem *Son* [The Dream, 1844], and the poem *Zapovit* [The Testament, 1845]. The last-named may be counted among the most popular Ukrainian revolutionary songs. In his lyrical political writings, S. frequently adopted the biblical, religious traditions inherent among the peasants. These traditions appealed to the Ukrainian people because they considered their battles for social and national liberation to be religious struggles. S.'s poem *Maria*, a secular paraphrase on the life of the Virgin Mary, represents a work of worldwide literary significance.

The poetic work of S., a synthesis of profound philosophical ideas, progressive politics, and high artistic mastery, represents the unsurpassed peak of the Ukrainian literature of the nineteenth century. S.'s originality, his close association with the lower classes, and his surprisingly wide breadth of culture and intellectual capacities enabled him to express perfectly the thoughts and feelings of the peasants of his Ukrainian homeland.

S.'s work continues to be alive in the hearts of the people, and to be a determinant factor in the development of Ukrainian culture and literature, exerting influences that go far beyond the borders of the Ukraine. Many of his works have been translated into numerous languages.

Editions: Povne zibranny tvoriv [Collected Works], 10 vols., Kiev, 1951–53; *Sobranniye sochinenii* [Collected Works], 5 vols., Moscow, 1955–56
Further Works: Kateryna [Catherine] (1838); *Khudozhnyk* [The Artist] (1856)
Selected English translations: Translations from S., tr. A. Stefan (1947)

SHIRVANZADE (Pseud. of *Movesian, Aleksandr*)
Born April 4, 1858, Shemakha (Azerbaidzhan); died August 7, 1935, Kislovodsk. Armenian novelist and playwright.

S. describes the rise and fall of the Armenian bourgeoisie from the 1880s to the establishment of Soviet power. His heroes are manufacturers and workers, artisans and peasants. His novel *Chaos* (1898) describes the decline of a Baku millionaire's family; in it S. included details of the social and political life of the times. He was, however, unable to comprehend the historical role of the proletariat.

Editions: Izbrannyye sochineniya [Collected Works] (in Russian), 3 vols., Tiflis, 1936–38
Further Works: Vardan Arumian (1902)

SHISHKOV, VYACHESLAV YAKOVLEVICH
Born October 3, 1875, Beshetzk (Province of Tver); died March 6, 1945, Moscow. Soviet Russian novelist.

The work of S. is almost entirely devoted to life in pre- and postrevolutionary Siberia. A number of minor works on these themes gradually led to the two high points of his work. The first of these was the novel *Ugryum reka* [The Dark Stream, 1933], in which S. showed the decline of a merchant family and depicted the past history of Siberia up to the time of the revolution. The second high point in S.'s work was the historical novel *Yemelyan Pugachov* (1938). This work, which was in three volumes, described the activities of Pugachev and the uprising of the people

 M. Y. Saltykov-Shchedrin

Serafimovich

T. Shevchenko

M. A. Sholokhov

Sholom-Aleykhem

in connection with the rising power of the social movement in the eighteenth century.

Editions: Sobraniye sochinenii [Collected Works], 8 vols., Moscow, 1960

SHOGENTZUKOV, ALI AHKHADOVICH
Born in 1900; died November 29, 1941. Kabardian Soviet poet and short-story writer; most important representative of Kabardian Soviet literature.

S., the son of a poor peasant family, was first employed as a teacher, but worked as a writer from 1935 on. S.'s poems and stories have shown him to be a talented poet and master of both his own language and the history of the Kabardian people. His verse novel *Kambot and Lyaza* (1932–36) is considered to be one of the most important works of Kabardian literature. In it S. depicts the powerful figures of the working people as they do battle against the despotism of the princes.

S. introduced Russian verse forms into Kabardian literature; he himself was greatly influenced by Lermontov. He translated Gorki's *Song of the Stormy Petrel* and *Song of the Falcon* into the Kabardian language.

SHOLOKHOV, MIKHAIL ALEKSANDROVICH
Born May 24, 1905, Khutor Krushiliny (Stanitza Vioshen-skaya). Soviet Russian novelist and short-story writer. One of the most important contributors to world literature.

S. is a member of the Supreme Soviet of the USSR, and a member of the Academy of Sciences. He has received numerous honorary doctoral degrees. S. comes from a Cossack family; in 1920 he took part in the battles against the armies of the White Guard. He has lived in Stanitza Vioshenskaya since 1926.

S. first became known as a writer at the age of eighteen. Between 1923 and 1926 he wrote a number of stories and novellas that first appeared individually. In 1926 these stories were published in two collections entitled *Donskiye rasskazy* [Stories from the Don] and *Lazorevaya step* [The Shimmering Steppe]. Using dramatic, highly emotional situations, S. here describes how the class battles that were taking place in the first half of the 1920s demanded a decision either for or against the revolution from each individual. He shows how such conflicts caused separations and heartache between adults and children, often with father and son or lover and beloved in opposite camps—*Rodinka* [The Birthmark] and *Shibalkovo* [The Shibalkovo Family].

S.'s stories about the simple, uneducated fighter for Soviet power are usually characterized by tragic, optimistic emotions (*Smertnyi vrag* [The Mortal Enemy]). The absorption of socialist, humanistic ideas into the minds of both child and woman are presented in emotionally accented terms in *Nakhalionok* [The Bastard] and in *Dvukhmuzhnyaya* [The Woman with the Two Husbands]. The very slow turning of the Cossacks from their original conservative position toward a gradual acceptance of Soviet power is also described by S. in *Chuzhaya krov* [Alien Blood], which has been made into a film.

S.'s greatest novel is *Tikhi Don* (Book I, 1928, Book II, 1929, Book III, 1933, Book IV, 1940. The entire work appears in English as two consecutive novels, *And Quiet Flows the Don* [1934] and *The Don Flows Home to the Sea* [1940]; these were later combined in one volume as *The Silent Don* [1942]). It is considered one of the world's most famous works of literature. S. was awarded the State Prize in 1941 for this work, which has been filmed twice, once in 1930 and again in 1958. In an artistically convincing manner and in epic and frequently highly dramatic scenes S. presents for the first time in Soviet literature the complex developmental problems of an entire people—the Don Cossacks. In this work S. discussed the initial move toward Soviet power of the politically prejudiced peasant classes, and the changes taking place in the social and political conditions in the Don region during the decade between 1912 and 1922, as well as the historical events and personalities of that period. S. traces, with great knowledge and understanding, the meaning of life and of man's responsibility for both his own acts and those of society, as well as the problem of individual happiness.

S. describes the customs and habits of the Don Cossacks, their peasant ties to the soil, and their enmity toward the non-Cossack population, to whom they deny the right to own land. In moving, frequently lyrical, episodic form, the author shows how the Cossacks suffered inhuman treatment at the time of the Imperialist war. These personal experiences promote the people's sympathy for the Bolsheviks, a feeling, however, that becomes fully effective only when their hopes of taking a separate path in the revolution fails in the face of reality. The working people among them finally come to realize that only Soviet power will do justice to their desire for a peaceful life. This basic theme is developed by individual characters and, in Books II and III, by the collective image of the people—the working Cossacks.

The central figure of this novel—and one of S.'s greatest artistic creations—is Grigori Melekhov. Melekhov's conscious break with the outdated moral views held by Khutor when he makes his decision in favor of the already married Aksinya, and his protest against the inhumanities of war, are evidence of his spontaneous readiness for progress. The tragic aspect of Grigori lies in the fact that he seeks to take a separate way in the socialist revolution even while he is fighting for it. This finally delivers him into the hands of his enemies. His guilt, which cannot be eradicated by his later re-entry into the Red Army, begins when, as one of the leaders of a counterrevolutionary uprising, against his own better judgment he leads his Cossacks against the Soviet forces and thereby causes much bloodshed. By the concluding chapter of this work it is apparent that Grigori Melekhov is a complete failure despite the fact that he himself had actually arrived at theoretical views similar to those held by the majority of the working Cossacks, whose representative he has been shown to be in the first two books. The basic character of the entire novel, however, is profoundly optimistic. In a symbolic, realistic manner, S. shows that the victory of the modern era in the formerly antiquated Don region is as incontrovertible and as ordered as the eternal cycle of natural processes.

S.'s novel *Podnyataya tzelina* (Book I, 1932, Book II, 1955–59;

Eng., *Virgin Soil Upturned*, 1935; Am., *Seeds of Tomorrow*, 1935) is of great significance. This work, which S. began in 1930, has been made into a film and received the Lenin Prize in 1960. In this novel, dramatic descriptions of situations are combined with masterful psychological characterization. The work is an integral whole despite the fact that the structures of the action are different in the two volumes. The main theme of the novel is the cooperation between the party and the people in the revolutionary reconstruction of a village. The development of socialist consciousness among the Don Cossacks is shown in the figure of Kondrat Maidannikov and in numerous secondary figures. Those exhibiting the richest inner life are the Communists Davydov, Nagulnov, and Razmiotnov; the White Guardists Polovtzev and Lyatyevski are shown to be empty and depraved. The striving for the re-establishment of the reactionary order in the Don region leads to the complete dehumanization of the emotionally unreliable kulak Ostronov, who always opposes Soviet power. S.'s socialist humanism and his appreciation of the simple man is also made evident by the author's repeated use of interspersed, novella-like sketches to describe his so-called secondary figures.

In his novel *Oni zrazhalis za rodinu* [They Fought for Their Homeland, 1943–59], which is as yet not complete, although a number of chapters were published in *Pravda*, S. describes the difficult military situation in the USSR in the summer of 1942, at the time when the fascist armies were pushing in the direction of Stalingrad. The parts of the work so far published are episodic in structure and are characterized by optimistic emotions. They are permeated with an awareness that gives the reader an idea of the sufferings of the people. The leading figures—for the first time in S.'s work—represent people from different parts of the Soviet country. The basic idea expounded in this novel—hate (in the name of humanity) considered as a necessary requirement for victory over the fascist enemy—may already be found in his sketch *Nauka nenavisti* (1942; The Science of Hatred, 1945). The biography of its hero, Lieutenant Gerasimov, resembles that of Andrei Sokolov, the hero of *Sudba cheloveka* (1956–57; One

Man's Destiny, and Other Stories, 1967), which first appeared in *Pravda* and was subsequently made into a film.

Sudba cheloveka occupies an important position in recent Soviet literature. It shows in concentrated, dramatic form the epic and at the same time poetic talents of S. As a driver at the front and later as a prisoner of war in fascist Germany, Sokolov is not the type of war hero usually found in novels. He nevertheless becomes a heroic figure, never developing into a self-centered, passive sufferer, but always acting in a humanistic manner because of his feeling of responsibility for his own acts and for those occurring around him. By bringing all his interests and energy to bear on behalf of those close to him and on his people suffering in the war he becomes the master of his own life. Andrei Sokolov embodies the best features of the Soviet Russian national character. A a literate non-party communist he is a symbol for the invincibility of the socialist way of life.

S. was awarded the Nobel Prize in 1965.

Editions: Sobraniye sochinenii [Collected Works], 8 vols., Moscow, 1956–60
Selected English translations: Tales of the Don, tr. H. C. Stevens (1962)

SHOLOM-ALEYKHEM (Pseud. of *Sholum Nokhumovich Rabinovich*)

Born March 2, 1859, Pereyaslav; died May 13, 1916, New York. Yiddish novelist.

S.'s literary activities go back to 1879. He wrote first in Hebrew but then turned to the Yiddish language. He wrote stories, novellas, novels, plays, sketches, poems, and essays. S. was the personal friend of many Russian writers, and corresponded with Chekhov and Gorki. He emigrated to the United States following the pogroms of 1905–06. S.'s democratic and humanistic views and his deep sense of responsibility for the fate of the eastern European Jews found expression in his novels and stories—works which have made him immortal as a popular Jewish writer.

S.'s fiction exhibits a sensitive humor which is reflected in both the lovingly presented traditional figures from the Jewish bourgeoisie and in a critically viewed reality. In his literary and critical essays S. favored a realistic view of reality.

Among S.'s most important works are the novels *Tevye der Milkhiker* [Tevye the Milkman, 1894], which contains stories from the lives of simple Russian Jews, and *Mottl Peysi dem Khazns* (1907; The Adventures of Mottle the Cantor's Son, 1953), the odyssey of a Jewish family from their beginnings in the Ukraine to their life in New York.

Further Works: Blondzende Shtern (1912; Wandering Star, 1952); *Altnay Kasrilevke* (1918; Inside Kasrilevke, 1948); *Funem Yarid* (1924; The Great Fair, 1955)
Selected English translations: Stories and Satires by S.A., tr. C. Leviant (1959)

SHTORM, GEORGI PETROVICH
Born September 25, 1898, Rostov-on-Don. Soviet Russian novelist.

S.'s work, which first became known in the 1930s, consists almost exclusively of historical novels. Among his early novels are *Povest o Bolotnikove* [Stories from Bolotnikove, 1930], *Trudy i dni Mikhaila Lomonosova* [The Deeds and Days of Mikhail Lomonosov, 1932], and *Na pole Kulikovom* [On the Kulikovo Field, 1938]. In 1946 he published his best-known novel, *Flotovodetz Ushakov* [Admiral Ushakov], in which he described the battles fought against Turkey in 1787–92 by the Russian Black Sea fleet under Ushakov.

Further Works: Stranitzy morskoi slavy [Stories about Sea Life] (1954); *Potaionny Radishchev* [Secretive Radishchev] (1965)

SIMEON POLOTZKI (Pseud. of *Simeon Petrovski-Sitnianovich,* formerly *Samuil Yemelyanovich*)
Born 1629, Polotzk; died August 25, 1680, Moscow. Russian poet and playwright.

S. P. received a theological education in Kiev, and later became court poet and tutor of the children of tsar Aleksis I Mikhailovich

(1645–76). S. P. was the first person to introduce syllabic poetic writing into Russia. In addition to theological and rhetorical papers he wrote two comedies, a book of psalms in verse (1680), hymns, and panegyric poems. His work shows the beginnings of a satirical presentation of monastic life.

S. P. founded the first Russian school for poets, which included among its members both Silvestr Medvedev (1641–91) and Karion Istomin (circa 1700).

Editions: Izbrannyye sochineniya [Selected Works], 1953

SIMONOV, KONSTANTIN (CYRIL) MIKHAILOVICH

Born November 28, 1915, Petrograd. Soviet Russian novelist, poet, playwright, and journalist.

S. studied at the Gorki Institute of Literature in Moscow in 1938. Among his first literary works we find the poems *Dom* [The House, 1935], and *Povest o tryokh bratyakh* [The Story of the Three Brothers, 1936], in which he regards himself as a contemporary of the social revolution. Beginning in the mid-1930s S.'s work gradually becomes characterized by antifascist themes. This is evident in his first volume of poems *Nastoya-shchiye lyudi* [True Men, 1938]. His collection of poems *Druzya i vragi* (1948; rev. ed., 1954; Friends and Foes, 1955) is dedicated to the worldwide fight against war and fascism. S. has written numerous sketches, poems, and stories about the heroic life of the simple Soviet people during World War II. His short novel *Dni i nochi* (1943; Days and Nights, 1945) is one of the great Soviet prose works on the battle of Stalingrad.

The first three novels—*Tovarishchi po oruzhiya, Zhivye i miortvyye*, and *Soldatami ne rozhdayutsya*—of the as yet unfinished series on World War II are based on S.'s personal experiences, and occupy an important place in Soviet war literature.

The novel *Tovarishchi po oruzhiya* [Comrade in Arms, 1952] deals with the battle of Soviet and Mongol troops against the Japanese aggressors in 1939. The tragic end of the Spanish civil war is also mentioned, and the novel ends with the liberation of the western regions of Byelorussia and the Ukraine.

In *Zhivyye i miortvyye* [The Living and Dead, 1959] S. outlined the tragic military events of June–November 1941, creating a story rich in episodes—a monument for the many true supporters of the Soviet whose sacrifices prevented catastrophe at that time. The theme of this work is continued in the novel *Soldatami ne rozhdayutsya* [Soldiers Are Not Born, 1964], which is about the battle of Stalingrad. A number of the characters who first appeared in the earlier novels of the cycle reappear, but in this later volume they are psychologically more motivated. The main idea of the novel—that men can learn to become soldiers but will never get used to war—is particularly well presented in the figure of General Serpilin. Stalin has also been well described in this work.

S.'s dramatic work, too, is characterized by some of the themes outlined above. A number of plays, including *Istoriya odnoi lyubvi* [The Story of a Love, 1939–40] and *Russkiye lyudi* (1942; Russian People, 1942), have themes closely connected with S.'s lyric poetry. The participation of Soviet soldiers in the civil war in Spain is the theme of S.'s play *Paren is pashevo goroda* [A Boy from Our Town, 1941], while the relationship of friends and enemies again appears in the drama *Ruski vopros* (1946; The Russian Question, 1947). S. discusses the idea of the responsibility of the living for the legacy of the dead in his drama *Chetvyorty* [The Fourth Man, 1961].

S. has also written a number of war and travel sketches. He was awarded State Prizes in 1942, 1943, 1946, 1947, 1949, and 1950.

Further Works: Voyennye dnevniki [War Diaries] (1945); *Chuzhaya ten* [Foreign Shadow] (1949); *Yuzhnyye povesti* [Southern Tales] (1962); *Kazhdy den dlinnyi* [Every Day Is Long] (1965)

SIMUSHKIN, TIKHON ZAKHAROVICH

Born June 26, 1900, Staraya Kutlya (Pensa). Soviet Russian novelist.

S. studied the problems of northern peoples at the University of Moscow, and was a member of the first Soviet expedition to visit the land of the Chukchi people in 1924. He was the co-author of the first grammar of the Chukchi language.

The complex transition from patriarchal conditions to the new order, the fierce arguments with the keepers of the old order, with ignorance, prejudices, and superstition, and the desire of the small community of the Chukchi for knowledge are vividly described in S.'s book *Chukotka* [In the Land of the Chukchi People, 1939] and in the novel *Alitet ukhodit v gory* (1948; Alitet Goes to the Hills, 1952), for which he was awarded the State Prize of 1949. His novel *Priklyucheniya Aivama* [Aivam's Adventure, 1955] describes the life of the Chukchi people of today.

SLONIMSKI, MIKHAIL LEONODOVICH

Born August 13, 1897, Pavolvsk. Soviet Russian novelist.

S. began his literary activities in 1917. His stories re-created events and people of the wartime period. During the revolution he became a member of "The Serapion Brothers" literary group.

In his novel *Lavrovy* [The Lavrovs, 1926, rev. ed., 1948], S. demonstrated how a man from the bourgeois intelligentsia found his way to acceptance of the revolution. In *Povest o Levine* [The Story of Eugene Levine, 1936] he showed the brave stand taken by the leader of the Bavarian Soviet republic during his trial in the 1920s. The short stories in *Pogranichniki* [Frontier Guards, 1937] show how heroism in man grows out of the everyday events of his daily life. *Strela* [The Arrow, 1945] represents a marked achievement among S.'s war stories. The theme of the progressive Russian intelligentsia during the early years of this century is dealt with in his novel *Inzhenery* [Engineers, 1950], while the spiritual and cultural backwardness of the simple people of the older society and the conquest of this backwardness by the events of the revolution are shown in his novel *Duzya* [Friends, 1954].

Further Works: Shestoi strelkovyi [The Sixth Rifle Battalion] (1922); *Foma Kleshniov* [Foma Kleshniov] (1930); *Pervyi god* [The First Year] (1949)

Slovo o polku Igoreve (The Lay of the Host of Igor)
An anonymous, heroic epic of strongly rhetorical character, this is considered to be the most prominent literary work of art in Old Russian literature.

Slovo o polku Igoreve has as its subject the unsuccessful military campaign of Prince Igor Sviatoslavich of Novgorod-Seversk against the nomadic tribe of the Polovetzy in 1185. This song was first discovered in 1795 by A. I. Musin-Pushkin, in the form of a manuscript copy from the sixteenth century which was later destroyed by the Moscow fire of 1812. It was first published in 1800. Because of its high idealism and great artistic values, *Slovo* has greatly influenced the subsequent development of Russian literature and art in general.

The song describes the fight of the southern Russian princedoms against the threat of invasion; the military campaign of Prince Igor up to the time of his defeat and imprisonment; the magnificent speech by the Grand Duke Sviatoslav reflecting the patriotic idea of Russian unity around Kiev and demanding unified action instead of civil war between the princes; and, finally, Igor's flight and his return, and the moving lament of Yaroslavna, which has all the fresh magic of the Russian folksong.

Masterful linguistic and creative power, utilizing contemporary genres and a strong, rhythmical prose, make *Slovo* a poetic work that has placed the Russian literature of the Middle Ages, with its humanistic, patriotic, and national aspects, alongside the best of world literatures.

Translation: Song of Igor's Campaign, tr. V. Nabokov (1960)

SMELYAKOV, YAROSLAV VASSILIYEVICH
Born 1913, Lutsk (Volhynia). Soviet Russian poet.
S. graduated in 1931 from the School of Polygraphy and subsequently worked as a typesetter. His first volumes of poems appeared in 1932 under the title *Rabota i lyubov* [Work and Love]. His poem *Strogaya lyubov* [Bittersweet Love, 1956], in which he re-created the period of the first Five-Year Plan as seen

through the eyes of a young student at a vocational school, is considered to be his most important work. He was awarded the State Prize in 1967 for his cycle of poems entitled *Den Rossii* [A Day of Russia].

SMUUL, JUHAN
Born February 18, 1922, on the island of Muhu. Estonian Soviet poet and novelist.

S. took part in World War II; in 1944 he was discharged from the army for medical reasons, and began work on the staff of the Leningrad newspaper *Rahva Hääl* [The People's Voice]. After his return to the Estonian SSR he continued working as a journalist. In 1955 S. was elected deputy to the Supreme Soviet of the Estonian SSR.

S. began his literary career during World War II. He later wrote the poems *Tormi poeg* [Son of the Storm, 1947], *Järvesuu poiste brigaad* [The Youth Brigade from Järvesuu, 1948], *Eesti poeem* [Estonian Poem, 1949], *Mina kommunistik noor* [I Am a Komsomol, 1953], and *Kirjad Sõgedate külast* [Letters from the Village of Sodegate, 1955]. In 1956 he published the play *Atlandix ookean* [The Atlantic Ocean]. In 1961 S. received the Lenin Prize for *Jäine raamat* [The Book about the Ice], in which he described the moral greatness of the Soviet people in the Antarctic, and the difficult conditions existing there.

S. has held the title of People's Writer of the Estonian SSR since 1955, and was awarded the State Prize in 1952.

Further Works: Jaapani meri, detsember [The Japanese Sea, December] (1963)

SNEGOV, SERGEI IOSIFOVICH
Born August 5, 1910, Odessa. Soviet Russian novelist.

S. studied mathematics and physics. He was a teacher in Leningrad, and later became an engineer in the northern part of Russia. He has been publishing stories and novels since 1955. Although his literary form is not always without faults, he depicted with some skill the ethical and moral conflicts arising in the course of the realization of the technical revolution.

SOBKO, VADYM MYKOLAIOVYCH
Born May 18, 1912, Moscow. Ukrainian Soviet novelist, short-story writer, and dramatist.

S., the son of an engineer, worked in the coalmines of the Donetz Basin and in the Kharkov Tractor Works. In 1938 he graduated from the Faculty of Philology of the University of Kiev. During the war years S. edited an army newspaper, and after the war worked for many years for the Soviet Military Administration in Germany.

S.'s thematically very diversified work encompasses novels, short stories, and plays, and includes the novel *Zaporuka miru* (1949; Guarantee of Peace, 1951). In the short story *Serdtze* [The Heart, 1950] S. describes the complex reconstruction of a democratic and peace-loving Germany in place of the present German Democratic Republic. He was awarded the State Prize in 1951.

Further Works: Shlyakh zori [The Way of the Star] (1948); *Za druhym frontom* [Behind the Second Frontline] (1949); *Zoryani kryla* [Starry Wings] (1950); *Zhyttya pochnayetsya znovu* [Life Begins Anew] (1950); *Sribrnyi korabel* [The Silver Ship] (1961)

SOBOLEV, LEONID SERGEYEVICH
Born July 20, 1898, Irkutsk. Soviet Russian novelist.

S. was educated in a naval training school. Between 1918 and 1931 he was a commander in the navy, and took part in both the civil war and World War II. He has been writing since 1925.

S.'s first novel, *Kapitalnyi remont* [Main Repair, 1932], describes the growing revolutionary activities of the sailors during World War I. S. already showed in this work the lyrical, colorful style and expert development of dramatic situations that was to be characteristic of his later writing. In his collection of short stories from the front, *Morskaya dusha* (1942; The Soul of the Sea, 1945), S. erected a monument to the heroic deeds of the

Soviet sailors in World War II. This work received the State Prize in 1943. The fate of a Soviet naval officer is the subject of S.'s short novel *Zelionyi luch* (1954; The Green Light, 1955).

S. has also worked as a journalist and publicity writer in the field of Kazakh literature.

SOFRONOV, ANATOLII VLADIMIROVICH
    Born January 19, 1911, Minsk. Soviet Russian playwright and poet.

S., the son of a clerk, spent his childhood in the Don region. In 1937 he attended the Faculty of Literature at the Rostov Institute of Pedagogy. During World War II S. worked first on an army newspaper and from 1940 on was a war correspondent with *Izvestiya*.

S.'s first collection of poems, *Solnechnyye dni* [Sun-filled Days], appeared in 1934. His second volume of poetry, *Nad Donomrekoi* [On the Don River], was published in 1938. Plays on contemporary themes occupy an important position in S.'s postwar work, in addition to lyric writings in which the song genre is strongly represented. S.'s first two plays, *V odnom gorode* [In a Town, 1946] and *Moskovski kharakter* [The Character of Moscow, 1948], were awarded State Prizes. His numerous visits to foreign countries, undertaken in his position as a member of the Peace Council of the USSR, yielded material for his book *Na pyati materikakh* [On Five Continents, 1958].

Further Works: Stepnyye soldaty [Soldiers of the Steppes] (1944); *Pered znamenem* [Before the Flag] (1948); *Inache zhit nelzya* [It Is Not Possible to Live Otherwise] (1952); *Don moi* [My Don] (1954); *Serdtze ne proshchayet* [The Heart Does Not Forgive] (1954); *Dengi* [Money] (1956); *Chelovek v otstavke* [A Retired Man] (1957); *Million za ulybku* [A Million for a Smile] (1961); *Ukhodysashchiye teni* [The Disappearing Shadows] (1965)

SOLOGUB (Pseud. of *Fiodor Kuzmich Teternikov*)
    Born March 1, 1863, St. Petersburg; died December 5, 1927, Leningrad. Russian novelist.

S., the son of a tailor, became a teacher, first in a provincial town and later in the capital city of St. Petersburg. From 1894 on he worked with other symbolists for the magazine *Severni vestnik* [The Messenger from the North]. S. was one of the leading representatives of decadence. Among his early works the novel *Melki bes* (1892; published 1905; Pettiness, 1922) gives a true picture of the depressing life led by the lower-middle classes but at the same time shows a strong tendency to concentrate on the abnormal and pathological aspects of that life. In his later work S. extolled the unreal world of fantasy and death as being the only way of life. His antirevolutionary, mystic novel *Tvorimaya legenda* [Dance of Death, 1907–10] gives a distorted picture of the revolutionary period of 1905–07. S. was never able to understand the meaning of the October revolution.

SOLOUKHIN, VLADIMIR ALEKSEYEVICH
Born June 14, 1924, Alepino (District of Vladimir). Soviet Russian poet and novelist.
After World War II, in which he participated, S. attended the Gorki Institute of Literature in Moscow, and subsequently worked as a journalist. His first volume of poems, *Dozhd v stepi* [Rain in the Steppe], appeared in 1953. His work was primarily concerned with the people and natural life of central Russia. His poems, which are frequently symbolistic in feeling, are aimed at attaining a conscious awareness of the beauties of nature. In his prose works, written in a style reminiscent of Turgenev and Paustovski, S. describes everyday events in a poetic manner, and, by combining lyric, epic, and political elements, succeeds in giving an impressive picture of the life of the village people.

Further Works: Vladimirskiye prosiolky [The Vladimir Crossroads] (1957); *Kaplya resy* [A Drop of Dew] (1960); *Svidaniye v Vyasnikakh* [A Meeting in Vynasniki] (1964); *Mat-matchekja* [Mother-Stepmother] (1964); *Razryv-trava* [Magic Grass] (1965)

SOLZHENITZYN, ALEKSANDR ISAYEVICH
Born December 11, 1918, Kislowodsk. Soviet Russian novelist.
S. became widely known with his first novel, *Odin Den Ivana*

Denisovicha (1962; One Day in the Life of Ivan Denisovich, 1963), which is about life in a work camp. Based on his own experiences, S. here shows the complex interrelationships that exist in such a camp. In his works published after 1963—*Sluchai na stanzii Krechetovka* (An Incident on the Train Station Krechetovka, 1968), *Matrionin dvor* (Matryona's House, 1963), and *V polsu dela* (For the Good of the Cause, 1964)—S. discusses problems of individual moral responsibility. These stories are somewhat didactic and moralistic; their abstract humanism tends to result in a rigid and aesthetic schematization. S.'s style is convincing because of the precision of the psychological observations and the detailed, compact development of the themes.

Further Works (not published in Russia): *V kruge pervum* (1968; The First Circle, 1968); *Rakovyi korpus* (1968; The Cancer Ward, 1968)

SOSYURA, VOLODYMYR MYKOLAIOVYCH
   Born January 6, 1898, Debaltzevo; died January 1, 1965, Kiev. Ukrainian Soviet poet.

S. was the son of a miner; he suffered much hardship as a child, and early found his way into the proletarian movement. He fought as a Red Guard in the civil war. In 1925 he graduated from the Kharkov Institute for Adult Education. He participated in World War II as a war correspondent for an army newspaper.

P. is considered to be one of the founders of Ukrainian Soviet lyric writing. His first verses were published in 1917. His collections *Poezii* [Poems] and *Chervona zyma* [Red Winter] appeared in 1921. The more than fifty collections of poems that have appeared since then represent a true poetic chronicle of the historical road taken by the Ukrainian people from the October revolution to the present time. Many of S.'s poems are today regarded as folksongs. Among his best-known poetic cycles are *Chervoni troyandy* [Red Roses, 1932], *Shchob sady shumily* [That the Gardens May Rustle, 1947], for which he was awarded the State Prize of 1948, and *Shchastya simy trudovoy* [The Happiness of the Working People, 1962].

With his melodic, image-rich verses S. has followed the great classical traditions of Ukrainian poetry. The strongly developed romantic and folksong-like features give his work its unique character.

STALSKI (Pseud. of *Gasanbekov Suleiman Hasanbekov*) Born May 18, 1869, Akhaga-Stal; died there November 23, 1957. Soviet poet of the Caucasian mountain tribe people (Lesghians); People's Poet of Dagestan.

S., the son of a poor Lesghian farmer, was orphaned at an early age. He was exploited and oppressed by the rich members of his home aul. He worked in the aul from the age of thirteen, as well as in Baku, in the vineyards of Derbent, on the Samarkand railroad, and at various other jobs. He was illiterate, and his works were at first circulated orally. From the early 1900s his poems, which he would recite from memory, were recorded by folklorists.

At the First Soviet Writers' Congress in 1934 Gorki referred to S. as "the Homer of the twentieth century." S. was familiar with the works of Pushkin and Lermontov, as well as those of the oriental poets Hafis, Nisama, Sadi, and Navoi. His early poems and songs were directed against social injustice and the oppression of the people in a class-oriented society. Following the victory of the socialist revolution, S. became one of the most popular Soviet poets of the Caucasus. His poems and patriotic songs on the life of the Soviet Dagestan village, collective work, and the people and nature of the Caucasus, have found wide distribution among the public. His works have been translated into Russian as well as into the languages of various other nationalities of the USSR. His poem *Sergo Ordzhonikidze* (1936) and *Thoughts about My Home Country* (1937) show S. to be an enthusiastic follower of Soviet power.

STANYUKOVICH, KONSTANTIN MIKHAILOVICH
Born March 25, 1843, Sevastopol; died May 20, 1903, Naples. Russian novelist.

S. was the son of an admiral. In 1860–63, as a member of the

Russian Navy, he took part in a journey around the world; the adventures of that voyage formed the basis for his book *Vokrug sveta na "Korshune"* [Around the World on H.M.S. "Hawk," 1895]. In the 1860s and 1870s he joined the revolutionary movement, and between 1885 and 1888 was exiled to Tomsk. In addition to contemporary novels of social criticism S. wrote *Morskiye rasskazy* [Sailors' Stories, 1886–1902], in which he described the everyday life and heroism of the simple sailor; these stories are regarded as his most mature work.

STAVSKI (Pseud. of *Vladimir Petrovich Kirpichnikov*)
Born in 1900, Pensa; died (killed in action) November 14, 1943. Soviet Russian novelist and playwright.

S. joined the Communist Party in 1918, and took part in the civil war. He started his literary career in 1921. S.'s books of sketches and, in particular, the novel *Razbeg* [The Start, 1931], which was later adopted for the stage, are among the most impressive descriptions of collectivization in Soviet literature. His volume of stories entitled *Silneye smerti* [Stronger than Death, 1932] and his drama *Voina* [War, 1941] dealt with the civil war. S.'s reports written from the frontline during World War II have been collected in the volume entitled *Frontovye zapisi* [Reports from the Front, 1942].

Further Works: O shchastye i muzhestve. Rasskazy i ocherki [About Happiness and Courage: Stories and Sketches] (1953)

STEIN (Pseud. of *Aleksandr Petroviich Rubinstein*)
Born September 15, 1906, Samarkand. Soviet Russian playwright.

S.'s first published work, which he co-authored with Y. Goryev and the brothers Tur, was *Neft* [Petroleum]. S. became widely known after 1945 for his plays *Zakon chesti* [Law of Honor, 1948], *Personalnoye delo* [A Personal Matter, 1954], *Gostinitza Astoriya* [Hotel Astoria, 1956], and *Okean* [The Ocean, 1961]. S. has used historical and contemporary themes in his dramatically acerbic plays, which are frequently concerned with the Red Navy and with military intelligence. He was awarded State Prizes in 1945 and 1951.

Further Works: Mezhdu livnyami [Between the Heavy Rains] (1946); *Prolog* [Prologue] (1955); *Vesseniye skripki* [Spring Violin] (1959); *Povest o tom kak voznikayut syuzhety* [Story about the Making of Plots] (1964)

STELMMAKH, MYKHAILO (Pseud. of *Mykhailo Panasovych*)
Born May 14, 1912, Dyakivtzy. Ukrainian Soviet poet and novelist.

S., the son of a peasant, studied at the Institute of Pedagogy in Vinnitza and became a country schoolteacher. During World War II he was the editor of a frontline newspaper, and was severely wounded in battle. After the war he worked for a number of years as a research assistant at the Institute of Folklore and Ethnography of the Academy of Sciences of the USSR.

S.'s first collection of poems *Dobryi ranok* [A Clear Morning] appeared in 1941. It was followed by *Provesan* [Early Spring, 1942] and *Ukrayini vilni zhyt* [The Ukraine Must Live in Freedom, 1944]. In his later work narrative prose gained in importance, its epic breadth combining well with S.'s lyrical fervor and vividness. In his most important work, the novel chronicle *Velyka ridnya* [Native Soil, 1945], S. tells of the rise of socialist awareness among the kolkhoz farmers of a western Ukrainian village. His civil war novel *Krov lyudska—ne vodytza* [Human Blood Is Not Water, 1957] takes place in the same village. In the latter novel, S. stirringly described the bitter class battles taking place in the country during the first years of Soviet power. The same theme is also treated in the novel *Khlib i sil* [Bread and Salt, 1958], which concludes S.'s epic novel cycle about the development of the Ukrainian village from the October revolution to the present.

S.'s last novel, *Pravda i kryvda* [Truth and Falsehood, 1961], also deals with village themes. The author relates how the brave and moral people of a kolkhoz completely destroyed during the war fight against poverty and injustice to attain a modest degree of justice and prosperity. S. was awarded the Lenin Prize of 1961.

STEPNYAK (Pseud. of *Sergei Mikhailovich Kravchinski*)
Born July 13, 1851, Novy Stardub (near Kherson); died December 23, 1895, London. Russian novelist and political journalist. An important member of the populist group.

S. was the son of an army surgeon. He became a professional revolutionary in 1872–73, and fought in the Balkans and in Italy. He was the leader of the secret terrorist organization *Zemlya i volya* [Country and Liberty], and editor of the newspaper of the same name. In 1878 he killed the hated Chief of Police Mesentzov; as a result he was forced to emigrate, and lived in London for seventeen years. He befriended both Plekhanov and F. Engels.

In his collection of sketches *La Russia sotteranea* (Italian, 1882; Eng., Underground Russia, 1883; Russian, Podpolnaya Rossiya, 1893) S. gave an impressive picture of the fight of the populists against tsarism. Among other novels of importance are *Andrei Kozhukhov* (Eng., The Career of a Nihilist, 1889; Russian, 1898) and the historical novel *Rossiya pod vlastyu tzarei* (2 vols., Eng., Russia under the Tsars, 1964; Russian, 1964).

STORY OF SORROW-TROUBLE, THE   See POVEST O GORE-ZLOCH-ASTII

SUDRABKALNS, JĀNIS (Pseud. of *Arvids Peine*)
Born May 17, 1894, Inčukalns. Latvian Soviet poet.
S. was the son of a schoolteacher. During World War I he was a surgeon's assistant, and since 1917 has been involved with both journalism and writing. His first volume of poems, *Spārnotā armada* [The Winged Armada, 1920], is filled with unrest and romantic dreams of the future. In his later work we find that the realistic discovery of the contradictions of capitalism become gradually more important. This can be seen in S.'s collection of poems *Pārvērtibas* [Transitions, 1923] and *Spuldze veja* [Lantern in

the Wind, 1931], as well as in the volumes of humorous and satirical poems entitled *Trubadurs ez ēzela* [The Troubadour on the Ass, 1921] and *Džentlmens cerinu frakā* [The Gentleman in the Lilac-Colored Tail Coat, 1924]. S. was an unreserved supporter of Soviet power in 1940, seeing in it the realization of his old dreams. His collection of poems *Brālu saimē* [A Family of Brothers, 1947], in which he hymns the idea of friendship among peoples, stands out among the work he published in Soviet Latvia. He was awarded the State Prize of 1948 for this work.

S. has also been successful in the genre of delicate lyric poetry, as can be seen in *Viena besdelīga lido* [A Swallow Flies, 1937] and *Besdelīgas atgriežas* [The Swallows Return, 1951]. S., who has translated many works of world literature, is regarded as following in the tradition of J. Rainis. He holds the title of People's Poet of the Latvian SSR.

Further Works: Cīruli ziemā (1939); *Cīruli sauc cīnā* (1942); *Cela maize* [Bread on the Road] (1944)

SUKHOVO-KOBYLIN, ALEKSANDR VASILYEVICH
Born September 28, 1817, Moscow; died March 24, 1903, Beaulieu (France). Russian realistic playwright.

S. came from a noble and cultured family; he was influenced by Gogol. S. created an important dramatic trilogy of social criticism, *Kartiny proshedshevo* [Pictures from the Past, 1869]. In this work S. utilized his personal knowledge of the declining nobility and of the corrupt and inefficient tsarist bureaucracy—he had once been suspected of having killed his mistress, and was liberated only in 1857 after seven years of detention pending investigation. This picaresque comic trilogy includes *Svadba Krechinskovo* (1885; Krechinsky's Wedding, 1961), *Delo* [The Trial, 1861], and *Smert Tarelkina* [The Death of Tarelkina, 1868].

SULFIYA, SULFIYA ISRAILOVA
Born 1915, Tashkent. Uzbekistanian Soviet poet.
In 1931 S. studied at the Institute of Pedagogy in Tashkent. In

her poems and prose writings she is concerned, above all, with
the involvement of the Uzbekistanian woman in the social life
of her people. The poems included in the volume *Pages from Life*
(1932) extol the happy life of the liberated woman who is taking
part in the socialist reconstruction of her country.

After World War II, S. criticized those women who had received a higher education but upon its completion retired into
private life. This was also the subject of her political essay *Conversations with Women Friends* (1952). Her lyrical poems *During the Days of Separation* and *In My Hands I Hold a Weapon,
On My Shoulder I Carry a Soldier's Coat*, written during the
war, were particularly popular with the soldiers.

SUMAROKOV, ALEKSANDR PETROVICH

Born December 4, 1717 or 1718, Vilmanstrand, Finland; died
October 23, 1777, Moscow. Leading Russian classicist and playwright.

S. was of noble birth. In 1756–61 he became director and cofounder with F. G. Volkov of the first Russian theater in St.
Petersburg. He later became the first Russian free-lance writer.
In everything he wrote, but especially in his odes, he made himself the voice of the enlightened progressive nobles opposing Catherine II. His tragedies, which included *Dmitri Samozvanetz*
(1771; Demetrius the Impostor, 1806), were also politically directed.

S. was involved in a number of important projects for the theoretical and practical rejuvenation of the Russian literary language.
An extremely versatile man, S. was the author of the first Russian
comic plays; they enjoyed great popularity for many years.

SURKOV, ALEKSEI ALEKSANDROVICH

Born October 13, 1899, Serednevo (District of Yaroslavl). Soviet Russian poet.

The views held by S., the son of a poor peasant, have been
decisively influenced by the experiences he underwent in the

K. M. Simonov

J. Smuul

V. M. Sosyura

Stalski

M. Stelmmakh

J. Sudrabkalns

A. H. Tammsaare   A. N. Tolstoi   L. N. Tolstoi

Group picture of contributors to *Sovremennik*
top A. N. Tolstoi, Grigorovich
bottom Goncharov, Turgenev, Drushinin, A. N. Ostrovski

civil war. He later became an editor and journalist, and during World War II worked as a war correspondent.

S., who was chairman of the Soviet Writers' Union, published his first poems in the 1920s. His major themes had already appeared in his first collections of poems entitled *Sapev* [The Prelude, 1930] and *Rovesniki* [Contemporaries, 1934]. His major theme was a recounting of the heroic deeds of the simple civil-war soldier, both during the period when he had to defend his country and in times of peace; he also wrote of the development of his contemporaries in the world of socialism and communism that was gradually gaining in importance.

S.'s patriotic poems and lyrics concerned with the problems of internationalism and of the battle for peace—in particular his volume *Miru—mir* [Peace to the World, 1947], for which he received the State Prize in 1951—have earned him the approbation of the public. His fervent poems, many of which have been set to music, frequently have for their hero an individual who in turn becomes a representative of the millions.

SÜTISTE, JUHAN (Pseud. of *Johannes Schütz*)

Born December 28, 1899, near Tartu; died February 2, 1945, Tallin (as a result of mistreatment during his imprisonment by the fascists). Estonian poet.

S.'s work formed a link between the best traditions of Estonian classic poetry and the characteristic features of the socialist epoch. His collections of verses and poems have been appearing since 1921. His most important poem, *Tuhas ja tules* [Ashes and Fire, 1938], is dedicated to the workers in the shale industry. S. has also published plays and travel sketches.

S. welcomed the institution of Soviet power in Estonia in 1940 with his poem *Maakera pöördub itta* [The Globe Is Turning toward the East, 1940]. The poems S. wrote secretly during his imprisonment by the fascists in 1942–44 have been published in the volume *Umbsed päevad* [Humid Days, 1945]. Following his liberation from fascism S. wrote a series of poems and the historical drama, published posthumously, entitled *Ristikoerad* [Dog

Knights, 1946], in which he described the fight of the Russians against the twelfth-century Teutonic knights.

SVETLOV, MIKHAIL ARKADYEVICH

Born June 17, 1903, Yekaterinoslav; died 1964, Moscow. Soviet Russian poet of the first Komsomol generation.

S. came from a working-class family. He became a leading member of the Komsomols, and took part in the civil war. He started to write poetry in 1917; his first volume *Relsy* [Rails] appeared in 1923.

S. has written many popular songs and poems with a predominantly emotional content, filled with optimistic romanticism and revolutionary fervor. He became famous following the publication in 1926 of his lyric poem *Grenada* [Granada], which tells of a young Red Army soldier who died on the Ukrainian steppe with the name of far-away Granada on his lips. The life and death of this soldier symbolizes the dream of the people for brotherly friendship between all nations of the world.

S. also wrote a number of verse dramas, and translated works from numerous foreign languages. The basic theme of his work is the humanity of the socialist revolution, and the romantic heights from which, when reached, many may aspire to even nobler deeds. S. was awarded the Lenin Prize in 1967.

Editions: Stikhi i pyesy [Poems and Plays], Moscow, 1957

SYDYKBEKOV, TUGELBAI

Born May 14, 1912, Ken-Sun. Kirghiz novelist.

Following a number of attempts at verse, in the 1930s S. turned to the genre of the novel, which at that time was new to Kirghiz literature. His first great success was *Bisdin samandyn kishileri* [People of Our Days, 1948], in which he described the battle of the Kirghiz farmers in the interior of the country during wartime. He was awarded the State Prize for this work in 1949. The complexities and problems of social change during collectivization are reflected in S.'s novel *Between the Mountains* (1956).

Further Works: Too baldary [Children of the Mountains] (1953)

TABIDZE, GALAKTION
Born November 18, 1892, Chkviisi, near Kutaisi; died March 17, 1959, Tiflis. Georgian Soviet poet.

T., the son of a peasant, attended a theological seminary. His early revolutionary poems *May 1st* (1908) and *Sun, Arise!* (1910) were very popular, while his later poems showed the influence of Russian symbolism.

T. was one of the first writers to support Soviet power, and in 1925 wrote his poem *We, the Poets of Georgia!* to celebrate it. T.'s work reflected the thoughts and emotions of growing socialist man, his readiness to defend his country and to fight for peace and friendship among peoples. All these themes appear in his collections of poetry entitled *Pacifism* (1930), *European Recollections* (1935), and *Moscow* (1947).

T. enriched Georgian poetry with new themes and images. He was People's Poet of the Georgian SSR from 1933 until his death in 1959.

Editions: Chsulebani [Collected Works], 7 vols., Tiflis, 1935–52

TAMMSAARE, A. H. (Pseud. of *Anton Hansen*)
Born January 30, 1878, Järva-Madise; died March 1, 1940, Tallinn. Estonian novelist.

T., the son of a peasant, studied in Tartu between 1907 and 1911, and subsequently worked as a journalist. He is known for his naturalistic stories and sketches about the lives of the peasants. His most important work, the five-volume novel chronicle *Tôde ja ôigus* [Truth and Justice] was written between 1926 and 1933. It depicts, against a broad social background, the fate of a peasant boy who can find neither right nor justice in capitalistic society.

T.'s last novel, *Pôrgupohja uus vanapagan* [The Devil with a Forged Passport, 1939], is a biting satire about the existing bourgeois order. T. also translated a great number of classical Russian and English works into Estonian.

Further Works: Kôrbôja peremees [The Farmer from Kôrboja] (1922); *Kuningal on külm* [The King Is Freezing] (1936)

TANK, MAKSIM (Pseud. of *Awhem Ivanavich Skurko*)
Born September 17, 1912, Pilkovshchyna (District of Molodechno). Byelorussian Soviet poet.

T., who comes from a peasant family, has been writing lyrics and epic poems since the early 1930s; this work is characterized by an optimistic romanticism. His first volume of poetry, *Na etapakh* [Behind the Lines, 1936], and his poem *Narach* (1937), in which he described the uprising of the fishermen of Lake Narach against the Polish estate owners, were suppressed by the Polish authorities. In his collection of poems *Shuravinavy tsvet* [Purple Color, 1937] and *Pad machtai* [Under the Mast, 1937], T. supported the idea of a socialist Byelorussia.

T.'s work is closely linked with the romantic traditions of Byelorussian folklore. In a number of poems he has written of the important questions of our times, and is especially concerned with the problem of humanism.

Editions: Sbor tvorov, Vershy i poemi [Collected Works, Poems, and Verses], 2 vols., Minsk, 1958

TENDRYAKOV, VLADIMIR FIODOROVICH
Born December 5, 1923, Makarovskaya (District of Voronezh). Soviet Russian novelist.

T. fought as a soldier in World War II; after the war he attended the Gorki Institute of Literature in Moscow, and worked as a journalist. His major themes are about the life of the Soviet farmer. T.'s work is characterized by a predilection for interesting destinies which pose challenging social and ethical problems to him as a novelist, and for characters who are placed in crucial situations requiring the making of definite decisions. T.'s ability to tell his stories in a psychologically absorbing manner have ensured him a considerable public.

T.'s best known works include the volume of short stories *Ukhaby* [The Quagmire, 1956], the novels *Za begushchim dniopm* [Day by Day, 1959] and *Svidaniye z Nefertiti* [Meeting

Nefertiti Again, 1964], and the short stories *Sud* [The Judgment, 1961] and *Rasskazy radista* [Stories of a Radio Operator, 1963].

Editions: Izbrannyye proizvedeniya [Selected Works], 2 vols., Moscow, 1963
Further Works: Sredi lesov [Among the Forests] (1954); *Chudotvornaya* [Miracle Worker] (1958); *Korotkoye zamykaniye* [Short Circuit] (1962)

TEUNOV, KHACHIM
Born in 1912, Aryk (northern Caucasus). Kabardino Soviet novelist and short-story writer.
T. graduated from the Institute of Pedagogy in Nalchik. Some of his early sketches appeared in 1929, but he became known more widely following the publication of his novels *Aslan* (1941), *The New Stream* (1946), and *Golden Morning* (1950). These form a trilogy about the fate of a number of generations of one family. T. has also written several literary portraits of Kabardino writers, as well as a book of literary essays entitled *Literature and Writers of Kabardino* (1958).

TIKHONOV, NIKOLAI SEMIONOVICH
Born December 4, 1896, St. Petersburg. Soviet Russian poet and novelist.
T. was a soldier during World I and volunteered for service in the Red Army during the civil war. In the 1920s and 1930s he traveled extensively through the USSR, Asia, and Europe. During World War II he lived in beleaguered Leningrad.
T.'s volumes of poetry *Orda* [The Horde, 1921] and *Braga* [Fermented Matter, 1922] reflected the romanticism and elemental strength of the revolution. After T. overcame certain experimental, formalistic tendencies, his work in the 1930s attained a significant level, as may be seen in the cycle of poems entitled *Stikhi o Kakhetia* [Poems on Kakhetia, 1935]. This cycle of poems is dedicated to the theme of the Soviet Orient, a region in which T. has always been particularly interested.

T.'s volume of poems *Ten druga* [The Shadow of a Friend, 1956], based on his western European impressions, contains a passionate condemnation of fascism and declares the poet's loyalty to the antifascist forces. Most important among these poems is *Kirov z nami* [Kirov Is with Us, 1941]. T.'s jewel-like poems here sometimes tend toward a balladlike style. In them he points to the revolutionary past (represented by the city of Kirov) and to the courage of the defenders of Leningrad as harbingers of a final victory over fascism.

T.'s postwar work is concerned with contemporary political problems. He has translated works from the literatures of Georgia, Armenia, Uzbek, Lithuania, and Hungary. T. was awarded State Prizes in 1942 and 1949; he is president of the Soviet Peace Committee and a member of the World Peace Council. He was awarded the Lenin Peace Prize in 1957.

Editions: Sobraniye sochinenii [Collected Works], 6 vols., Moscow, 1958–59
Further Works: Yurga (1931), *Stranitzy vospominanii* [Reminiscences] (1961)

TIOTKA (Pseud. of *Aloiza Stepanovna Pashkevich*)
Born July 3, 1876, Peshchany (District of Vilna); died February 5, 1916. Byelorussian poet.

T. came from a peasant family and graduated as a teacher from a St. Petersburg college. Because of her revolutionary activities she was persecuted by the courts; she emigrated to Galicia (then part of Austria), returning home only in 1913. In Minsk she published a magazine and founded several schools. Impressed by the revolution of 1905, she wrote a number of volumes of poetry. These recount the distress of the Byelorussian people, and call for the overthrow of autocracy and the establishment of democratic institutions.

Editions: Vybranyya tvory [Selected Works], Minsk, 1952

TOGOLOK, MOLDO (Pseud. of *Baimbet Abdrakhamonv*)
Born June, 1860, Kurtka; died there January 4, 1942. Kirghiz
poet and folklorist.

As a farm laborer, a physician, and a teacher, T. became familiar
with the hard life led by the peasants as well as their rich folklore, which he recorded. His love songs and laments tell of the
country's injustices, especially toward the Kirghiz women. In his
song *Ösgörüsh* [Revolution, 1918], T. supported the October
revolution. His very popular poem *Atkantan and Süigenbai*
(1923) tells of the love of two young people under the new social
conditions.

In 1936 T.'s style changed somewhat, becoming more lyrical;
in his poems he wrote of the events that had occurred during the
reconstruction period and during the early months of the war.

Editions: Chygyrmalar [Works], 2 vols., Frunse, 1954–55
Further Works: Nassijat (1923); *Erkindik* (1927)

TOKOMBAYEV, AALY (Pseud. of *Balka Chalkar*)
Born November 7, 1904, Chon-Kemin. Kirghiz poet and short-
story writer.

T., the son of a workingman, graduated in 1927 from the
University of Tashkent and then worked as an editor. He is a
member of the Academy of Sciences of the Kirghiz SSR and a
member of both the Presidium of the Writers' Union of the
USSR and of that of the Kirghiz SSR.

T.'s poems, stories, and essays have been appearing since 1924.
Among his most important works is *Tutkun Marat* [The Prisoner
Marat, 1928], a poem about the struggles of the German working
class. This poem is an attempt to link folkloristic traditions with
the achievements of Mayakovski. *Küünüm syry* [The Secret of
the Melody, 1941] is a charming story written in the form of an
improvised legend. The poems *Kytaidagy dsholugushuu* [Meeting
in China, 1950] and *Ös kösüm menen* [With My Own Eyes,
1953] reflect the conflicts in the mind of an industrious peasant
during the period of collectivization.

Further Works: Dsharalangan dshürök [The Wounded Heart] (1941)

TOKTOGUL SATYLGANOV
Born April, 1864, Cholpon-Ata; died December 29, 1933. Folklorist; one of the founders of Kirghiz Soviet literature.
T.S., who was a poor herdsman, early felt the need to protest against social injustice. He voiced this need in songs accompanied by the *komus* (a stringed instrument); these songs were only occasionally written down by his listeners.
In his lyric form *Alymakan*, T.S. lamented the impossibility of achieving happiness with the beloved Alymakan, who is married to a rich man. T.S. was violently persecuted following the publication of a number of satires, including *Besh kaman* [The Five Boars], a poem filled with hate against five tyrants and with compassion for seven peasant families who had been cruelly mistreated. In 1898 he was sentenced to death on the basis of perjured testimony; his sentence was commuted, however, and he was exiled to Siberia; he escaped from Siberia in 1910. In his song *Kandai ayal tuudu eken Lenindei uuldu* [What a Mother Has Borne the Heroic Lenin!, 1919], he welcomed the October revolution and the changes it brought about for the Kirghiz peasants. *Eldi karachy* [Look at My People, 1928], like other late works, shows the lyric enrichment of traditional poetic images and Kirghiz verse forms.
Editions: Toktogul [A Collection of His Works], Frunse, 1950

TOLSTOI, ALEKSEI KONSTANTINOVICH
Born September 5, 1817, St. Petersburg; died October 10, 1875, Krasny Rog (District of Chernigov). Russian novelist.
Following an extensive journey through Europe, which included a visit with Goethe, T. entered the civil service. Between 1837–40 he worked in the diplomatic service at the Russian mission in Frankfurt, Germany, and then at the Russian court. In 1867 he published a collection of lyric poems, mostly concerned with nature. Using the joint pseudonymn Kosma Prutkov, T., together with the brothers A. M. and V. M. Shemchushnikov, had already become known as an author of political satires. *Son Popova* [The Dream of State Councillor Popova, 1873, published

1878] was also a satire, despite the fact that T. by that time was in favor of "pure art" and the idealization of pre-Petrian Russia. T.'s historical novel about the times of Ivan the Terrible, *Knyaz Serebryanny* (1862; A Prince of Outlaws, 1927), is still widely read.

Further Works: Smert Ivan Groznovo [The Death of Ivan the Terrible] (1866); *Tsar Fiodor* (1868; *Tsar Fiodor,* tr. A. Hayes, 1924); *Tsar Boris* (1870)

TOLSTOI, ALEKSEI NIKOLAYEVICH

Born January 10, 1883, Nikolayvsk (now Pugachov), in the District of Samara (now Saratov); died February 23, 1945, in the Sanatorium Barvikhin. Soviet Russian novelist.

T. was brought up on the estate of his stepfather; his mother was a novelist. He studied at the Institute of Technology in St. Petersburg between 1901–06, and at a technical school in Dresden in 1906. In 1918 he emigrated to France; he visited Berlin in 1921, and returned to Russia in 1923. T. appeared at many international antifascist congresses; he was a Deputy of the Supreme Soviet of the USSSR.

T.'s work is characterized by an extraordinary richness of theme. His topics included the dissolute life led by the Russian estate owners; decadence; the Russian intelligentsia and the Russian emigrants; the decline of capitalism; the new man born during the revolution; the Russian people during the periods of change; the times of Ivan the Terrible; the "time of trouble" (1604–1613); the epoch of Peter I; the fight of the Soviet people against the fascist invaders. The central themes of his work, however, are the fate of Russia and the revolution, the problems of civilization and the happiness of man.

Before the October revolution T. was a critical realist, and, beginning in 1908, described the decline of the Russian nobility in his novels. These included *Mishuka Nalymov* (1910) and *Khromoi barin* (1912; The Lame Prince, 1950). During the period he spent abroad T. wrote the novel *Detstvo Nikity* (1920; Nikita's Childhood, 1945), an idyll about his own childhood that reflected much of T.'s nostalgia for his own country. The small hero of the story, Nikita, discovers strange things in the Russian countryside, in nature, and among the simple village peasants. The charm of a carefree childhood is closely intertwined with the novelist's love for his homeland.

T. was one of the founders of Soviet science fiction. His novel *Aelita* (1922) describes a revolution on Mars, while in *Giperboloid inzhenera Garina* (1925; The Garin Death Ray, 1950) he predicted the tendencies toward imperialist development that were to come ten years later, indicating the grave danger the weapons of mass anihilation could pose for humanity. T.'s characters already show evidence of fascist immorality, while T. himself appears here as one of the first antifascist writers.

T. was the author of more than forty plays. A number of these are adaptations of the works of foreign dramatists, including Büchner, Čapek, and Hasenclever.

Between 1920–41 T. wrote his novel trilogy *Khozhdeniye po mukam* (Vol. I, 1920–21; rev. ed., 1925, *Siostry* [The Sisters]; Vol. II, 1922–28, *Vosemnadtzaty god* [The Year 1918]; Vol. III, 1940–41, *Khmuroye utro*). Vols. II and III of this trilogy were published in English as *Ordeal* (1953) and *Darkness and Dawn* (1936), while an abridged version of the complete trilogy appeared in English in 1932 under the title *Imperial Majesty*. T. received the State Prize in 1943 for this work. Its main theme is the complex and difficult road traveled by the Russian intelligentsia to reach a positive attitude toward the revolution. *Khozhdeniye* is a great novel of socialist realism—it gives an excellent picture of the period, showing the important events of the civil war, the varied stratification of Russian society, the fight of the Russian people against counterrevolution and foreign intervention.

T. also wrote the noteworthy historical novel *Piotr pervy* (1929–45; Peter the First, 1959), for which he received the State Prize of 1941. In this novel Tsar Peter is seen as a significant historical figure closely related to the important events of his time, fighting against medieval barbarism albeit with barbaric means. Its high artistic quality and veracity, its wealth of ideas and its unique linguistic quality have made *Piotr* the most important historical novel in Soviet literature.

After the October revolution T.'s work became imbued with a philosophical profundity and a great fertility of thought and ideas; his writing was characterized by monumental design and broad perspectives, by intense optimism and a belief in the future, and by language of a classical simplicity. As a master of the Russian language, whose work represents the close link between Soviet literature and classical Russian traditions, T. has become one of the most popular Soviet novelists. Many of his works have been translated.

Editions: Sobraniye sochinenii [Collected Works], 15 vols., Moscow, 1949–53
Further Works: Pokhozhdeniye Nevsorova ili Ibikus [Adventures of Nevsorov or Ibikus] (1924); *Khleb* [Bread] (1936); *Rasskazy Ivana Sudareva* [Tales of Ivan Sudarev] (1942–44); *Ivan Groznyi* [Ivan the Terrible] (1942–44)

TOLSTOI, LEV NIKOLAYEVICH

Born September 9, 1828, Yasnaya Polyana (near Tula); died November 20, 1910, Astapovo. Russian novelist and political writer; leader of Russian critical realism.

T. came from an aristocratic family; he studied law in Kazan in 1844–47, and later made reform attempts on his estate in Yasnaya Polyana. In the years 1851–53 he participated—first as a soldier, later as an officer—in the battles in the Caucasus and, in 1854–55, in the Crimean War.

After resigning from the army in 1856, T. gradually became involved with literary circles in St. Petersburg. Between 1857 and 1860 he traveled extensively in Western Europe, visiting France, Switzerland, Italy, Germany, Belgium, and England. Between 1859 and 1862 T. was largely occupied with his practical and theoretical teaching activities. He established schools for peasant children in Yasnaya Polyana and elsewhere, and, following the philosophy of Rousseau, developed a system of free education, the basic principles of which he discussed in his journal

Yasnaya Polyanan (1862) and in his essay *O narodnom obrazo-vanii* [On Public Education, 1874].

After the abolition of serfdom, T., in the years between 1862 and 1863, acted as an arbitrator between estate owners and peasants, trying to protect the interests of the latter as far as possible. His ideological search, which had resulted in an early alienation from his own class, led T. to a complete break with feudal capitalistic society in 1880. In a series of declarative essays —*Ispoved* (1879–82; A Confession, 1921), *Tak chto zhe nam delat?* [What Then Should We Do?, 1882–86], *V chom moya vera* (1883; What I Believe, 1921), and *Rabstvo nashevo vremeni* (1900; Slavery of Our Times, 1900)—T. attacked the basic foundations of the existing social order, rejecting all forms of exploitation and oppression. He also rejected the Orthodox Church, which excommunicated him in 1901.

Despite his profound social criticism, T. was not in favor of using force. He searched for a way to overcome class divisions by disseminating his moralistic religious teachings (Tolstoiism). Tolstoiism was based on a nonviolent opposition to evil, on total forgiveness, and on the moral self-improvement of the individual by an unselfish love for his fellow men. The roots of T.'s contradictory, utopian, and regressive teachings may be found—as has been demonstrated by V. I. Lenin in his essays on Tolstoi (including *Lev Tolstoi kak zerkalo russkoi revolyutzii* [Lev Tolstoi as the Mirror of the Russian Revolution, 1908])—in T.'s self-established position as a representative of the patriarchal peasantry and in his inability to comprehend the worldwide historical role of the working class.

During the last years of his life T. enjoyed great moral authority; he openly attacked the excesses of the tsarist government in his many political writings, including *Ne mogu molchat* [I Cannot Keep Silent, 1908]. Since T. was unable to realize his ideals completely while remaining within the circle of his family he secretly left his home in Yasnaya Polyana on November 10, 1910. He died a few days later at the railway station of Astapovo.

T. began his literary career in 1851. As a realistic writer who combined an epic breadth of thought and a profound psychological analysis (see his *Dialectics of the Soul*, after Chernyshevski) with the study of actual ideological problems, T. early showed his brilliant artistic capabilities. These are evident in his early autobiographical trilogy which is composed of *Detstvo* (Vol. I, 1852), *Otrochestvo* (Vol. II, 1854), and *Yunost* (Vol. III, 1857); the work was published in English in one volume in 1951 under the title *Childhood, Boyhood, Youth*. The central theme of T.'s early narrative work, the critical presentation of the war, may be found in his Causasian stories *Nabeg* (1853; The Raid, 1889), and *Rubka lesa* [The Clearing, 1855], as well as in the famous *Sevastopolskiye rasskazy* (1855–56; Sevastopol, 1916)—stories which were based on T.'s experiences at the defense of Sevastopol during the Crimean War.

T. described the social problems of the Russian villages in his stories *Utro pomeshchika* [The Morning of an Estate-Owner, 1856], *Polikushka* (1862), and *Kholstomer* [The Canvas Measurer, 1863–88]. Bourgeois life as contrasted with life close to nature was the subject of *Lutzern* (1857) and the novel *Kazaki* (1862; The Cossacks, 1960). The problems of love and marriage were the subject of *Semeinoye shchastye* (1859; Family Happiness, 1953).

The gradual development of T.'s thought toward a view of art that was close to the people came to a climax in 1862 with the publication of his essay *Krestyanskim rebyatam u nas ili nam u krestyankikh rebyat?* [Who Should Learn to Write from Whom: The Peasant Children from Us, or We from the Peasant Children?]. This was written when T. was attempting to overcome a temporary enthusiasm for "pure art." In his pamphlet *Chto takoye iskusstvo* (1897–98; What Is Art?, 1960), T. presented his views on aesthetics.

The first major peak in T.'s work may be considered to be his novel *Voina i mir* (1863–69; War and Peace, 1949). Here, against the background of the Napoleonic wars in general and the French campaign of 1812 in particular T. has depicted the individual fates and ideological problems of the period. He showed that the Russian people were the true conquerors of Napoleon, and allowed his main characters—Pierre Bezukhov, Andrei Bolkonski, and Natasha Rostova—to find their way to an understanding of the real truth in the simple Russian man.

In his second great novel, *Anna Karenina* (1873–77; Eng., 1957), T. was concerned with the immediate present. In the tragic fate of his heroine T. exposed the depraved views of morality and marriage held by contemporary Russian society, while in the figure of Levin he demonstrated the social and intellectual conflicts produced by the advance of capitalism. T.'s novel, with its skillful interweaving of plots, its profound depths of characterization, and its brilliant use of language, is one of the masterpieces of literature. *Anna Karenina*, together with *War and Peace*, established the worldwide reputation of both the author and the Russian novel itself.

Following the change in his ideological views, T. gave expression to his new ideas in *Narodnyye rasskazy* [Popular Stories, 1885–86]. He also wrote a number of other short stories, among which *Smert Ivavna Ilyicha* (1885; The Death of Ivan Ilyich, 1925) and *Kreitzerova sonata* (1887–89; The Kreutzer Sonata, 1924) are important because of their sharp criticism of the bourgeois family and its morality. In the 1880s T. turned toward the drama in order to use the stage for the further propagation of his ideas. He wrote the plays *Vlast tmy* (1886; The Power of Darkness, 1967), *Plody prosvestsheniya* (1890; The Fruits of Enlightenment, 1911), and *Zhivoi trup* (1900; The Living Corpse, 1939).

T.'s last novel, *Voskreseniye* (1899; Resurrection, 1957), contained a critical presentation of all the significant aspects of contemporary society—the state, the judiciary, the church, and private ownership of the land. The heroine of this novel, Katyusha Maslova, T. chose from among the people. The religious, moralistic overtones associated with the transformation of Nekhlyudov does not significantly weaken the strong accusatory note of the work. The same may be said of T.'s important later stories, including

Hadzhi Murat (1904; Hadji Murad, 1928) and *Posle bala* [After the Ball, 1903].

During the revolution of 1905 T. regarded himself as the spokesman of the Russian peasantry. He wrote an antiwar speech addressed to the Peace Congress in Stockholm in 1910. T.'s work greatly influenced world literature, especially the writers R. Rolland, J. Galsworthy, G. Hauptmann, T. Mann, A. Zweig, and A. Seghers.

Editions: Polnoye sobraniye sochinenii [Complete Works], 92 vols., Moscow–Leningrad, 1928–58; *Sobranye sochinenii* [Collected Works], 20 vols., Moscow, 1960–65
Further Works: Sapiski markiora [Notes of a Scorekeeper] (1853); *Metel* [Snowstorm] (1856); *Tri smerti* [Three Deaths] (1859); *Rasskazy iz "Novoi Azbuki" i "Russkikh knig dlya chteniya"* [Stories from "The New Alphabet" and "The Russian Reader"] (1872–75); *I svet vo tme svetit* [The Earth Shines in Darkness] (1911); *O narod nom obrazovanii* [On Popular Education] (1874); *Khozyain i rabotnik* [The Master and the Laborer] (1894–95); *O Shekspire i o drame* [On Shakespeare and the Drama] (1903–04)

TREDYAKOVSKI, VASILII KIRILLOVICH
Born March 5, 1703, Astrakhan; died August 17, 1769, St. Petersburg. Russian philologist and poet.

T., the son of an orthodox priest, studied in Holland and Paris; between 1730 and 1759 he was a professor at the St. Petersburg Academy. One of the first of the Russian classicists, T.'s writings on Russian poetry (1735 and 1752) anticipated the later efforts of Lomonosov and Sumarokov. He is considered to be the creator of modern Russian poetry. T. was the author of the first significant Russian odes—including one written in 1734 on the capture of Danzig—and of the rationalistic poem *Feoptiya*, written in 1754 and published in 1963. T. was also a skillful translator—his *Tilemakhida* (1766) is a free translation of Fénelon's educational novel *Télémaque*—and the creator of a scientific terminology of philology.

T. was the first Russian poet to use tonal principles in his work, and he thus prepared the way for a new and more adaptable form of expression. He advocated the replacement of the syllabic metre in Russian verse with a more regularly accented one.

Editions: Izbrannyye stikhotvoreniya [Selected Poems], Moscow–Leningrad, 1963

TRENEV, KONSTANTIN ANDREYEVICH

Born June 2, 1876, Romashovo (District of Kharkov); died May 19, 1945, Moscow. Soviet Russian playwright.

While still a young teacher and editor, T. began to write realistic stories of social criticism, influenced by the ideas expressed by Lev Tolstoi. In 1905 these stories appeared in collected form. T.'s discussions of actual problems, especially the situation of the peasants and the life of the intelligentsia, which he treated from the democratic point of view, led him to side with the workers' movement.

After 1917 T. concerned himself exclusively with literature; he wrote numerous dramas on contemporary and historical themes. His best and most successful work was the civil war drama *Lyubov Yarovaya* (1926). Here the necessity for a clear decision in favor of the socialist revolution is demonstrated in the conflict between the heroine Lyubov Yarovaya and her husband. Following and expanding the dramatic traditions established by A. Ostrovski, T. inserted numerous dramatic episodes into his plots. His most prominent historical dramas are *Pugachovshchina* [The Revolt of Pugachev, 1925] and a play about the revolution entitled *Na beregu Nevy* [On the Banks of the River Neva, 1937]. T.'s efforts to depict contemporary problems have not met with similar success.

During World War II, T. wrote short stories, sketches, and essays on patriotic themes. He was awarded the State Prize in 1941.

Editions: Izbrannyye proizvedeniya [Selected Works], 2 vols., Moscow, 1955
Further Works: Zhena [The Wife] (1928); *Yasnyi log* [The Bright Valley] (1931); *Opyt* [Experience] (1933); *Gimnazisty* [High-School Students] (1935); *Anna Luchinina* (1941)

TRETYAKOV, SERGEI MIKHAILOVICH
Born June 21, 1892, Riga (Latvia); died August 8, 1939.
Soviet Russian poet and dramatist.
T., who studied law before becoming a writer, came from a
family of teachers. He was associated with Mayakovski's magazine *Lef*, for which he wrote. He also supported the establishment of a proletarian theater. In 1924–25, T. worked as a lecturer
in Russian at Peking University. He later became a foreign correspondent for *Pravda*, and also held jobs as a radio reporter, press
photographer, and translator. He was the friend of B. Brecht—
who wrote a poem on the occasion of T.'s death—J. R. Becher,
F. Wolf, and other German writers and artists.
T. first started writing poems, dramas, sketches, novels, and
film scripts in 1913. In 1924, in collaboration with Mayakovski,
he wrote a code of labor laws in verse. Among his best-known
works are the dramas *Slyshish, Moskva?* [Can You Hear Me,
Moscow?, 1924] and *Rychi, Kitai!* (1926; Roar, China!, 1932).
He also wrote a contemporary novel on collectivization entitled
Vyzov [Military Leaders, 1930] and the biographical novel *Den
Shi-Kua* (1930) which is presented in the form of an interview.

TRIFONOV, YURII VALENTINOVICH
Born August 28, 1925, Moscow. Soviet Russian novelist.
T. is the son of a clerk. During World War II he took part in
the building of a canal in Turkmenia, and worked in an aircraft
plant. In 1949 he graduated from the Gorki Institute of Literature
in Moscow.
T.'s first major work was the novel *Studenty* (1950; Students,
1953), for which he was awarded a State Prize. His novel *Uto-
leniye zhazhdy* [Thirst, 1963] describes the building of the Kara-
Kum canal. This dynamic story reflects the problems of the moral
changes in man during the rise of communism.

TROYEPOLSKI, GAVRIIL NIKOLAYEVICH
Born November 29, 1905, Novospaskoye (District of Voronezh). Soviet Russian novelist.

T. graduated in 1924 from an agricultural school; he worked for a number of years as a teacher and, since 1930, has been a rural economist.

T. began to write in the 1930s (his story *Dedushka* [Little Grandfather] appeared in 1937), but it was only after 1948 that he became fully involved with writing. His best-known work is the short-story cycle *Iz zapisok agronoma* [From the Writings of an Agronomist, 1953]. Based on his own experiences as an agronomist, this work is a vivid description of the situation existing in the Soviet villages in the early 1950s.

TSVETAYEVA, MARINA IVANOVNA

Born September 26, 1892, Moscow; died August 31, 1941, Yelabera. Soviet Russian modernist poet.

T. studied Old French literature at the Sorbonne. She left Russia in 1922, and traveled to Berlin, Prague, and Paris, returning to the Soviet Union in 1939. Fairy-tale motifs, historical themes, and love predominate in her romantic, expressive poems. One of her best known, written in 1922, is *Tsar-Devitza* [The Tsar's Bride]. Shortly before the outbreak of World War II, T. wrote a cycle of violently bitter poems on the crucial events following the Nazi invasion of Czechoslovakia. She committed suicide in 1941.

Editions: Izbrannoye [Selected Works], Moscow, 1961
Further Works: Vecherinii al'bom [The Evening Album] (1910); *Volshebnyi fonar* [The Magic Lamp] (1912); *Iz dvukh knig* [From Two Books] (1913); *Versty I* [Miles] (1922); *Stikhi Bloku* [Poems for Blok] (1922); *Razluka* [Separation] (1922); *Proza* [Prose] (1953); *Lebedinyi stan* [Swans' Abode] (1958)

TUGLAS (Pseud. of *Friedebert Mihkelson*)

Born March 2, 1886, Tartumaa. Estonian Soviet novelist, literary critic, and historian.

T. participated in the revolution of 1905 in Tartu, and at the same time became prominent as a writer; he was an active member and a principal leader of the literary group *Noor Eesti* [Young Estonia]. T. was arrested in 1903 because of his revolutionary activities, and was forced to emigrate. Between 1907 and 1917 he lived in Finland and Paris, traveling widely in Europe. After his return to Estonia in 1917 T. exerted a great influence on the literary life of the country. In 1905–07 he wrote realistically, concentrating on revolutionary, romantic works. During the reactionary years following the revolution he turned toward symbolism, but in the 1930s again returned to a more realistic style. Among his most significant works are the story *Hingemaa* [The Land of Souls, 1906] and the novel of childhood impressions *Väike Illimar* (1937). T. holds the title of People's Writer of the Estonian SSR.

Editions: Teosed [Works], 8 vols., Tallinn, 1957–60

TUKAI, GABDULLA (Pseud. of *Gabdulla Muhammed Tukayev*)
  Born April 26, 1886, Kushlauch (District of Kazan); died March 24, 1913. Tatar poet and political journalist.
  T. was one of the founders of realism in Tatar literature; he created the Tatar literary language as it is used today. T. was influenced by the classical Russian literature of the nineteenth century, and by M. Gorki. He first started writing poetry in 1902, and, impelled by the events of the revolution of 1905–07, became the spokesman of liberty.
  Liberty, the welfare of the Tatar people, and equal rights for women were the main subjects of T.'s poems, including the dramatic *Shurale* (1907). T. urged his countrymen to fight against tsarism, at the same time guiding them toward a deeper friendship with the Russian people by introducing them to Russian progressive literature.
  T., who was the cofounder of a number of Tatar newspapers and magazines, worked as a political journalist and critic.

Editions: Stikhi i poemy [Verses and Poems] (in Russian), Moscow, 1946; *Izbrannoye* [Selected Works], Moscow, 1957

TUMAIAN, OVANES
Born February 19, 1869, Dsekh (now Tumanyan); died March 23, 1923, Moscow. Armenian poet and translator of Russian and Western European literary works.

Vivid language, visual forms, and a strong sense of humor characterize T.'s versatile poetic and critical work, the traditions of which are continued in contemporary Armenian Soviet literature.

T.'s poems formulated the protests of the people against both native and foreign oppression before the October revolution, and supported the idea of friendship between peoples. His most important poems are those dealing with the prerevolution Armenian village—*Maro* (1922)—and the history of the Armenian people —*The Fall of Tmkaberd* (1905).

Editions: Izbrannyye proizedeniya [Selected Works] (in Russian), Moscow–Yerevan, 1952; *Skazky i legendy* [Fairy Tales and Legends] (in Russian), Yerevan, 1952

TURGENEV, IVAN SERGEYEVICH
Born November 9, 1918, Orel; died September 3, 1883, Bougival, near Paris. Russian novelist.

T., who came from a noble family, studied first in Moscow and St. Petersburg (1833–37) and later in Berlin (1838–41), where he, like Engels, attended Schelling's lectures. In Berlin both he and his friend Bakunin made intensive studies in Hegelian philosophy. T. intended to become a professor of philosophy, but gradually turned toward writing.

T.'s early works, the poems *Steno* (1834), *Parasha* (1843), and numerous others from the same period exhibit features characteristic of romanticism, although they are, nonetheless, still linked with more serious observations and philosophical thoughts.

T.'s close friendship with Belinski, who made many valuable suggestions to the author concerning his work, commenced in 1843. In 1847 Belinski and T. traveled together through Germany and France. Between 1847 and 1852 the magazine *Sovremennik* published T.'s *Zapiski okhotnika* (A Sportsman's Notebook, 1950), a collection of very effective sketchlike stories about the lives of the peasants, their moral strength, and the cruel effects on them of serfdom. The book proved to be an effective tool for the antifeudal democrats, and made its author immediately known abroad. The tsarist government thereupon used T.'s obituary of Gogol, published in 1852, to have him arrested. He was imprisoned for a month and then exiled to his estate in Spaskoye near Orel from 1852 to 1853. It was during this period of exile that T. wrote his story *Mumu* (1852; Eng., 1945), which is similar in style to *Zapiski okhotnika*.

In 1853 T. returned to St. Petersburg, where he became one of the leading contributors to *Sovremennik*. His dramas *Bezdenezhye* [A Poor Gentleman, 1846] and *Mesyatz v derevne* (1850; A Month in the Country, 1952), among others, are regarded as precursors of the lyric drama of Chekhov. T.'s novels *Rudin* (1856; Eng., 1950), *Dvoryanskoye gnezdo* (1858; A Nobleman's Nest, 1947), *Nakanune* (1859; On the Eve, 1958), and *Otzy i deti* (1862; Fathers and Sons, 1961), like his best short stories *Asya* (1858) and *Pervaya lyubov* (1860; First Love, 1950), are concerned with the analysis of the progressive members of the Russian intelligentsia. All T.'s works were responsive to the newest tendencies in Russian intellectual life; they contained extremely pointed discussions on all the decisive Russian problems of the time. According to T., the foremost intellectuals among the nobility were actually able to discover and see the weaknesses of their own time, and to propagate humanistic ideas, although they were not able to initiate the decisive impulses that would bring about development and progress. Rudin, for instance, in the novel of the same name, preaches progressive ideals but founders on his inability to practice what he preaches. His love for the girl Natalya—the first of T.'s famous heroines—who strives to bring Rudin's ideas to fruition is shattered on the rocks of his irresolution and passivity.

T. also attempted to picture in his novels the young democratic intellectuals who, from the late 1850s, gradually began to play an increasingly important role in the intellectual life of Russia.

Insarov in *Nakanune*, a Bulgar, dies without having achieved anything of particular importance, while Yelena in the same novel, who has divorced herself from her nobility and is unafraid of the hard life at Insarov's side, looks only toward the future. The democrat Bazarov in *Fathers and Sons* most clearly represents for T. a person who understands the best avenues to be taken after the fiasco caused by the progressive Russian nobility in their attempt to achieve a kind of freedom. Bazarov is characterized by an aggressive opposition to all forms of authority, and by a philosophically overexaggerated materialism.

The fact that T. continued to impose certain restrictions on his characters is due, on the one hand, to the inability of T. the nobleman to understand the activities of the revolutionary democrats, Chernyshevski and Dobrolyubov among them. His break with *Sovremennik* in 1860 and his errors in the interpretation of the agrarian reforms of 1861 may be regarded as being partly due to that inability.

T.'s position and the increasing pressures of tsarism resulted in the publication of a number of works dealing with pessimistic themes, including the novel *Dym* (1867; Smoke, 1949). From the early 1860's T. lived almost constantly abroad, spending the years 1862–71 in Baden-Baden. He propagated Russian literature in Europe, and had a considerable number of friends among German and French writers. Despite his long absence from Russia, T. recognized the rise of the progressive forces there during the early 1870s. In his novel *Nov* [Something New, 1869–71] T. welcomed the struggle of the revolutionary populists, although he did not overlook their weaknesses. A way out from stagnation was possible for him only through the transformation of Russia by democratic forces. Toward the end of his life T. published the important collection *Stikhotvoreniya v prose* [Poems in Prose, 1878–82].

Editions: Sobraniye sochinenii [Collected Works], 12 vols., Moscow, 1954–58; *Polnoye sobraniye sochinenii i pisem* [Complete Works and Letters], 28 vols., Moscow–Leningrad, 1960–

Selected English translations: The Novels of I. T., tr. C. Garnett; 17 vols., 1919–23; *The Plays of I. T.*, tr. M. S. Mandell (1924); *Hamlet and Don Quixote*, tr. R. Nichols (1950)

TURZUN-ZADE, MIRZO
Born May 2, 1911, Karatag. Tadzhik Soviet poet.

T. was influenced by Lahuti and Aini, and by Tadzhik-Persian classical literature. His first collection, a selection of his works entitled *Bairoqi zafar* [The Flags of Victory], appeared in 1932. In 1939, in cooperation with A. Dehoti, T. wrote the libretto for the first Tadzhik opera, *Surisi Vose'* [The Vose Revolt], which was about the peasant revolt of 1885–87. At that time he also wrote a number of poems on life in his homeland.

T. has repeatedly utilized the theme of internationalism in his work, as can be seen in the volume entitled *Qissaji Hinduston* [Indian Ballad, 1947], for which he received the State Prize of 1948, and *Sadoji Osijo* [The Voice of Asia, 1956]. For the latter work and for his poem *Hasani-arobakas* [Hassan the Waggoner, 1954], which convincingly reflects the changes in the awareness of the Tadzhik people, T. was awarded the Lenin Prize of 1960.

Editions: Asarhoji muntakhab [Selected Works], 3 vols., Dushanbe, 1962

TVARDOVSKI, ALEKSANDR TRIFONOVICH
Born June 21, 1910, Sargoye (District of Smolensk). Soviet Russian lyric poet.

T., the son of a blacksmith, attended school in his village, and then worked as a blacksmith. Between 1936 and 1939 he studied at the Faculty of Philology at the University of Moscow. During the war he was a journalist. Between 1910–70 T. was the editor-in-chief of the magazine *Novy mir*.

T. has become justly famous for his poems. In *Strana Muraviya* [The Land Muravia, 1934–36], a folkloristic poem, T. describes how the peasant Nikita Morgunok searches in vain for a kolkhoz-free dreamland but finally is able to find happiness working for the kolkhoz. *Vasilii Tiorkin*, written between 1941 and 1945 as a result of T.'s meetings with soldiers at the front, is a poem that tells of the experiences and thoughts of the simple Soviet soldier, to whom it is dedicated. It became one of the most popular works of Soviet wartime literature, and was awarded the State Prize in 1946. The lyric chronicle *Dom u dorogi* [The House at the Wayside, 1946], for which T. received the State Prize of 1947, gives a poetic rendering of the author's thoughts on war and peace, life and death, construction and destruction, as well as his comments on the sufferings of the Soviet civilian population during the war.

T.'s poem *Za dalyu dal* [A Distant Place beyond Distant Places], one of the most important works of postwar Soviet literature, was written between 1950 and 1960, and received the Lenin Prize in 1961. The poem represents an artistic generalization of our time. Its hero travels across the Volga and the Urals through Siberia; in his reminiscences, thoughts, and impressions the reader gradually acquires a poetic, harmonious picture of distant places, including Russia and Siberia. Interwoven with these poetic landscapes are images of our own time, the past, and the future.

Editions: Stikhotvoreniya i poemy [Poems and Verses], 2 vols., Moscow, 1957; *Izbrannyye proizvedeniya* [Selected Works], 4 vols., Moscow, 1960–61
Further Works: Tiorkin na tom svete [Tiorkin in the Other World] (1963)

TYCHYNA, PAVLO (*Pavlo Hryhorovych*)
Born January 27, 1891, Pisky; died September 16, 1967, Kiev. Ukrainian Soviet poet and literary historian.

T., the son of a village priest, graduated in 1913 from the theological seminary in Chernyhiv and then studied at the Kiev Institute of Commerce. Following work as a journalist during World War II, in the postwar years T. occupied a number of extremely high governmental positions. He also became a member of the Academy.

T. was one of the founders of Ukrainian literature. His personal acquaintance with the democratic Ukrainian writer M. M. Kotzyubynsky was of great importance to his literary development. T.'s first two collections of poems, *Sonyashni klarnety* [Sun Clarinets, 1918] and *Pluh* [The Plough, 1920], were outstanding for their originality and style, despite the fact that some of these poems still showed certain features characteristic of constructivist experimentation. With the collection of poems *Viter z Ukrayiny* [Wind from the Ukraine, 1924], T. gradually linked his work with the new socialist reality. His later volumes gave permanent expression to the vitality and optimism of the Soviet people. They included *Chuttya odnoi rodyny* [Feelings of a Family, 1938], for which T. received the State Prize of 1941; *Stal i nizhnist* [Steel and Tenderness, 1941]; *Mohutnist nam dana* [The Power Has Been Given to Us, 1953]; and *My svidomist lyudstva* [We Are the Conscience of Humanity, 1957]. T.'s poems, which frequently use well-known motifs and melodies from old Ukrainian airs, are extremely versatile with respect to their themes, and exhibit an unusual musicality.

Aside from his poetic work, T. is also a well-known figure in the field of Ukrainian children's literature. He has also published numerous essays on literary theory, as well as a number of scientific papers. His translations of works from different literatures, including a number of non-Slavic ones, are of great artistic value.

Editions: Tvory [Selected Works], 6 vols., Kiev, 1961–62

TYNYANOV, YURII NIKOLAYEVICH

Born October 18, 1894, Reshitza (District of Vitebsk); died December 20, 1943, Moscow. Soviet Russian novelist.

T., the son of a physician, graduated in 1918 from the Faculty of History and Philology of the University of Petrograd. Between 1921 and 1930 he lectured at the Leningrad Institute of Art History on the history of Russian poetry. After 1921 he published a series of literary essays. Despite the fact that theoretically T.

was a formalist, these collections of essays contain a number of stylistically valid studies on Dostoyevski and Gogol. T.'s explorations in the history of literature may be regarded as preliminary studies for his historical novels about the time of the Decembrist revolt. These novels represent a brilliant chapter in the history of that genre in Soviet literature.

T.'s novel *Kyukhlya* [Wilhem Küchelbecker the Poet, 1935] is dedicated to a friend of Pushkin. Kuchelbecker here represents one of the noble revolutionaries of the period, yet loses none of his own individuality in the process. T.'s novel *Smert Vazir-Mukhtara* (1929; Death and Diplomacy in Persia, 1938), which has frequently been unfairly criticized, is about the tragic fate of the poet Griboyedov, who in 1829 was torn to pieces by a fanatical Persian mob. T. was unable to complete his novel *Pushkin* (Parts I and II, 1936; Part III, 1943), which he had designed on the grand scale; the three parts already published deal with Pushkin's life up to the time of his exile. T.'s artistic ability to make the spirit of the past come alive from documentary sources reached a peak in this work.

T.'s short stories *Podporuchnik Kizhe* [Second Lieutenant Kizhe, 1927] and *Maloletni Vitushishnikov* [The Young Vitushishnikov] are historic anecdotes of great force; both stories are biting satires about the time of Paul I. *Voskovaya persona* [The Guard Man, 1931] exhibits certain formalistic tendencies.

T. is well known for his translations of H. Heine.

TYUTCHEV (Pseud. of *Fiodor Ivanovich Tyutchev*)
Born December 5, 1803, Ovstug (District of Oryol); died July 27, 1873, Tzarskoe Selo. Russian poet.

T. came from the nobility, and after graduation from the University of Moscow in 1821 served in the diplomatic corps at the Russian legations in Munich (1822–27) and Turin (1837–39). He continued to live in Munich until his return to Russia in 1844. After his return he worked in the censor's office of the Foreign Ministry in St. Petersburg. Politically T. was a monarchist. He sided with the Slavophiles, but, especially after the Crimean War, did not deny that tsarist Russia was internally weak. During the last years of his life T. supported the independence movements among the western and southern Slavs, and was a representative of Pan-Slavism.

T. was deeply involved with German intellectual thought. He was a friend of Heinrich Heine, whose poems he translated into Russian; many of his aesthetic views were influenced by the philosophy of Schelling, whom he knew personally, and by the work of Goethe. His poem *Na dreva chelovechestvya vysokom* [On the High Tree of Humanity, 1832] is dedicated to the memory of Goethe.

T.'s poems of the 1820s and 1830s were romantic and metaphoric in form. They reflected the transience of man's activities in the face of an eternal Nature, taking the decline of the Russian nobility as an example of such transitoriness. The poem *Ot zhizni toi, chto bushevala zdes* [On the Life that Once Stirred Here So Mightily, 1871] is a fine example of T.'s work of this period. In *O chom ty voyesh, vetr nochnoi* [Nightwind, of What Do Your Breezes Sing?, 1837], *Son na morye* [The Dream on the Sea, 1830], and *Volna i duma* [Waves and Thoughts, 1851], poems dealing with the philosophy of nature in symbolic form, T. depicts the relations between man and the cosmos and between intellectual awareness and the inchoate origins of our being. In other nature poems, including *Vesenniye vody* [Spring Billows, 1832] T. has used the seasons as a symbol for the rhythms of human life.

By the 1840s T.'s poems showed a tendency toward an impressionistic, realistic style. His love lyrics of this period—in addition to the great early (1836) love poem *Ya pomnyu vremya zolotoye* [I Remember that Golden Time]—are among the most profound creations of Russian poetry. *O, kak ubistvenno my lyubim* [Oh, How Destructive Is My Love, 1851] and *Poslednaya lyubov* [Last Love, 1852–54] are among poems included in the cycle T. dedicated to Y. A. Deniseva, the woman he loved. *Russkoi zhen-*

shchine [To A Russian Woman, 1848–49] and *Sliozy lyudskiye* [Human Tears, 1850] show T.'s deep compassion and social understanding.

T. has translated the works of Goethe (including parts of *Faust*), Schiller, Lamartine, and other foreign writers.

Editions: Stikhotvoreniya, pisma [Poems, Letters], Moscow, 1957
Selected English translation: A selection of T.'s work is included in *Pushkin, Lermontov, T.,* tr. V. Nabokov (1947)

TYUTYUNNYK, HIRYHORI MYKHAILOVYCH

Born April 23, 1920, Shilovka; died August 29, 1961, Kiev. Ukrainian Soviet poet and novelist.

T. came from a very poor village family. He took part in World War II as a partisan. In 1946 he graduated from Kharkov University, and subsequently worked as a teacher of foreign languages. Following a successful start as a poet during the closing years of the 1930s, T. turned toward the writing of fiction in 1950. His most important work, the novel *Vyr* [The Whirlpool, 1960], which is the first part of what was originally destined to be a trilogy, describes the social changes in the Ukrainian villages before the war, and the events leading up to them. The novel is also symbolic of the trials undergone by the Ukrainian people during the difficult years of fascist invasion and occupation.

TZERETELI, AKAKI

Born June 21, 1840, Shvitori; died there February 8, 1915. Georgian poet.

T., who came from a noble family, attended the high school in Kutaisi; from 1859, while a student of Orientalism at St. Petersburg, he was ideologically influenced by the ideas of the Russian revolutionary democrats. He was one of the leaders of the Georgian liberation movement, and a founder of critical realism in Georgian literature.

T. saw in art a means by which he could educate the people. His early poems—*The Harvesters' Song* (1863), *Confessions of a Peasant* (1863), and *Lullaby* (1864)—already showed his com-

M. Turzun-zade

I. S. Turgenev

A. T. Tvardovski

P. Tychyna

Tyutchev

L. Ukrayinka

A. Upits

N. V. Uspenski

E. Vilde

V. V. Vishnevski

passion for the oppressed people and his sympathy toward the liberation movement. The poems of this period also harbored a strong opposition to the serfdom system and to national oppression. These ideas became more strongly emphasized in T.'s historical poems, including *Tornika Eristavi* (1884) and *Natela* (1900), and in his dramas such as *Medeja* (1897). T.'s famous poem *To the Workers!* appeared in 1880. His poem *Spring,* written shortly after the assassination of Alexander II in 1881, also became very well known. T. welcomed the revolution of 1905 and in the same year translated the "Internationale" into Georgian. In his novel *Bashi-Achugi* (1895–96) he described the seventeenth-century fight of the Georgian people against foreign invaders. His autobiographical *My Adventures* (1895–1908) presented a realistic picture of the conditions existing in Georgia in the second half of the nineteenth century. The poems *Firefly* (1871), *Song of Songs* (1882–1900) and *Suliko* (1895) have been set to music and have become well known outside Georgia.

Editions: Chsulebata sruli: krebuli, tkhmet tomad [Complete Collection of Works], 15 vols., Tbilisi, 1950

TZYDENDAMBAYEV, CHIMIT

Born 1918. Buryat-Mongol poet and novelist.

T. first started writing in 1930. In his poems and verses he has drawn lyric portraits of the heroes of collectivization and industrialization. He has also described the Buryat-Mongol collective villages, and the beauties of his homeland. His well-turned prose attained a respected position with the publication of his story *Bansarov's Inkwell* in 1948. T. is currently occupied with the completion of the third volume of his novel trilogy on the nineteenth-century Buryat scholar Dorshi Bansarov. The first two volumes of this work—*Dorshi, syn Bansara* [Dorshi the Son of Bansar, 1953] and *Vdali ot rodnykh stepei* [Far from the Native Steppes, 1959]—have earned him the undivided approbation of the Buryat public.

UKRAYINKA, LESYA (Pesud. of *Larysa Petrivna Kosach-Kvitka*) Born February 25, 1871, Novhorod-Volynski; died August 1, 1913, Surami (Georgia). Ukrainian poet.

U. came from a noble family, and received an excellent education. She spoke several European languages, having traveled frequently for reasons of health. Despite severe illness, her life was closely connected with the fight of the revolutionary labor movement. She translated the most important works of both Marx and Engels into Ukrainian.

U.'s work was consistent with the best traditions of Ukrainian literature. In her highly individualistic poems, which were closely linked with popular Ukrainian poetry and folklore, she extolled the fight of her people against tsarist autocracy. Her poetry reached its climax with the song cycle *Nevilnychi pisni* [Slave Songs, 1896]. Using mythological and biblical themes, U. called for social and national liberation of the Ukrainian people. Her numerous historical, philosophical dramas and poems include *Kassandra* (1903–07), *Vayilonsyi polon* [The Babylonian Captivity, 1903], *Na ruyinakh* [On the Ruins, 1904], and *Orgiya* [Orgy, 1913]. In her most significant work, the romantic, fairytale drama *Lisova pisnya* [Forest Song, 1911–12], U. employed Ukrainian folklore to depict in rhythmically versatile stanzas the dissatisfaction of the simple man with his environment, and his desire for a free and beautiful life.

In her intimate, vivid poems, which were filled with unique melody, U. symbolized the conflict between the individual and society, a conflict she tried to solve in the interest of the people. Her poetic work greatly influenced the subsequent development of Ukrainian culture and literature.

U.'s works have been translated into many other languages, most of them Slavic. Her own translations of the works of Western European classical writers are of considerable literary value.

Editions: Tvory [Collected Works], 5 vols., Kiev, 1951–56

ULUG-SODA, SOTYM
Born September 11, 1911, Varsik. Tadzhik playwright, novelist, and literary historian.

U. was the son of a poor farmer; between 1941–44 he served at the front as a war correspondent. His literary merit was first recognized with the publication of his plays *Shodmon* (1939) and *Dar otas* [In the Fire, 1945]. His novel *Navobad* [Rejuvenated Soil], which was about an agricultural community during the postwar years, appeared in 1949. The autobiographical *Subhi gavoniji mo* [The Dawn of Our Lives] followed in 1954. U. is best known for his drama based on the life of the Tadzhik poet Rudaki—here, in rapidly changing scenes, U. shows his hero as a versatile character who must prove himself in harsh conflicts and defend his love for the oppressed Nigina. The film based on his play *Rudaki* has been greatly praised in the Near East and Central Asia.

UPITS, ANDREJS
Born December 5, 1877, Vidzeme (County of Skrīvers). Latvian Soviet novelist.

U. came from a poor peasant family; he studied privately in order to pass the examination required of teachers, passing it in 1896. He taught for about eleven years, but after 1908 devoted himself exclusively to literature. He was imprisoned twice, once by the German imperialists in 1918 and again in 1920 by the nonsocialist Latvian government, for his insistence on upholding Soviet power. The Latvian government, however, liberated him after numerous protests had been made on his behalf. During World War II U. lived in the Kirov region of the USSR.

U.'s work, which is characterized by socialist realism, encompasses all the major genres of literature. His novels and masterful short stories stand out among his works from the prerevolutionary period. He began his great Robežniek cycle with *Jauni avoti* [New Sources, 1909] and *Zida tikla* [Silken Nets, 1912], which tell of the involvement of the Latvian peasants with the revolution of 1906–07. This cycle became a trilogy when U. added

Ziemelis [North Wind, 1921]. The work was later extended still further when in 1932 and 1933 respectively U. added *Jāṇa Robežnieka pārnākšana* [The Return of Jan Robežniek] and *Jāṇa Robežnieka nāve* [The Death of Jan Robežniek]. U.'s plays, especially *Balss un atbass* [The Voice and the Echo, 1911], have earned great acclaim. After World War II he published the socio-historical novel *Zaḷā zeme* [The Green Land, 1945], for which he received the State Prize. U. has held the title of People's Writer of the Latvian SSR since 1943, and has been a member of the Academy of Sciences of the Latvian SSR since 1946.

USPENSKI, NIKOLAI VASILYEVICH
Born in 1837, Stupino; died November 2, 1889, Moscow. Democratic Russian novelist.

In realistic sketches U. described the exploitation and oppression of the serfs; these sketches were collected in *Porosionok* [The Piglet, 1858] and *Khorosheye zhitio* [A Beautiful Life, 1858]. Other themes employed in his sketches and stories included the development of the Russian village bourgeoisie; the agrarian reforms of 1861, which were directed against the interests of the people; and the reaction of the liberal noble estate owners to these reforms.

U. broke with the magazine *Sovremennik*, in which some of his best works had been published, following a journey abroad in 1861. He spent the last years of his life in poverty and died, a suicide, in 1889.

Editions: Sobraniye sochinenii [Collected Works], Moscow–Leningrad, 1931

UTKIN, IOSIF PAVLOVICH
Born May 15, 1903, Chingan, China; died November 13, 1944. Soviet Russian poet.

U. attended the high school in Irkutsk. He participated in both the civil war and World War II.

U. started to write poetry in 1923. His melodic, emotion-stressed poems deal with episodes from the civil war and World War II; he has also written delicate, intimate lyrics. Some of U.'s works, including his early (1926) *Povest o ryzhem Motele* . . . [The Story of Red-Haired Motel . . .], are interwoven with a gentle sense of humor.

Editions: Stikhi i poemy [Poems and Verses], Moscow, 1956

VAARANDI, DEBORA

Born October 1, 1916, Võru. Estonian Soviet poet.

V. studed in Tartu between 1936 and 1940. She worked as a journalist following the re-establishment of Soviet power in Estonia. Her first book, *Põleva laotuse all* [Under a Burning Sky, 1945], contains poems written during the war. Her later work is for the most part concerned with the socialist reconstruction and the revolutionary past of her country.

V. has translated a number of works written by Soviet Russian poets. She holds the title of Meritorious Writer of the Estonian SSR.

Further Works: Selgel hommikul [In the Clear Morning] (1950); *Luuletused* [Poems], (1959); *Unistaja aknal* (1959)

VAGIF, MOLLA-PANAKH

Born 1717, Salakhly; died 1797, Shusha. Azerbaidzhani poet.

V. became very popular both because of his activities as an educationalist and as Vizier of the Khan of Karabakh. He opposed the Persian Shah and favored friendship with Russia.

V.'s simple, expressive lyrics drew their inspiration from the rich store of traditional Azerbaidzhani folklore. His ideological view is characterized by optimism and by the belief in the force of idealistic reasoning. In his poems *The Cranes* (1756), *The Violet* (1756), and *Two Beautiful Girls Are Singing Your Praises* (1756), V. extolled the beauties of nature and earthly love, at the same time condemning the feudal conditions of his era. V.'s influence on Azerbaidzhani poetry has been extraordinarily great.

Editions: Asarlary [Works], Baku, 1945

VALIKHANOV, CHOKAN
Born in 1835, near Airtausk; died October, 1865, near Alma-Ata. Kazakh democratic humanist, traveler, and folklorist.
V. was the son of a nobleman; he studied between 1847 and 1853 at the School for Cadets in Omsk. He later traveled through Kirghizia and met many Russian Orientalists. Between 1860 and 1861 he lived in St. Petersburg.
V. was the author of many scholarly essays on the history and culture of central Asia. He also recorded sections of the Kirghiz epic poem *Manas*. V. was a firm believer in cooperation with democratic Russian culture.

Editions: Izbrannyye proizvedeniya [Selected Works] (in Russian), Alma-Ata, 1958

VASHA-PSHAVELA (Pseud. of *Luka Rasikashvili*)
Born July 26, 1861, Chargali; died July 10, 1915, Tbilisi. Georgian poet and playwright.
V., the son of a village clergyman from the region of Pshavia, attended a teachers college, where he became acquainted with the Greek and Roman classics as well as with those of Western Europe and of the Russian revolutionary democrats. After 1882 he worked as a teacher.
V.'s early poems already showed the influence of the folklore of the mountain people. He continued to utilize these traditions in his pictures of the life, thoughts, feelings, and history of these people as depicted in his numerous poems, stories, and plays. Many of V.'s works showed the conflict between the freedom-loving individual and the patriarchal standards of life in his mountain homeland. These aspects of V.'s poems are especially evident in *Aulda Ketelauri* (1888) and *Guest and Host* (1893), and in his drama *The Outcast* (1894). V.'s works, which exhibit a markedly patriotic spirit, are distinguished for their diversity and lyricism.

Editions: Chsulebani [Works], 7 vols., Tbilisi, 1930–56

VENCLOVA, ANTANAS

Born January 7, 1906, Trempiniai (now in the county of Kapsukas). Lithuanian Soviet poet.

V., who comes from a peasant family from the Suvalkija region of Lithuania, graduated from the University of Kaunas in 1932. While still young he took part in the fight against the fascists and in the battle for Soviet power. In 1930–31 he was an editor for *Trecias frontas*. Between 1940–41 he was Lithuanian People's Commissar for Education.

During World War II, V. was highly praised for his poems, which have been collected in *Obelis kur augalota* [Where the Tall Appletree Stands] published in 1945. During the postwar years, V. has been active and successful in both his literary and political activities. In 1959 he published the novel *Gimimo diena* [The Birthday]. Between 1954–59 he was president of the Lithuanian Writers' Union; he has been a longtime member of the Peace Committee of the USSR, and is a Deputy of the Supreme Soviet. He was awarded the State Prize in 1952.

Editions: Rinktine [Selected Works], Kaunas, 1950

VENEVITINOV, DIMITRII VLADIMIROVICH

Born September 26, 1805, Moscow; died March 27, 1827, St. Petersburg. Russian romanticist; a member of Pushkin's circle.

V. was in agreement with the aims of the Decembrist movement. His philosophically profound metaphysical poems, which are noted for their humanism as well as for their elegiac quality, were greatly influenced by the idealism of the German philosopher Schelling.

V. wrote numerous poems in an anacreontic vein. He was also a prominent literary critic and translator.

Editions: Polnoye sobraniye stikhotvorenii [Complete Works], Leningrad, 1960

VERESAYEV (Pseud. of *Vikentii Vikentyevich Smidovich*)

Born January 16, 1867, Tula; died June 3, 1945, Moscow. Soviet Russian novelist.

V., the son of a physician, himself worked for many years as a doctor. In the 1890s he joined the legal Marxists. He was one of the group of progressive writers who followed in the steps of Gorki.

V.'s early stories—*Bez dorogi* [Without a Road, 1895] and *Dva kontza* [Two Corpses, 1899–1903]—continue the tradition of critical realism and are distinguished for their apparent political tendencies. *Zapiski vracha* (1901; Confessions of a Physician, 1904) reached a large public because of its open denunciation of the abuses existing at that time within the tsarist health services. In his short story *Na povorote* [At the Turn, 1902], V. described the growing revolutionary trends in Russian society and the negative role played by the liberal bourgeois intelligentsia. V. wrote a number of essays on literary decadence during the period of revolutionary suppression under R. A. Stolypin (1869–1911—Minister-President and Interior Minister under the last ruling tsar).

After the October revolution V. attempted to demonstrate in his writings the road the intelligentsia should follow to revolution and socialism. These works included, among others, the novels *V tupike* (1922; The Deadlock, 1928) and *Siostry* (1933; The Sisters, 1936). During his last active years V. produced a series of memoirs, including *Vospominaniya* [Recollections, 1936] and *Nevydumannyye rasskazy o proshlom* [True Stories from the Past, 1940].

Editions: Sochineniye [Works], 4 vols., Moscow, 1947–48

VERSHIGORA, PIOTR PETROVICH

Born May 16, 1905, Severinovka; died March 27, 1963, Moscow. Soviet Russian novelist.

V. was an actor and a producer before turning to literature. During World War II he fought as the commander of a partisan unit. His novel *Lyudi s chistoi sovestyu* [People with a Clear Conscience, 1946], for which he was awarded the State Prize of 1947, describes the heroic fight of the Soviet partisans in the regions occupied by the enemy.

In his later works—*Karpatski reid* [Raid through the Carpathian Mountains, 1950] and *Reid na San i Vislu* [Raid on the Rivers San and Vistula]—V. continued to depict the activities of the partisans. The novel *Dom rodnoi* [My Parents' Home, 1962] describes the difficulties encountered in the reconstruction of a country destroyed by war.

VESIOLYI, ARTION (Pseud. of *Nikolai Ivanovich Kochkurov*) Born September 29, 1899, Samara; died December 2, 1939. Soviet Russian novelist.

V. came from a working-class family. He took part in both the October revolution and the civil war, at the same time working as a journalist. In 1922 he studied in Moscow at the Bryusov Institute of Art and Literature and later at the University of Moscow. He was a member of the Pereval group and of RAPP.

V. started to publish plays and stories in 1919. His major work is the novel *Rossiya krovyu umytaya* [Bloodstained Russia, 1932].

V. was chiefly concerned with the changes taking place among the masses as a result of the October revolution and the civil war. The liberation of Siberia by Yermak has been taken by V. as the subject for one of his major works, the historical novel *Gulya-Volga* [Marching Volga, 1932].

VIENUOLIS (Pseud. of *Antanas Zukanskas*) Born April 7, 1882, Užožeriai; died August 17, 1957, Anykščiai. Lithuanian playwright and novelist.

V. came from a peasant family. He lived in the Caucasus from 1904, then in Moscow; he returned to Lithuania in 1918. In the pre-Soviet period, V. was a critical realist; his masterful stories *Paskenduole* [The Suicide, 1909], *Vežys* [Cancer, 1925], and *Jšduketere* [The Foster-Daughter, 1945], among others, exposed bourgeois society and its morals.

V.'s novel *Puodžiunkiemis* [The Game Is Finished, 1947] was his first work of socialist realism. Here he gave a sweeping picture of the development of the Lithuanian village in the bourgeois

state and during the beginning of the fascist occupation. V. held
the title of People's Artist of the Lithuanian SSR.

Editions: Răstai [Works], 7 vols., Vilnius, 1953–55
Further Works: Prieš diena (1924); *Prieblandoje* (1936–45)

VILDE, EDUARD

Born March 4, 1865, Pudivere (northern Estonia); died December 26, 1933, Talling. Estonian novelist and playwright; most
significant representative of critical realism in Estonian literature.

V., the son of an estate laborer, worked for more than twenty
years as a journalist following his graduation from high school.
His first acquaintance with Marxist teachings, which were to
strongly influence his subsequent work, took place in the years
1895–96. His novel *Külmale maale* [To Siberia, 1896] represents
the first successful novel of critical realism to emerge from Estonia.
Raudsed käed [The Iron Hand, 1898] described the exploitation
of the proletariat. In the historical trilogy *Mahtra sõda* [Uprising
in Mahtra, 1902], *Kui Anija mehed Tallinnas käisid* [The Envoys
from Anija, 1902], and *Prohvet Maltsvet* [The Prophet Maltsvet,
1908], V. clearly showed that the only way for the people to
attain social justice could be through their own endeavors.

In 1905 V. took part in the revolutionary movement, and subsequently was forced to emigrate. During his emigration he wrote
stories, sketches, and plays, in which he scathingly denounced
the reactionary Estonian bourgeoisie. V. returned to his homeland
after the February revolution of 1917; from that time until his
death he was chiefly concerned with the preparation of his complete works for publication.

Editions: Works, 33 vols., n.d.

VINOKUROV, YEVGENII MIKHAILOVICH

Born October 22, 1925, Bryansk. Soviet Russian poet.

During World War II V. served as a platoon commander in
the Red Army. His poems, which have been appearing in print
since 1948, give a detailed, sensitive picture of the inner world

of the young people who grew up during the war. V. seeks through philosophy an answer to the problems of life. V.'s first volume of poems, *Stikhi o dolge* [Poems on Duty], appeared in 1951.

Further Works: Muzyka [Music] (1964)

VIRTA, NIKOLAI YEVGENYEVICH
Born December 19, 1906, Bolshaya Lasovka (District of Tembov). Soviet Russian novelist and playwright.

V. is the son of a village priest. He started to write in 1923, and his first novel *Odinochestvo* (1935; Alone, 1935) received the State Prize of 1941. This work, which is distinguished by its profoundly psychological depiction of the enemies of Soviet power, shows the defeat of a kulak revolt during the civil war, in accordance with socialist law. T. Khrennikov later composed an opera, *V buryu* [In the Storm, 1939], based on this novel.

V. frequently depicted the problems of country people, as in his novel *Krutyye gory* [Steep Mountains, 1965], which is about the changes that took place after September, 1953. V. also wrote a number of plays, including *Dali-daniye ne oglyadnyye* [Unbounded Distances, 1957]. The film script *Stalingradskaya bitva* [The Battle of Stalingrad, 1949] to some degree shows the influence of the so-called theory of nonconflict, as well as features of the personality cult.

Further Works: Zagovor (1938); *Povesti poslednikh* [Stories from the Last Years] (1956); *Letom nebo vysokoye* [In the Summer the Sky Is High] (1959); *Step, da step krugom* [Steppes All around You] (1960); *Trii kamnya very* [Three Stones of Faith] (1960)

VISHNEVSKI, VSEVOLED VITALYEVICH
Born December 21, 1900, St. Petersburg; died February 28, 1951, Moscow. Soviet Russian playwright.

V. came from the progressive bourgeois intelligentsia. During the revolution he became a member of the Communist Party and fought in both the army and navy on various fronts during the civil war. V.'s first writings were published between 1921–22.

In 1929, following the publication of his epic drama *Pervaya konnaya* [The First Cavalry Army], his name became known throughout the Soviet Union. The basic themes of V.'s work include the revolution; the formation of the "new man" under the stress of battle; the Russian soldier; and the development of the Soviet army.

V.'s search for the romantic heroic drama found perfect expression in his play *Dramaticheskie proiznedeniya* (1932; An Optimistic Tragedy, 1937), in which he described the party's fight for revolutionary discipline and the destruction of anarchy in the Red Navy. The play is concerned with a small number of communists under the leadership of a female commissar who reform a section of the Red Navy and turn it into a dedicated battle unit. The conflicts thus arising between individual and social morale are depicted with vivid clarity. V.'s film script *My, iz Kronshtadta* [We, the Kronstadt Sailors, 1933–36] is concerned with a similar theme. Revolution and the civil war are the subject of *Voina* [War, 1929–39] and of the novel-length film script *My, ruski narod* [We, the Russian People, 1937].

V.'s dramatic art endeavors to synthesize the human element with history, and then to involve the spectator in it to the greatest possible degree. Taking advantage of the great demand for a new form of drama and the rejection of traditional dramatic forms, V. arrived at an individual, forceful, and laconic style. During World War II V. was an officer and a frontline correspondent in Leningrad; his play *U sten Leningrada* [Before the Walls of Leningrad, 1944] was first staged in that city. The artistic value of his last work, *Nezabyvayemy 1919* [The Unforgettable 1919, 1950], was greatly impaired by a historically distorted presentation of Stalin. V. was a close friend of Friedrich Wolf, who translated *Optimisticheskaya tragediya* [An Optimistic Tragedy] into German; V. himself translated a number of Wolf's plays into Russian. It was in part due to his friendship that V. became so well acquainted with German socialist literature.

Editions: Sobraniye sochinenii [Collected Works], 6 vols., Moscow, 1954–61

VLADIMOV (Pseud. of *Georgii Nikolayevich Volosevich*)
Born February 19, 1931, Kharkov. Soviet Russian novelist.
V. graduated with a law degree in 1953 from the University
of Leningrad. His first published work included a number of
critical essays on literary themes.
V.'s novel *Bolshaya ruda* [The Great Bronze], which appeared
in 1961, analyzed the moral development of a present-day youth
with considerable psychological depths and understanding.

VOROVSKI, VATZLAV VATZLAVOVICH
Born October 27, 1871, Moscow; died May 10, 1923, Lausanne
(Switzerland). Russian revolutionary; Soviet diplomat and literary
critic.
V., whose father was a Polish engineer, studied at the Moscow
Technical School in 1891–97. V. was involved in revolutionary
activities, and became a Bolshevist in 1903. In 1905 he worked
with Lenin, who greatly valued his talents as a political writer,
and with Lunacharski. During the years following the revolution
of 1905, V., who was the leader of a Bolshevist group in Odessa,
combined party work with extensive literary activities.
Critical essays on literature occupy an important position in
V.'s total work. In these essays he opposed the idealistic concepts
of decadence and defended the materialist theory of art. He outlined the role and function of art in social life, demonstrating
that literature, like any other ideology, exhibits class character
in a class-oriented society. V. attributed great importance to
ideology for the true reflection of reality; he made profundity
and generality in the interpretation and presentation of the significant aspects of reality, as well as Lenin's principles of free
national development, the guiding criteria for the critical evaluation of literary works of art.
The themes of V.'s essays encompass both contemporary, early
twentieth-century literature and the classic Russian literature of
the nineteenth century. He stresses the rich heritage of the revolutionary democrats, and considers them to be the forerunners
of Marxism.

V.'s work reached its peak in his essays on literary decadence and on M. Gorki. He analyzed Gorki's development in connection with the new changes in the approach to reality, changes that pointed out fresh, clear-cut roads for the writer, and provided him with ways in which to personify his socialist ideals. V.'s essays also discussed the question of the new aims of art present in the third, or proletarian, phase of the Russian liberation movement.

Editions: Sochineniya [Works], 3 vols., Moscow, 1931–33

VOVCHOK, MARKO (Pseud. of *Maria Oleksandivna Vilinskaya-Markovich*)

Born December 22, 1834, Yekaterinovka (District of Orel); died August 10, 1907, Nalchik (Caucasus). Revolutionary democratic Ukrainian-Russian novelist and translator.

V. came from the Russian landed gentry. In 1851 she married the well-known progressive Ukrainian folklorist A. V. Markovich. During the years between 1859 and 1867 she lived in France, Germany, Switzerland, and Italy, and met many prominent European intellectuals including Flaubert, Jules Verne, Herzen, Turgenev, and Pisarev; she supported the democratic movement despite severe persecution. In 1878 she was forced to leave St. Petersburg and live in the provinces; she joyfully welcomed the Russian revolution of 1905.

V.'s considerable literary output—which in time showed a marked development from romanticism to critical realism—is dominated by novels and stories of social criticism. In these stories V. described the difficult life led by the peasants and the poverty prevalent in the cities, using a strong, rhythmic language that frequently borrows from folklore.

V. first became known for her volume of sketches entitled *Narodni opovidannya Marko Vovchka* (1857). Two years later this work appeared in a translation by Turgenev under the title *Ukrainian National Stories.* She also published the volume *Rasskazy iz narodmovo russkovo byta* [Stories from Russian National Life, 1869]; both these works were widely praised.

V.'s poetic work, which was directed against the feudal order, is also partly aimed at a criticism of the established church; it was greatly admired by the public. The anticlerical novel *Zapiski prichotnika* [Notes of an Artist, 1870] and the collection of satirical stories *Skazki i byl* [Fairy Tales and Reality, 1874] are outstanding. V. was a skillful translator of Western European belletristic writings, including those of Jules Verne. She also translated scientific works, among them those of Darwin and Brehm. V.'s own works have been translated into the various Slavic languages as well as into French, German, English, and Danish.

Editions: Polnoye sobraniye sochinenii [Complete Works], 7 vols., Saratov, 1896–99; *Sobraniye sochinenii* [Collected Works], 3 vols., Moscow, 1957

VOZNESENSKI, ANDREI ANDREYEVICH
Born May 12, 1933, Moscow. Soviet Russian poet.
Until 1957 V. studied at the Institute of Architecture in Moscow. His poems, which have been appearing since 1958, are sustained by highly complex word and sound associations; frequently they can only be understood with considerable difficulty.
In 1959 V. wrote the poem *Mastera* [The Masters] using historical material. His poem *Treugolnaya grusha* [The Three-cornered Pear], based on impressions obtained in America, was published in 1962. *Lonshyumo* [Lonjumeau], a poem dedicated to the memory of Lenin, appeared in 1963.
V.'s most important work is the poem *Osa* (1962). This poem, which is in the form of the diary of the girl Osa, deals with the eternal theme of good and evil in our own century. The poem is made up of both verse and prose, the prose sections reflecting the world of inanimate capitalist automation.

VURGUN (Pseud. of *Samed Vekilov*)
Born March 21, 1906, Salakhly; died May 27, 1956, Baku. Azerbaidzhani poet and dramatist.
V. was a village teacher. In 1929 he began to study at the

University of Moscow. He later did postgraduate work at the Azerbaidzhani Institute of Literature and Linguistics.

V.'s literary career began in 1926 with the publication of a number of lyric poems, including *The Blue Lake* and *Be Prepared!* The free Soviet man and the friendship among the peoples of the Caucasus were the major themes of his first two collections of poems, *The Oath* (1930) and *The Lantern* (1932). V.'s first long work, *Komsomol Poem* (1932–34)—a poetic study of the battles against the enemies of Soviet power—became one of the first important poems of Azerbaidzhani Soviet literature. V.'s poem *Azerbaidzhani* (1935), in which he praised the beauties of his homeland and of free labor, became very popular.

V.'s first play, written in 1938, was the heroic drama *Vagif*, the central figure of which was the eighteenth-century Azerbaidzhani poet and humanist Vagif. Here, as in *Khanlar* (1938–39) and *Farhad: Shirin* [Farhad and Shirin, 1941] in which he used themes borrowed from the work of Nizami, V.'s aim was to re-create some of the unforgettable pages of the Azerbaidzhani past. V.'s dramas are permeated with a revolutionary fervor, patriotism, and a great love of liberty. During the war, V. worked on his great dramatic poem *Man* and on the *Poem on Baku*. Confidence in an ultimate victory, hatred for fascism and for the enemies of peace, mingled with a strong sense of pride in the achievements of communism are characteristic of both his war and postwar poems. V. held the title People's Poet of the Azerbaidzhani SSR, and was awarded State Prizes in 1941 and 1942.

Editions: Istigbal taranassi. Sheilar va poemalar [Melody of the Future: Poems and Verses], Baku, 1947; *Dram assarlary* [Dramatic Works], Baku, 1950

VYAZEMSKI, PRINCE PYOTR ANDREYEVICH

Born July 23, 1792, Moscow; died November 22, 1878, Baden-Baden (Germany). Russian poet, literary critic, and journalist; friend of Pushkin and a brother-in-law of Karamzin.

During his youth V. was influenced by Decembrist views. These are reflected in his political writings as well as in his poems, which in his lifetime were extraordinarily popular. His liberal attitudes changed in 1829. As a literary critic, V. wrote a well-received essay on the writings of D. I. Fonvisin (1745–92). He supported both progressive romanticism and the principles of populism; in 1818 he became the first author to apply the term *narodnost* to the populist movement.

In addition to political satires such as *Negodovaniye* [Indignation, 1820] and *Russki bog* [The Russian God, 1828] (a translation of which was found among the papers of Karl Marx's literary estate), V.'s writing consisted for the most part of elegies, open letters, sophisticated epigrams, and magazine essays.

Editions: Stikhotvoreniya [Poems], Moscow–Leningrad, 1962

VYSHENSKYI, IVAN
Born circa 1550, in the District of Lvov; died circa 1620, in the Greek monastery on Mt. Athos. Ukrainian writer.

It is assumed that V. came from a city family. In about 1580 he went to Mount Athos in Greece; he remained in the monastery there until his death. From within the monastery he fought against the policies of the Catholic church in the Ukraine by issuing open letters to the clergy and by writing polemic tracts. He was sharply critical of the social structure existing in his country, a structure based on social inequality, and he demanded the establishment of religious asceticism as the basis of life.

V.'s polemic tracts, which have had a decisive influence on the dominant politics and philosophical thinking of the people of the Ukraine, are written in a forceful, emotional style, rich in rhetoric. V. may be regarded as the precursor of the satire in Ukrainian literature.

Editions: Sochineniya [Works], Moscow, 1955, and Kiev, 1959

WASILEWSKA, WANDA (In Russian, *Vanda Vasilevskaya*)
Born January 22, 1905, Cracow; died July 29, 1964, Kiev. Soviet novelist of Polish descent, writing in Polish.

Between 1923–27 W. studied philology at the University of Cracow. She later worked as a teacher, and took part in the revolutionary movement in Poland. In 1939 she went to Lvov and became a Soviet citizen. During World War II she was active in journalism and politics. She was President of the Union of Polish Patriots in the USSR, Deputy of the Supreme Soviet of the USSR, and a member of the World Peace Council.

W.'s first work appeared in 1921. Her writing during the 1930s —which included the short story *Oblicze dnia* [The Face of the Day, 1934] and the novels *Ojczyzna* (1935) and *Ziema v jarzmie* [Soil under the Yoke, 1938]—give a multifaceted picture of the conditions and social battles in prewar Poland. In addition to numerous stories and novels about the war and contemporary events, W. has written the trilogy *Piesna nad vodami* [Song over the Waters, 1935–45], in which she described developments in Volhynia during the war and during postwar socialist reconstruction. She was awarded State Prizes in 1943, 1946, and 1952.

Editions: Sobraniye sochinenii [Collected Works] (in Russian), 6 vols., Moscow, 1954–55
Further Works: Po prostu milosc [Just Love] (1944); *V borbe rovkovoi* [In Battle] (1960)

WEIDENBAUMS, EDWARDS

Born October 3, 1867, Glaznieki near Cesis; died May 24, 1892, Tartu. Latvian poet.

W., the son of a peasant, graduated from Riga high school despite considerable economic difficulties; he studied law in Tartu (Estonia), but died shortly before he was to receive his degree.

W. studied the question of Marxism, and in 1886 published the first Marxist paper written in Latvian. His poems, which were both revolutionary and satirical, were distributed in handwritten copies and were greatly appreciated by both the revolutionary intelligentsia and the workers. W.'s satire was directed against the bourgeoisie and the church.

Editions: Kopoti raksti 1 – 2, sej. [Works], Riga, 1960

YANOVSKY, YURII IVANOVYCH
Born August 27, 1902, Yelizavetgrad (now Kirovograd); died February 25, 1954, Kiev. Ukrainian Soviet novelist.
Y., the son of a factory clerk, attended the School of Electrical Engineering in Kiev between 1922–23. During World War II and in the postwar years he occupied responsible positions as a reporter; he was present at the Nuremburg war crime trials in 1946. Y.'s first works were published in 1924, and since then he has written in all the literary genres. His most important work, the civil war novel *Vershnyky* [The Rider, 1935], is concerned with the fight of the Red Army to establish Soviet power in the Ukraine. Y. was awarded the State Prize in 1948.

Editions: Tvory [Works], Kiev, 1954
Further Works: Kyyivski opovidannya [Kiev Stories] (1949); *Dochka prokurora* [The Daughter of the Public Prosecutor] (1954); *Myr* [Peace] (1956)

YASHIN (Pseud. of *Aleksander Yakovlevich Popov*)
Born March 27, 1913, Bludnovo (District of Volodga). Soviet Russian poet and novelist.
Y. is from a peasant family; he became a village teacher. His first collection of poems, *Pesni Severu* [Songs to the North], appeared in 1934. In 1940 Y. published the poem *Mat* [The Mother], and in 1949 completed his verse novel *Aliona Fomina*, for which he was awarded the State Prize in 1950.
Between 1951–56 Y. wrote a number of lyrical portraits of his Soviet contemporaries, together with poems describing the movement of the people toward the virgin lands. Y. has also written short stories, some of which are controversial from the artistic point of view. They include *Rychagi* [Levers, 1956] and *Vologodskaya svadba* [Wedding in the Volga, 1962].

Editions: Izbrannyye stikhotvoreniya [Selected Poems], Moscow, 1857; *Gody zhizni* [Years of Life: Selected Poems], Moscow, 1961

YASIENSKI, BRUNO (In Russian, *Yasenski*)
Born July 17, 1901, Klimontov; died October 20, 1941. Polish
novelist. Wrote in Russian after 1929.

Y., the son of a physician, began to write in 1918. In 1925 he
emigrated from Poland to France, where he joined the Communist Party. Following the publication of his satirical fantasy *Ya
Zhgu Parizh* [I Burn Paris Down, 1928], Y. was deported from
France. He later entered the Soviet Union, where he continued
to write. In 1933 he published a series of political satires, including *Nos* [The Nose], in which he ridiculed the racial theories
of the German fascists. His unfinished novel *Zagovor ravnodu-
shnykh* [The Conspiracy of Indifferent Men] was published in
1956.

Editions: Izbrannyye proizvedeniya [Selected Works], 2 vols., Moscow

YAZYKOV, NIKOLAI MIKHAILOVICH
Born March 4, 1803, Simbirsk; died January 7, 1847, Moscow.
Russian romantic poet and contemporary of Pushkin.

Y., who was of noble birth, studied in both St. Petersburg and
Dorpat (Tartu) between 1822–29. His youthful fire and enthusiasm led him to side with the Decembrists and Pushkin. After
1831 Y. joined the reactionary Slavophile movement.

Y.'s historical ballads, including *Pesn barda vo vremya vlady
chestva Tatar v Rossi* [The Song of the Bard during the Rule
of the Tatars over Russia, 1823] and *Novgorodskaya Pesnya
1170* [Novgorod Song: 1170, 1825], as well as his elegies and
songs such as *Rodina* [Homeland, 1825], breathe patriotism and
love of liberty. His exuberant *Pesni* [Songs], in which he praised
freedom, friendship, and wine, are still popular today and are
frequently set to music.

Editions: Stikhotvoreniya: poemy [Poems and Verses], Leningrad,
1958

YEFREMOV, IVAN ANTONOVICH
Born April 22, 1907, Vyritza, near St. Petersburg. Soviet Russian paleontologist and novelist.

Y., who is well known in the field of science, participated in a number of scientific expeditions into Asia. He studied geology and holds a Ph.D. in biology. Writing since 1944, Y. has published science fiction as well as the two-volume historical work *Velikaya duga* [The Great Arc, 1949–53]. He first became known as a writer following the publication of his novel *Tumannost Andromedy* (1957; Andromeda, 1959), which was about the intellect of communist man in the third millennium.

Further Works: Lezviye britvy [Razor Blades] (1963)

YESENIN, SERGEI ALEKSANDROVICH

Born October 3, 1895, Konstantinovo (District of Ryazan) (now Yesenino); died December 27, 1925, Leningrad. Soviet Russian poet.

Y. came from the family of a small landowner. His extraordinary natural talents were already evident in his impressive verses on Russian village life, published in 1910. His literary talents developed gradually, first becoming evident in Moscow in 1912, and later in St. Petersburg, where he lived in an isolated, upper middle-class milieu.

Y. took for his theme the lives of the Russian village people he knew so well; he sang with love and tenderness of the Russian countryside. In their fresh vividness and extraordinary musicality, which is often akin to folk poetry, his impressive, image-rich verses hymn the simple beauties of life. The true value of Y.'s poems are impaired at times by a certain outmoded tendency to idealize reality.

Y.'s complex ideologic and artistic development was accelerated by the events of the October revolution, which forced him to see the world from the socialist point of view. He endeavored to show that he was in emotional agreement, at least subjectively, with socialism, as may be seen in some of his most important poems and verses. These include *Pugachov* [Pugachev, 1921]; *Anna Snegina* (1925); *Russ sovyetskaya* [Soviet Russia, 1924]; and *Stansy* [Stanzas, 1924]. A series of poems on Lenin also indicate that Y. endeavored to reach a literary position that was close to reality. These poems are impressive because of their honesty and passion, and because of the smooth amalgamation of political fervor and specific poetic sentiments. Negative influences exerted by petite-bourgeois literary circles, however, prevented the further development of these beginnings. The constant pressure of such influences forced Y. into an emotional dilemma which eventually led to his suicide.

The best of Y.'s work, a masterful presentation of the Russian people, their land, and their history, belongs to the immortal inheritance of Russian lyric writing.

Editions: Sobraniye sochinenii [Collected Works], 5 vols., Moscow, 1961

YEVTUSHENKO, YEVGENII ALEKSANDROVICH
Born July 18, 1933, Sima. Soviet Russian poet.

The popularity of Y.'s poems, which have been appearing in print since 1949, is due for the most part to the provocative aggressiveness of such anti-imperialist lyrics as *Khotyat li ruskiye voiny?* [Do the Russian People Want War?], as well as to his ruthless exposure of certain aspects of Soviet life (*Nasledniki Stalina* [Stalin's Heirs, 1962]).

A number of Y.'s poems are dedicated to the memory of the fallen heroes of the Soviet Union—*Svadby* [Weddings, 1955] and *Partizanskiye mogily* [Partisan Graves, 1957] among others. The poems *Opyat na stantizii Zima* [Again at the Zima Station, 1963] and *Bratskaya GES* [The Hydroelectric Station at Bratsk, 1965] indicate that Y. has overcome the temporary departure from the party line for which he was criticized in 1963.

Further Works: Razvedchiki gryadushchevo [Secret Service Men of the Future] (1952); *Yabloko* [An Apple] (1960); *Babyi Yar* (1961); *Nezhnost* [Tenderness] (1962); *Uzmakh ruki* [A Wave of the Hand] (1962)
Selected English translations: A Precocious Autobiography (1963); *The Poetry of Y.Y., 1953–65* (Russian/Eng. text), (1965)

M. Vovchok

Vurgun

V. A. Zhukovski

S. A. Yesenin

ZABOLOTZKI, NIKOLAI ALEKSEYEVICH
Born May 7, 1903; died October 14, 1958. Soviet Russian poet. Z. came from Kazan. In his first collection of poems, *Stolbizy* [Stakes, 1929], he described the unhappy life of the bourgeoisie. The relationship between man and nature are the main themes of Z.'s poems; his views have been greatly influenced by the ideas expressed by the scientist K. Ziolkovski. While in *Stolbizy* man was simply the miserable counterpart to a glorious nature, by the 1930s Z. had gradually come to realize that man himself is the most perfect of nature's creations—it is man who exerts a constant influence on an imperfect nature. Z. sums up this philosophy in the poem *Sever* [The North], written in 1938. This particular philosophy also explains Z.'s frequent depiction of natural phenomena disguised in human form, as well as his stress on the basically philosophical character of these phenomena.

S. has translated many poetical works of Georgian and other literatures into Russian. He was also the author of a modern Russian version of *Slovo o polku Igoreve* [The Lay of the Host of Igor].

Editions: Stikhotvoreniya [Poems], Moscow, 1957

ZADASA, GAMZAT
Born August 21, 1877; died June 11, 1951. Avar Soviet poet and playwright.

Z., the son of a poor farmer, started to write poetry when he was fourteen. Deeply involved with the life of his people, Z. aimed his satirical, barbed verse at retardation, superstition, and religious prejudice. His most important themes were friendship between peoples and equality of women. In 1934 he participated in the first Soviet Writers' Congress.

Toward the end of the 1930s Z., although primarily a poet, became prominent as a dramatist. His patriotic poems on the war years have been collected in a volume entitled *For Our Homeland* (1946). The poem *Herdsman's Saga* (1951) offers an impressive picture of the mountain people of the northern Caucasus.

Z. received the State Prize in 1951 for a collection of his selected poems published in 1950. He held the title of People's Poet of Dagestan, which he received in 1934.

Editions: Izbrannoye [Selected Works], Moscow, 1951 and 1955

ZADONSHCHINA

The most important narrative from among several dealing with the victory of the Russians under Dmitri Donskoi over Mamai's Tartar army in 1380 on the battlefield of Kulikovo. Z., written toward the end of the fourteenth century by the priest Sofronia from Ryazan, shows the influence of national poetry, especially of *Slovo o polku Igoreve* [The Lay of the Host of Igor]. The epic advocates Russian unity under the leadership of the Moscow princes.

ZAKRUTKIN, VITALII ALEKSANDROVICH

Born March 27, 1908, Feodosiya. Soviet Russian novelist.

Z. graduated from the Herzen Institute in 1936. His stories and sketches from World War II have been published in several volumes, among them *Korichnevaya chuma* [The Brown Plague, 1941] and *Sila* [Strength, 1942]. The civil war is the subject of Z.'s novel *U morya Azovskovo* [At the Sea of Azov, 1946]. He received the State Prize for his novel *Plavuchaya stanitza* (1950; Floating Stanitza, 1954), in which he describes the everyday life of the Soviet fishermen. The decay of the old world and the beginning of the new is the subject of the novel *Sotvoreniya mira* [The Creation of the World, 1955–56].

ZALYGIN, SERGEI PAVLOVICH

Born December 6, 1913, Durasovka (Ufa). Soviet Russian novelist and short-story writer.

Z., a graduate in the technical sciences, is a scientific worker in the Siberian Division of the Academy of Sciences of the USSR.

Severnyye rasskazy [Northern Stories; Book I, 1947; Book II, 1950] is based on Z.'s wartime impressions of the inhabitants of the Soviet north. The stories describe the difficult, self-sacrificing lives of the northern people and their constant struggle with an unrelenting nature.

Since 1950 Z. has been writing sketches and stories about life in the Soviet villages. His story *Na Irtyshe* [On the Irtysh, 1964], in which certain problems of collectivization are regarded from a contemporary view, has aroused considerable interest.

Further Works: Svideteli [Witnesses] (1956); *Tropy Altaya* [Altai Trails] (1962); *Bliny, Rasskazy* [Pancakes: Short Stories] (1963)

ZAMYATIN, YEVGENII IVANOVICH

Born February 1, 1884, Lebedyan (Tambov); died March 10, 1937, Paris. Russian novelist and short-story writer.

Z. studied shipbuilding at the Polytechnic Institute in St. Petersburg. He joined the revolutionary movement of 1905–07 and was subsequently persecuted. In 1916 Z. went to England; he returned to Russia in 1917 and worked for various magazines. He left the Soviet Union permanently in 1932 and settled in France, where he died in 1937.

Z.'s early stories show the influence of critical realists such as Leskov and Gogol. His best work from the artistic point of view —the story *Uyezdnoye* [Smalltown Affairs]—appeared in 1913; in it Z. mercilessly satirized the primitive life of the Russian lower middle-classes. He exposed the inhuman character of capitalist society in *Ostrovityane* [The Islands, 1922] and in *Lovetz chelovekov* [The Man-Catchers, 1918]. He was opposed to the October revolution, and his postrevolutionary works, including *Poshchera* (1920; The Cave, 1933), are extremely pessimistic.

Z.'s extraordinary novel of the twenty-sixth century, *My* [We], published in England in 1924, is a sensational attack on the Soviet social order. It has been greatly praised in capitalist countries, and had a considerable influence on the works of A. Huxley and G. Orwell.

Editions: Sobraniye sochinenii [Collected Works], 4 vols., Moscow, 1929; *Izbrannoye* [Works], Moscow, 1965

ŽEMAITĖ (Pseud. of *Julija Beniusevičiutė-Žymantienė*)
Born May 31, 1845, Bukante, near Platelia; died December 7,
1929, Marijampole. Novelist; foremost representative of Lithu-
anian critical realism. Z. came from an impoverished Polish landowner's family. She
turned to literature, after a hard life on the land, at the age of
forty-eight. Z. welcomed both the 1905 revolution and the October revolution; in 1917 she joined the Lithuanian Socialist Union.
Z.'s works give a panoramic view of Lithuanian village life at
the end of the nineteenth and the beginning of the twentieth
century. Her major themes include a commentary on the existing
class differences and the underprivileged position of women; the
unmasking of clericalism, the fight against tsarist oppression, and
a description of the sufferings caused by the feudal system. These
themes are already evident in her first cycle of stories, *Laime
nutekejimo* [The Happiness of Marriage, 1895–98], as well as in
such masterpieces as *Marti* [The Daughter-in-Law, 1896] and
Petras Kurmelis (1896–98). Z. is also well known for the dramas
Valsčiaus sūdas [The County Court] and *Musų gerasis* [Our Old
Fellow, 1899–1900] and for short stories such as *Prie dvaro* [At
the Estate, 1902], *Kelionē i Šidlava* [The Voyage to Sidlava, 1906],
and *Du kankintiniai* [The Two Tortured Ones, 1902]. Her *Auto-
biografija*, which she never completed, was published in 1916.

Editions: Raštai [Works], 4 vols., Kaunas, 1958

ZHITIYE ALEKSANDRA NEVSKOVO (The Life of Aleksandr Nevski)
The biography of the conqueror of the Teutonic knights, Aleksandr Nevski. Written in the traditional form of a saint's life, this
work was compiled at the end of the thirteenth century. It has
certain features in common with the "war epic," a poetic form
that appeared in southern Russia at about the same time.

ZHITKOV, BORIS STEPANOVICH
Born September 11, 1882, Novgorod; died October 19, 1958,
in Moscow. Soviet Russian author of children's books.

Z., the son of a teacher, studied in Odessa, Novorosisk, and St. Petersburg. In 1910 he worked as a laborer in Denmark, where he met Lenin, and, in 1912, traveled around the world by sea. From 1924 until his death Z. was active in the field of literature. Using events and backgrounds inspired by his travels, he created fascinating adventure stories, among them *Morskiye istorii* [Sea Stories, 1925], animal and hunting stories, and a dictionary for preschool children entitled *Chto ya videl* [What Have I Seen?, 1939].

ZHUKOVSKI, VASILII ANDREYEVICH

Born February 9, 1783, Mishenskoye (Tula); died April 24, 1852, Baden-Baden (Germany). Leading representative of Russian romanticism.

With the publication of *Lyudmila* (1808) and *Svetlana* (1812) —both imitations of G. A. Bürger's *Lenore*—Z. became the founder of Russian romantic ballad writing. His dreamlike, resigned attitude is reflected in numerous elegies, including *Vecher* [The Evening, 1806], *Teon i Eshin* (1814), and *Slavyanka* (1815).

During the War of 1812, in which he participated as a volunteer, Z. wrote the ode *Pevetz vo stane russkikh voinov* [The Bard in the Camp of the Russian Warriors]. A creator of new verse forms and of intensely lyrical love and nature poetry, Z. exerted a permanent influence on Pushkin and on Russian poetry as a whole. His poetry reflected true humanism; his political conservatism, however, endowed his work with occasional mystic, idealistic features.

Z.'s translations of the *Odyssey* and of Oriental, English, French and German poetic works are regarded as exemplary.

ZLOBIN, STEPAN PAVLOVICH

Born November 24, 1905, Moscow; died September 15, 1965. Soviet Russian novelist.

Z.'s sketches and stories first became known in 1924. He subsequently turned his attention to the genre of the historical novel, taking his themes from the broad, popular movements in Russian history, the leaders of which he described in a fluent, psychologically impressive manner. His main work, the eventful novel *Stepan Razin* [Stenka Razin, 1951], is notable for its convincing characterizations and its accurate historical detail. *Stepan Razin* received the State Prize in 1952.

Further Works: Salavat Yulayev (1929); *Ostrov Buyan* [The Island Buyan] (1948); *Propavshiye bez vesti* [Lost without a Trace] (1962)

ZORIN, LEONID GENRIKHOVICH
Born February 3, 1924, Baku. Soviet Russian playwright.

Z., who graduated from the Faculty of Philology of the University of Azerbaidzhan and from the Gorki Institute of Moscow, has written dramas and satirical comedies on contemporary themes. His play *Druzya i gody* [Friends and Years, 1961] has enjoyed great success.

Further Works: Sokoly [Falcons] (1941); *Dobryaki* [The Goodhearted] (1958); *Dion* (1965)

ZOSHCHENKO, MIKHAIL MIKHAILOVICH
Born August 10, 1895, Poltava; died July 22, 1958, Leningrad. Soviet Russian satiricist.

Z., the son of an artist, studied law in St. Petersburg. He volunteered for the army in World War I, but was discharged for medical reasons. Between 1918 and 1919 he fought as a volunteer in the ranks of the Red Army; he later worked in various professions.

Z.'s literary career started in 1921 when he joined the "Serapion Brothers" literary group. Z.'s satirical, humorous short stories, in which he ridiculed the little bourgeois man-in-the-street, have earned him a permanent place in Soviet literature. Z. preferred to tell his stories in the first person, a technique that permitted him to expose the complacency and limitations of the narrator by using comic turns of expression and a lively vernacular style. In some of his stories Z. juxtaposed scenes exposing the disgusting environment of the petit bourgeois and his dreams for a truly humane relationship growing from a socialist society.

Z. has also written numerous magazine features and comedies. His well-written stories on Lenin (1940–41), produced for the young reader, have been particularly admired by the public.

Further Works: Rasskazy [Short Stories] (1923); *Vrazhayemye grazhdanye* [Respected Citizens] (1926)
Selected English translations: The Woman Who Could Not Read, and Other Tales (1940)